$$E = \frac{mc^2}{\sqrt{1 - \frac{v^2}{c^2}}}$$

« For us believing physicists, the demarcation between past, present and future has merely the significance of but a persistent illusion. »

To Vero Besso and Bice Rusconi, March 21, 1955

« In classical physics, we had one clock, one time flow for all observers in all co-ordinate systems.
Time, and therefore such words as 'simultaneously', 'sooner', 'later' had an absolute meaning independent of any co-ordinate system.
Absolute time and the inertial co-ordinate system were abandoned by the relativity theory.
The background for all events was no longer the one-dimensional time and the three-dimensional space-continuum, but the four-dimensional time-space continuum, another free invention, with new transformation properties. »

From *The Evolution of Physics*

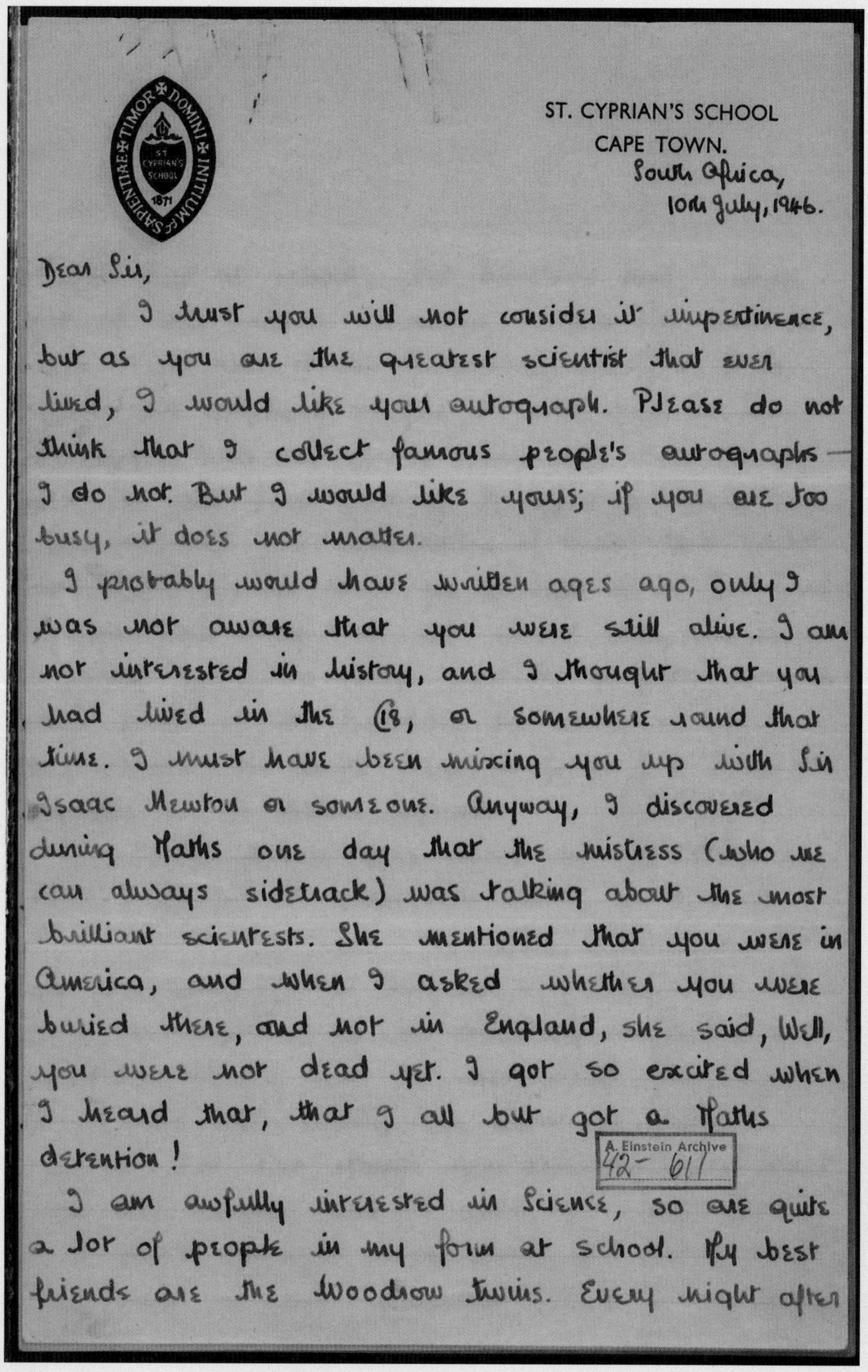

ST. CYPRIAN'S SCHOOL
CAPE TOWN.
South Africa,
10th July, 1946.

Dear Sir,

I trust you will not consider it impertinence, but as you are the greatest scientist that ever lived, I would like your autograph. Please do not think that I collect famous people's autographs — I do not. But I would like yours; if you are too busy, it does not matter.

I probably would have written ages ago, only I was not aware that you were still alive. I am not interested in history, and I thought that you had lived in the C18, or somewhere round that time. I must have been mixing you up with Sir Isaac Newton or someone. Anyway, I discovered during Maths one day that the mistress (who we can always sidetrack) was talking about the most brilliant scientists. She mentioned that you were in America, and when I asked whether you were buried there, and not in England, she said, Well, you were not dead yet. I got so excited when I heard that, that I all but got a Maths detention!

I am awfully interested in Science, so are quite a lot of people in my form at school. My best friends are the Woodrow twins. Every night after

↑ From a letter by Myfanwy Williams who was "awfully interested in science" and used to discuss astronomy with her friend. In his reply of August 25, 1946, referring to Myfanwy's assumption that he might have died a century ago, Einstein concedes:

« I have to apologize to you that I am still among the living. There will be a remedy for this, however. »

ALBERT

THE PERSISTENT ILLUSION OF TRANSIENCE

EINSTEIN

ALBERT EINSTEIN ARCHIVES (ED.)
ZE'EV ROSENKRANZ BARBARA WOLFF

MAGNES PRESS
THE HEBREW UNIVERSITY OF JERUSALEM

Original edition: *Albert Through the Looking-Glass, 1998*

German edition, revised and substantially enlarged:
Albert Einstein – privat und ganz persönlich, 2004;
2nd revised edition 2005

French edition, revised and substantially enlarged:
Albert Einstein – derrière l'image, 2005

Spanish edition, revised and substantially enlarged:
Albert Einstein – detrás de la imagen, 2007

English edition, revised and substantially enlarged:
Albert Einstein – The Persistent Illusion of Transience, 2007

Cover and pages 3, 4, 5, 7: Albert Einstein, Princeton 1941
Photos by Trudi Dallos

Published by:
The Albert Einstein Archives
Magnes Press
The Hebrew University of Jerusalem

Graphic design: Poste 4, Strasbourg
Layout: Gala Prepress Ltd.

ISBN: 978-965-493-325-4
Printed in Israel

FOREWORD OF THE PRESIDENT OF THE HEBREW UNIVERSITY OF JERUSALEM

The book presented here should give the reader a view, admittedly limited, of one of the most universal symbols of the twentieth century, one of the greatest intellects of all ages. Albert Einstein has become a myth, a symbol, a paradigm of scientific revolution. But the personal papers of Einstein which are stored at The Hebrew University's Jewish National & University Library reveal that there is much that is hidden behind the myth.

Paradoxically, Einstein's image as reflected by this book is far from two-dimensional. Einstein's theory of relativity constitutes one of the most profound revolutions in the human perception of the world in which we live, and represents one of the most significant contributions to human knowledge. Another revolution in scientific thought, arguably even more profound, is that of quantum mechanics. Einstein's ongoing struggle with the theory of quantum mechanics increasingly isolated him from the mainstream of scientific thought and could have turned him into a tragic figure. But despite this, none of the creators of quantum mechanics has been as mythified in the public eye as Einstein.

What was so special about the figure of Einstein that it captured the collective imagination of the twentieth century? Our Einstein Archives provides some of the answers. It reveals to us a complex, multifaceted person, a man of contradictions and paradoxes. This brilliant intellect, unfettered by the chains of existing paradigms, created through his special and general theories of relativity one of the most far-reaching breakthroughs in the history of human thought. At the same time he was so adamant in his convictions that he was unwilling to accept the other revolution in twentieth century science, the theory of quantum mechanics.

Although a dedicated pacifist, Einstein felt compelled to advocate the development of nuclear weapons in light of the threat of a Nazi bomb as part of the horrible destructive capacity of the German war machine.

Although he did not believe in the concept of a personal God, he was a lifelong atheist deeply influenced by his Jewish identity, by a concept of peoplehood and the unique role of the Jewish people in the unfolding saga of human civilization.

Even in his relations with The Hebrew University one finds the same contradictions. One of its founding fathers, Einstein was at one time one of its most severe critics, joining with Chaim Weizmann in challenging the lines of development and leadership expressed by Judah L. Magnes, the then head of the institution. Despite this, he chose The Hebrew University as the permanent repository for his personal and scientific manuscripts, papers and correspondence.

I believe that these tensions reveal the complexity of the real Albert Einstein and explain perhaps, at least in part, why he and no other person became such a symbol of the twentieth century.

Prof. Menachem Magidor
President
The Hebrew University of Jerusalem

PREFACE OF THE CURATOR OF THE ALBERT EINSTEIN ARCHIVES

The publication of *Albert Einstein – The Persistent Illusion of Transience* marks a new and outstanding accomplishment in the varied activities of the Albert Einstein Archives. When the original version, *Albert Through the Looking Glass*, dating from 1998, came close to being sold out during the course of the year 2005, I realized that there was a definite need for a new English-language edition and I brought up the idea of producing the present volume. Nine years after the first publication we are happy to have a successor in the form of a revised and expanded version with an up-to-date design. This volume comes as a welcome addition to a series that, at this time, includes German, French and Spanish editions.

We are pleased that we can now offer a book that emphasizes Einstein's contacts with the United States, the United Kingdom and Australia. While the 2002 version of "The Einstein Scrapbook" highlighted Einstein's relationship with the North American continent, this is the first time the Archives has published chapters on Einstein's interaction with the British and the larger Anglophone world. Some of its material has already been displayed in local exhibitions in England and Australia in previous years, but has now been adapted for this book.

The bulk of the workload fell on Barbara Wolff for which she deserves our gratitude and full recognition. This book would not have come into being if not for the groundbreaking work of my predecessor Ze'ev Rosenkranz, who started it all. His contribution is still a substantial part of this book. My earnest appreciation goes to Hai Tsabar of Magnes Press for his part in this successful collaboration. My heartfelt thanks go to them and to all those who have assisted us in realizing this project.

Einstein's relationship to the English language was not an easy one. His heavy German accent in English was famous. He had a hard time getting used to spoken English and never felt comfortable with written English. In 1944, after living for ten years in the United States, he mentions this problem in a letter to his friend, Max Born: "But I cannot write in English, because of the treacherous spelling. When I am reading, I only hear it and am unable to remember what the written word looks like." Einstein had indeed never been taught English at school and his Swiss matriculation certificate of 1896 shows marks for all subjects, except one: English Language and Literature.

As the curator of the Albert Einstein Archives I am glad to present to you this book that will surely take its appropriate place among the many publications about Einstein that are currently available to the interested reader.

Dr. Roni Grosz
Bern Dibner Curator
Albert Einstein Archives
The Hebrew University of Jerusalem

PREFACE OF THE FORMER CURATOR OF THE ALBERT EINSTEIN ARCHIVES

More than a half century after his death, Albert Einstein's countenance is one of the most recognizable images on this planet. Therefore, it is particularly apt that this volume be available to a global audience.

Einstein burst onto the world stage when he was forty years old. In November 1919, British astronomers announced the verification of his general theory of relativity. From that moment on, journalists began reporting Einstein's every public utterance, every minute detail of his travel itineraries around the globe, and every published attempt at further developing his scientific theories.

Einstein's iconic standing has only increased since his death in 1955. His celebrity status reached a peak at the very end of the twentieth century when TIME Magazine selected him as "Person of the Century". The year 2005 – designated the international Einstein Year – saw a virtual frenzy of Einstein-related activities, celebrating the centenary of his annus mirabilis, his miracle year in 1905, when over the course of merely six months, from March to September, Einstein published four landmark papers which shook the foundations of modern physics. The recent unsealing of a large amount of family correspondence, which had been closed to public view, has brought about an even greater interest in Einstein's private life.

Albert Einstein was a multi-faceted human being. Throughout his life, he was engaged in a broad spectrum of diverse activities, many of which are reflected in this book.

We are all familiar with the public image of Albert Einstein – the aged, absent-minded professor in a worn-out sweater with unruly hair and soulful eyes. But who was the man behind the popular myth and the public façade? What was Albert Einstein really like as a person? How do we reconcile the multifarious images we have of Einstein: the delicate and slow-developing child; the brash and overconfident adolescent and young man; the middle-aged, at times diffident, individual thrust onto the world stage; the theoretical physicist who revolutionized modern physics at a young age, yet became increasingly isolated from the scientific community in his later years; the loyal scientific colleague who had to navigate the precarious waters of academia; the radical pacifist who became a figurehead of the international peace movement; the German Jew of Swabian origin who adopted both Swiss and American citizenships; the devoted and warmhearted friend; the difficult (and at times exasperating) husband; the doting father who placed arduous demands on his sons; and the romantic lover? One of the most authentic ways to gain a closer insight into the real historical figure of Albert Einstein is to examine the historical documents he produced and left behind.

The purpose of this volume is to present the reader with choice documents and images which reflect the diversity of Einstein's life and work. The material is drawn from Einstein's personal papers and photograph collection and augmented by additional material mainly from the Albert Einstein Archives.

In selecting the archival material for the original edition, I have been guided by my close familiarity with Einstein's personal papers. It was, admittedly, a very personal selection – the chosen items are cultural artifacts to which I developed a special relationship. Yet the reproduced material represents some of the most significant items in Einstein's personal papers. Ultimately, I sought to incorporate a wide variety of materials in order to present the entire scope of the private and public selves of Albert Einstein.

Ze'ev Rosenkranz
Historical Editor
Einstein Papers Project
The California Institute of Technology

This book has a rather long history.
It owes its first edition, under the title *Albert Through the Looking-Glass*, to the former curator of the Albert Einstein Archives. The *Looking-Glass* was, so to speak, an expanded by-product of an exhibition which, under the curatorship of Ze'ev Rosenkranz, had opened in 1995 at the Jewish National and University Library in Jerusalem. Outside of Israel the distribution of the book was rather limited, while enhanced versions of the exhibition were soon to be seen on four continents.

As the International Year of Physics 2005 approached, it became obvious that a German edition of *Albert Through the Looking-Glass* should be planned. By that time, Ze'ev Rosenkranz had left the Albert Einstein Archives and I took on the task to tend to this publication. It turned out to be much more difficult than expected, as none of the publishers I contacted were ready to produce such an expensive book.

It was by fortunate coincidence that the director of the Historical Museum in Bern, Peter Jezler, and his team, planning a comprehensive exhibition on Einstein, first in Ulm, Germany, and later in Bern, Switzerland, took to the book project and assumed the risk and responsibility. Together we published the substantially enhanced German version with a completely new design in March 2004, followed by an even more elaborated French edition in 2005.

The success which these beautifully designed volumes achieved encouraged us to envision additional editions in different languages yet with the same appealing design and inspired by the same idea. Like the traveling exhibitions, each volume would be augmented by documents and texts that would particularly concern the readers of the respective language.

Thus the new English version contains additional material illustrating Einstein's connection with Great Britain and Australia, as well as with the United States.
Other new items come from a collection of family letters released only recently and published here for the first time.

Albert Einstein – The Persistent Illusion of Transience does not claim to be an ultimate comprehensive portrait of Albert Einstein. I hope, though, that this lack will be compensated for by the authenticity of the documents from which Albert Einstein speaks to the reader directly. Just as Ze'ev Rosenkranz's selection of documents for the original edition was a personal one, so my compilation of old and new documents is not free of personal preferences. The freedom to be creative has certainly contributed to the pleasure I had in composing this book.

I am especially indebted to Hananya Goodman who, in extensive sessions, with great patience converted my German-English raw material into impeccable English texts, and to Rama Hermony who was exceptionally responsive to all my ideas regarding the graphic design of this volume.

Barbara Wolff
Albert Einstein Archives
The Hebrew University of Jerusalem

Around 1940

ALBERT EINSTEIN (1879-1955)
CONTENT

The earliest known photograph of Albert Einstein, 1882

TIMELINE 1879→1955

1879
Born March 14 at 11:30 AM in Ulm, Germany

1880
Einstein family moves to Munich

1885–1888
Pupil at Catholic elementary school in Munich
Private lessons in Judaism at home

Munich, 1893

1888–1894
Pupil at Luitpold-Gymnasium, Munich

1894
Parents move to Milan
Six months later, Einstein leaves Gymnasium without completing his schooling and joins his family in Italy

1895–1896
Pupil at cantonal school in Aarau, Switzerland
Renounces his Württemberg citizenship, thereby also renouncing his German citizenship

1896–1900
Student at the School for Mathematics and Science Teachers at the Polytechnic (later the Federal Institute of Technology), Zurich

1901
First scientific paper is published in the *Annalen der Physik*
Acquires Swiss citizenship

1901–1902
Temporary teaching position at school in Schaffhausen and Winterthur, Switzerland

Bern, 1903

1902
Daughter ["Lieserl"] born to Einstein and Mileva Marić in her hometown in Hungary. Appointed as technical expert third class at the Swiss Patent Office in Bern

1903
Marriage to Mileva Marić in Bern
Joins with Conrad Habicht and Maurice Solovine to discuss ideas in their "Akademie Olympia"
In a letter from Einstein to Mileva "Lieserl" is mentioned for the last time

Bern, 1905

1904
Son Hans Albert born in Bern

1905
Einstein's **annus mirabilis**: completes papers on light quanta Brownian motion, and special theory of relativity

1906
Receives Ph.D. from Zurich University
Promoted to technical expert second class at the Swiss Patent Office

1907
Discovers the principle of equivalence

1908
Appointed lecturer at Bern University

1909
Appointed Associate Professor of theoretical physics at Zurich University
Resigns from Patent Office

1910
Second son Eduard born in Zurich

1911
Predicts bending of light

Prague, 1912

1911–1912
Professor of theoretical physics at German University of Prague

1912–1914
Professor of theoretical physics at the Federal Institute of Technology, Zurich

1913
Appointed member of the Royal Prussian Academy of Sciences and professor at Friedrich Wilhelm University (without teaching obligations)

1914
With wife and sons goes to Berlin
Separates from Mileva, who returns with both children to Zurich
Signs anti-war "Manifesto to Europeans"

Berlin, 1916

1915
Joins pacifist "New Fatherland League"
Completes logical structure of the general theory of relativity

1916
Publication of the general theory of relativity

1917
Writes first paper on cosmology
Appointed Director of Kaiser Wilhelm Institute for Physics in Berlin

1917–1920
Suffers from a liver ailment, a stomach ulcer, jaundice and general weakness – his cousin Elsa takes care of him

1919
Divorces Mileva Marić
Marries his cousin Elsa
Kurt Blumenfeld stimulates Einstein's interest in Zionism
Bending of light observed during solar eclipse in West Africa and Brazil
Announcement at joint meeting of Royal Society and Royal Astronomical Society that Einstein's theories have been confirmed by eclipse observations
Sensational headlines in *The Times* and *The New York Times*:
Einstein becomes a world figure

Leiden, 1920

1920
Mass meeting against the general theory of relativity in Berlin mainly motivated by anti-Semitism
Appointed special visiting professor at Leiden University

Vienna, 1921

1921
First visit to the U.S. with Chaim Weizmann: fund-raising tour for the future Hebrew University
Lectures at Princeton University on theory of relativity

Tokyo, 1922

1922

Completes first paper on unified field theory
Visit to Paris contributes to normalization of French-German relations
Joins Committee on Intellectual Cooperation of the League of Nations
Lecture tours in Japan and China
Awarded Nobel Prize in Physics for 1921

1923

Coming from Japan visits Palestine: holds inaugural scientific lecture at future site of The Hebrew University in Jerusalem, named first honorary citizen of Tel Aviv
Visit to Spain
Nobel Prize lecture in Göteborg, Sweden
Edits first collection of scientific papers of The Hebrew University

With Niels Bohr, mid-1920s

1924

The "Einstein-Institute" in Potsdam, Germany, housed in the "Einstein-Tower" starts its activities

1925

Trip to South America: lectures in Argentina, Brazil and Uruguay
Joins Board of Governors and Academic Council of The Hebrew University

Scharbeutz, Germany, 1928

1927

Begins intense debate with Niels Bohr on the foundations of quantum mechanics

1928

Suffers temporary physical collapse – enlargement of the heart is diagnosed

On board the *Belgenland*, 1930

1930

Intensive activity on behalf of pacifism

1930–1932

Scholar in Residence at California Institute of Technology for three winter semesters; spends rest of the year in summer house in Caputh near Berlin

1932

Public correspondence with Sigmund Freud on the nature of war
Appointed faculty member at The Institute for Advanced Study, Princeton
Plans to divide his time between Berlin/Caputh and Princeton
Leaves Germany for the United States but does not know it will be for good

Hans Albert, Bernhard and Albert Einstein, Caputh, 1932

1933

After Nazi rise to power declares that he will not return to Germany as long as human rights are not respected there
Resigns from Prussian Academy of Sciences and German citizenship
Spends spring and summer in Belgium and Oxford
Emigrates to U.S. in October
Why War? published

1934

Collection of essays *The World* As *I See It* published

1935

The Einstein-Podolsky-Rosen paradox published

1936

Elsa Einstein dies

With step-daughter Margot, New York, 1939

Mid-1940s

1938
Publication of *The Evolution of Physics* coauthored with Leopold Infeld

1939
Signs famous letter to President Franklin D. Roosevelt recommending U.S. research on nuclear weapons

1940
Acquires U.S. citizenship while retaining Swiss citizenship

1942
Manhattan Project to build U.S. atomic bomb; Einstein is not involved because he is considered a security risk

1943
Works as consultant with the Research and Development Division of the U.S. Navy Bureau of Ordnance, section Ammunition and Explosives

1944
Newly handwritten copy of his 1905 paper on special relativity auctioned for six million dollars in Kansas City, as a contribution to the American war effort

1945
Shattered by the extent of the Holocaust of European Jewry
Shocked by the nuclear bombing of Hiroshima and Nagasaki

1946
Becomes chairman of the Emergency Committee of Atomic Scientists, whose aim is arms control and furthering the peaceful use of nuclear energy
Expresses public support for the formation of a world government

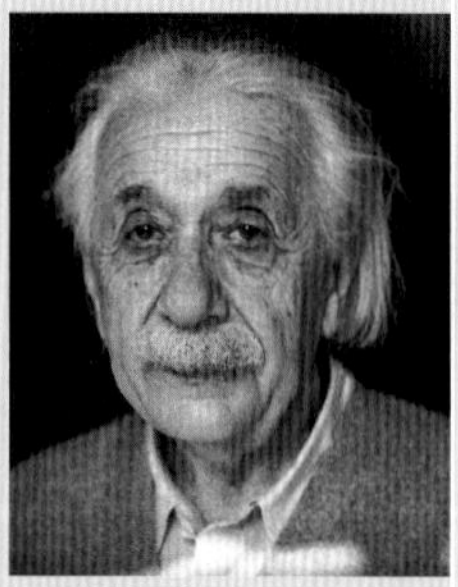

Early 1950s

1948
First wife, Mileva Marić, dies in Zurich
Intact aneurysm of the abdominal aorta disclosed

1949
Publication of *"Autobiographical Notes"*

1950
Signs Last Will and Testament: The Hebrew University named as the ultimate repository of his personal papers
Collection of essays *Out of My Later Years* published

1952
Offered presidency of the State of Israel after Chaim Weizmann's death

1953
Public support for individuals under investigation by the House Un-American Activities Committee

1955
Co-signs the Russell-Einstein Manifesto warning of the nuclear threat
Rupture of the aortic aneurysm
Dies April 18 at 1:15 AM in Princeton Hospital at the age of 76
Body cremated and ashes scattered at an undisclosed place

Winter 1951
Photo by Alan Windsor Richards

Herr Albert Einstein von Ulm,
geboren den 14. März 1879,
besuchte die aargauische Kantonsschule & zwar die III. & IV. Klasse
der Gewerbeschule.
1
Albert Einstein

EINSTEIN'S PERSONAL LIFE

« I am truly a 'lone traveler' and have never belonged to my country, my home, my friends, or even my immediate family, with my whole heart; in the face of all these ties, I have never lost a sense of distance and a need for solitude – feelings which increase with the years. »

From *What I Believe*, 1930

↑ Ulm, Bahnhofstrasse B no. 135
where Einstein was born.

« Dear Mr. Erlanger!

I thank you cordially for the thoughtful present. The house is quite nice to be born in, for on that occasion one actually does not yet have any great aesthetic needs. First one rather bawls at the loved ones without worrying much about reasons and circumstances.

Yours A. Einstein »

FAMILY BACKGROUND AND EDUCATION

Einstein's ancestors had settled in rural Swabia in Southern Germany before 1700. His parents already belonged to the urban, acculturated, Jewish middle class. Albert, their first child, was born in Ulm in 1879. Two years later, after the family's move to Munich, his sister Maja was born.

Albert was a solitary, dreamy boy, and his parents expressed concern about their child's slow development. Yet, by the time he reached primary school, his early difficulties disappeared. Contrary to popular belief, Einstein proved to be a rather good pupil.
At an early age, encouraged by his uncle and father, who together ran a small factory producing electrical devices, Albert began to take a special interest in mathematics and science.

He attended the Catholic elementary school in the neighborhood, then went to the Luitpold-Gymnasium, a prestigious and progressive high school.
After his parents moved to Italy, Einstein left high school at the age of 15, defending this decision later by his dislike of the authoritarian, militaristic atmosphere he encountered there. He completed his school education in Switzerland in 1896.

↙↓ Letter to Max Erlanger, thanking him for the photograph, April 16, 1929

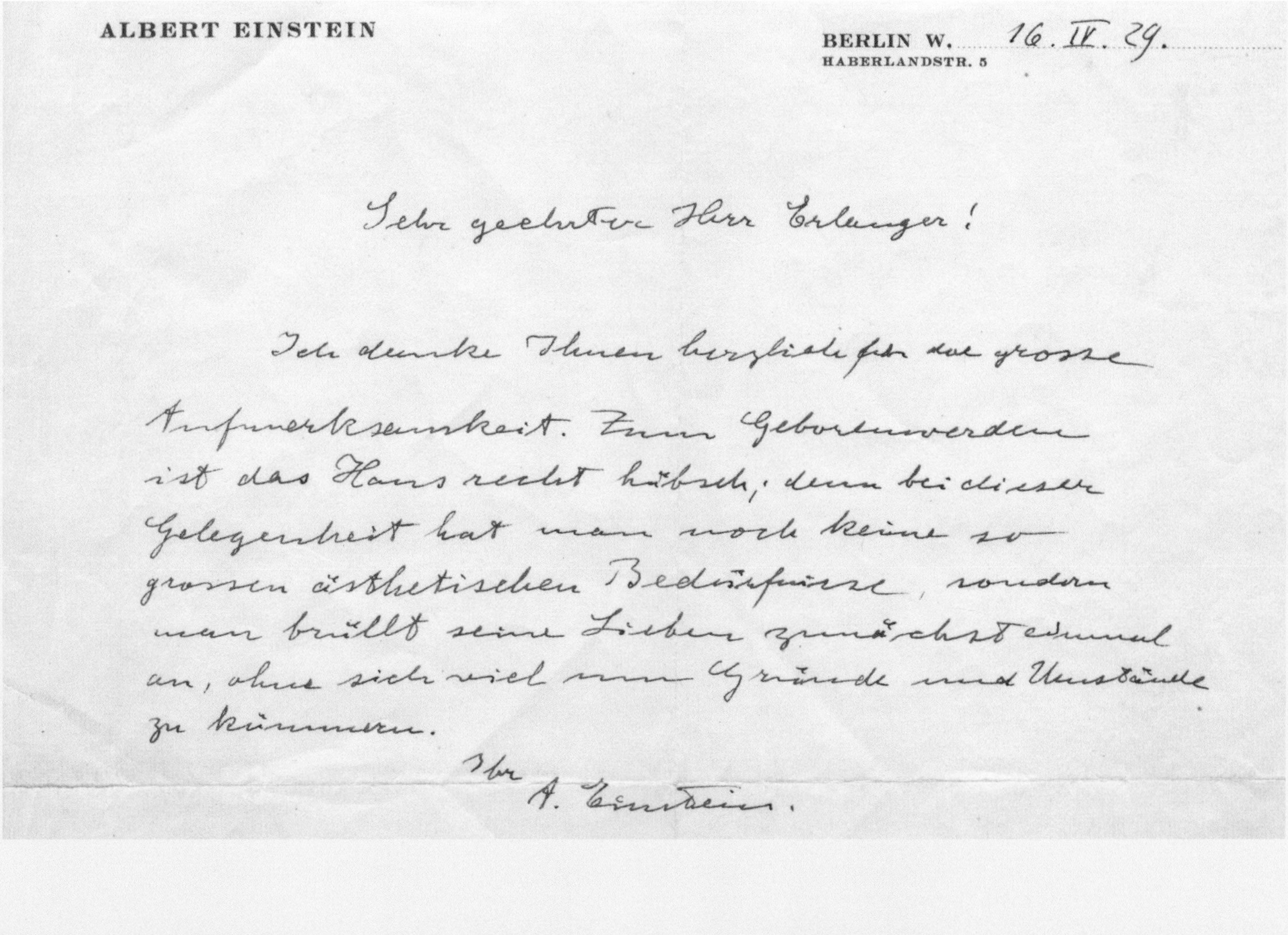

ALBERT EINSTEIN

BERLIN W. 16. IV. 29.
HABERLANDSTR. 5

Sehr geehrter Herr Erlanger!

Ich danke Ihnen herzlich für die grosse Aufmerksamkeit. Zum Geborenwerden ist das Haus recht hübsch; denn bei dieser Gelegenheit hat man noch keine so grossen ästhetischen Bedürfnisse, sondern man brüllt seine Lieben zunächst einmal an, ohne sich viel um Gründe und Umstände zu kümmern.

Ihr
A. Einstein.

A. a.

2

Geburtsurkunde.

Nr. 224

Ulm am 15. März 1879.

Vor dem unterzeichneten Standesbeamten erschien heute, der Persönlichkeit nach bekannt,

der Kaufmann Hermann Einstein

wohnhaft zu Ulm Bahnhofstraße B. No. 135

israelitischer Religion, und zeigte an, daß von der

Pauline Einstein geborene Koch, seiner Ehefrau,

israelitischer Religion,

wohnhaft bei ihm

zu Ulm in seiner Wohnung

am vierzehnten März des Jahres

tausend acht hundert siebenzig und neun vormittags

um elf ein halb Uhr ein Kind männlichen

Geschlechts geboren worden sei, welches den Vornamen

Albert erhalten habe.

*

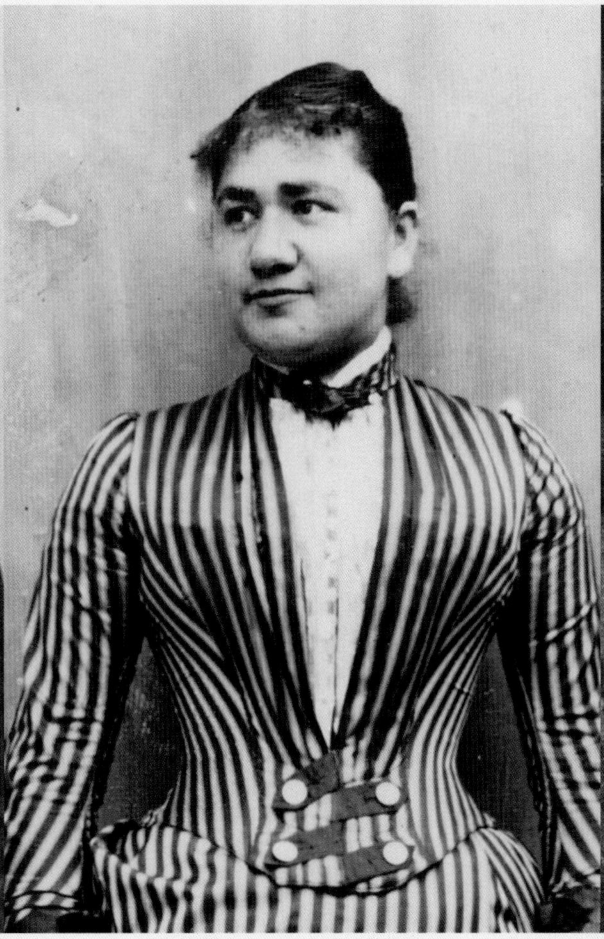

↑ Einstein's father, Hermann Einstein, a kind-hearted man, unsuccessful merchant, fond of German literature.

↑ Einstein's mother, Pauline Einstein, née Koch, a strong personality and a talented pianist.

↑ Albert Einstein (5 years old) with his sister Maja (3 years old), 1884

« The merchant Hermann Einstein, residing at Ulm, Bahnhofstraße B, No. 135, of the Jewish faith, reported that his wife, Pauline Einstein, née Koch, of the Jewish faith, who lives with him at his Ulm residence gave birth on March 14, 1879 at 11:30 in the morning to a child of male sex who was given the first name Albert. »

←↑ Birth certificate, Ulm, issued on March 15, 1879

↑ Luitpold-Gymnasium, Munich 1889. Of the fifty-two boys, Albert alone manages a slight smile (first row, third from right).

« Albert entered Gymnasium at the age of $9^1/_2$. In accord with the school's humanistic orientation, primary emphasis was placed on classical languages, Latin and later Greek, while mathematics and the natural sciences received less emphasis. The clear, rigorous logical structure of Latin suited his talents, but Greek and modern foreign languages were never his forte. His Greek professor, to whom he once submitted an especially poor paper, went so far in his anger to declare that nothing would ever become of him. And in fact, Albert Einstein never did attain a professorship of Greek grammar. »

↑ From "Albert Einstein – A Biographical Sketch" by his sister, Maja Winteler-Einstein.

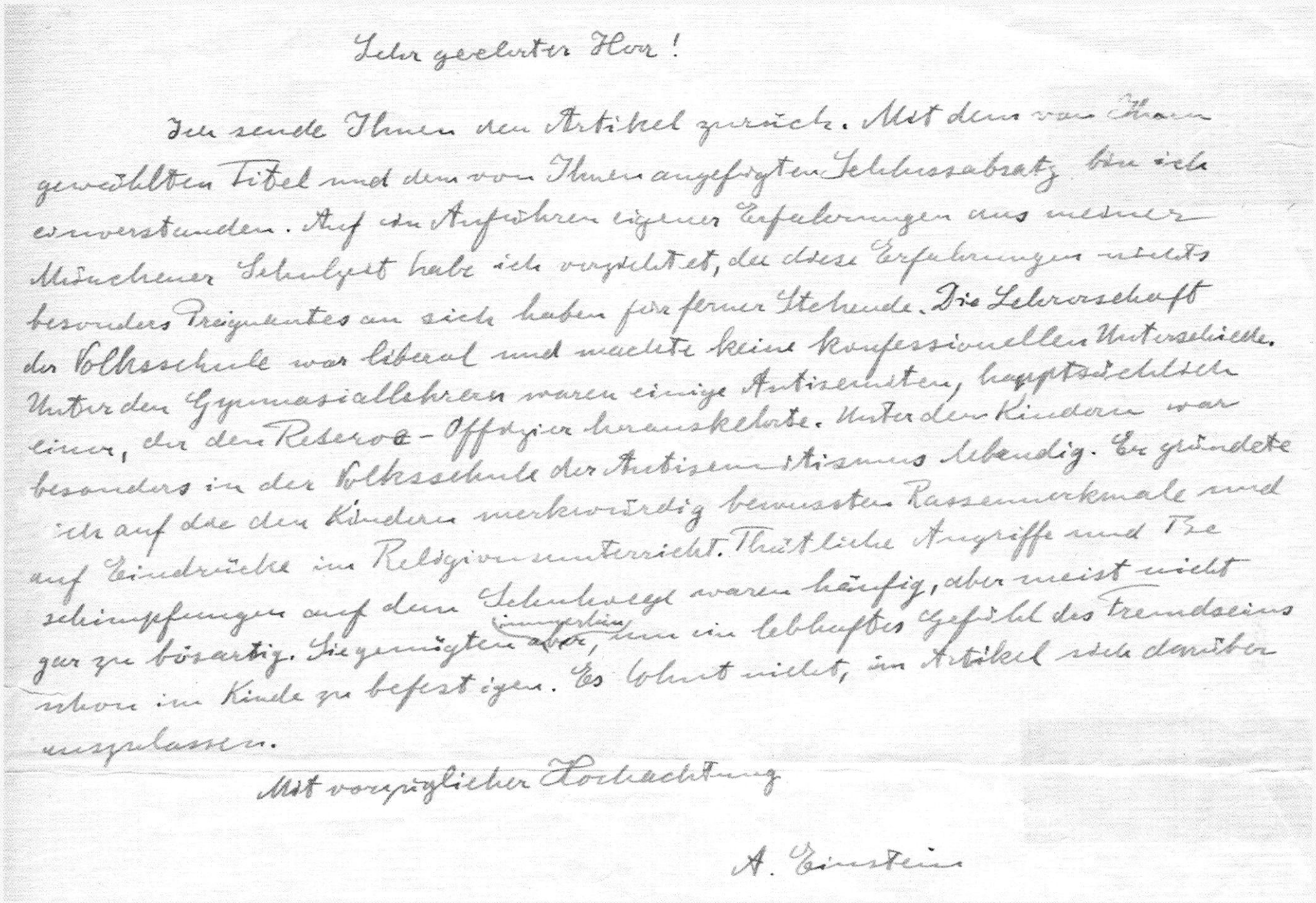

Sehr geehrter Herr!

Ich sende Ihnen den Artikel zurück. Mit dem von Ihnen gewählten Titel und dem von Ihnen angefügten Schlussabsatz bin ich einverstanden. Auf das Anführen eigener Erfahrungen aus meiner Münchener Schulzeit habe ich verzichtet, da diese Erfahrungen nichts besonders Prägnantes an sich haben für ferner Stehende. Die Lehrerschaft der Volksschule war liberal und machte keine konfessionellen Unterschiede. Unter den Gymnasiallehrern waren einige Antisemiten, hauptsächlich einer, der den Reserve-Offizier herauskehrte. Unter den Kindern war besonders in der Volksschule der Antisemitismus lebendig. Er gründete sich auf die den Kindern merkwürdig bewussten Rassenmerkmale und auf Eindrücke im Religionsunterricht. Thätliche Angriffe und Beschimpfungen auf dem Schulwege waren häufig, aber meist nicht gar zu bösartig. Sie genügten immerhin aber, um ein lebhaftes Gefühl des Fremdseins schon im Kinde zu befestigen. Es lohnt nicht, im Artikel sich darüber auszulassen.

Mit vorzüglicher Hochachtung

A. Einstein

↑↗ Draft of a letter to Paul Nathan, political editor of the *Berliner Tageblatt*, with regard to an article Einstein had written about "Assimilation and Anti-Semitism," April 3, 1920

« …The teaching faculty at elementary school was liberal and did not make any denominational distinctions. Among the secondary school teachers there were a few anti-Semites, one in particular, who flaunted his rank as reserve officer. Among the children anti-Semitism was alive particularly at elementary school. It was based on the children's remarkable awareness of racial characteristics and on impressions left from religious instruction. Active attacks and verbal abuse on the way to and from school were frequent but usually not all that serious. They sufficed, however, to establish an acute feeling of alienation already in childhood… »

↑ Studio portrait of the 14-year-old Albert Einstein, 1893

« Due to its liberal atmosphere and to the unpretentious seriousness of its teachers who did not rely on any imposed authority, the Cantonal School at Aarau left an unforgettable mark on me. Comparing it with the six years of schooling at a German, authoritarian high-school, I became acutely aware of how much more superior is an education favoring independence of action and personal responsibility, to a training based on drill, external authority and ambition. »

→ From "Autobiographical Sketch", first published in *Schweizerische Hochschulzeitung* 28, 1955

→ Matriculation certificate,
Aargau Cantonal School,
Aarau, Switzerland,
October 3, 1896.
The highest possible grade was six

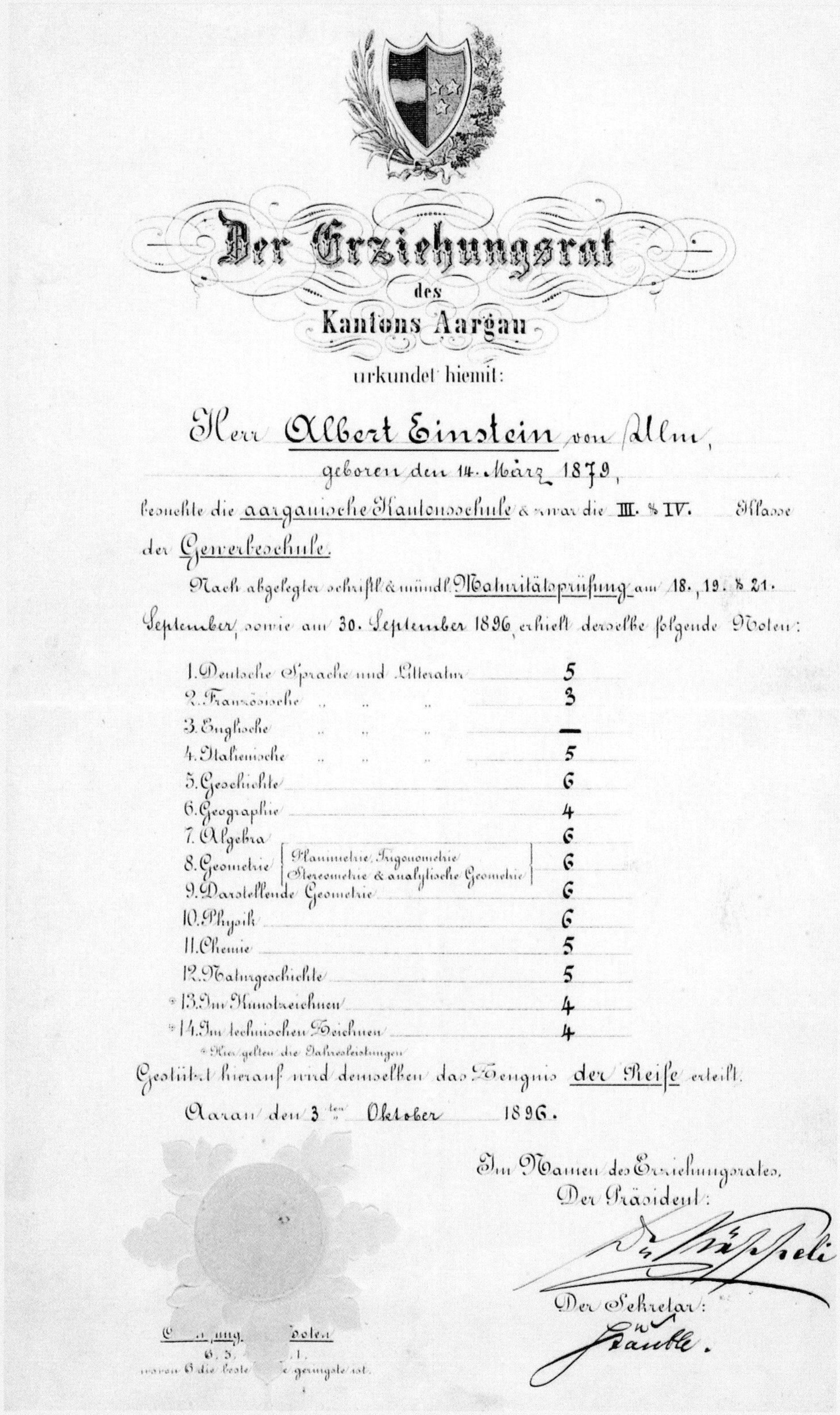

The Board of Education of the Canton Aargau hereby certifies that:
Mr. Albert Einstein of Ulm, born on March 14, 1879, attended the Aargau Kantonsschule, namely the third and fourth classes of the vocational school.
After taking the written and oral school-leaving examination held on September 18, 19, 21 and 30, 1896, he received the following marks:

1. German 5
2. French 3
3. English . . . . -
4. Italian 5
5. History 6
6. Geography 4
7. Algebra 6
8. Geometry 6
9. Descriptive Geometry . . . 6
10. Physics 6
11. Chemistry 5
12. Natural History 5
13. Artistic Drawing 4
14. Technical Drawing 4

Based on these marks, the above is granted the matriculation certificate.

Aarau, October 3, 1896

PERSONALITY AND FAMILY LIFE

By adolescence, Albert had evolved into a self-confident, even brash young man. He clearly exuded a great deal of attraction for the opposite sex, and established a few close friendships with fellow students, some of which lasted until the end of his life.

While studying at the Zurich Polytechnic, he fell in love with Mileva Marić, a fellow student. She was the daughter of a well-to-do Serbian country gentleman and honored official in the Hungarian bureaucracy, and one of the first women to study physics at the Polytechnic.

Many tender letters reflect his passionate relationship with Mileva Marić.
During his most scientifically fruitful years at the turn of the century when Einstein developed his early revolutionary theories, Mileva was not only his "sweet little one," but functioned also as his ideal sounding board. Yet, the search for evidence of Mileva's autonomous contribution to Einstein's scientific work has proved unsuccessful.

The first years of their relationship were warm and affectionate. Mileva gave birth to their daughter in 1902. Yet because neither of them had a secure income at the time, and because Einstein's parents opposed such a union, they did not marry until a year later. All traces of the daughter after the age of two seem to have been lost. There has been some speculation as to her fate – she may have been put up for adoption or she may have died at a young age. Albert and Mileva went on to have two sons, Hans Albert, born in 1904, and Eduard, born in 1910.

Apparently, Mileva could hardly overcome the loss of her daughter, suffering increasingly from melancholy. By around 1909 their marriage began to crumble and they became more and more estranged. In 1912 Albert got involved with his divorced cousin, Elsa.

Upon Einstein's move to Berlin in 1914, he and Mileva separated. They were divorced in 1919, and soon afterwards he married Elsa, who had two daughters, Margot and Ilse, from her previous marriage.

↑ Mileva, Hans Albert and Albert Einstein, Bern, 1904

↑ Eduard, Mileva and Hans Albert Einstein, Berlin, July 1914

« When you will be my dear little wife, we will zealously work on science together, so as not to become old philistines, right? My sister seemed to me so philistine. You must never get that way, it would be awful for me. You must always remain my witch and my urchin. I long very much for you. »

← From a letter to his future wife, Mileva Marić, December 28, 1901

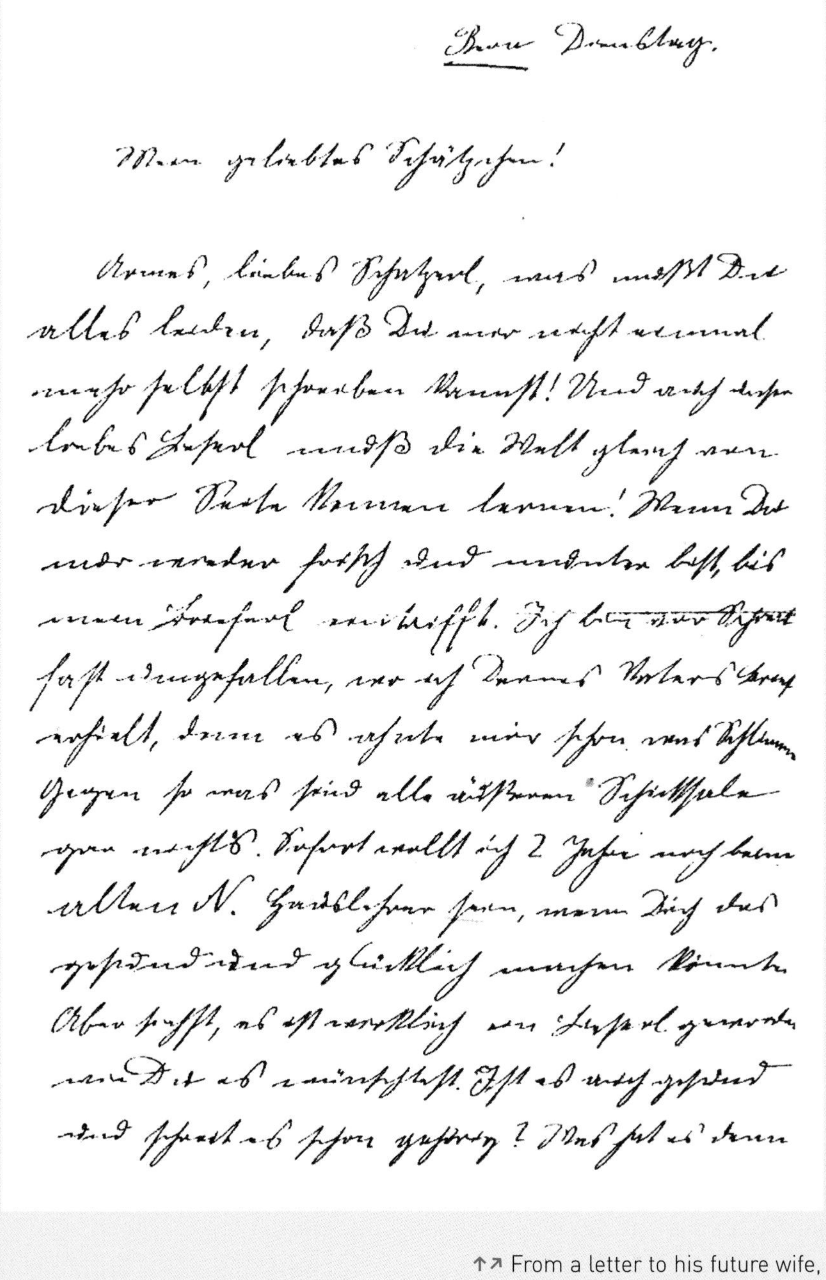
Bern Dienstag.

Mein geliebtes Schätzchen!

↑↗ From a letter to his future wife, Mileva Marić, February 4, 1902

« My beloved sweetheart!

Poor, dear sweetheart, what you've had to suffer if you can't even write to me yourself anymore! And our dear Lieserl too must get to know the world from this aspect right from the beginning! I hope you will be up and around again by the time my letter arrives. I was frightened out of my wits when I got your father's letter, because I had already sensed something wrong. External fates are nothing compared to this. At once I felt like remaining a tutor at old N[üesch]'s for two more years if that could bring you health and happiness. But you see, it has really turned out to be a Lieserl, just as you wished. Is she healthy, and does she already cry properly? What are her little eyes like? Whom of us does she resemble more? Who is giving her milk? Is she hungry? She must be completely bald. I love her so much and don't even know her yet! Couldn't you have a photograph made of her in the meantime until you've regained your health? Will she soon be able to turn her eyes toward something? Now you can make observations. I'd like once to make a Lieserl myself – it must be so fascinating! She certainly can cry already, but to laugh she'll learn much later. Therein lies a profound truth. When you feel a little better you must make a drawing of her! »

« Dear Papa,

I received your postcard and did not reply to it sooner because I always have very much homework. Mama has come home again in the meantime and has a nurse. We are tremendously happy. When Mama came home we had a celebration. I had practiced a sonata by Mozart, and Tete had learnt a song. We are very glad that Mama is here again, for we are not so alone. Mama can at least listen while I'm playing the piano and does Latin a bit with me. It's much nicer this way. We are slaving away in Latin: we've already had the 1st, 2nd, 3rd + 4th conjugation and the 1st, 2nd, 3rd, 4th+ 5th declension. The life insurance bill arrived a while ago and comes to 139.7 francs.

In letzter Zeit habe ich immer an einem Schiff gearbeitet, das ich aus einem einfachen Holzschiffchen gemacht habe.
Es kann sehr gut fahren und ich habe viel Freude daran.
Viele Grüße
Dein Albert.

Recently, I was working steadily on a ship I just made out of a simple wood carving.
It can sail very well and I have lots of fun with it.

Many greetings, yours, Albert »

↑ Letter from Hans Albert to his father, Albert Einstein, November 1916

↑ Eduard and Hans Albert Einstein, Arosa, July 1917

« My dear Albert,

I was most pleased with your ship [...]. You should know that when I was your age this was my favorite hobby as well. I really would like to have a closer description of it. Does the hull consist of two parts? Is it solid or hollow? How did you taper it at the bow? Is that which is sticking out downwards at the stern a rudder or only a weight? Where do you let it float?
I so much wish to see you both again...»

↑ From the father's answer to his son, Hans Albert, November 26, 1916

↑ Ilse and Margot Löwenthal,
later Einstein,
Elsa's daughters,
Berlin, around 1912

« I love her as much as if she were my own daughter, perhaps even more, since who knows what kind of brat she would have become [had I fathered her]. »

↑ About his stepdaughter Margot. From a letter to Elsa, May 1924

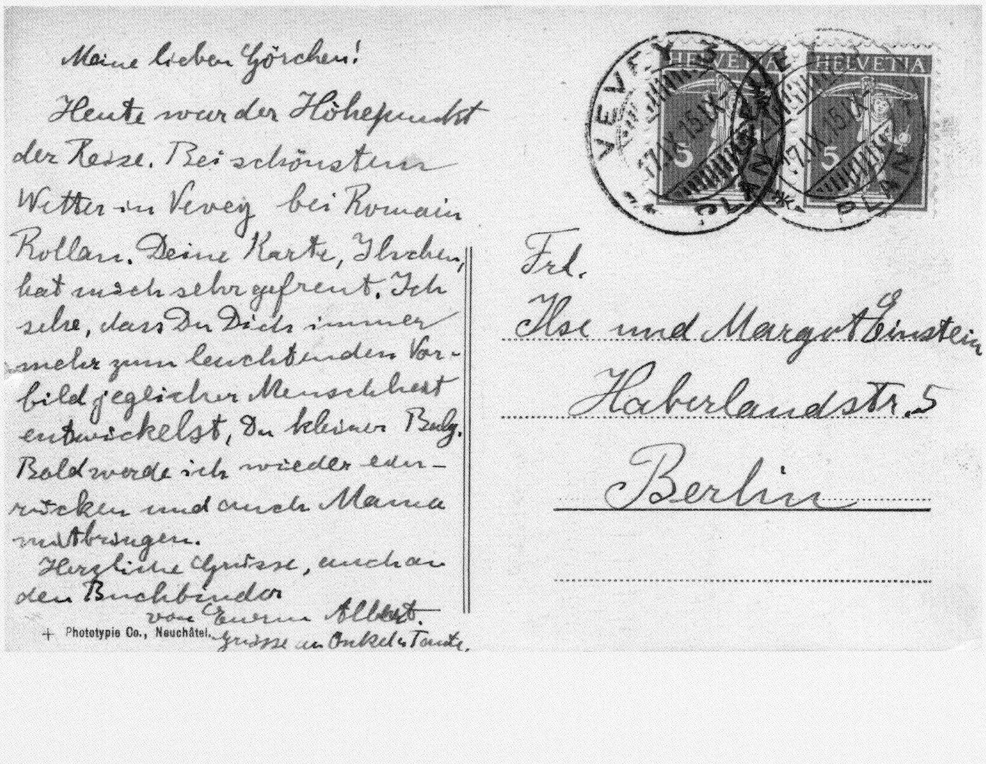

Meine lieben Görchen!
Heute war der Höhepunkt der Reise. Bei schönstem Wetter in Vevey bei Romain Rollan. Deine Karte, Ilschen, hat mich sehr gefreut. Ich sehe, dass Du Dich immer mehr zum leuchtenden Vorbild jeglicher Menschheit entwickelst, Du kleiner Balg. Bald werde ich wieder einrücken und auch Mama mitbringen.
Herzliche Grüsse, auch an den Buchbinder
von Eurem Albert.
Grüsse an Onkel u. Tante.

+ Phototypie Co., Neuchâtel.

Frl.
Ilse und Margot Einstein
Haberlandstr. 5
Berlin

«My dear little gals!

Today was the highpoint of the trip. With the most beautiful weather at Vevey [I visited] Romain Rollan[d]. Your card, Ilschen, gave me much pleasure. I see that you are more and more developing into a radiant model for all mankind, little urchin. Soon I'll march right in again and bring Mama back as well.

Kind regards... »

←↑ Postcard to his future step-daughters, Ilse and Margot, September 17, 1915

Albert's sons remained with Mileva in Zurich, and he would come to visit them or take them on vacations. A moving correspondence between father and sons indicates mutual affection and bears witness of Albert's efforts not to lose contact with the boys; even in letters to his second wife Einstein expresses his pleasure and pride in the boys.

Understandably, Einstein's relationship with Hans Albert was strained by the divorce and complicated by war-time conditions. In later years, the father strongly disapproved of his first son's association with an older woman whom the young man later married. Even so, no one was to doubt how much Einstein loved his children. He had a special affection for his younger son, Eduard, a highly sensitive boy with musical and literary talents. After Eduard was diagnosed with schizophrenia as a young adult, he spent many years of his life in a mental institution. A dismal photograph shows father and son during Einstein's last visit in 1933, before leaving Europe for good.

Elsa had no particular scientific ambitions and was much less Einstein's intellectual match than Mileva. Yet she provided him with comfort and protected him from intrusions that his growing fame brought about.

She clearly enjoyed sharing in his popularity. Though he was certainly not the most faithful of husbands and sought intimacy in a number of extramarital affairs, he cared for her deeply and appreciated her attention and homemaking qualities.

With Mileva, Einstein had not only dreamed about a sort of gypsy life during their student years, but as a married couple still maintained a bohemian existence, rejecting middle class values.

With his second wife, Elsa, he reverted to the secure bourgeois lifestyle of the "Philistines" that he so liked to ridicule.

Albert and Elsa moved to Princeton in 1933 with Albert's secretary, Helen Dukas. In 1934, they were joined by Elsa's daughter, Margot. After Elsa's death in 1936, Einstein lived a quiet life, working at the Institute for Advanced Study and taking long summer vacations with family and friends. In 1938, Hans Albert, Frieda and their two sons immigrated to the U.S. In 1939 Albert's sister, Maja, arrived from Italy where racist laws endangered her life. Her brother opened his home for her and she shared it with him, Margot and Helen Dukas until her death in 1951.

↓ Albert and Elsa Einstein on board the *Kitano Maru* during their voyage to the Far East, 1922

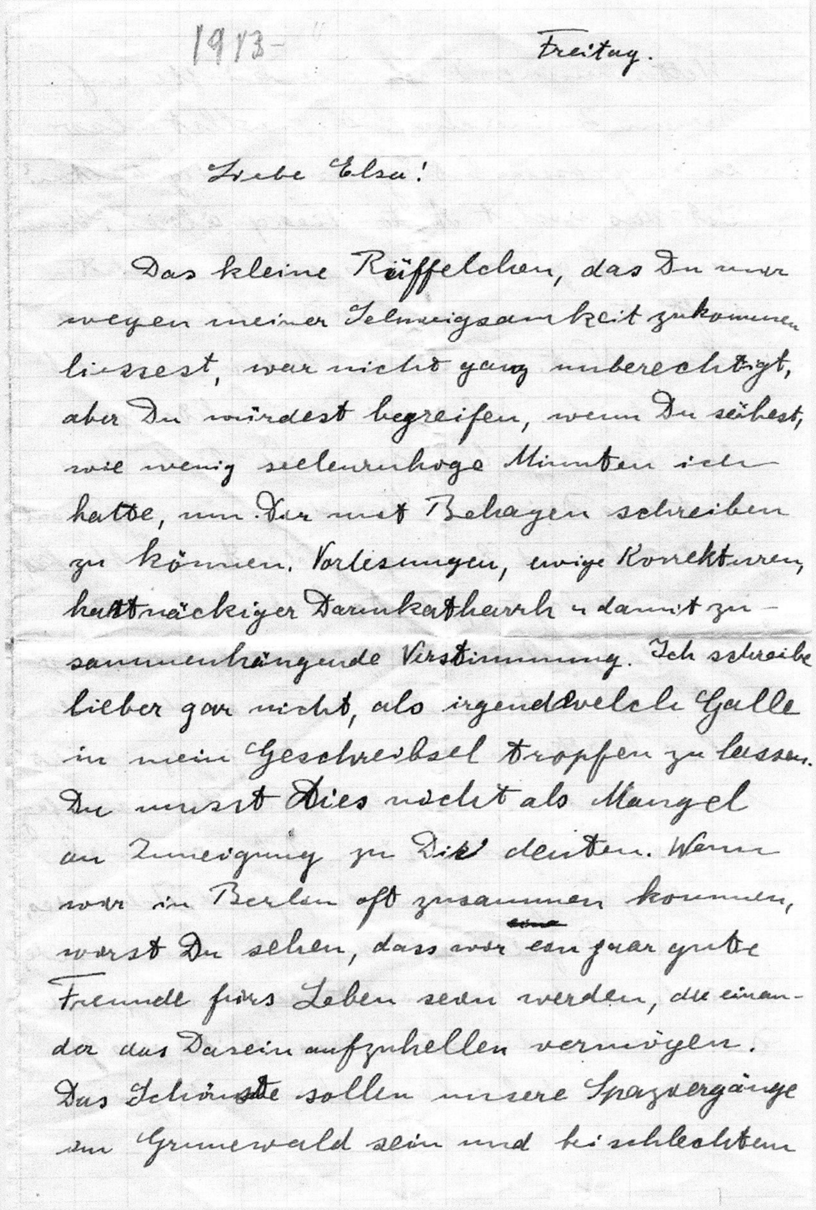
1913-

Freitag.

Liebe Elsa!

Das kleine Rüffelchen, das Du mir wegen meiner Schweigsamkeit zukommen liessest, war nicht ganz unberechtigt, aber Du würdest begreifen, wenn Du sähest, wie wenig seelenruhige Minuten ich hatte, um Dir mit Behagen schreiben zu können. Vorlesungen, ewige Korrekturen, hartnäckiger Darmkatharrh u. damit zusammenhängende Verstimmung. Ich schreibe lieber gar nicht, als irgendwelche Galle in mein Geschreibsel tropfen zu lassen. Du musst Dies nicht als Mangel an Zuneigung zu Dir deuten. Wenn wir in Berlin oft zusammen kommen, wirst Du sehen, dass wir ein paar gute Freunde fürs Leben sein werden, die einander das Dasein aufzuhellen vermögen. Das Schönste sollen unsere Spaziergänge im Grunewald sein und bei schlechtem

↑↗ Letter to his cousin,
Elsa Einstein,
November 7, 1913

« Dear Elsa!

The little scolding you gave me because of my silence was not totally unjustified; but you would understand it if you saw how few were the calm moments in which I could have written to you in peace and quiet. […] You must not interpret this as a lack of affection for you.
When we start meeting frequently in Berlin you will see that we will become good friends for a lifetime, who will be able to brighten each other's existence. The most beautiful thing will be our walks in the Grunewald forest and, in inclement weather, our rendezvous in your small room. So you want to give a big extemporaneous reading? […] People like me are happy when they don't have to make a public presentation – and you are doing it of your own volition. Still, I'm impressed by your courage. Yet, by no means would I like to attend it. Because only as a private gift and product of the moment do I love the words from out of your mouth, the more spontaneously, the better! If you were to recite me the most beautiful poem no matter how divinely, my pleasure would not even approach the pleasure I felt when I received the mushrooms and goose cracklings you prepared for me. I know how the psychologist would interpret this but I wouldn't be ashamed and you would certainly not despise the primitive side of my nature that is revealed by this, even if you would smile a little. »

« Dear Tete,*

When I read your letters I am very much reminded of my youth. In one's thoughts, one tends to set oneself against the world. One compares one's own strengths with everything else, one alternates between despondency and self-assurance. One has the feeling that life is eternal and that everything that one does and thinks is so important. Yes, one feels as if one were the first and only fellow who has gone through all this. Yet this heroism is rather embarrassing and can only be corrected by humor and by one's somehow turning with the social machine. [...] All my life I have troubled myself with problems and am always – as on the first day – inspired by the fact that cognition in the scientific and artistic sense is the best thing we possess. My love of these things has never diminished and will stay with me till I breathe my last.

You were also born for this and your words to the contrary only derive from the fear of not being able to achieve anything worthwhile. Dear Tetel,* therefore I somehow take pity on you. But there is an easy solution: to become just a little cog in the large machinery so that no one can demand anything else. One is a thinking and feeling creature privately and for one's own pleasure. If one hears the angels singing a couple of times during one's life, one can give the world something and one is a particularly fortunate and blessed individual. Yet if this is not the case, one is nevertheless a small particle of the soul of one's generation and that is also beautiful. Think about this carefully, so that you don't fall victim to the devil of ambition and vanity. And keep in mind: not the desire for the achievement but love of the things themselves can lead to something worthwhile. Be that as it may, you bring me great joy because you're not going through life mindlessly but rather seeing and thinking. I would like to be with you again soon. Couldn't you come here during your Easter holidays? (I don't dare to ask you to come during Christmas so that Mama will not be left on her own.) »

* Nickname for Eduard

↑ Eduard Einstein, around 1925

↖↑ Letter to his younger son, Eduard, 1928/1929

→ From a letter by Michele Besso to Albert Einstein, June 19, 1937. Since they had met in Zurich in 1896, a close friendship bound Einstein and Besso together. In a moving letter in 1928 Besso acknowledges that he owes Einstein his wife, and therefore his son and his grandson, his job and thus his financial security, and even his appreciation of the sciences. Einstein, for his part, could rely on Besso not only as an ideal sounding board during the years of his highest scientific productivity, but as a true friend who would stand by and take care of Mileva and the sons whenever there was a need.

« Yesterday evening [I heard] a powerful series of Händel's pieces, the last one being the beautifully delicate prelude (Bach-Busoni Choralvorspiele, Heft I, No.5, Ich ruf zu Dir, Herr) beautifully delicately played by Eduard Einstein. There is something questionable about his body: overweight; timidity that prevents him from going out, did not leave the apartment for one year – the visiting friend does not always get to see him. But again, three times lately: complete, well composed, highly original discourses in the psychological field: presented somewhat harshly [...], as if breaking through a curtain of great shyness... »

← Mileva, Hans Albert (left) and Eduard, and Hans Albert's wife, Frieda, Zurich, about 1930

↑ Albert and Elsa Einstein at the Grand Canyon National Park, February 28, 1931
Photo by El Tovar Studio

Throughout his life, Einstein was in many respects a radical non-conformist and rejected societal norms. Despite his outspoken sympathies for certain political objectives, he was not willing to join any political party.

He reserved a special sarcasm for every form of pomp and circumstance, and took the weaknesses of his fellow men as well as his own foibles with good humor. His roaring, childlike laughter left a deep impression on all those who met him.

Colleagues and friends observed Einstein's striking ability to distance himself from his feelings and to belittle the importance of emotional issues. Einstein himself described his attitude in respect of emotions as "inwardly little involved" and claimed that this detachment had been a necessary prerequisite for his total dedication to his first love: science.

In an even broader sense he enjoyed an exceptional independence since, first in Berlin, later in Princeton, he held positions that permitted him to dedicate himself entirely to his research, without any teaching obligations and with few other responsibilities.

Einstein died of a rupture of an aortic aneurysm in 1955 at the age of 76. He was cremated and his ashes scattered at an undisclosed place.

« I always loved solitude, a treat which tends to increase with age. It is a strange thing to be so widely known and yet be so lonely. But it is a fact that this kind of popularity – as it has become the case with me – is forcing its victim into a defensive position which leads to isolation. »

→ From a letter to Ernesta Marangoni, October 1, 1952

→ The sender of the letter, a left-wing politician and psychotherapist, planned to carry out a study of politicians based on Individual Psychology, to be published in the weekly magazine *Die Weltbühne*, and asked Einstein to participate. Einstein had very limited confidence in psychoanalysis and other techniques that seemed irrational to him. He may have shyed away from looking deeply into his own inner life.
Here is the response to the suggestion that he undergo an "analysis," or rather an investigation.

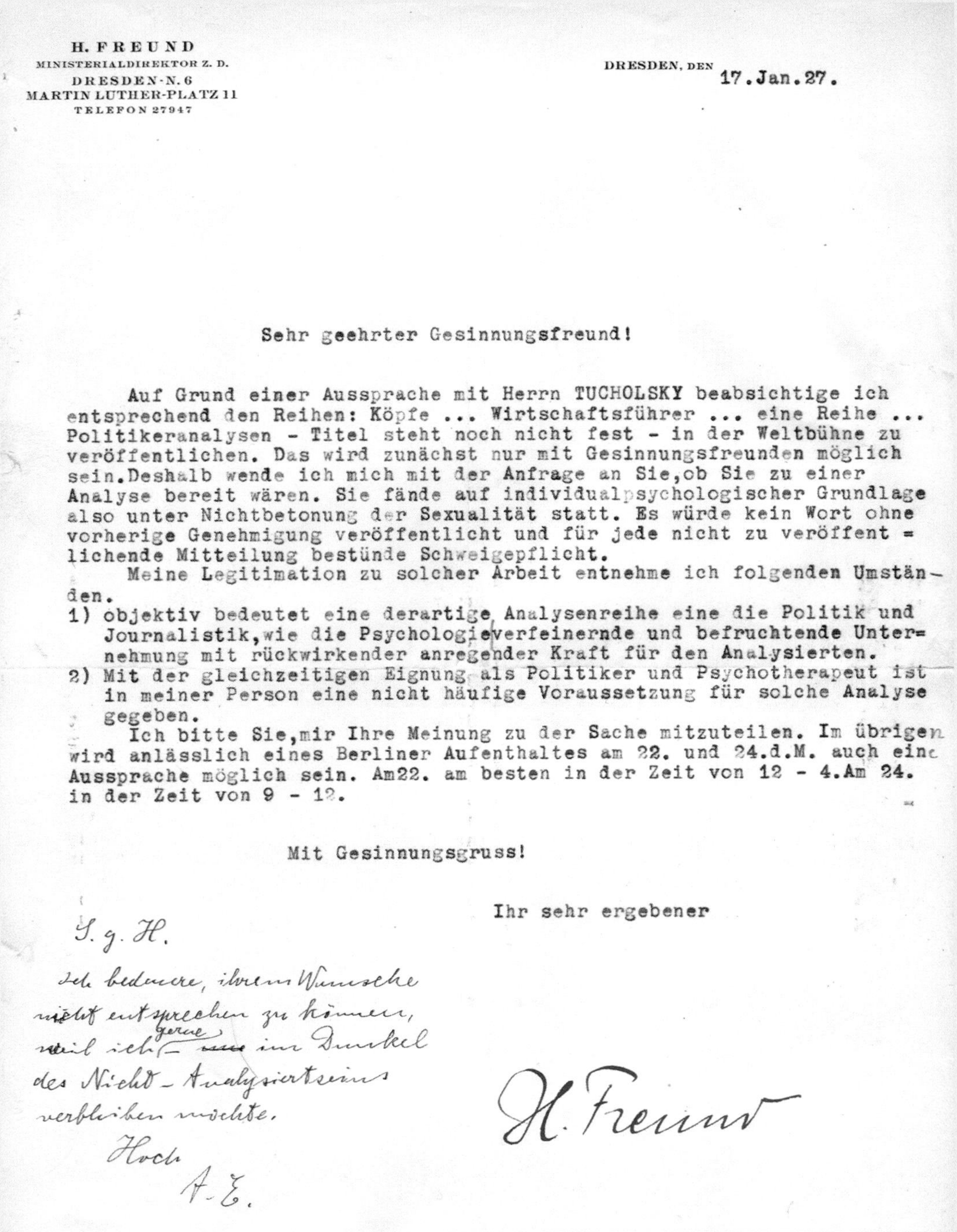

H. FREUND
MINISTERIALDIREKTOR Z. D.
DRESDEN-N. 6
MARTIN LUTHER-PLATZ 11
TELEFON 27947

DRESDEN, DEN 17.Jan.27.

Sehr geehrter Gesinnungsfreund!

Auf Grund einer Aussprache mit Herrn TUCHOLSKY beabsichtige ich entsprechend den Reihen: Köpfe ... Wirtschaftsführer ... eine Reihe ... Politikeranalysen - Titel steht noch nicht fest - in der Weltbühne zu veröffentlichen. Das wird zunächst nur mit Gesinnungsfreunden möglich sein. Deshalb wende ich mich mit der Anfrage an Sie, ob Sie zu einer Analyse bereit wären. Sie fände auf individualpsychologischer Grundlage also unter Nichtbetonung der Sexualität statt. Es würde kein Wort ohne vorherige Genehmigung veröffentlicht und für jede nicht zu veröffent = lichende Mitteilung bestünde Schweigepflicht.

Meine Legitimation zu solcher Arbeit entnehme ich folgenden Umständen.

1) objektiv bedeutet eine derartige Analysenreihe eine die Politik und Journalistik, wie die Psychologie verfeinernde und befruchtende Unter= nehmung mit rückwirkender anregender Kraft für den Analysierten.
2) Mit der gleichzeitigen Eignung als Politiker und Psychotherapeut ist in meiner Person eine nicht häufige Voraussetzung für solche Analyse gegeben.

Ich bitte Sie, mir Ihre Meinung zu der Sache mitzuteilen. Im übrigen wird anlässlich eines Berliner Aufenthaltes am 22. und 24.d.M. auch eine Aussprache möglich sein. Am 22. am besten in der Zeit von 12 - 4. Am 24. in der Zeit von 9 - 12.

Mit Gesinnungsgruss!

Ihr sehr ergebener

H. Freund

S. g. H.

Ich bedauere, Ihrem Wunsche nicht entsprechen zu können, weil ich gerne ~~sehr~~ im Dunkel des Nicht-Analysiertseins verbleiben möchte.

Hoch

A. E.

↑ Letter by H. Freund to Einstein, January 17, 1927 including the draft of Einstein's reply. It is unknown whether it was ever sent.

« I regret that I cannot accede to your request, because I should like very much to remain in the darkness of not having been analyzed. »

Peconic Bay Long Island.
20. VII. 38.

Liebe Mileva!

Mit dem Bürgerrecht ist es so: Als ich 1914 nach Berlin kam, war ich ausschliesslich schweizer Bürger. Dies hatte ich für meine Annahme der Stelle in Berlin zur Bedingung gemacht, und sie wurde auch angenommen. Solange ich mit Dir verheiratet war, war ich also ausschliesslich Schweizer Bürger. Erst 1919 drang die Akademie in mich, neben dem schweizer Bürgerrecht auch das deutsche zu akzeptieren. Ich war so dumm und gab damals nach. Dies hatte nämlich zur Folge, dass sie 1933 mir alles wegnahmen, was ich in Deutschland besass. Dich und die Kinder geht dies aber nichts an. 1933 gab ich das deutsche Bürgerrecht auf und besitze also nur noch das schweizerische.

Was nun das Haus betrifft, so weisst Du ja selbst, dass ich eine erhebliche Summe letztes Jahr hineingesteckt habe. Es zu halten würde ich überhaupt nicht in der Lage sein. Wenn also die Gläubiger darauf drängen, so müssen wir es aufgeben. Nun ist erstens zu bedenken, dass das Geld, was ich Tetel monatlich gebe, in Yugoslavien bequem für Euch beide ausreicht. Ferner könnte man Deinen dortigen Besitz durch Übertragung auf Deine Schwester oder Tetel sichern. Das Bedenken wegen der geistigen Anregung kommt nicht in Betracht. Von Zeit zu Zeit ein paar Bücher und Musikalien lassen sich leicht auftreiben. Und für die medizinische Hilfe gebe ich keinen Dreck. Die monatliche Zahlung an Tetel habe ich testamentarisch festgelegt, und zwar so, dass sie allem andern vorangeht. Um diese Zahlung zu sichern, solang Tetel lebt, reicht es auf jeden Fall, wenn nicht in Amerika eine Finanzkatastrophe grossen Stils eintritt. Wenn Euch also die feinen Leute

« Dear Mileva!

The matter of the nationality is the following: When I arrived in Berlin in 1914, I was solely a Swiss citizen. I had made that a condition of my accepting the position, and it was accepted. Therefore, while I was married to you, I was solely a Swiss citizen. Only in 1919, the Academy pressed me to accept the German citizenship along with the Swiss one. At that time I was so silly, and conceded.
The result was that in 1933 they confiscated all the property I had in Germany.
However, none of this regards you and the kids.
In 1933 I renounced the German citizenship and now have only Swiss citizenship.
As far as the house is concerned, you know yourself what a considerable sum I have invested last year. I would certainly not be in a position to keep it. Thus, if the creditors insist, we will have to give up on it. Now, firstly you have to keep in mind that the money I'm sending for Tetel each month would be enough to provide a comfortable life for both of you in Yugoslavia. Moreover, one could safeguard your property there by signing it over to the name of your sister or of Tetel. I disregard any qualms about the lack of intellectual stimulation [there]. From time to time, one can easily ferret out a couple of books and musical scores. For the medical coverage I won't give a dirty penny.
For the monthly allowance for Tetel I made provisions in my will, namely that payment for him would be given first. In any case, unless a financial catastrophe on a grand scale occurs in America, this payment is guaranteed as long as Tetel is alive.

←↑ Letter to his first wife, Mileva, July 20, 1938

in Zürich Euer letztes wegnehmen, so geht ruhig nach Yougoslavien. Dort ist es überhaupt sicherer, denn auf die lieben Schweizer ist überhaupt kein unbedingter Verlass. Sie haben damals auch keinen Finger gerührt, als die saubern Deutschen an mir ihr Schurkenstückchen trieben. Ich sähe Euch lieber in Serbien.

Albert ist in Greenville in South-Carolina und schreibt sehr befriedigt (und sehr wenig). Ich habe ihm ein schönes Auto gekauft, ohne dass er doch nicht auskommen kann. So habe ich in diesem Jahr viel Geld für ihn ausgegeben, aber dafür ist er auch dauernd versorgt und hat eine interessante Arbeit. Es ist ein wahres Glück, dass er mit der scheusslichen Fr. zufrieden ist.

Ich habe dieses Jahr etwas Wunderbares in meiner Wissenschaft gefunden. Dies wird sich später wahrscheinlich als entscheidender Fortschritt herausstellen.

Tetel lasse ich herzlich für seinen Brief danken. Ich freue mich, dass er Lust zum Schreiben hatte. Herzliche Grüsse an Euch beide von Deinem

Albert.

Therefore, when the nice folks in Zurich take away all your savings, just move quietly to Yugoslavia. There you will actually be in a safe place, as one can hardly rely on the dear Swiss without reservation. They did not lift a finger at the time when the German bastards played their dirty tricks with me. I would prefer knowing you were in Serbia.

Albert is in Greenville, South Carolina, satisfied [with his situation], and writes rather sparsely. I bought him a pretty car, as without it he would certainly not get by. Thus, I spent a lot of money on him this year, but at least he got lasting security and found an interesting job. Lucky for him he is pleased with that nasty Fr[ieda].
This year I made a wonderful discovery in my science. Later, it will probably turn out to be a crucial advancement.
Please give my warmest thanks to Tetel for his letter. I am happy that he felt like writing. Heartfelt regards to both of you, yours Albert »

←↑ Financial problems, ailing health, bitterness and mistrust on both sides had overshadowed the years following the separation, and the war had added to the burden.
Even in later years, tensions would flare up from time to time, and discord could not always be excluded; but an amicable relationship between Albert and Mileva again became possible, based essentially on the joint care of their sons.
This quite sympathetic letter may exemplify what Einstein meant when he once, after the marriage fell apart, said to Mileva that he would remain loyal to her, in his own way.
Mileva's preceding letter had raised the question of Einstein's nationality. She may have been afraid of expulsion in case Switzerland would be annexed or join Germany. Her main concern, however, was that, under those circumstances, Eduard might be taken as a hostage.
Einstein tries to dispel her worries, thereby surprisingly mistaking the official German version of his naturalization for what actually happened. Contrary to his description in this letter, the question of his citizenship only came up on the occasion of the Nobel Prize award in 1922, and it was more than one year later that Einstein agreed upon a retroactive assigning of the German citizenship in addition to the Swiss citizenship.
In the matter of the house, too, Einstein shows appreciation for Mileva's problems. We understand from the letter that he is supporting her and Eduard, as well as Hans Albert in the U.S., not only with words, but with considerable sums of money, although he does not always favor the costly medical treatments that Eduard underwent. Einstein suggests rather than imposes a way out of Mileva's financial straits which would have solved one problem immediately. A move to Yugoslavia, though, would have placed Mileva and Eduard in the middle of a war zone shortly afterwards. Yet Einstein is hardly to blame for not having anticipated what may have prevented Mileva from following his suggestion.
Physics is mentioned here only incidentally as it no longer represents a shared topic of conversation.

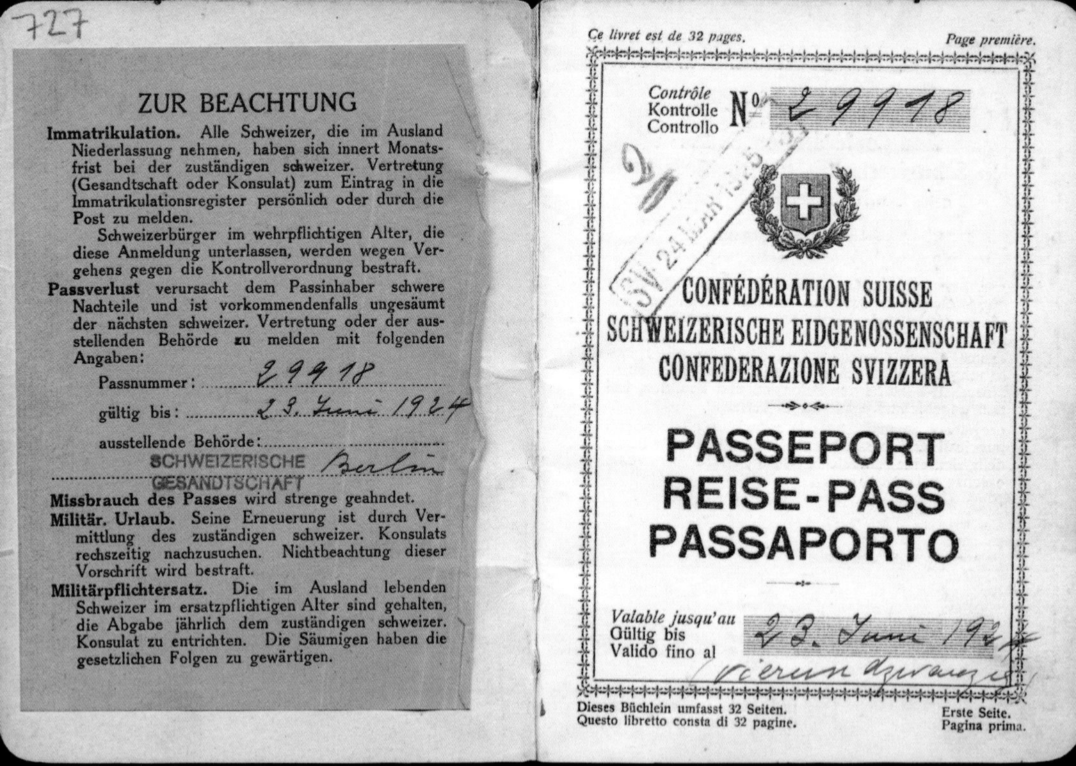
727

ZUR BEACHTUNG

Immatrikulation. Alle Schweizer, die im Ausland Niederlassung nehmen, haben sich innert Monatsfrist bei der zuständigen schweizer. Vertretung (Gesandtschaft oder Konsulat) zum Eintrag in die Immatrikulationsregister persönlich oder durch die Post zu melden.

Schweizerbürger im wehrpflichtigen Alter, die diese Anmeldung unterlassen, werden wegen Vergehens gegen die Kontrollverordnung bestraft.

Passverlust verursacht dem Passinhaber schwere Nachteile und ist vorkommendenfalls ungesäumt der nächsten schweizer. Vertretung oder der ausstellenden Behörde zu melden mit folgenden Angaben:

Passnummer: 29918

gültig bis: 23. Juni 1924

ausstellende Behörde: SCHWEIZERISCHE GESANDTSCHAFT Berlin

Missbrauch des Passes wird strenge geahndet.

Militär. Urlaub. Seine Erneuerung ist durch Vermittlung des zuständigen schweizer. Konsulats rechtzeitig nachzusuchen. Nichtbeachtung dieser Vorschrift wird bestraft.

Militärpflichtersatz. Die im Ausland lebenden Schweizer im ersatzpflichtigen Alter sind gehalten, die Abgabe jährlich dem zuständigen schweizer. Konsulat zu entrichten. Die Säumigen haben die gesetzlichen Folgen zu gewärtigen.

Ce livret est de 32 pages. *Page première.*

Contrôle Kontrolle Controllo N° 29918

CONFÉDÉRATION SUISSE
SCHWEIZERISCHE EIDGENOSSENSCHAFT
CONFEDERAZIONE SVIZZERA

PASSEPORT
REISE-PASS
PASSAPORTO

Valable jusqu'au Gültig bis Valido fino al 23. Juni 1924 vierundzwanzig

Dieses Büchlein umfasst 32 Seiten. Questo libretto consta di 32 pagine. Erste Seite. Pagina prima.

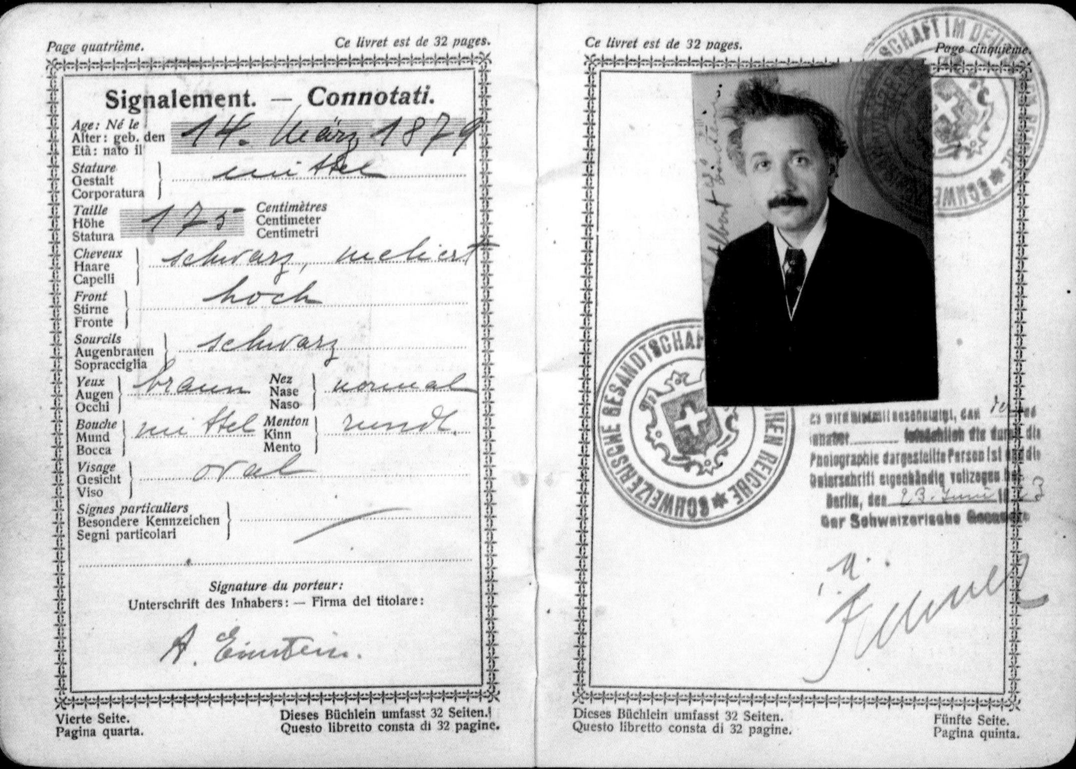
Page quatrième. *Ce livret est de 32 pages.*

Signalement. — Connotati.

Age: Né le Alter: geb. den Età: nato il — 14. März 1879

Stature Gestalt Corporatura — mittel

Taille Höhe Statura — 175 *Centimètres* Centimeter Centimetri

Cheveux Haare Capelli — schwarz, meliert

Front Stirne Fronte — hoch

Sourcils Augenbrauen Sopracciglia — schwarz

Yeux Augen Occhi — braun; *Nez* Nase Naso — normal

Bouche Mund Bocca — mittel; *Menton* Kinn Mento — rund

Visage Gesicht Viso — oval

Signes particuliers Besondere Kennzeichen Segni particolari —

Signature du porteur: Unterschrift des Inhabers: — Firma del titolare:

A. Einstein.

Vierte Seite. Pagina quarta. Dieses Büchlein umfasst 32 Seiten. Questo libretto consta di 32 pagine.

Ce livret est de 32 pages. *Page cinquième.*

SCHWEIZERISCHE GESANDTSCHAFT IM DEUTSCHEN REICHE

Es wird hiermit bescheinigt, dass ... die umseitig ... durch die Photographie dargestellte Person ist und die Unterschrift eigenhändig vollzogen hat.

Berlin, den 23. Juni 1923

Der Schweizerische Gesandte

Dieses Büchlein umfasst 32 Seiten. Questo libretto consta di 32 pagine. Fünfte Seite. Pagina quinta.

↑↗ Einstein's Swiss passport, issued in June 1923. When, in 1925, the Swiss authorities refused to issue him a diplomatic passport, in order to ease his traveling, the German ministry for foreign affairs was glad to step into the breach. On his trip to Latin America, Einstein, now officially a German citizen, traveled on a German diplomatic passport.

Reg. Nr. 2060 Gebühr

Berlin, den 2. August 1923

Bayerische Gesandtschaft.

~~Einreise nach München Nürnberg~~ Lautrach vorbehaltlich der Aufenthalts~~genehmigung~~ der Polizeibehörde ~~vorgenehmigt~~. Persönliche polizeiliche Meldung innerhalb 24 Stunden nach Ankunft vorgeschrieben.

I. V. Sommer

BAYER. GESANDTSCHAFT IN BERLIN.

VISTO – CONSULADO GERAL DOS ESTADOS UNIDOS DO BRASIL ... MONTEVIDEO

BRASIL REPUBLICA DOS ESTADOS UNIDOS DO BRASIL JOSÉ BONIFACIO 1822 SELLO CONSULAR 4.000 Rs

Dr Alberto Conrado

Consul Geral

Recebi $ 2,40 ouro

Conrado

Nr. 7

Grenzstelle ...heim Ausgereist 4 OKT. 1924

Nr. 1 Grenzstelle Bertheim Ein – Ausgereist 7. FEB 1925

Nr. 1523 Taxe: M. 2.40

Gesehen auf der Schweizerischen Gesandtschaft zu Berlin und verlängert auf 6 Monate bis zum 12. Januar 1925 (fünfundzwanzig) für die Reise und zum Aufenthalt in allen Staaten Europas

12. Juli 1924

i. A. Fehlmann

SERVICE CONSULAIRE SUISSE IMMATRICULATION

Bayer. Grenzpolizei Austritt Passau 3 JUL 1924

Grenzpolizeistelle Lindau i. B.

Oesterr. Grenzpolizei Eintritt

Österreichische Sichtvermerkmarke für Einmalige Einreise

Österreich 4. MÄR 2... Feldkirch.

↑ Albert Einstein on a Princeton street, in the background his secretary Helen Dukas, holding leash for Chico, the dog, early 1950s

↑ Albert Einstein with Helen Dukas and Chico, in their Princeton garden.
Photo by Abraham Mandelstam

« Of all the communities available to us there is not one I would want to devote myself to, except for the society of the true searchers, which has very few living members at any time. »

← From a letter to his friend, the physicist Max Born, April 29, 1924

↙↓ From a letter to his biographer, Philipp Frank, 1940

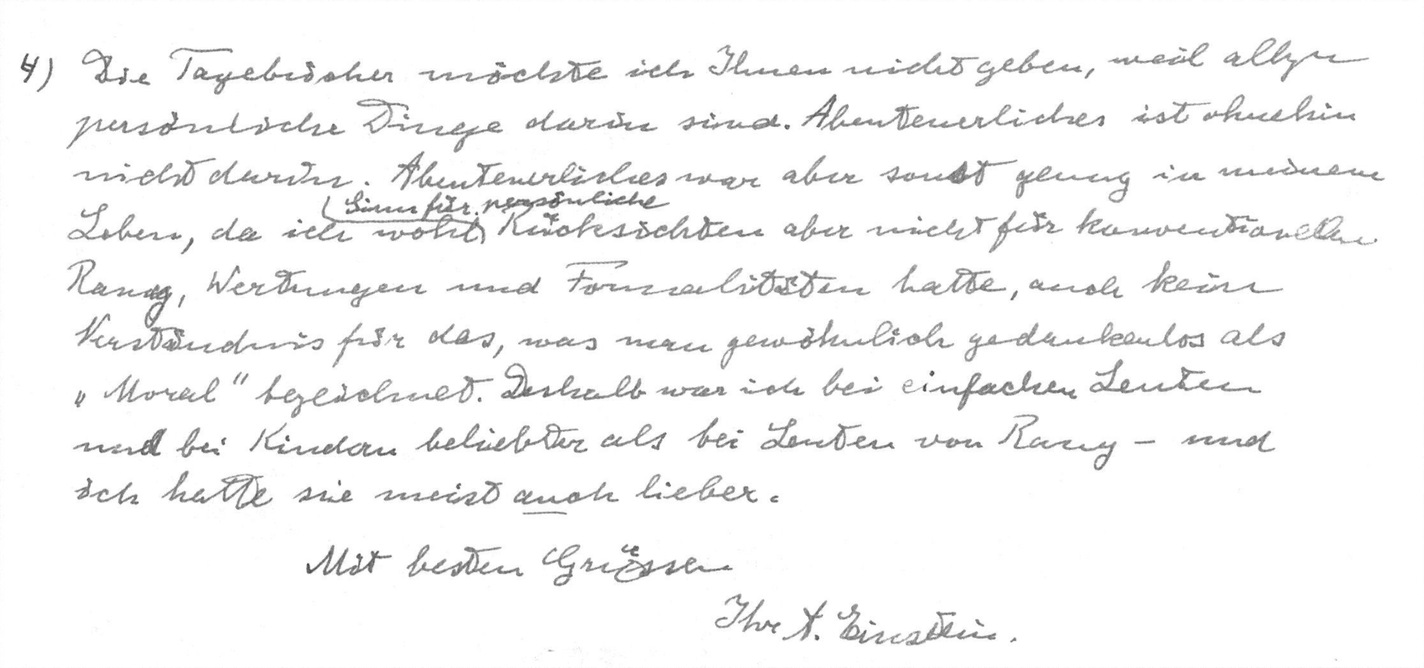

4) Die Tagebücher möchte ich Ihnen nicht geben, weil allzu persönliche Dinge darin sind. Abenteuerliches ist ohnehin nicht darin. Abenteuerliches war aber sonst genug in meinem Leben, da ich wohl Sinn für persönliche Rücksichten aber nicht für konventionellen Rang, Wertungen und Formalitäten hatte, auch kein Verständnis für das, was man gewöhnlich gedankenlos als „Moral" bezeichnet. Deshalb war ich bei einfachen Leuten und bei Kindern beliebter als bei Leuten von Rang – und ich hatte sie meist auch lieber.

Mit besten Grüssen

Ihr A. Einstein.

« I prefer not to make my diaries available to you, as they contain things too personal. They don't contain anything adventurous, anyway. Adventures, though, I experienced plenty, as I was inclined to respect individuals, but not conventional status or standards, and formalities; nor did I appreciate what, in general, is mindlessly called 'morals.' That is why ordinary people and children were more fond of me than socialites; and, mostly, I preferred them, too. »

← Albert Einstein with assistants
Valentine Bargmann and
Peter G. Bergmann,
Princeton, October 2, 1940.
Photo by Lucien Aigner

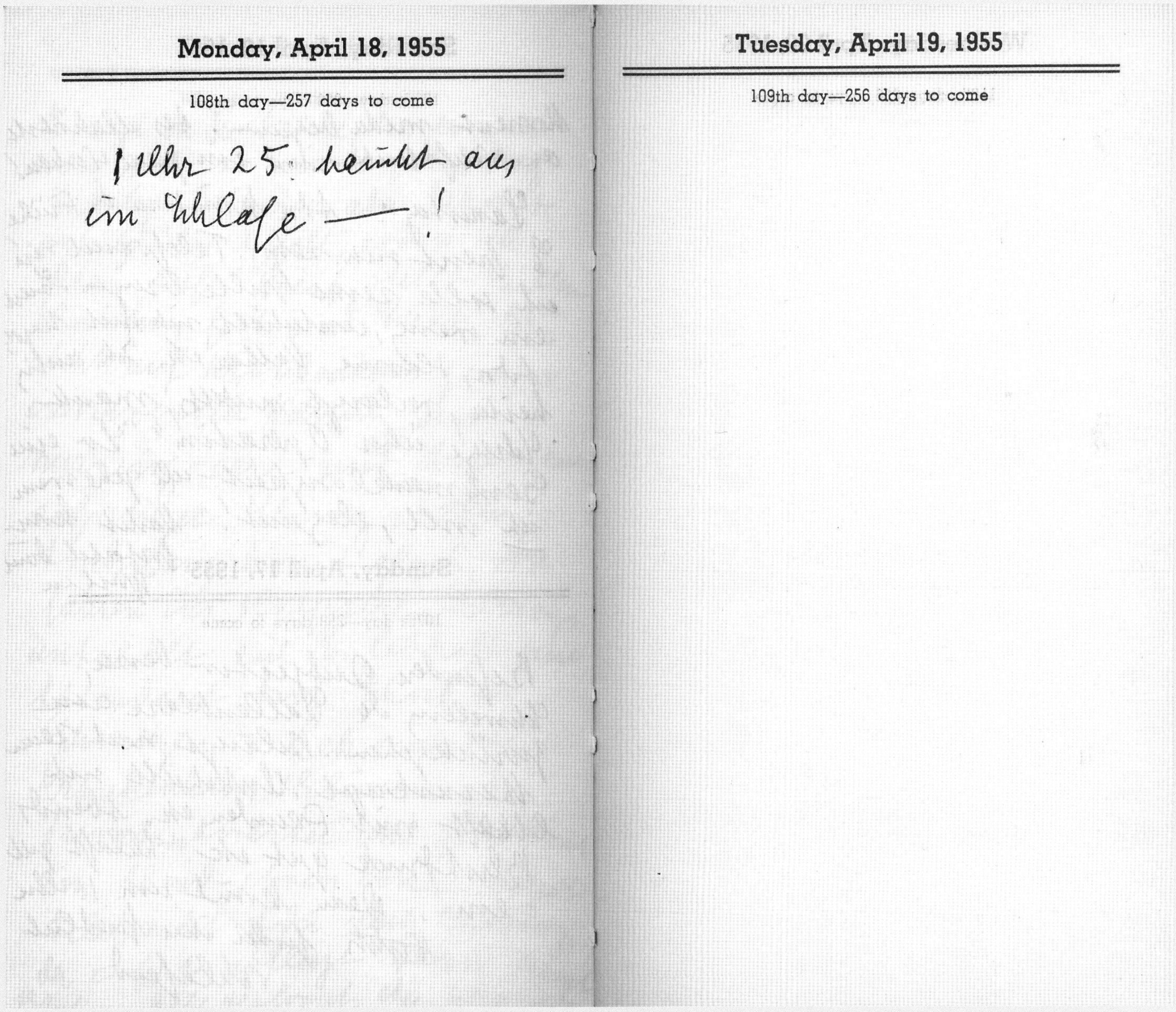

Monday, April 18, 1955

108th day—257 days to come

1 Uhr 25: haucht aus
im Schlafe —— !

Tuesday, April 19, 1955

109th day—256 days to come

1:25 a.m.: drew his last breath while asleep – !

↑ Page of Helen Dukas' diary the day Einstein passed away.

2

EINSTEIN'S SCIENTIFIC ACHIEVEMENTS

« When the blind beetle crawls over the surface of a globe, he doesn't realize that the track he has covered is curved.
I was lucky enough to have spotted it. »

An answer Einstein used to give to journalists when asked how he had become so famous.

EINSTEIN'S SIGNIFICANCE

Albert Einstein's contribution to modern physics is simply unique. His scientific career was a constant quest for the universal and immutable laws which govern the physical world.
Einstein's theories span the fundamental questions of nature, from the very large to the very small, from the cosmos to sub-atomic particles. He overturned the established concepts of time and space, energy and matter. As the father of the theory of relativity and as a major contributor to quantum theory Einstein played a crucial role in establishing the two pillars of 20th century physics.
Einstein was a theoretical physicist; his only concrete tools being pencil and paper.
It has been said that his true abilities lay in a penetrating and intuitive grasp of the workings of the natural world, and the "thought experiment" - an imagined scenario as used in philosophy, physics and other fields, leading from well-structured hypothetical questions to a theoretical conclusion.
Yet, Einstein was not a purely abstract thinker. He conceived the world in concrete images and strove to translate them into words and equations that could be understood by others.
Einstein's work must be viewed within the context of the evolution of modern physics. He did not create airtight perfect physical theories that were to last forever. He was well aware that his theories were based on a long history of previous efforts of the scientists who had preceded him. Moreover, Einstein declared that just as his theories had gone beyond Newton's, sooner or later someone would have to go beyond his own.

« Where the world ceases to be the scene of our personal hopes and wishes, where we face it as free beings admiring, asking, and observing, there we enter the realm of Art and Science. If what is seen and experienced is portrayed in the language of logic, we are engaged in science. If it is communicated through forms whose connections are not accessible to the conscious mind but are recognized intuitively as meaningful, then we are engaged in art. Common to both is the loving devotion to that which transcends personal concerns and volition. »

→ "What Do the Artistic and Scientific Experiences Have in Common?" Contribution to *Menschen, Zeitschrift neuer Kunst*, February 4, 1921, upon the request of its co-editor, Walter Hasenclever. Here, as repeatedly elsewhere, Einstein presented his ideal of escaping from merely personal concerns to a higher realm.

→ The cosmic genius at work.
Cartoon by Lou Grant

→ From "Induction and Deduction in Physics," *Berliner Tageblatt*, December 25, 1919

« The truth of a theory can never be proven. For one never knows if future experience will contradict its conclusions; and furthermore there are always other conceptual systems imaginable which might coordinate the very same facts. »

← As a student at the Zurich Polytechnic, ca.1898

→ Reflection about his friendship with Marcel Grossmann. From Einstein's condolence letter to Grossmann's widow, September 20, 1936

« He, an exemplary student, me, unorderly and dreamy. He, aligned with the teachers and easily grasping everything, me, remaining aloof and unsatisfied, little popular. But we were good friends, and our discussions at the Metropol, every few weeks having ice coffee together, evoke some of my nicest memories. Then the end of our studies – me, suddenly abandoned by everybody, at a loss with life. Yet he stood by me, and it was thanks to him and his father that, a couple of years afterwards, I found employment at Haller's patent office. That was a sort of lifesaving without which I might not have died, but intellectually I would have withered. »

THE EARLY YEARS

Einstein's interest in science and technology was initially stimulated by his uncle and father. A student who used to come for dinner once a week acquainted the twelve-year-old Albert with popular science books and philosophy which obviously left a deep impression. At the age of sixteen, Albert wrote his first physics essay. By the time he had completed his secondary education, he was certain of his vocation: the study of physics, especially in its theoretical aspects.

In 1896, Einstein entered the Zurich Polytechnic as a student of the School for Mathematics and Science Teachers. In retrospect he will confess that he perceived himself as a "veritable idiot", feeling overfed with information and having to struggle to find his sense of balance. This may have been the reason why he often skipped his classes and, instead, delved into books. His knowledge of theory eventually resulted primarily from self-instruction.

Upon completion of his studies in 1900, Einstein tried to obtain a position in academia, but his efforts met with no success. Not until June 1902 did he find employment at the Swiss Patent Office in Bern.

Although he was now isolated from the scientific community, he kept abreast of significant developments in physics through scientific publications.

Working with the many-sided aspects of patent applications offered him an important source of inspiration. Other impulses evolved from discussions with Michele Besso and from debating on literature, philosophy and science in the framework of the informal study group he had created with two friends, playfully called the "Olympia Academy."

It was during this period as a patent clerk, unknown to the scientific world, that he developed and published his first groundbreaking theories.

Hiemit wird bescheinigt, daß
Herr Albert Einstein von Ulm, Deutschland
unterm 2. August 1900 das Diplom der eidg. polytechnischen Schule als „Fachlehrer in mathemat. Richtung"
erhalten hat.
Zürich, den 2. August 1900.
Der Präsident des schweiz. Schulrathes:

→ Wallet-sized Mathematics Teaching Certificate, August 2, 1900

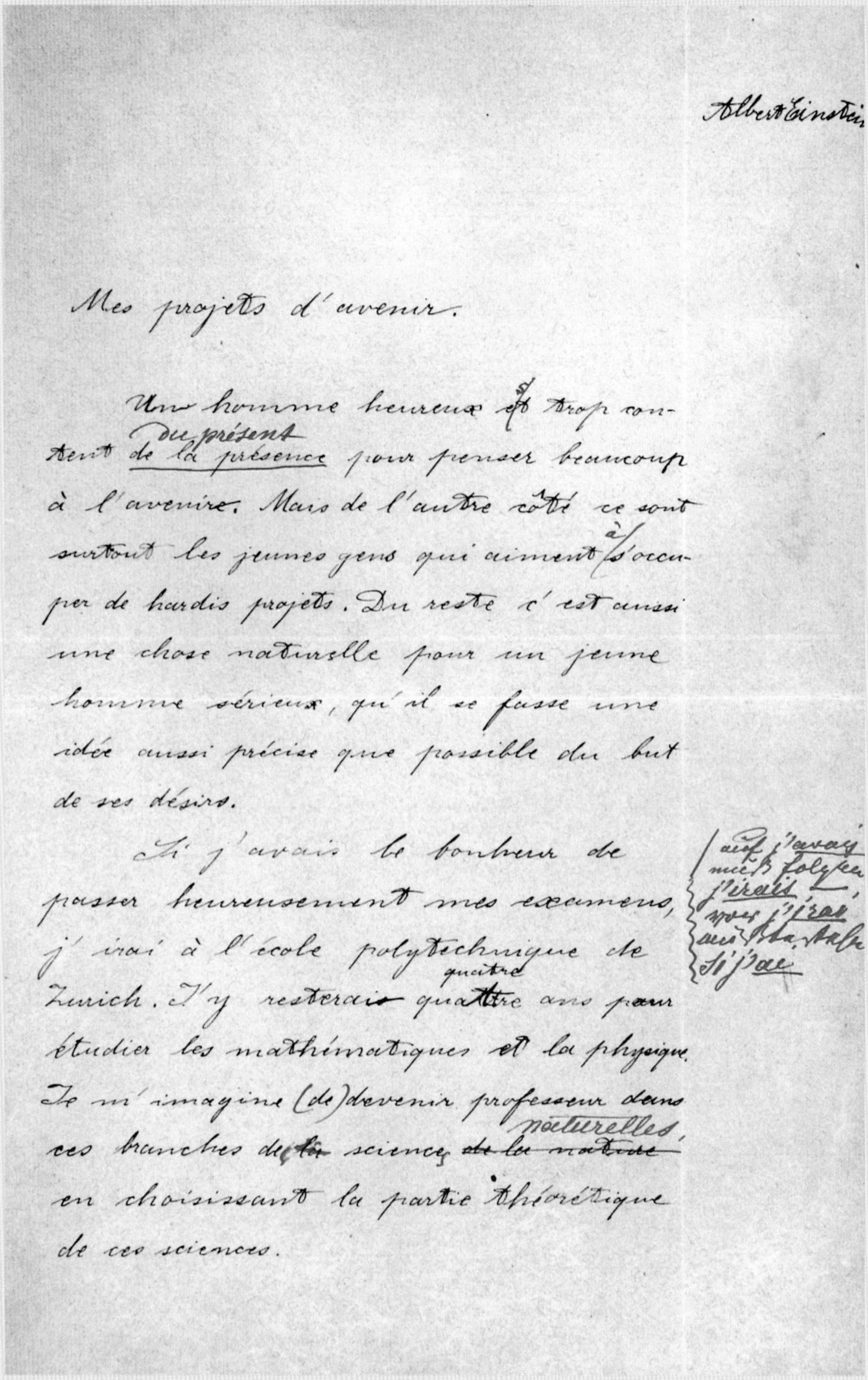

Albert Einstein

Mes projets d'avenir.

Un homme heureux est trop content du présent ~~de la présence~~ pour penser beaucoup à l'avenir. Mais de l'autre côté ce sont surtout les jeunes gens qui aiment à s'occuper de hardis projets. Du reste c'est aussi une chose naturelle pour un jeune homme sérieux, qu'il se fasse une idée aussi précise que possible du but de ses désirs.

Si j'avais le bonheur de passer heureusement mes examens, j'irai à l'école polytechnique de Zurich. J'y resterais quatre ~~quattre~~ ans pour étudier les mathématiques et la physique. Je m'imagine (de) devenir professeur dans ces branches de ~~la~~ science naturelles ~~de la nature~~, en choisissant la partie théorétique de ces sciences.

↑↗ In his French composition for the final school examination, Einstein exactly describes his plans for the future. September 1896

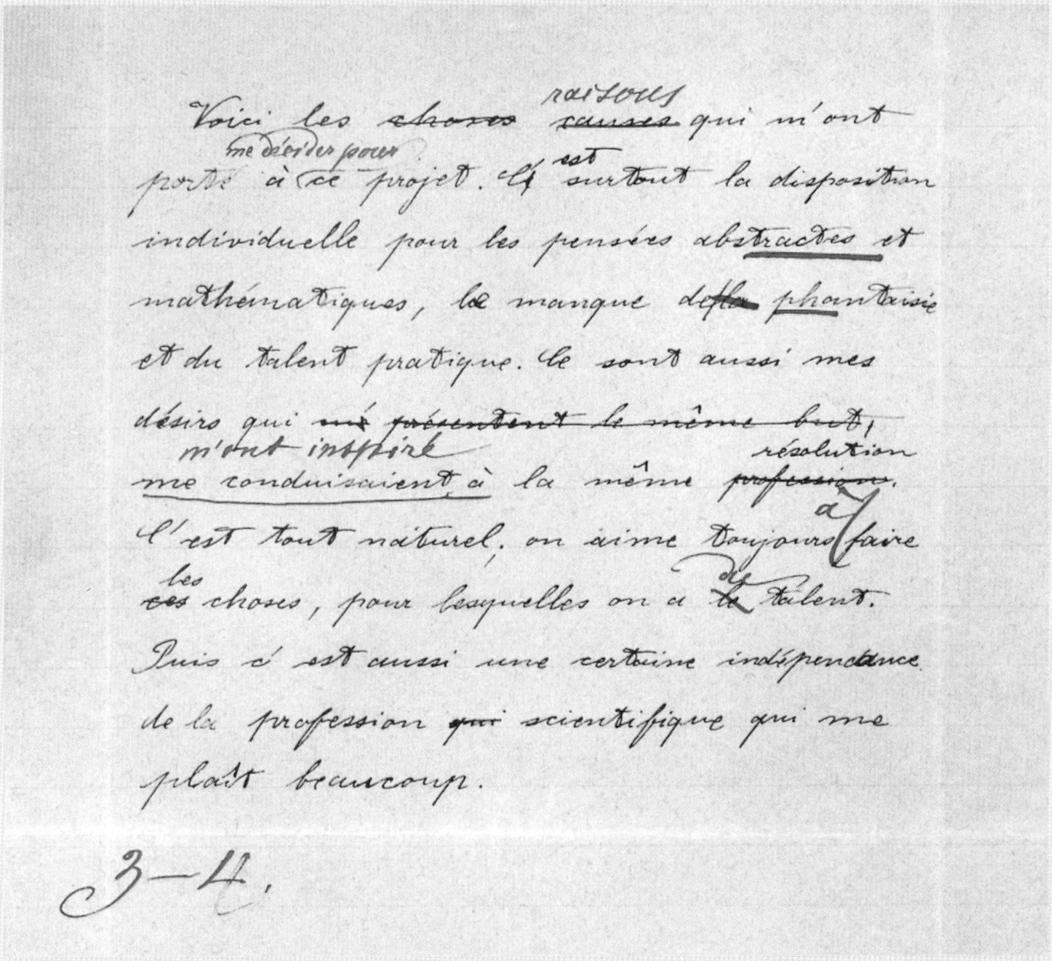
Voici les ~~choses~~ ~~causes~~ raisons qui m'ont ~~porté à~~ me décider pour ce projet. C'est surtout la disposition individuelle pour les pensées abstractes et mathématiques, le manque de la phantaisie et du talent pratique. Ce sont aussi mes désirs qui ~~me présentent le même but,~~ ~~m'ont inspiré~~ me conduisaient à la même ~~profession~~ résolution. C'est tout naturel, on aime toujours à faire les choses, pour lesquelles on a du talent. Puis c'est aussi une certaine indépendance de la profession ~~qui~~ scientifique qui me plaît beaucoup.

3–4.

«My plans for the future.

A happy man is too satisfied with the present to dwell too much upon the future. But on the other hand, young people like to contemplate bold projects. Also, it is natural for a serious young man to envision his desired goals with the greatest possible precision.
If I am lucky and successfully pass my examinations, I shall enroll in the polytechnic school in Zurich. I shall stay there four years to study mathematics and physics. I envisage that I will become a teacher of these branches of natural science, opting for the theoretical part of these sciences.
Here are the reasons that have brought me to this plan. They are, above all, my individual inclination for abstract and mathematical thinking, a lack of imagination and of practical sense. Even my desires led me to this same decision. That is quite natural; everybody likes to do things for which he has a talent. Moreover, it is a certain independence offered by the scientific profession that greatly appeals to me. »

↑ The members of the "Akademie Olympia": Conrad Habicht, Maurice Solovine, Albert Einstein. Bern, around 1903

« It was no doubt a beautiful time, in Bern, when we ran our merry 'Academy' which was definitely less childish than those respectable [Academies] that I became more intimately acquainted with later on. »

→ From a letter to Maurice Solovine, November 25, 1948

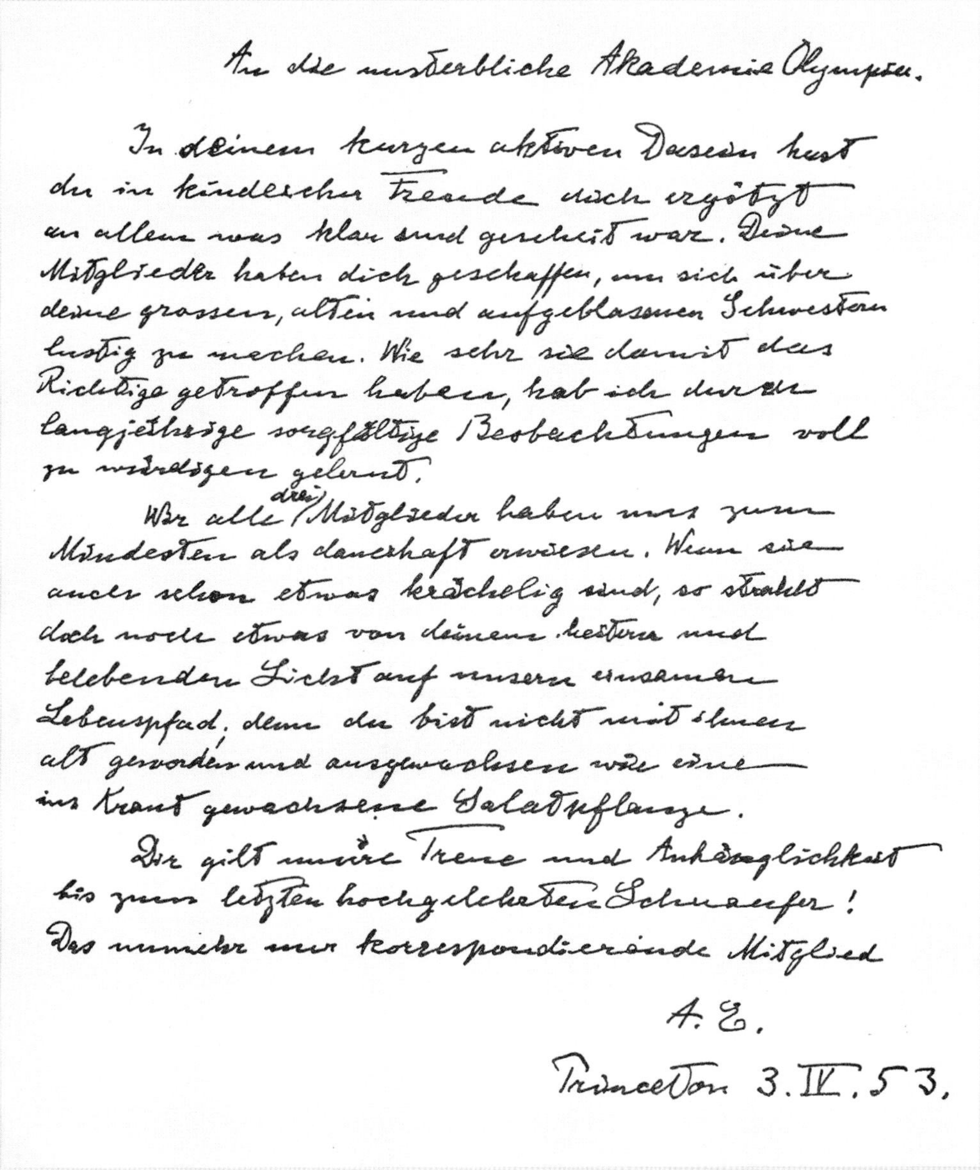
An die unsterbliche Akademie Olympia.

In deinem kurzen aktiven Dasein hast du in kindlicher Freude dich ergötzt an allem was klar und gescheit war. Deine Mitglieder haben dich geschaffen, um sich über deine grossen, alten und aufgeblasenen Schwestern lustig zu machen. Wie sehr sie damit das Richtige getroffen haben, hab ich durch langjährige sorgfältige Beobachtungen voll zu würdigen gelernt.

Wir alle drei Mitglieder haben uns zum Mindesten als dauerhaft erwiesen. Wenn sie auch schon etwas krächelig sind, so strahlt doch noch etwas von deinem heitern und belebenden Licht auf unsern einsamen Lebenspfad, denn du bist nicht mit ihnen alt geworden und ausgewachsen wie eine ins Kraut gewachsene Salatpflanze.

Dir gilt meine Treue und Anhänglichkeit bis zum letzten hochgelehrten Schnaufer!

Das nunmehr nur korrespondierende Mitglied

A. E.

Princeton 3. IV. 53.

↑↗ Reminiscence, shared with Maurice Solovine. April 3, 1953

« To the immortal Olympia Academy.

In your short active life, dear Academy, you took a childish delight in all that was clear and reasonable. Your members created you to make fun of your big, old and pompous sister Academies. I learned fully to appreciate just how well your members' mockery hit the mark through long years of careful observation.
We three have, at least, all proved durable. Though somewhat decrepit, we still follow the solitary path of our life by your bright, inspiring light. For, unlike [us], you did not grow old and shapeless like an overgrown head of lettuce.
To you belongs my loyalty and devotion until the last learned gasp!

A.E. – now only a corresponding member. »

THE ANNUS MIRABILIS

For more than two hundred years, the basic laws of motion and gravitation as postulated by Newton in the 17th century had prevailed. However, by the end of the 19th century serious cracks had developed in the Newtonian edifice. Firstly, Newton had regarded light as a stream of particles, while subsequent experiments showed that light was wave-like. Secondly, the newly discovered theory of electromagnetism did not fit into the Newtonian system. Various hypotheses, including the ether theory, were put forward, yet none of them was totally satisfactory. Some of these hypotheses foreshadowed Einstein's scientific breakthroughs. However, it was his scientific genius which brought all these elements together and created something entirely new.
In the course of one year – 1905 – Einstein published four papers which revolutionized the concepts of time and space, energy and matter, and resolved some of the fundamental issues which had been baffling physicists for several decades. The year 1905 is known as Einstein's *annus mirabilis*, his miracle year, as 1666 had been for Isaac Newton.

Einstein's first classic paper, which offered an explanation of the photoelectric effect, introduced a radically new understanding of the structure of light. His second paper dealt with Brownian motion and proved the existence of molecules. The two other papers Einstein published in 1905 were even more significant for the development of modern physics. They dealt with the nature of space and time and the dynamics of individual moving bodies. Einstein's new theory eventually became known as the special theory of relativity.

« The arguments and calculations to be carried out are among the more difficult ones in hydrodynamics, and only a person possessing perspicacity and training in the handling of mathematical and physical problems could dare to tackle them, and it seems to me that Mr. Einstein has proved that he is capable of working successfully on scientific problems; I would therefore recommend that the dissertation be accepted. »

↑ From the expert opinion by Alfred Kleiner on Einstein's dissertation, July 1905

→ Albert Einstein. dressed up in his checkered suit tailor-made for the expert at the patent office.
Photo by Lucien Chavan, around 1905

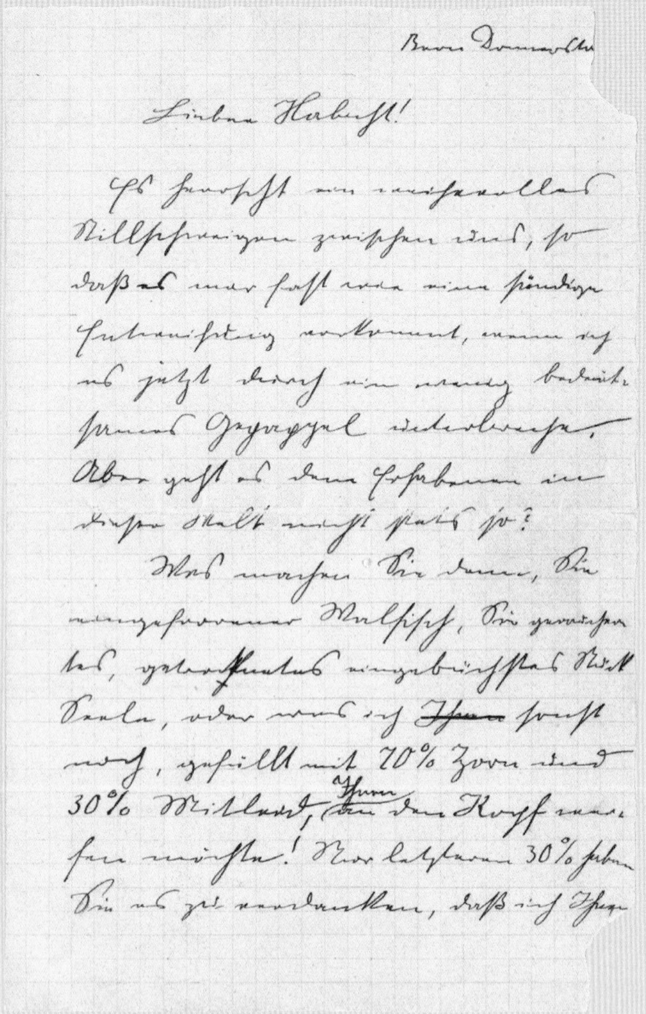

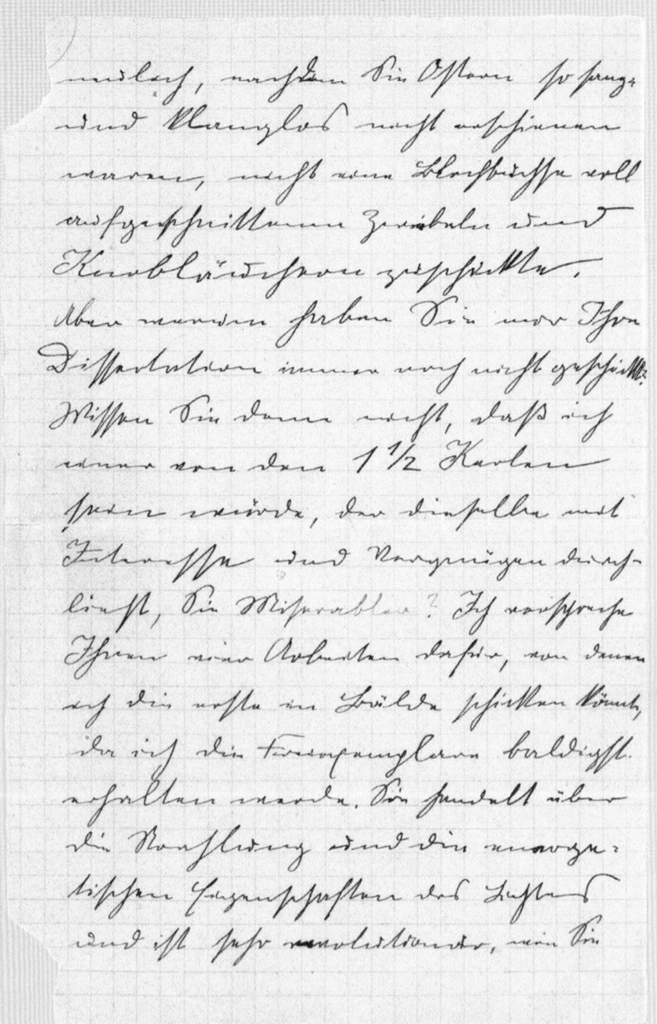

« Dear Habicht!

Such a solemn air of silence has descended between us that I almost feel as if I am committing a sacrilege when I break it now with some inconsequential babble. But is this not always the fate of the exalted ones of this world?
So what are you up to, you frozen whale, you smoked, fried, canned piece of soul […]

[…] But why have you still not sent me your dissertation. Don't you know that I am one of the $1^1/_2$ fellows who would read it with interest and pleasure, you wretched man? I promise four papers in return, the first of which I might send you soon, since I will soon get the complimentary reprints. The paper deals with radiation and the energy properties of light and is very revolutionary, as you...

↑↗ Letter to Conrad Habicht, May 1905

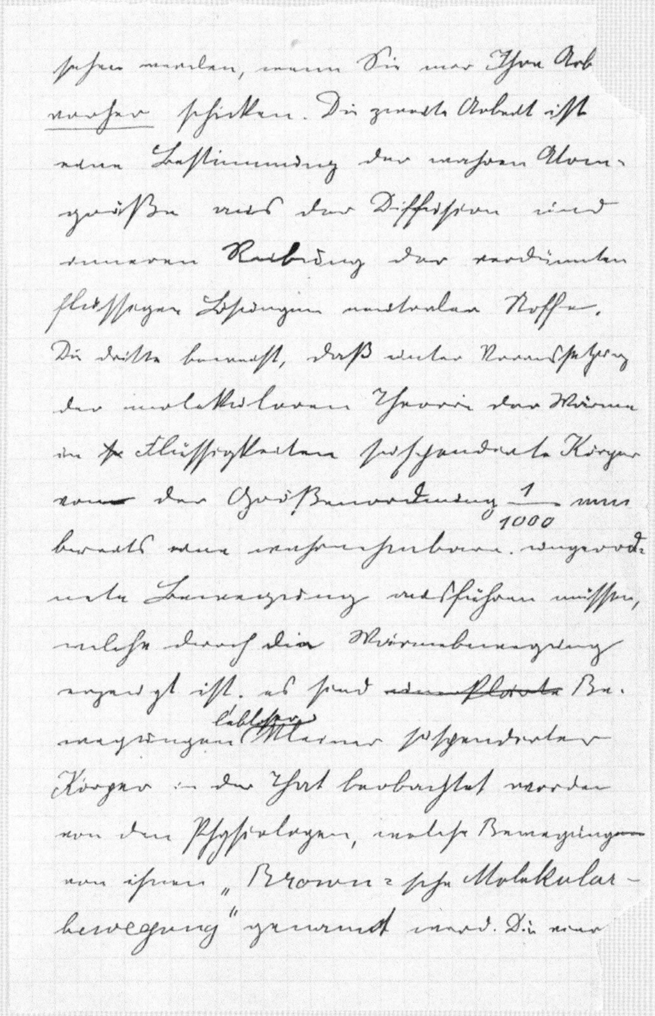
sehen werden, wenn Sie mir Ihre Arb[eit]
vorher schicken. Die zweite Arbeit ist
eine Bestimmung der wahren Atomgröße aus der Diffusion und
inneren Reibung der verdünnten
flüssigen Lösungen neutraler Stoffe.
Die dritte beweist, daß unter Voraussetzung
der molekularen Theorie der Wärme
in Flüssigkeiten suspendierte Körper
von der Größenordnung $\frac{1}{1000}$ mm
bereits eine wahrnehmbare ungeordnete
Bewegung ausführen müssen,
welche durch die Wärmebewegung
erzeugt ist. Es sind ~~[illegible]~~ Bewegungen lebloser kleiner suspendierter
Körper in der That beobachtet worden
von den Physiologen, welche Bewegungen
von ihnen „Brown'sche Molekularbewegung" genannt wird. Die vier

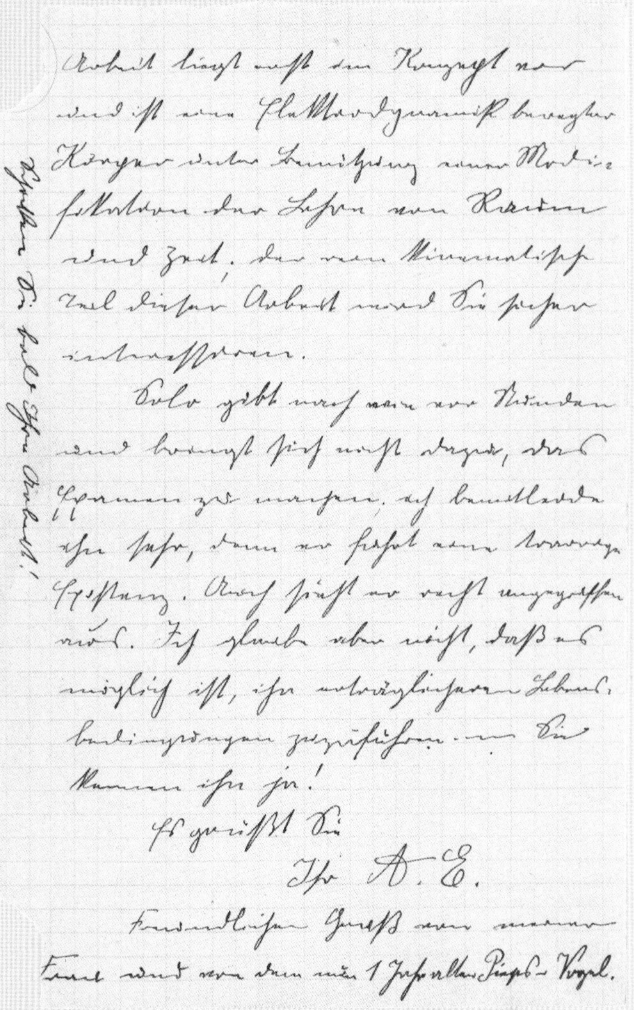
Schicken Sie bald Ihre Arbeit!

Arbeit liegt erst im Konzept vor
und ist eine Elektrodynamik bewegter
Körper unter Benützung einer Modi-
fikation der Lehre von Raum
und Zeit; der rein kinematische
Teil dieser Arbeit wird Sie sicher
interessieren.

Solo gibt noch immer Stunden
und bemüht sich nicht dazu, das
Examen zu machen; ich bemitleide
ihn sehr, denn er führt eine traurige
Existenz. Auch sieht er recht angegriffen
aus. Ich glaube aber nicht, daß es
möglich ist, ihm erträglichere Lebens-
bedingungen zu verschaffen — Sie
kennen ihn ja!

Es grüßt Sie
Ihr A. E.

Freundlichen Gruß von meiner
Frau und von dem nun 1 jährigen Piepsvogel.

...will see if you send me your work <u>first</u>. The second paper is a determination of the true sizes of atoms from the diffusion and the viscosity of dilute solutions of neutral substances. The third proves that on the assumption of the molecular theory of heat bodies on the order of magnitude 1/1000 mm, suspended in liquids, must already perform an observable random motion that is produced by thermal motion; in fact, physiologists have observed (unexplained) motions of suspended small, inanimate, bodies, which motions they designate as 'Brownian molecular motion.' The fourth...

...paper is only a rough draft at this point and is an electrodynamics of moving bodies which employs a modification of the theory of space and time [...]
Greetings from your A.E.
[...]
Send me your paper soon! »

THE PHOTOELECTRIC EFFECT

In 1900, the German physicist, Max Planck, had proposed that heat and light radiated from hot objects are emitted or absorbed in discrete chunks of energy he called "quanta." In his paper of 1905, Einstein adopted Planck's theory enthusiastically and used it to explain the photoelectric effect. This effect occurs when a light beam hits a metallic target and causes it to emit electrons. Einstein postulated that a light beam really does consist of a stream of quanta (photons), and thus gave the light quantum a physical reality. This seemed to contradict a century of accumulated evidence that light is a form of wave. In fact, light is both particle and wave. This wave-particle duality lies at the heart of the new quantum physics, developed in the 1920s, and forms the basis of our current understanding of the sub-atomic world. Intriguingly, it was for his explanation of the photoelectric effect, and not for the theory of relativity, that Einstein received the Nobel Prize in Physics. Applications of the photoelectric effect include the television, remote-control devices, automatic door openers and the DVD player.

↑ Bern, in front of the house where Einstein lived, 1903

6. ***Über einen***
die Erzeugung und Verwandlung des Lichtes
[1] ***betreffenden heuristischen Gesichtspunkt;***
von A. Einstein.

Zwischen den theoretischen Vorstellungen, welche sich die Physiker über die Gase und andere ponderable Körper gebildet haben, und der Maxwellschen Theorie der elektromagnetischen Prozesse im sogenannten leeren Raume besteht ein tiefgreifender formaler Unterschied. Während wir uns nämlich den Zustand eines Körpers durch die Lagen und Geschwindigkeiten einer zwar sehr großen, jedoch endlichen Anzahl von Atomen und Elektronen für vollkommen bestimmt ansehen, bedienen wir uns zur Bestimmung des elektromagnetischen Zustandes eines Raumes kontinuierlicher räumlicher Funktionen, so daß also eine endliche Anzahl von Größen nicht als genügend anzusehen ist zur vollständigen Festlegung des elektromagnetischen Zustandes eines Raumes. Nach der Maxwellschen Theorie ist bei allen rein elektromagnetischen Erscheinungen, also auch beim Licht, die Energie als kontinuierliche Raumfunktion aufzufassen, während die Energie eines ponderabeln Körpers nach der gegenwärtigen Auffassung der Physiker als eine über die Atome und Elektronen er-
[2] streckte Summe darzustellen ist. Die Energie eines ponderabeln Körpers kann nicht in beliebig viele, beliebig kleine Teile zerfallen, während sich die Energie eines von einer punktförmigen Lichtquelle ausgesandten Lichtstrahles nach der Maxwellschen Theorie (oder allgemeiner nach jeder Undulationstheorie) des Lichtes auf ein stets wachsendes Volumen sich kontinuierlich verteilt.

Die mit kontinuierlichen Raumfunktionen operierende Undulationstheorie des Lichtes hat sich zur Darstellung der rein
[3] optischen Phänomene vortrefflich bewährt und wird wohl nie durch eine andere Theorie ersetzt werden. Es ist jedoch im Auge zu behalten, daß sich die optischen Beobachtungen auf zeitliche Mittelwerte, nicht aber auf Momentanwerte beziehen, und es ist trotz der vollständigen Bestätigung der Theorie der Beugung, Reflexion, Brechung, Dispersion etc. durch das

↑ The first of the four epoch-making papers of 1905 is the only one Einstein himself considers "very revolutionary." It was submitted to the *Annalen der Physik* on March 18, 1905

BROWNIAN MOTION

Einstein's second paper of 1905 dealt with Brownian motion, the agitated dance performed by microscopic particles suspended in fluids. Einstein did not set out to explain this phenomenon, but rather worked out, on theoretical grounds alone, how the particles ought to behave. The significance of this paper was that it convinced scientists that Brownian motion is caused by the motion of the molecules and that therefore molecules must really exist.

↑ Bern, around 1905

5. ***Über die von der molekularkinetischen Theorie der Wärme geforderte Bewegung von in ruhenden Flüssigkeiten suspendierten Teilchen;***
von A. Einstein.

In dieser Arbeit soll gezeigt werden, daß nach der molekularkinetischen Theorie der Wärme in Flüssigkeiten suspendierte
Körper von mikroskopisch sichtbarer Größe infolge der Molekularbewegung der Wärme Bewegungen von solcher Größe
ausführen müssen, daß diese Bewegungen leicht mit dem
Mikroskop nachgewiesen werden können. Es ist möglich, daß
die hier zu behandelnden Bewegungen mit der sogenannten
„Brownschen Molekularbewegung" identisch sind; die mir
erreichbaren Angaben über letztere sind jedoch so ungenau,
[1] daß ich mir hierüber kein Urteil bilden konnte.

Wenn sich die hier zu behandelnde Bewegung samt den
für sie zu erwartenden Gesetzmäßigkeiten wirklich beobachten
läßt, so ist die klassische Thermodynamik schon für mikroskopisch unterscheidbare Räume nicht mehr als genau gültig
anzusehen und es ist dann eine exakte Bestimmung der wahren
Atomgröße möglich. Erwiese sich umgekehrt die Voraussage
dieser Bewegung als unzutreffend, so wäre damit ein schwer-
wiegendes Argument gegen die molekularkinetische Auffassung
[2] der Wärme gegeben.

§ 1. Über den suspendierten Teilchen zuzuschreibenden osmotischen Druck.

Im Teilvolumen V^* einer Flüssigkeit vom Gesamtvolumen V seien z-Gramm-Moleküle eines Nichtelektrolyten gelöst. Ist das Volumen V^* durch eine für das Lösungsmittel, nicht aber für die gelöste Substanz durchlässige Wand vom reinen Lösungs-

↑ In his paper about Brownian motion Einstein substantiates the existence of molecules. It was submitted to the *Annalen der Physik* on May 11, 1905

THE SPECIAL THEORY OF RELATIVITY

Einstein first set out on the trail to the special theory of relativity by thinking about the nature of light. One thought experiment that stirred his imagination, since the days he read Aaron Bernstein's popular science books, originated in the question about what he would see if he could travel alongside a beam of light, at the same speed as the light. The problem could not be solved using the conventional theorems and forced Einstein to find a new path to a solution.

Einstein's special theory of relativity is based on two fundamental postulates. Firstly, in accordance with Newton, the laws of physics are held to be exactly the same for all observers who move at constant velocity relative to one another. Secondly, adopting Maxwell's electromagnetic theory, Einstein claimed that for such observers, light always moves through empty space at a constant speed, regardless of how the source of light is moving relative to the observer.

Einstein's special theory of relativity constitutes a novel analysis of space and time. It shook the foundations of Newtonian physics. In Newton's universe, both duration and length were absolute and universally the same, no matter what the circumstances. In Einstein's new relativistic world, the measurement of time and length depends on the relative motion of the observers – especially if the observers are traveling close to the speed of light. A basic assumption of the special theory is the constancy of the speed of light. This assumption leads to all the amazing predictions of the special theory which defy common sense: a ruler moving at a high velocity will seem to shrink and get heavier, while a fast-moving clock will seem to run slower.

→ With this paper Einstein introduces a new view of space and time. It was submitted to the *Annalen der Physik* on June 30, 1905

In 1908, the mathematician, Hermann Minkowski, provided a geometrization of Einstein's special theory. In addition to the three known dimensions of space, he postulated that time could be considered a fourth dimension. Space and time would be regarded as a union, now known as "spacetime." It was Minkowski's geometrization of the special theory which led to widespread acceptance of Einstein's ideas among physicists.

3. *Zur Elektrodynamik bewegter Körper;* *von A. Einstein.*

Daß die Elektrodynamik Maxwells — wie dieselbe gegenwärtig aufgefaßt zu werden pflegt — in ihrer Anwendung auf bewegte Körper zu Asymmetrien führt, welche den Phänomenen nicht anzuhaften scheinen, ist bekannt. Man denke z. B. an die elektrodynamische Wechselwirkung zwischen einem Mag-
[1] neten und einem Leiter. Das beobachtbare Phänomen hängt hier nur ab von der Relativbewegung von Leiter und Magnet, während nach der üblichen Auffassung die beiden Fälle, daß der eine oder der andere dieser Körper der bewegte sei, streng voneinander zu trennen sind. Bewegt sich nämlich der Magnet und ruht der Leiter, so entsteht in der Umgebung des Magneten ein elektrisches Feld von gewissem Energiewerte, welches an den Orten, wo sich Teile des Leiters befinden, einen Strom erzeugt. Ruht aber der Magnet und bewegt sich der Leiter, so entsteht in der Umgebung des Magneten kein elektrisches Feld, dagegen im Leiter eine elektromotorische Kraft, welcher an sich keine Energie entspricht, die aber — Gleichheit der Relativbewegung bei den beiden ins Auge gefaßten Fällen vorausgesetzt — zu elektrischen Strömen von derselben Größe und demselben Verlaufe Veranlassung gibt, wie im ersten Falle die elektrischen Kräfte.

Beispiele ähnlicher Art, sowie die mißlungenen Versuche, eine Bewegung der Erde relativ zum „Lichtmedium" zu kon-
[2] statieren, führen zu der Vermutung, daß dem Begriffe der absoluten Ruhe nicht nur in der Mechanik, sondern auch in der Elektrodynamik keine Eigenschaften der Erscheinungen entsprechen, sondern daß vielmehr für alle Koordinatensysteme, für welche die mechanischen Gleichungen gelten, auch die gleichen elektrodynamischen und optischen Gesetze gelten, wie
[3] dies für die Größen erster Ordnung bereits erwiesen ist. Wir wollen diese Vermutung (deren Inhalt im folgenden „Prinzip
[4] der Relativität" genannt werden wird) zur Voraussetzung erheben und außerdem die mit ihm nur scheinbar unverträgliche

THE EQUIVALENCE OF ENERGY AND MASS

Einstein's special theory of relativity also led to the formulation of the most famous scientific equation of all, $E = mc^2$. This formula, which in his paper of September 1905 appeared in a slightly different form, shows the equivalence of energy and mass and states that they are interchangeable: just as some forms of energy can, under the right circumstances, be turned into mass, so mass can, under the right circumstances, be turned into other forms of energy. As c represents the speed of light, namely nearly 300,000 km/sec, or 186,282.397 miles/second, or almost one foot per nanosecond, one understands from this equation that a tiny amount of matter is equivalent to a vast quantity of energy. However, utilizing this energy technologically was not considered feasible in 1905. It was only with the discovery of nuclear fission in the late 1930s that one of the technological applications of Einstein's formula became a possibility. Much to Einstein's regret it brought about, first of all, the development of nuclear weapons.

↑ ©1997 by Sidney Harris

13. *Ist die Trägheit eines Körpers von seinem Energieinhalt abhängig?*
von A. Einstein.

Die Resultate einer jüngst in diesen Annalen von mir publizierten elektrodynamischen Untersuchung¹) führen zu einer sehr interessanten Folgerung, die hier abgeleitet werden soll.

Ich legte dort die Maxwell-Hertzschen Gleichungen für den leeren Raum nebst dem Maxwellschen Ausdruck für die elektromagnetische Energie des Raumes zugrunde und außerdem das Prinzip:

Die Gesetze, nach denen sich die Zustände der physikalischen Systeme ändern, sind unabhängig davon, auf welches von zwei relativ zueinander in gleichförmiger Parallel-Translationsbewegung befindlichen Koordinatensystemen diese Zustandsänderungen bezogen werden (Relativitätsprinzip).

Gestützt auf diese Grundlagen²) leitete ich unter anderem das nachfolgende Resultat ab (l. c. § 8):

Ein System von ebenen Lichtwellen besitze, auf das Koordinatensystem (x, y, z) bezogen, die Energie l; die Strahlrichtung (Wellennormale) bilde den Winkel φ mit der x-Achse des Systems. Führt man ein neues, gegen das System (x, y, z) in gleichförmiger Paralleltranslation begriffenes Koordinatensystem (ξ, η, ζ) ein, dessen Ursprung sich mit der Geschwindigkeit v längs der x-Achse bewegt, so besitzt die genannte Lichtmenge — im System (ξ, η, ζ) gemessen — die Energie:

$$l^* = l \frac{1 - \frac{v}{V} \cos \varphi}{\sqrt{1 - \left(\frac{v}{V}\right)^2}},$$

wobei V die Lichtgeschwindigkeit bedeutet. Von diesem Resultat machen wir im folgenden Gebrauch.

[1] 1) A. Einstein, Ann. d. Phys. 17. p. 891. 1905.
2) Das dort benutzte Prinzip der Konstanz der Lichtgeschwindigkeit ist natürlich in den Maxwellschen Gleichungen enthalten.

42*

↑ As early as mid-September, Einstein had drawn new conclusions from his former paper about the "Electrodynamics of Moving Bodies." They resulted later in the most popular equation of all time. This paper was submitted to the *Annalen der Physik* on September 27, 1905

THE GENERAL THEORY OF RELATIVITY

In 1908, Einstein eventually acquired a position as a lecturer at the University of Bern. In subsequent years, he rose through the academic hierarchy, taking up posts at the universities of Zurich and Prague and at the Zurich Polytechnic.
In 1913, he was appointed a member of the Prussian Academy of Sciences. This position was associated with a professorship, without teaching obligations, at the University of Berlin, and the direction of the future Kaiser Wilhelm Institute for Physics.
Einstein had begun work on a generalization of his theory of relativity shortly after the publication of his special theory in 1905. The special theory of relativity only applies in special circumstances – to objects moving at constant speeds in straight lines. A general theory of relativity would include an explanation for objects which move in curved paths and experience acceleration. The most important kind of accelerated motion, which makes planets move through space along curved paths and describes the fall of an apple to the ground, is caused by gravity.

In 1907, Einstein had what he later described as the "happiest thought of [his] life: for an observer falling freely from the roof of a house there exists – at least in his immediate surroundings – no gravitational field." This insight led Einstein to the postulation of the "equivalence principle" which states that in order for the acceleration caused by gravity to cancel out the force of gravity (leaving the observer in a state of "free fall"), the acceleration and gravity must be exactly equivalent to one another.
Einstein lacked the mathematical tools to make immediate progress and put aside the problem of gravity for over three years. In 1911, he realized that the equivalence principle implied an important and measurable effect: a ray of light passing near to the sun would be bent. In 1912, his old friend Marcel Grossmann introduced him to the non-Euclidian geometry developed by Bernhard Riemann that was required for the further development of a general theory.
Einstein completed the general theory of relativity in 1915 and confided to his friend Michele Besso: "The boldest dreams have now been fulfilled." Published in 1916, the general theory overturned Newton's theory of gravity.
In Newton's universe, gravity was regarded as a force by which a large mass attracts other masses. The planets were thought to be held in their elliptical orbits around the sun by the force of gravity. In Einstein's universe, gravity is not regarded as an exterior force, but rather as a property of space and time or "spacetime." As gravity affects all matter indiscriminately, the response of a body to gravity is independent of its mass. Gravity is not tied closely to an object itself, but is embedded in the backdrop of spacetime through which an object moves.

→ Einstein as a young lecturer, Prague 1912.
Photo by J.F. Langhans

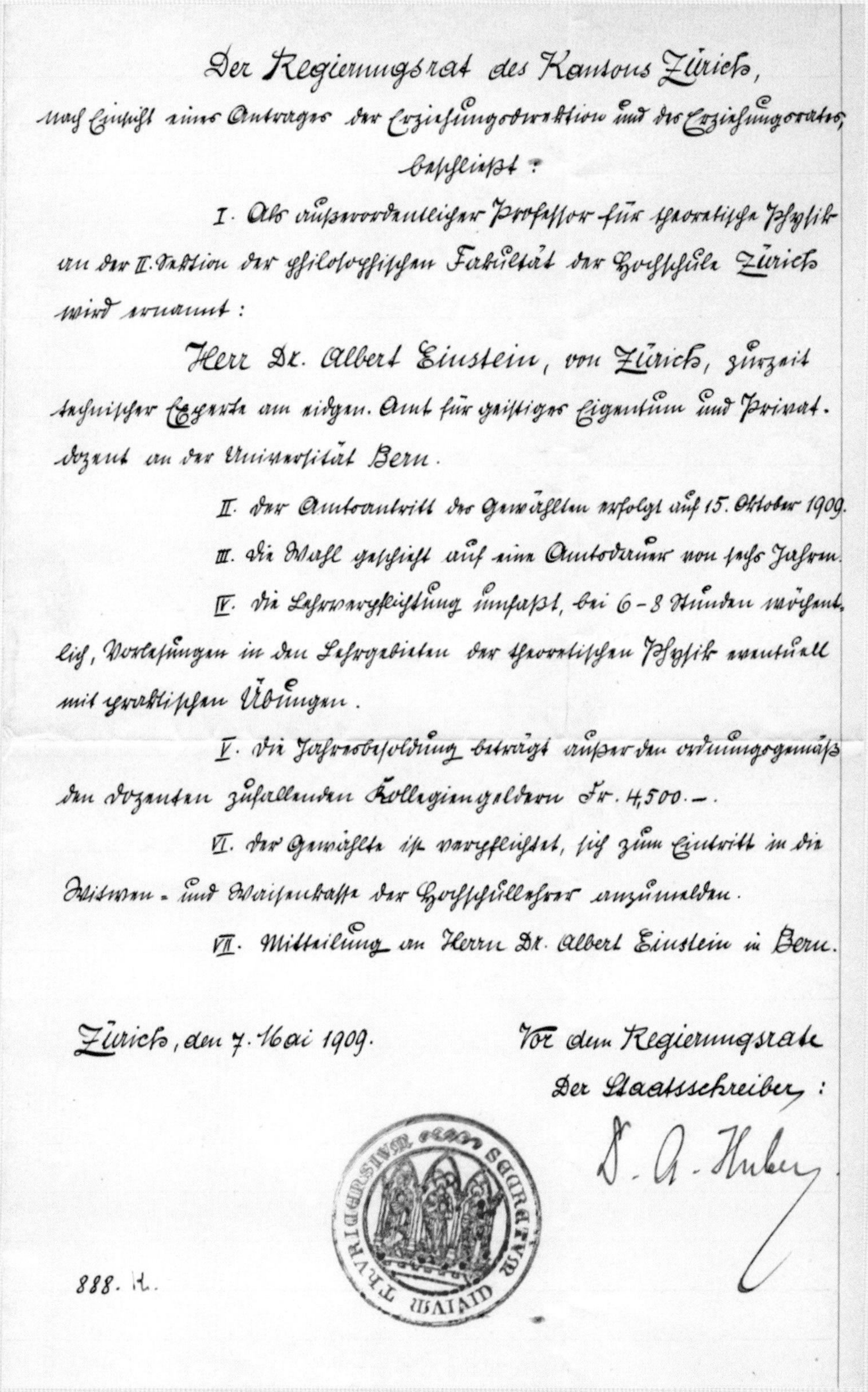

Der Regierungsrat des Kantons Zürich,

nach Einsicht eines Antrages der Erziehungsdirektion und des Erziehungsrates,

beschliesst:

I. Als ausserordentlicher Professor für theoretische Physik an der II. Sektion der philosophischen Fakultät der Hochschule Zürich wird ernannt:

Herr Dr. Albert Einstein, von Zürich, zurzeit technischer Experte am eidgen. Amt für geistiges Eigentum und Privatdozent an der Universität Bern.

II. Der Amtsantritt des Gewählten erfolgt auf 15. Oktober 1909.

III. Die Wahl geschieht auf eine Amtsdauer von sechs Jahren.

IV. Die Lehrverpflichtung umfasst, bei 6-8 Stunden wöchentlich, Vorlesungen in den Lehrgebieten der theoretischen Physik eventuell mit praktischen Übungen.

V. Die Jahresbesoldung beträgt ausser den ordnungsgemäss den Dozenten zufallenden Kollegiengeldern Fr. 4,500.–.

VI. Der Gewählte ist verpflichtet, sich zum Eintritt in die Witwen- und Waisenkasse der Hochschullehrer anzumelden.

VII. Mitteilung an Herrn Dr. Albert Einstein in Bern.

Zürich, den 7. Mai 1909.

Vor dem Regierungsrate
Der Staatsschreiber:
Dr. A. Huber

888. R.

← On May 7, 1909, Einstein was appointed associate professor of theoretical physics at the University of Zurich for a period of six years. Einstein accepted the obligation to lecture 6-8 hours per week at a salary not higher than his earnings at the patent office: 4,500 Swiss francs per year.

Space and time are no longer merely the passive arena in which material bodies act out their roles, but are themselves part of the action.
Einstein's curved four-dimensional spacetime "continuum" is often likened to a suspended rubber sheet stretched taut but deformed wherever heavy objects – stars, galaxies or any other matter – are placed on it.

↑ Einstein at his Berlin study, around 1916

Thus, a massive body like the sun curves the spacetime around it and the planets move along these curved pathways of spacetime. As the physicist, John Wheeler, put it: "matter tells space how to bend; space tells matter how to move."
The general theory predicted exactly to what extent a light beam would be bent when it passes near the sun. This prediction was confirmed by observations made by an expedition led by the British astronomer Arthur Eddington during a total eclipse of the sun in May 1919.

Following the development of more sophisticated technology in the 1960s, both the special and the general theories of relativity have repeatedly been verified through experiments involving rockets, atomic clocks, satellites and astronauts. One of the predictions of the general theory was that the universe must be expanding, thereby forming the basis for the "big bang" theory. Furthermore, the general theory has been essential in explaining the behavior of bizarre stellar objects within the expanding universe such as black holes and quasars.

« I would so much like to do something to keep our colleagues from the various fatherlands united. Is not our little clutch of assiduous intellectuals our only 'fatherland' for which such as we seriously care? Should even these people have a mindset that is solely a function of residence? »

↑ About the difficulty to maintain an international scientific dialogue during the war years; to Paul Ehrenfest, August 23, 1915

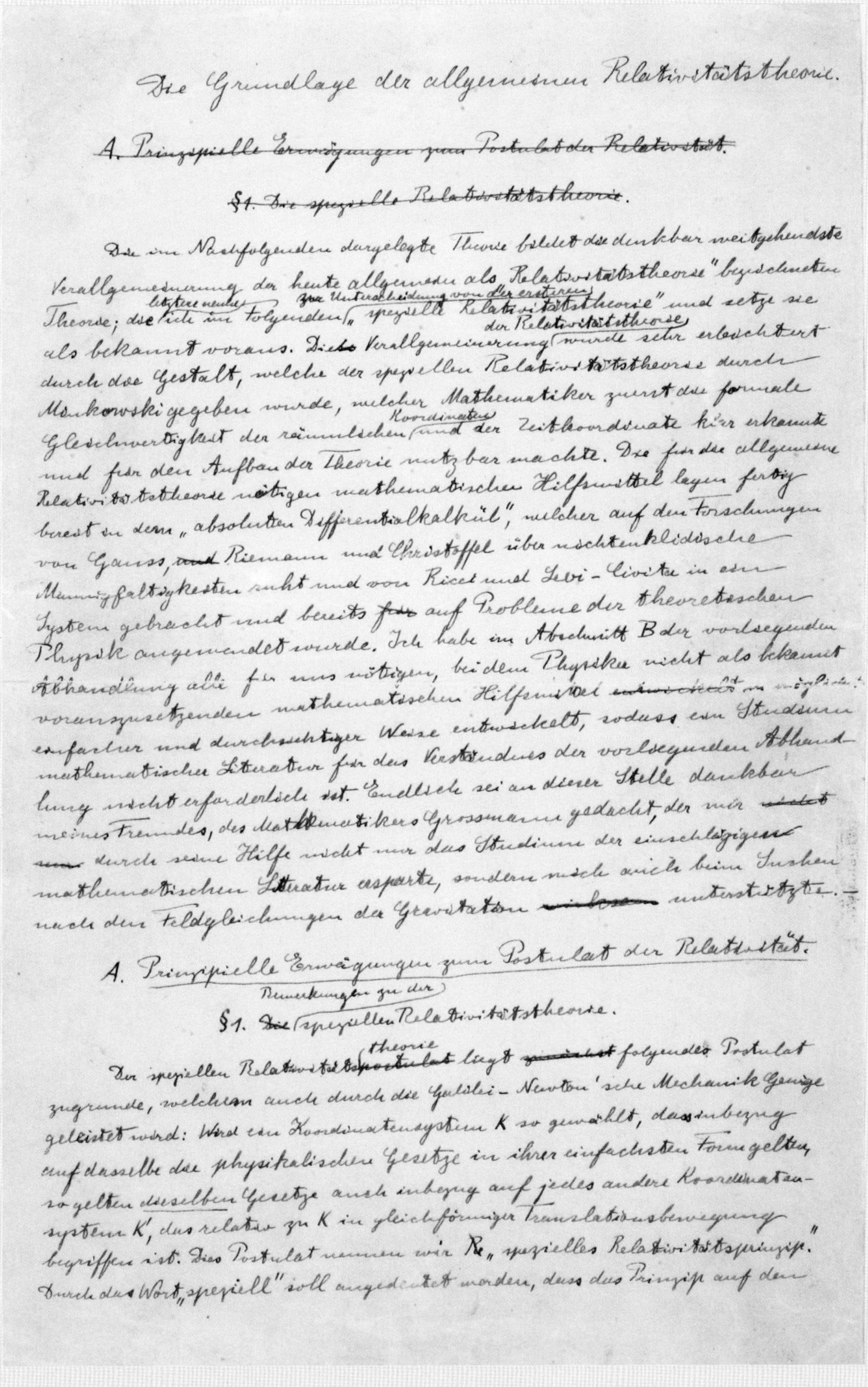

Die Grundlage der allgemeinen Relativitätstheorie.

~~A. Prinzipielle Erwägungen zum Postulat der Relativität.~~

~~§1. Die spezielle Relativitätstheorie.~~

Die im Nachfolgenden dargelegte Theorie bildet die denkbar weitgehendste Verallgemeinerung der heute allgemein als „Relativitätstheorie" bezeichneten Theorie; die letztere nenne ich im Folgenden zur Unterscheidung von der ersteren „spezielle Relativitätstheorie" und setze sie als bekannt voraus. Die Verallgemeinerung der Relativitätstheorie wurde sehr erleichtert durch die Gestalt, welche der speziellen Relativitätstheorie durch Minkowski gegeben wurde, welcher Mathematiker zuerst die formale Gleichwertigkeit der räumlichen Koordinaten und der Zeitkoordinate klar erkannte und für den Aufbau der Theorie nutzbar machte. Die für die allgemeine Relativitätstheorie nötigen mathematischen Hilfsmittel lagen fertig bereit in dem „absoluten Differentialkalkül", welcher auf den Forschungen von Gauss, ~~und~~ Riemann und Christoffel über nichteuklidische Mannigfaltigkeiten ruht und von Ricci und Levi-Civita in ein System gebracht und bereits ~~für~~ auf Probleme der theoretischen Physik angewendet wurde. Ich habe im Abschnitt B der vorliegenden Abhandlung alle für uns nötigen, bei dem Physiker nicht als bekannt vorauszusetzenden mathematischen Hilfsmittel in möglichst einfacher und durchsichtiger Weise entwickelt, sodass ein Studium mathematischer Literatur für das Verständnis der vorliegenden Abhandlung nicht erforderlich ist. Endlich sei an dieser Stelle dankbar meines Freundes, des Mathematikers Grossmann gedacht, der mir durch seine Hilfe nicht nur das Studium der einschlägigen mathematischen Literatur ersparte, sondern mich auch beim Suchen nach den Feldgleichungen der Gravitation unterstützte.

A. Prinzipielle Erwägungen zum Postulat der Relativität.

§1. Bemerkungen zu der speziellen Relativitätstheorie.

Der speziellen Relativitätstheorie liegt folgendes Postulat zugrunde, welchem auch durch die Galilei-Newton'sche Mechanik Genüge geleistet wird: Wird ein Koordinatensystem K so gewählt, dass in bezug auf dasselbe die physikalischen Gesetze in ihrer einfachsten Form gelten, so gelten dieselben Gesetze auch in bezug auf jedes andere Koordinatensystem K', das relativ zu K in gleichförmiger Translationsbewegung begriffen ist. Dies Postulat nennen wir „spezielles Relativitätsprinzip". Durch das Wort „speziell" soll angedeutet werden, dass das Prinzip auf den

← "The Foundation of the General Theory of Relativity" Manuscript of the article published in *Annalen der Physik* (1916). The article was the first systematic exposé of the general theory of relativity. This manuscript was donated to The Hebrew University in Jerusalem on the occasion of its opening in 1925.

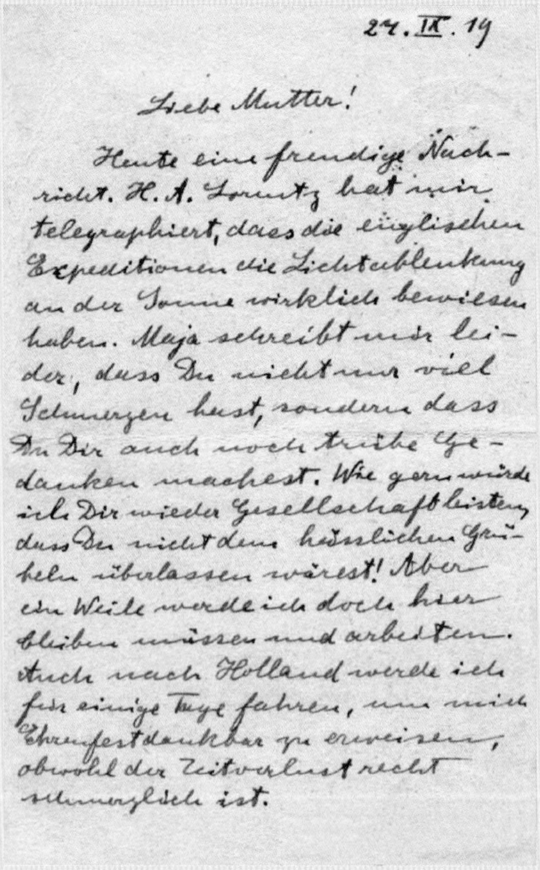

27. IX. 19

Liebe Mutter!

Heute eine freudige Nachricht. H. A. Lorentz hat mir telegraphiert, dass die englischen Expeditionen die Lichtablenkung an der Sonne wirklich bewiesen haben. Maja schreibt mir leider, dass Du nicht nur viel Schmerzen hast, sondern dass Du Dir auch noch trübe Gedanken machest. Wie gern würde ich Dir wieder Gesellschaft leisten, dass Du nicht dem hässlichen Grübeln überlassen wärest! Aber eine Weile werde ich doch hier bleiben müssen und arbeiten. Auch nach Holland werde ich für einige Tage fahren, um mich Ehrenfest dankbar zu erweisen, obwohl der Zeitverlust recht schmerzlich ist.

Postkarte

Ich wünsche Dir von Herzen gute Tage. Es küsst Dich innig Dein Albert

Grüsse an die Schwester, Frau ... und Fl. Doktor. Nächstes Mal ausführlicher!

Frau

Pauline Einstein

Sanatorium Rosenau

Luzern (Schweiz)

Abs. A. Einstein
Haberlandstr. 5
Berlin.

Dear Mother,

Today some happy news. H. A. Lorentz telegraphed me that the British expeditions have definitely verified the deflection of light by the sun. Maja writes me, to my dismay, that you're not only in a lot of pain but that you have gloomy thoughts as well. How much I would like to keep you company again so that you aren't left to such nasty musing. But I will have to stay here for a while and work. I will also be traveling to Holland for a few days to show my gratitude to Ehrenfest, even though the loss of time is quite painful. I truly wish you good days.
Affectionately yours,

Albert

↑↗ Einstein's mother Pauline was suffering from abdominal cancer and Einstein, expecting her impending death, hurried to share with her the so far unofficial results of the British expedition: the photographs taken by astronomer Arthur Eddington and his teams had demonstrated that Einstein's predictions were correct.
Postcard to Pauline Einstein, September 27, 1919

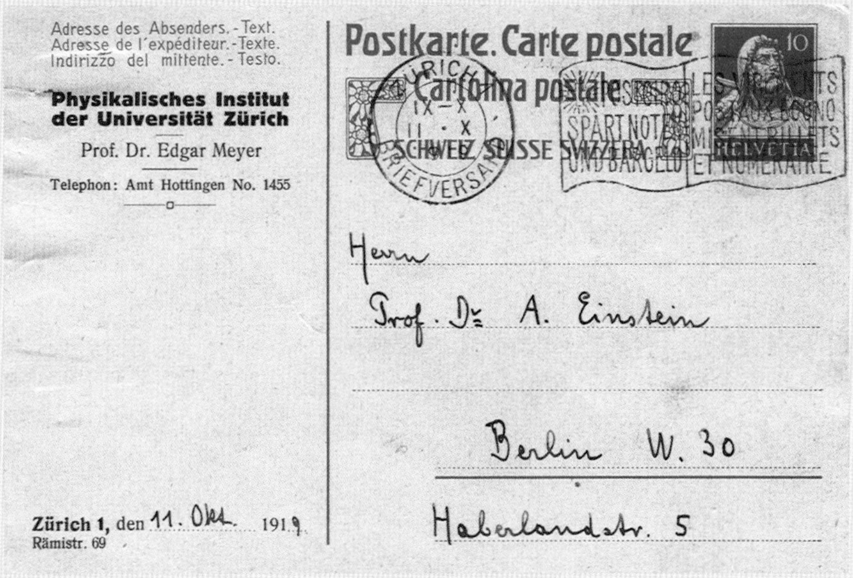
Adresse des Absenders. - Text.
Adresse de l'expéditeur. - Texte.
Indirizzo del mittente. - Testo.

Physikalisches Institut der Universität Zürich

Prof. Dr. Edgar Meyer

Telephon: Amt Hottingen No. 1455

Zürich 1, den 11. Okt. 1919
Rämistr. 69

Postkarte. Carte postale. Cartolina postale
SCHWEIZ SUISSE SVIZZERA

Herrn
Prof. Dr. A. Einstein
Berlin W. 30
Haberlandstr. 5

↙↓ Postcard from Zurich colleagues, October 11, 1919

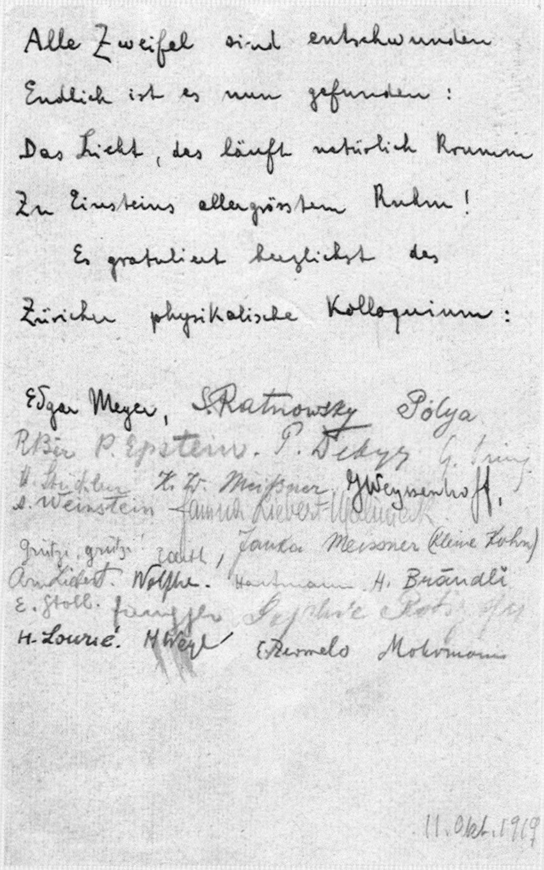
Alle Zweifel sind entschwunden
Endlich ist es nun gefunden:
Das Licht, das läuft natürlich krumm
Zu Einsteins allergrößten Ruhm!
Es gratuliert herzlichst das
Züricher physikalische Kolloquium:

Edgar Meyer, S. Ratnowsky, Pólya
P. Epstein, P. Debye
H. Brändli
E. Stoll
H. Lourié, H. Weyl

11. Okt. 1919

« All doubts have now been spent
At last it has been found:
Light naturally is bent
To Einstein's great renown!

Hearty congratulations from
The Zurich physics colloquium:

Edgar Meyer [and 24 other
signatories] »

← With colleagues at Leiden Observatory, September 26, 1923. Front row: Arthur Stanley Eddington, Hendrik Antoon Lorentz. Back row: Einstein, Paul Ehrenfest, Willem de Sitter.

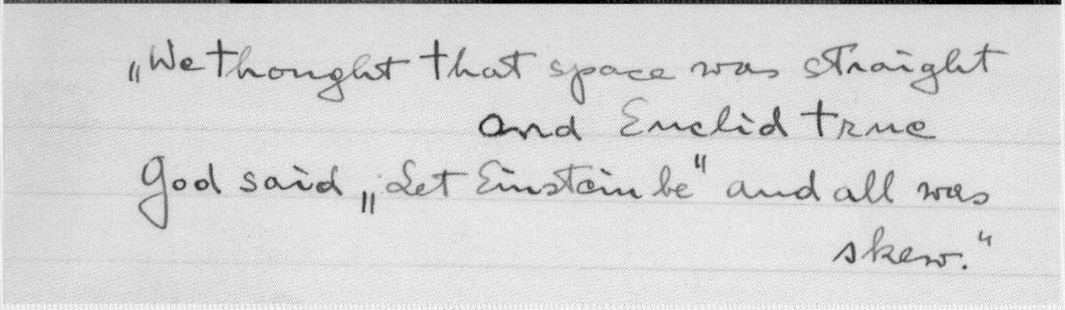

„We thought that space was straight
and Euclid true
God said „Let Einstein be" and all was
skew."

← From a letter by Paul Ehrenfest, February 8, 1920

Nature and nature's laws lay hid in night,
God said, "Let Newton be," and all was light.

It did not last; the devil howling "Ho!
Let Einstein be!" restored the status quo.

God rolled His Dice, to Einstein's great dismay:
"Let Feynman be!" and all was clear as day.

↑ Alexander Pope wrote the famous epitaph for Sir Isaac Newton in 1730;
Sir John Collings Squire added a couplet in the 1920s;
the last two lines were composed by Stephen G. Brush in 1994

THE BRITISH CONNECTION 1

It started with a bang on November 6, 1919, when, at a joint meeting of the Royal Society and the Royal Astronomical Society in London, the Astronomer Royal, Sir Frank Dyson, made the following announcement: The measurements recorded by two British expeditions during the eclipse of May 29, 1919, did not support Newton's long-accepted theory of gravity. Instead, as Arthur Stanley Eddington, astrophysicist at Cambridge and Einstein's British "prophet" had advocated, they agreed with the predictions regarding the bending of the light of Einstein's general theory of relativity.

Prudently, *The London Times* of the following day reported "Newtonian Ideas Overthrown" only on page 12, considering that this "Revolution in Science" might wound national feelings. Yet the news spread quickly, and soon "every driver and every drover" were talking about Einstein's theory. Already in December 1919, the overwhelming majority of the Royal Astronomical Society council had agreed to award Einstein its gold medal. However, a small group of "irreconcilable" patriots overthrew this motion the following month. It was only in1926 that a better international spirit made it possible to award Einstein the RAS Gold Medal, one year after the Royal Society had honored Einstein with its highly esteemed Copley Medal.

In June 1921, returning from a fundraising tour in the United States, with Chaim Weizmann, Einstein visited England for the first time. After delivering a lecture on relativity to an audience of more than 500 people at Manchester University, and another one on Zionist aspirations to Jewish students, he was received in London by Viscount Haldane, the important British Liberal politician, an intellectual with a lifelong interest in German idealist philosophy. At a splendid dinner in his honor at Haldane's home, Einstein met the Archbishop of Canterbury, as well as Arthur S. Eddington, Lord Rothschild, George Bernard Shaw and other British dignitaries. On June 13, Einstein gave a lecture at King's College. After having spoken for over an hour in German, without notes, he was given a standing ovation. Thus, a first step was made towards the reconciliation between the "perfidious Albion" and the "Hun."

Having established personal contact, Einstein kept in touch with British scientists and intellectuals.

→ Einstein and A.S.Eddington, Cambridge, June 1930. To the initiative of the Cambridge astrophysicist Einstein owed what in 1919 was considered the conclusive proof of general relativity over the Newtonian model.

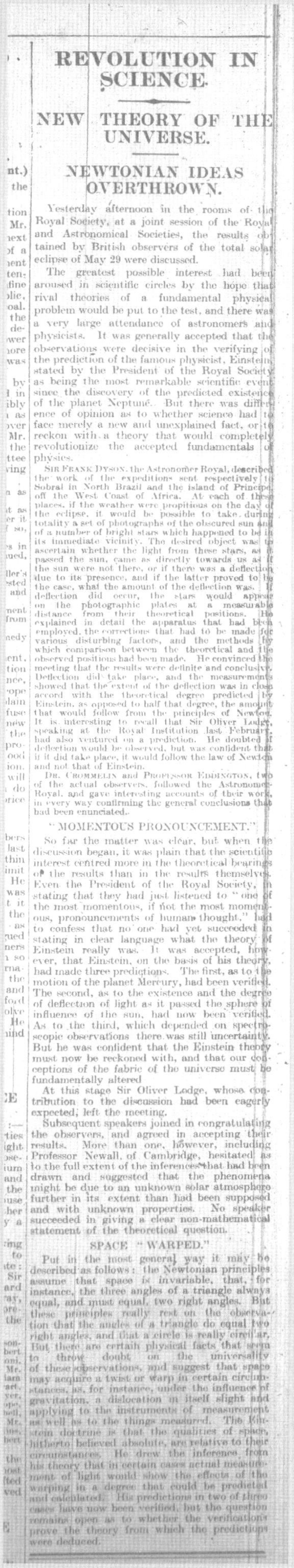

REVOLUTION IN SCIENCE.

NEW THEORY OF THE UNIVERSE.

NEWTONIAN IDEAS OVERTHROWN.

Yesterday afternoon in the rooms of the Royal Society, at a joint session of the Royal and Astronomical Societies, the results obtained by British observers of the total solar eclipse of May 29 were discussed.

The greatest possible interest had been aroused in scientific circles by the hope that rival theories of a fundamental physical problem would be put to the test, and there was a very large attendance of astronomers and physicists. It was generally accepted that the observations were decisive in the verifying of the prediction of the famous physicist, Einstein, stated by the President of the Royal Society as being the most remarkable scientific event since the discovery of the predicted existence of the planet Neptune. But there was difference of opinion as to whether science had to face merely a new and unexplained fact, or to reckon with a theory that would completely revolutionize the accepted fundamentals of physics.

SIR FRANK DYSON, the Astronomer Royal, described the work of the expeditions sent respectively to Sobral in North Brazil and the island of Principe, off the West Coast of Africa. At each of these places, if the weather were propitious on the day of the eclipse, it would be possible to take during totality a set of photographs of the obscured sun and of a number of bright stars which happened to be in its immediate vicinity. The desired object was to ascertain whether the light from these stars, as it passed the sun, came as directly towards us as if the sun were not there, or if there was a deflection due to its presence, and if the latter proved to be the case, what the amount of the deflection was. If deflection did occur, the stars would appear on the photographic plates at a measurable distance from their theoretical positions. He explained in detail the apparatus that had been employed, the corrections that had to be made for various disturbing factors, and the methods by which comparison between the theoretical and the observed positions had been made. He convinced the meeting that the results were definite and conclusive. Deflection did take place, and the measurements showed that the extent of the deflection was in close accord with the theoretical degree predicted by Einstein, as opposed to half that degree, the amount that would follow from the principles of Newton. It is interesting to recall that Sir Oliver Lodge, speaking at the Royal Institution last February, had also ventured on a prediction. He doubted if deflection would be observed, but was confident that if it did take place, it would follow the law of Newton and not that of Einstein.

DR. CROMMELIN and PROFESSOR EDDINGTON, two of the actual observers, followed the Astronomer-Royal, and gave interesting accounts of their work, in every way confirming the general conclusions that had been enunciated.

"MOMENTOUS PRONOUNCEMENT."

So far the matter was clear, but when the discussion began, it was plain that the scientific interest centred more in the theoretical bearings of the results than in the results themselves. Even the President of the Royal Society, in stating that they had just listened to "one of the most momentous, if not the most momentous, pronouncements of human thought," had to confess that no one had yet succeeded in stating in clear language what the theory of Einstein really was. It was accepted, however, that Einstein, on the basis of his theory, had made three predictions. The first, as to the motion of the planet Mercury, had been verified. The second, as to the existence and the degree of deflection of light as it passed the sphere of influence of the sun, had now been verified. As to the third, which depended on spectroscopic observations there was still uncertainty. But he was confident that the Einstein theory must now be reckoned with, and that our conceptions of the fabric of the universe must be fundamentally altered

At this stage Sir Oliver Lodge, whose contribution to the discussion had been eagerly expected, left the meeting.

Subsequent speakers joined in congratulating the observers, and agreed in accepting their results. More than one, however, including Professor Newall, of Cambridge, hesitated as to the full extent of the inferences that had been drawn and suggested that the phenomena might be due to an unknown solar atmosphere further in its extent than had been supposed and with unknown properties. No speaker succeeded in giving a clear non-mathematical statement of the theoretical question.

SPACE "WARPED."

Put in the most general way it may be described as follows: the Newtonian principles assume that space is invariable, that, for instance, the three angles of a triangle always equal, and must equal, two right angles. But these principles really rest on the observation that the angles of a triangle do equal two right angles, and that a circle is really circular. But there are certain physical facts that seem to throw doubt on the universality of these observations, and suggest that space may acquire a twist or warp in certain circumstances, as, for instance, under the influence of gravitation, a dislocation in itself slight and applying to the instruments of measurement as well as to the things measured. The Einstein doctrine is that the qualities of space, hitherto believed absolute, are relative to their circumstances. He drew the inference from his theory that in certain cases actual measurement of light would show the effects of the warping in a degree that could be predicted and calculated. His predictions in two of three cases have now been verified, but the question remains open as to whether the verifications prove the theory from which the predictions were deduced.

→ Placed next to headlines like "The Glorious Dead" and "Armistice Day Observance," the readers of *The London Times* would find this column on page 12 of the November 7, 1919 issue.

« ...After the lamentable breakdown of the old active intercourse between men of learning, I welcome this opportunity of expressing my feelings of joy and gratitude toward the astronomers and physicists of England. It is thoroughly in keeping with the great and proud traditions of scientific work in your country that eminent scientists should have spent much time and trouble, and your scientific institutions have spared no expense to test the implications of a theory which was perfected and published during the war in the land of your enemies. [...] I cannot forbear to express my personal thanks to my English colleagues for their work; for without it I could hardly have lived to see the most important implication of my theory tested. »

↑↘ From an article published in *The London Times*, November 28, 1919

« Today in Germany I am called a German man of science, and in England I am presented as a Swiss Jew. If ever I come to be considered a 'bête noire,' the descriptions will be reversed and I shall be regarded as a Swiss Jew by the Germans and as a German man of science by the English. »

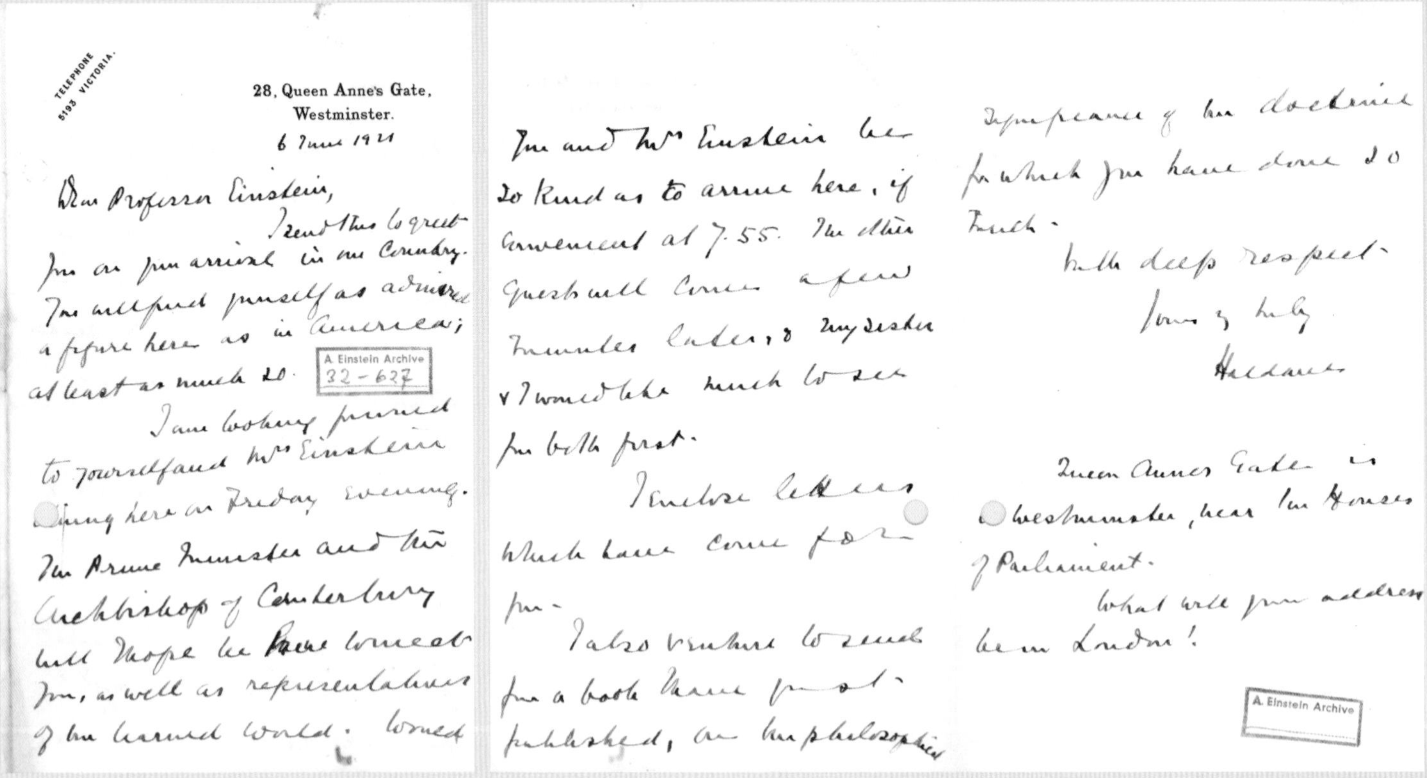

TELEPHONE 5193 VICTORIA.

28, Queen Anne's Gate,
Westminster.
6 June 1921

Dear Professor Einstein,

I send this to greet you on your arrival in our Country. You will find yourself as admired a figure here as in America; at least as much so.

I am looking forward to yourself and Mrs Einstein dining here on Friday evening. The Prime Minister and the Archbishop of Canterbury will I hope be here to meet you, as well as representatives of the learned world. Would you and Mrs Einstein be so kind as to arrive here, if convenient at 7.55. The other guests will come a few minutes later, & my sister & I would like much to see you both first.

I enclose letters which have come for you.

I also venture to send you a book I have just published, on the philosophical significance of the doctrine for which you have done so much.

With deep respect.
Yours truly
Haldane

Queen Annes Gate is in Westminster, near the Houses of Parliament.

What will your address be in London?

A. Einstein Archive 32-627

A. Einstein Archive

↑ "A dazzling and diverse array of superstars, representing science, the theater, the military, politics, and the church" turned up at the dinner party Viscount Haldane had arranged for his guest.
Letter by Viscount Haldane, June 6, 1921

« Venerated Lord Haldane!
Still fresh and yet like a dream, I hold in my mind the amazing experience I had in England. This country with its admirable intellectual and political tradition has made a deep and long-lasting impression upon me, greater than I expected. I am full of gratitude for the unique welcome given to me and especially for the fine way the leading authorities expressed their inclination for an international reconciliation. [...] With cheerful respect and admiration, yours Albert Einstein. »

↑ From Einstein's letter to Viscount Haldane, June 21, 1921

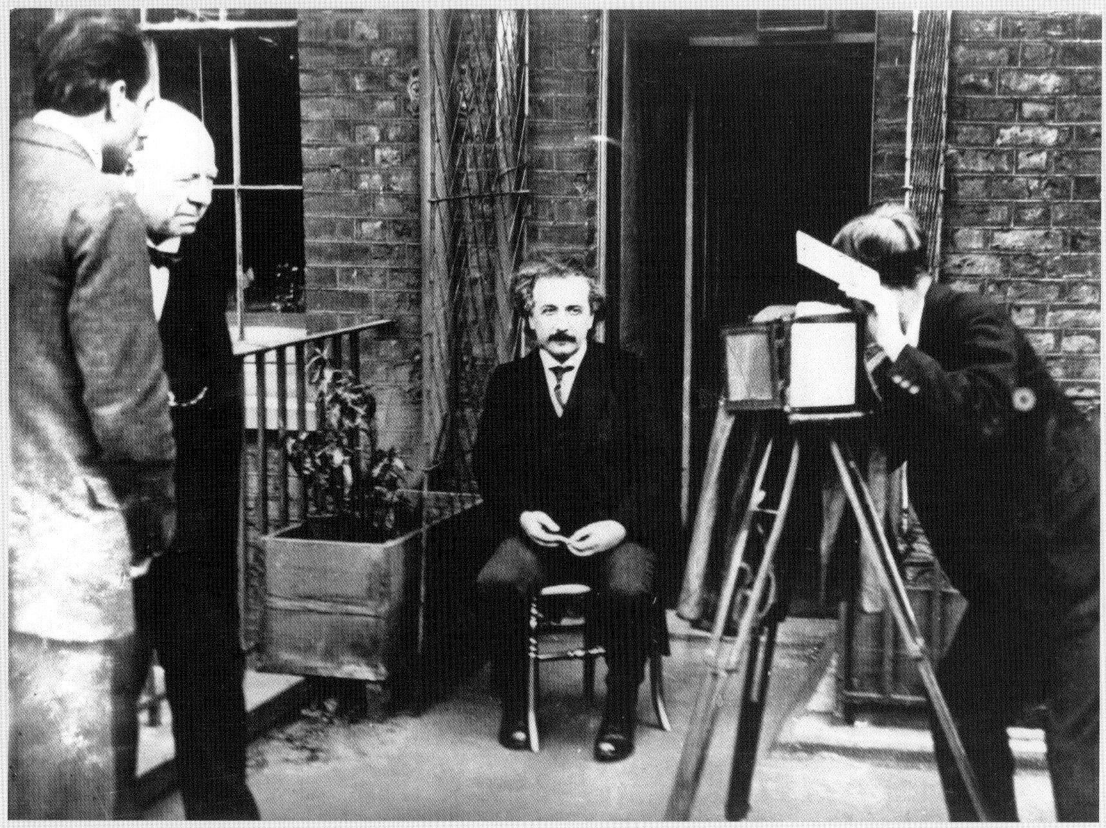

→ Already in 1921, when asked his profession, Einstein might have replied "photographer's model." Here he is sitting for the photographer in Viscount Haldane's garden in London, June 11, 1921

« It may be said at once that Einstein's lecture at King's College on Monday was [...] a superb performance. It is probable that no better lecturer than Einstein exists; certainly the present writer has never heard a lecturer as good. I know of only one lecturer, Mr. Jeans, who is as fluent [...], but even Mr. Jeans is unable to cover so much ground, without hurry and without obscurity, within the hour. Einstein had no notes, no hesitations and no repetitions, and the logical order in which he expounded his ideas was masterly beyond praise. One sat wondering how much of this exquisite performance was being wasted upon the audience; to how many was this carefully precise German an unintelligible noise? »

↑ From a review in *The Nation & The Athenaeum*, June 18, 1921

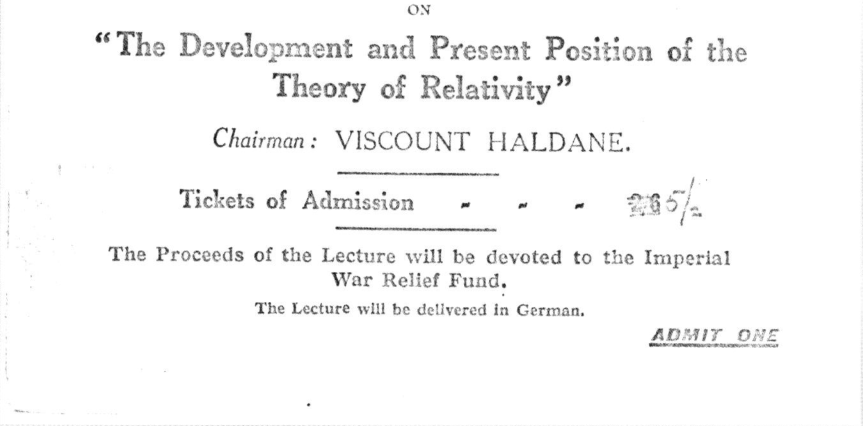

University of London, King's College.

A PUBLIC LECTURE

WILL BE GIVEN ON

Monday THURSDAY, JUNE 9th 13th, at 5.15 p.m.

By PROFESSOR EINSTEIN

ON

"The Development and Present Position of the Theory of Relativity"

Chairman: VISCOUNT HALDANE.

Tickets of Admission - - - 2/6 5/-

The Proceeds of the Lecture will be devoted to the Imperial War Relief Fund.

The Lecture will be delivered in German.

ADMIT ONE

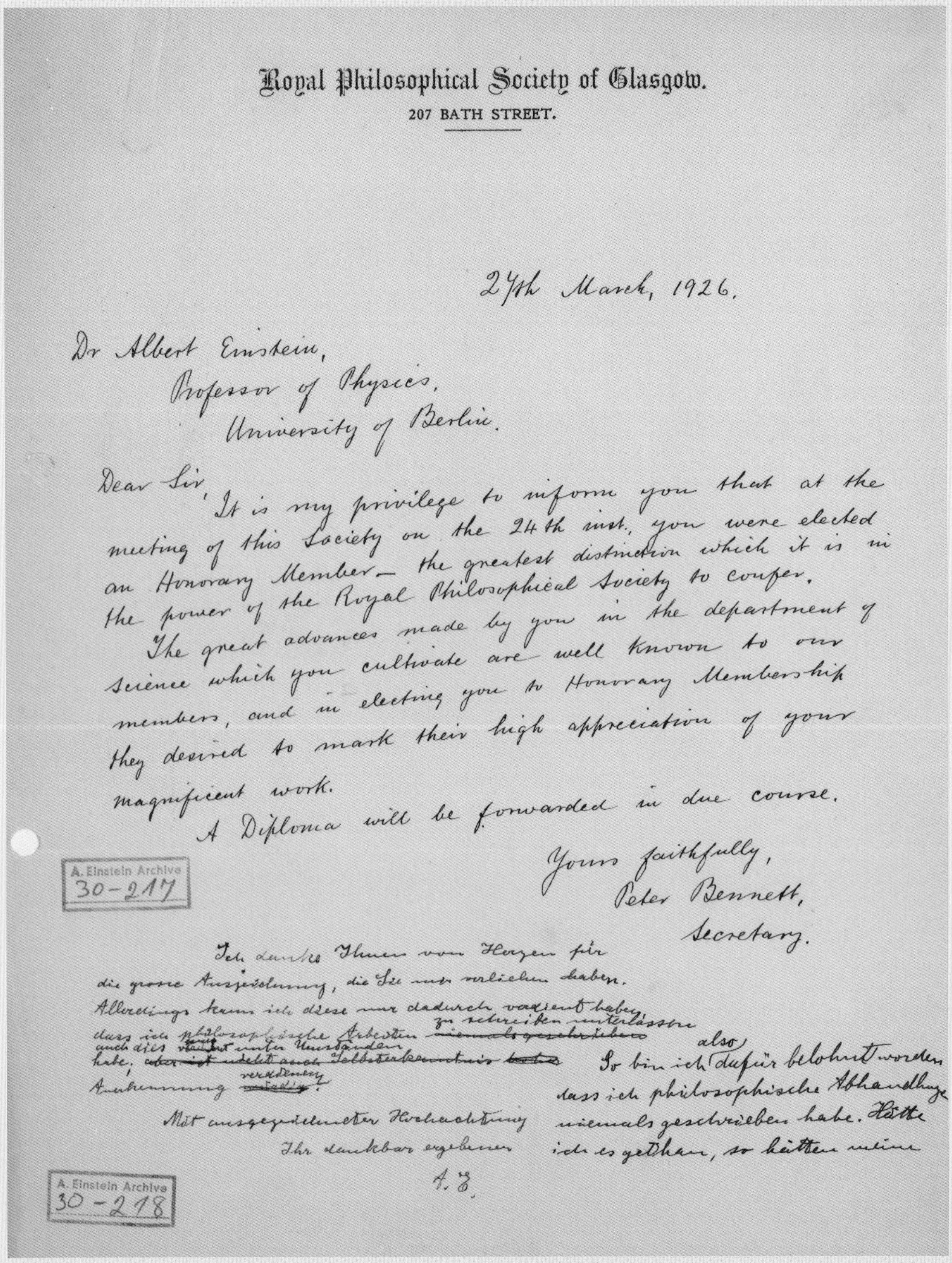

Royal Philosophical Society of Glasgow.
207 BATH STREET.

27th March, 1926.

Dr Albert Einstein,
Professor of Physics,
University of Berlin.

Dear Sir,
It is my privilege to inform you that at the meeting of this Society on the 24th inst. you were elected an Honorary Member — the greatest distinction which it is in the power of the Royal Philosophical Society to confer.

The great advances made by you in the department of science which you cultivate are well known to our members, and in electing you to Honorary Membership they desired to mark their high appreciation of your magnificent work.

A Diploma will be forwarded in due course.

Yours faithfully,
Peter Bennett,
Secretary.

A. Einstein Archive 30-217

Ich danke Ihnen von Herzen für die grosse Auszeichnung, die Sie mir verliehen haben. Allerdings kann ich diese nur dadurch verdient haben, dass ich philosophische Arbeiten zu schreiben unterlassen habe; auch dies verdient unter Umständen Anerkennung!

So bin ich also dafür belohnt worden, dass ich philosophische Abhandlungen niemals geschrieben habe. Hätte ich es gethan, so hätten meine

Mit ausgezeichneter Hochachtung
Ihr dankbar ergebener
A. E.

A. Einstein Archive 30-218

↑→ Letter from the Royal Philosophical Society of Glasgow including draft of Einstein's reply, April 27, 1926

« I thank you from my heart for the great distinction which you have awarded me. Admittedly, I may have deserved it by merely refraining from writing any philosophical treatise; under certain circumstances, even that can merit recognition. »

THE AUSTRALIAN CONNECTION

The observations of the British astronomers of 1919 had a flaw which was discovered only subsequently: the mirror which reflected the light into the telescope camera was slightly bent. Therefore, scientists required a more precise verification. The next opportunity to test Einstein's theory was provided by the solar eclipse of September 1922. This eclipse could only be observed on a narrow strip spanning from the Horn of Africa across the Indian Ocean to Australia. Due to technical improvements, the light could be collected directly by the telescopes' lenses. Therefore, these eclipse tests were seen as crucial in confirming or refuting the theory of relativity. Einstein was invited to visit Australia during the solar eclipse by the Universities of Sydney, Melbourne and Adelaide, yet he politely declined.

An expedition group led by Prof. William W. Campbell of the Lick Observatory in California set up its instruments at Wallal on the north-west coast of Australia.

Other independent teams of astronomers spread out through the continent with their telescopes. Observations were made as well at Christmas Island in the Indian Ocean by a British and a German-Dutch contingent, but these were unsuccessful due to bad weather.

Seven months after the eclipse, on April 12, 1923, Einstein was informed by Campbell that the results from his expedition had been the most successful. Overwhelming evidence had now been found that light from 140 bright stars was bent as it passed near the sun.

At the April meeting of the Royal Astronomical Society, A. S. Eddington who four years earlier lead the expedition to the island of Principe, presented the results of the Lick expedition to his colleagues. Recalling the two expeditions of 1919, he introduced his report with a quote from Lewis Carroll's poem *The Hunting of the Snark*:
"'What I tell you three times is true.'
The stars have now said it three times to three separate expeditions, and I am convinced that their answer is right."

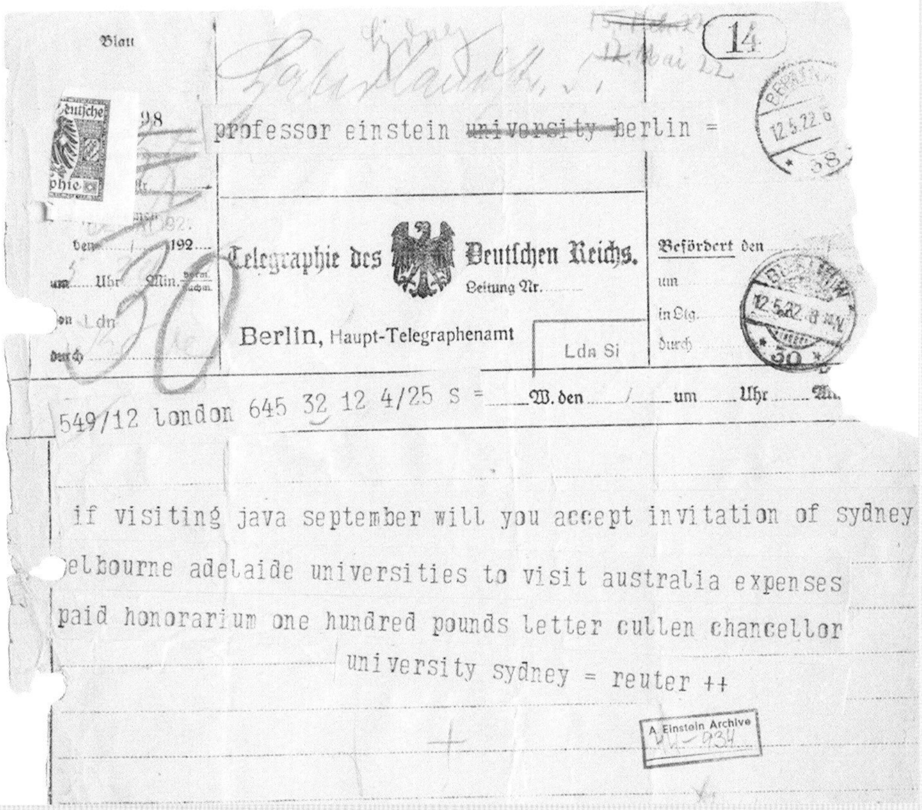
Telegraphie des Deutschen Reichs.
Berlin, Haupt-Telegraphenamt

professor einstein ~~university~~ berlin =

549/12 london 645 32 12 4/25 s =

if visiting java september will you accept invitation of sydney melbourne adelaide universities to visit australia expenses paid honorarium one hundred pounds letter cullen chancellor university sydney = reuter ++

→ Telegram from the University of Sydney inviting Albert Einstein to visit Australia in September 1922, May 12, 1922

→ Einstein's secretary, Ilse, drafted the reply on the back of the telegram from Sydney: "Thanks for kindly invitation, impossible to accept because too much occupied." May 15, 1925

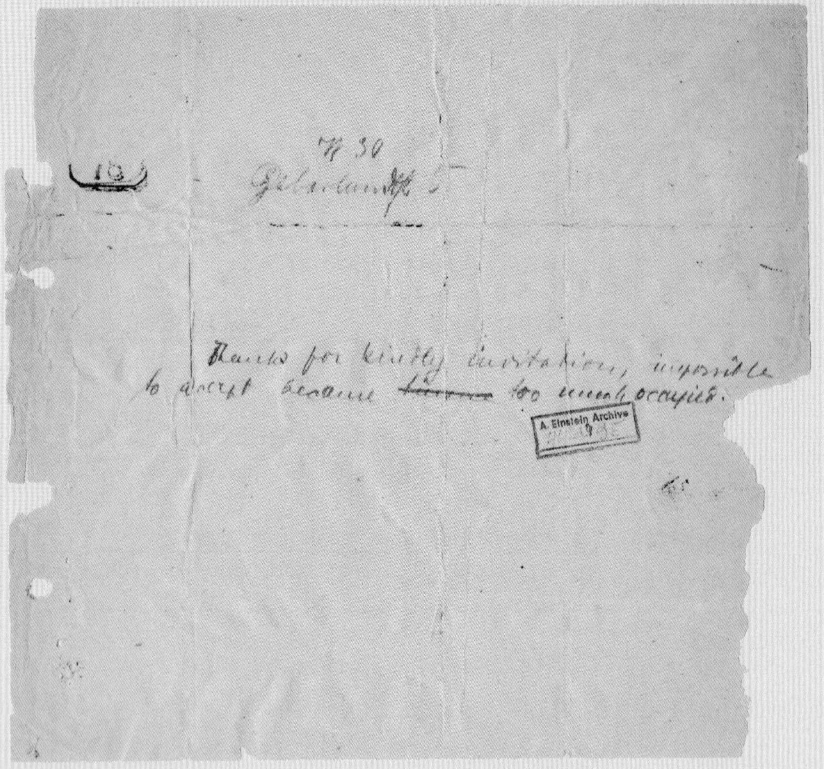
Thanks for kindly invitation, impossible to accept because ~~because~~ too much occupied.

A. Einstein Archive

↑ Lick observatory expedition, September 1922
Expedition supplies being landed through the surf at Wallal, a dry, isolated site where the eclipse would last the longest.

TOTAL ECLIPSE OF THE SUN.

SUCCESSFUL OBSERVATIONS.

(FROM OUR CORRESPONDENTS.)

PERTH (W. AUSTRALIA), SEPT. 21.

It was cloudless at Wallal to-day, and the observations of the eclipse were most successful.

The observers have been mainly photographing the sun's corona and investigating shadow bands. The visibility of the stars was satisfactory. A characteristic corona was displayed, and there were sunspots of the minimum type. One streamer was three million miles in length. Some of the photographs taken are being developed immediately, but no important results can yet be announced.

ADELAIDE, SEPT. 21.

Ideal conditions prevailed in Central Australia and also in Adelaide during the solar eclipse, so that highly important results are expected from the observations.

The scientific expedition posted on Cordillo Downs included the Government Astronomer, Professor Dodwell, who used a tower telescope lent by the Lick Observatory for the purpose of testing the Einstein effect. Professor Kerr Grant, of Adelaide University, measured the actinic value of the sunlight and the corona by photo-electric methods, and undertook spectroscopic determinations. Professor Dodwell has sent a message reporting complete success under perfect observing conditions.

→ Clipping from *The Times*, September 22, 1922, reporting on the success of the solar eclipse observation at Wallal, Western Australia, in Central Australia and in Adelaide.

→ Completely new equipment was designed for the Lick observatory expedition, allowing photographs of a large area around the sun, with many more star images, without distortion. The photo shows spectrographs on a makeshift mount, Wallal, September 1922

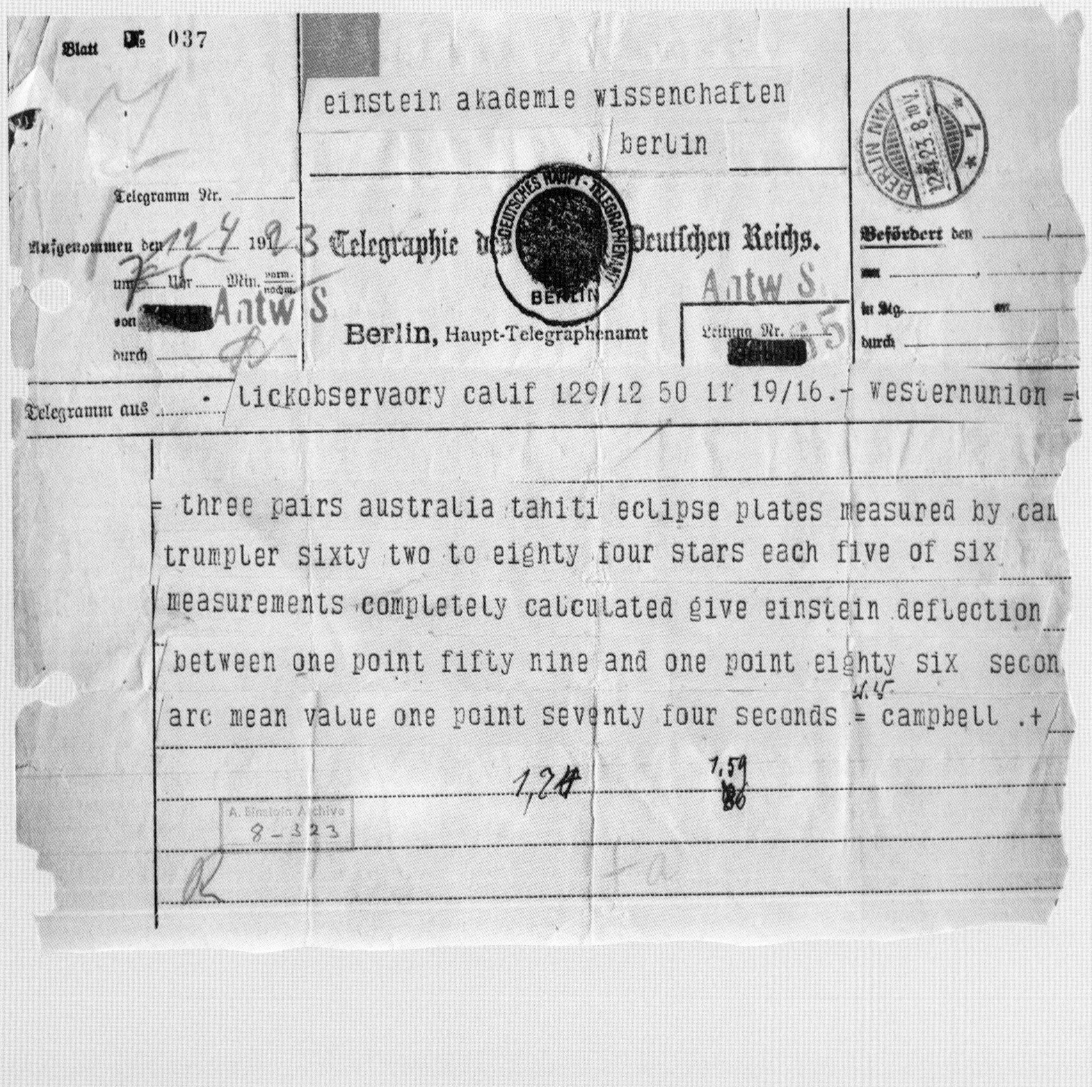

Blatt № 037

einstein akademie wissenchaften
berlin

Telegramm Nr.
Aufgenommen den 12.4.1923
um 7.45 Uhr Min.
von [redacted] Antw S
durch

Telegraphie des Deutschen Reichs.
Berlin, Haupt-Telegraphenamt

Antw S
Leitung Nr. [redacted]

Befördert den
um
in Stg.
durch

Telegramm aus lickobservaory calif 129/12 50 11 19/16.- westernunion =

= three pairs australia tahiti eclipse plates measured by cam
trumpler sixty two to eighty four stars each five of six
measurements completely calculated give einstein deflection
between one point fifty nine and one point eighty six secon
arc mean value one point seventy four seconds = campbell .+

A. Einstein Archive
8-323

←Telegram from William Wallace Campbell, Lick Observatory, California, informing Einstein that the measurements from the eclipse observations in Australia had confirmed Einstein's theory of the deflection of light.
April 12, 1923

THE NOBEL PRIZE

Since 1910 nearly every year Einstein's name was among those nominated for the Nobel Prize in Physics. In 1922 the Physics Committee was finally prepared to give the prize to Einstein for the year 1921, during which no prize had been awarded.

The official announcement was not made until November 1922, while Einstein was on a lecture tour in Japan. The citation states that Einstein received the 1921 Nobel Prize "for his services to theoretical physics and in particular for his discovery of the law of the photoelectric effect." Relativity was not mentioned in the citation, mainly because at that time the Swedish Academy considered it too controversial, both scientifically and politically.

When Einstein gave his delayed Nobel Prize lecture in Göteborg in July 1923, he ignored the wording of the citation and spoke on the theory of relativity, although at this time he was already itching to deal with new ideas, namely a unified field theory.

↑ Nobel Prize in Physics, 1921: Gold medal with an inscription taken from Virgil's Aeneid, loosely translated "And they who bettered life on earth by newfound mastery".
The two female figures represent Nature and the Genius of Science, the latter holding up the veil which covers the cold and austere face of the former.

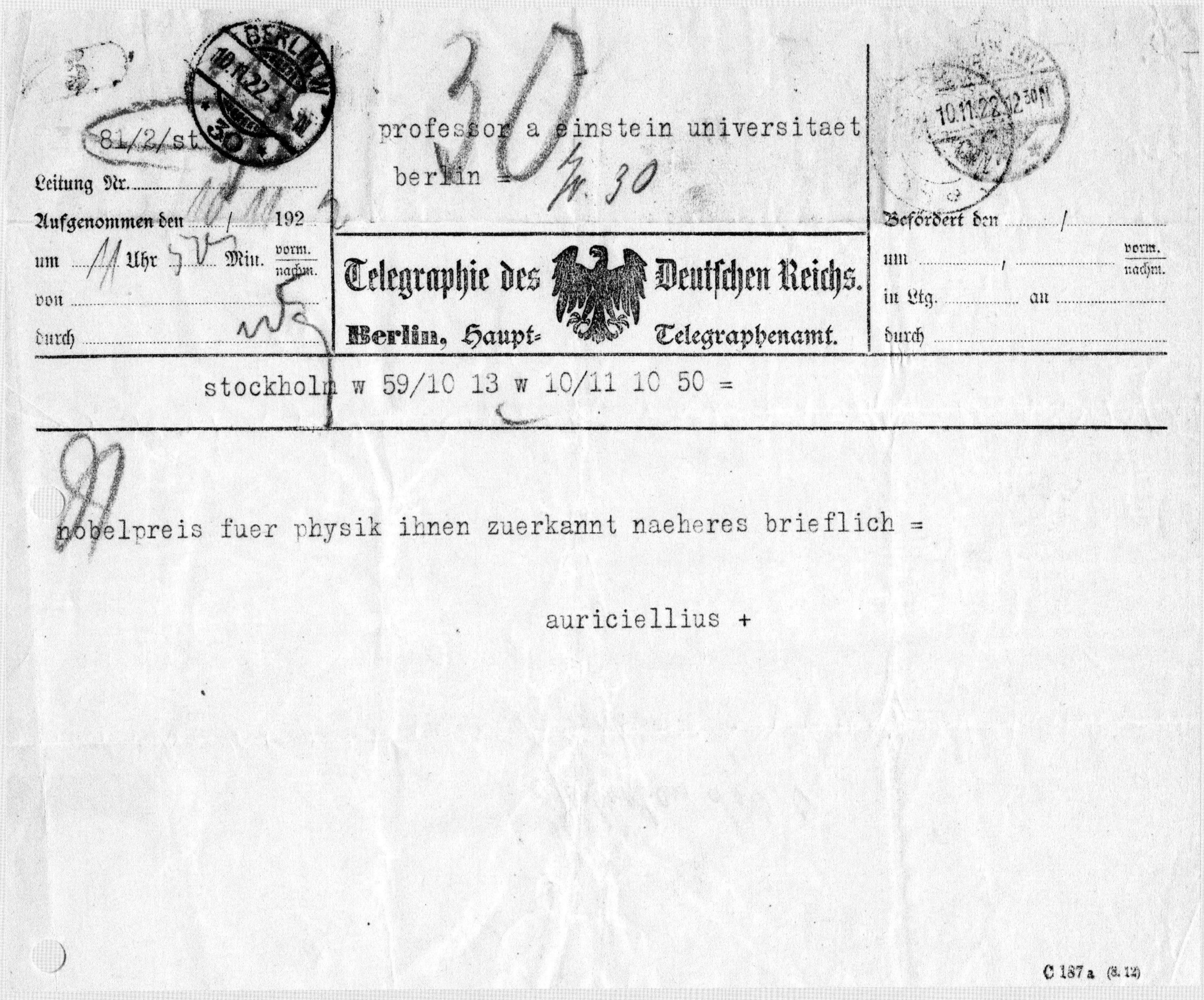

81/2/st

Leitung Nr.

Aufgenommen den 192

um ...... Uhr ...... Min. vorm. nachm.

von

durch

professor a einstein universitaet

berlin =

Telegraphie des Deutschen Reichs.

Berlin, Haupt-Telegraphenamt.

Befördert den

um .... vorm. nachm.

in Ltg. .... an

durch

stockholm w 59/10 13 w 10/11 10 50 =

nobelpreis fuer physik ihnen zuerkannt naeheres brieflich =

auriciellius +

C 187 a (8. 12)

« Nobel Prize in Physics awarded to you details by letter = Auriciellius »

↑ Telegram sent on behalf of the Nobel Committee by the secretary of the Swedish Academy of Sciences, Christopher Aurivillius, whose name appears misspelled on the telegram. November 10, 1922
The message reached Einstein through radio transmission on the ship to Japan.
Surprisingly, no mention of it is made in his travel diary.

KUNGLIGA SVENSKA VETENSKAPS-AKADEMIEN

har vid sitt sammanträde den 9 November 1922 i enlighet med föreskrifterna i det av

ALFRED NOBEL

den 27 November 1895 upprättade testamente beslutat att, oberoende av det värde som, efter eventuell bekräftelse må tillerkännas relativitets- och gravitationsteorien, överlämna det pris, som för 1921 bortgives åt den som inom fysikens område har gjort den viktigaste upptäckt eller uppfinning, till

84-27

↑↗ Nobel Prize in Physics, 1921: Certificate from the Royal Swedish Academy of Sciences, Stockholm, dated December 10, 1922

ALBERT EINSTEIN

för hans förtjänster om den teoretiska fysiken, särskilt hans upptäckt av lagen för den fotoelektriska effekten.

Stockholm den 10 December 1922

Kgl. Vet. Ak:s Præses.

Chr. Aurivillius

Kgl. Vet. Ak:s Sekreterare

→ At Paul Ehrenfest's home in Leiden, early November 1920: Albert Einstein, Paul Ehrenfest, Paul Langevin, Heike Kamerlingh-Onnes and Pierre Weiss.

« Soon I'll be fed up with relativity. Even such a thing fades away when one is too involved with it. »

↑↓ From a postcard to Elsa, Prague, January 8, 1921

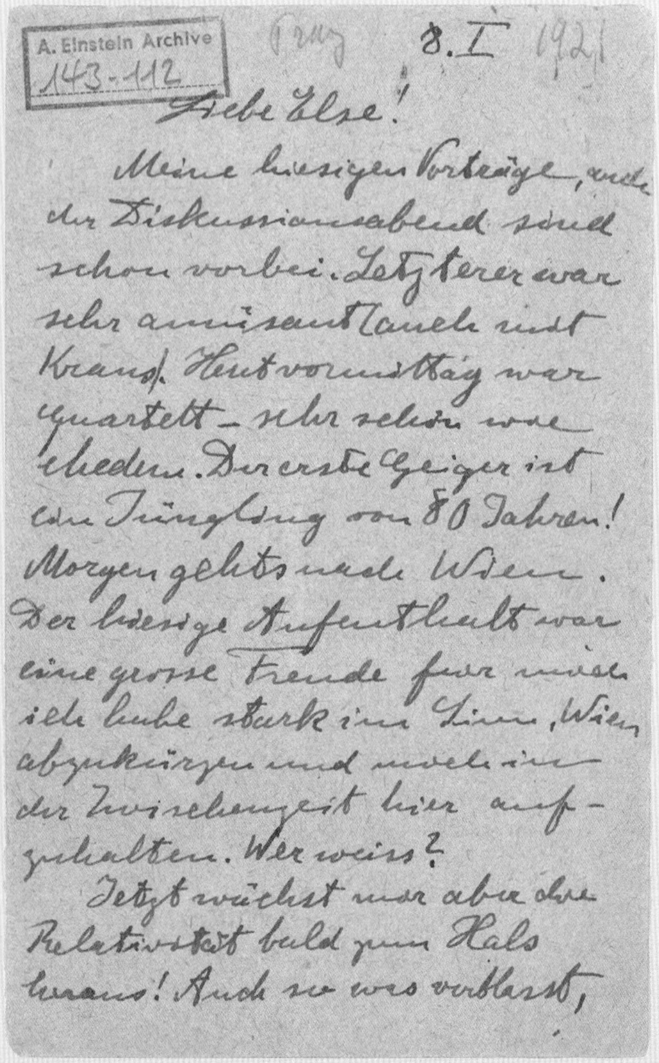

A. Einstein Archive 143-112

Prag 8. I 1921

Liebe Else!

Meine hiesigen Vorträge, und der Diskussionsabend sind schon vorbei. Letzterer war sehr amüsant (auch nicht Krampf). Heut vormittag war Quartett – sehr schön wie ehedem. Der erste Geiger ist ein Jüngling von 80 Jahren! Morgen gehts nach Wien. Der hiesige Aufenthalt war eine grosse Freude für mich. Ich habe stark im Sinn, Wien abzukürzen und mich in der Zwischenzeit hier aufzuhalten. Wer weiss?

Jetzt wächst mir aber die Relativität bald zum Hals heraus! Auch so was verblasst,

Frau Elsa Einstein
Haberlandstr. 5
Berlin

A. Einstein Archive 143-112

wenn man zuviel damit zu thun hat. Von der Stadt hab ich wenig gesehen, weil ich lang geschlafen & Nachmittags wieder. So war es gar nicht anstrengend. Gestern Abend ward Riesengesellschaft für mich gegeben, wobei ich, statt auf die vielen Reden zu antworten, geigte! Herzliche Grüsse an Euch alle Euer Albert.

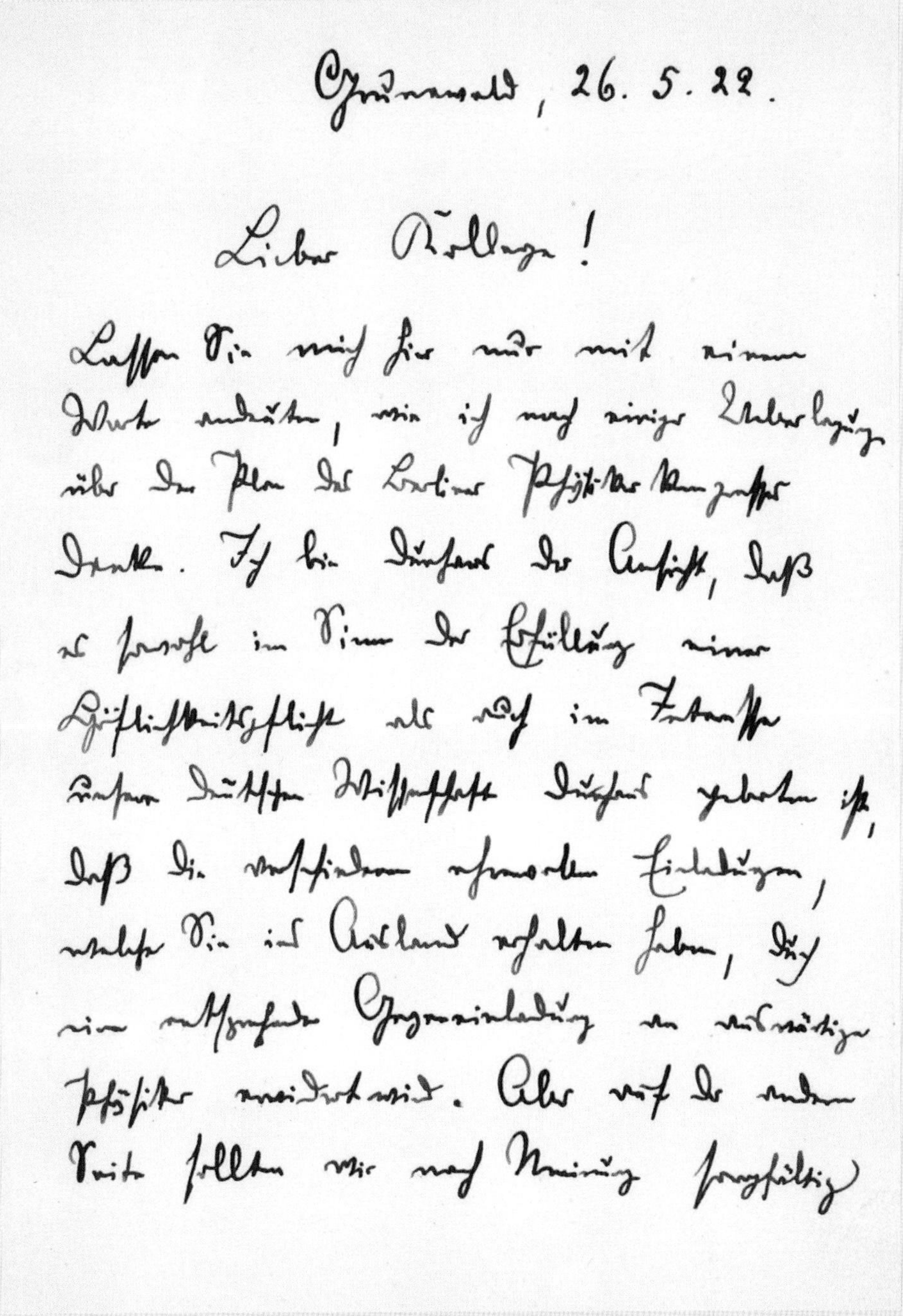

Grunewald, 26. 5. 22.

Lieber Kollege!

Lassen Sie mich hier nur mit einem Worte andeuten, wie ich nach einiger Ueberlegung über den Plan des Berliner Physikerkongresses denke. Ich bin durchaus der Ansicht, daß es sowohl im Sinne der Erfüllung einer Höflichkeitspflicht als auch im Interesse unserer deutschen Wissenschaft durchaus geboten ist, daß die verschiedenen ehrenvollen Einladungen, welche Sie ins Ausland erhalten haben, durch eine entsprechende Gegeneinladung an auswärtige Physiker erwidert wird. Aber auf der andern Seite sollten wir nach Meinung sorgfältig

« Dear colleague!

[…] I am, by all means, of the opinion that it is advisable, both as a fulfillment of an obligation of politeness and for the benefit of German science, to reciprocate, by invitations to foreign physicists, the various honorable invitations that you received from foreign countries. »

↑↗ Letter from Max Planck, May 26, 1922. Here Planck discusses the re-establishment of ties between German and other European physicists, which were severed during the First World War. Einstein as a representative of Berlin's scientific community, whom German authorities even considered a major "cultural asset" was in the position to act as a mediator.

QUANTUM THEORY

Following the publication of the general theory of relativity, Einstein resumed his work on sub-atomic processes. In his 1905 paper on the photoelectric effect, Einstein had laid the foundation for the quantum theory. In the period from 1916-1925, he made two additional major contributions to quantum theory. Firstly, he confirmed that photons carry momentum. Secondly, he introduced the notion of stimulated emission of radiation – a concept which eventually led to the development of the laser.

In the mid-1920s, two separate mathematical descriptions of the behavior of electrons were developed by Erwin Schrödinger and Werner Heisenberg. These descriptions formed the basis for a crucial new phase in quantum theory called quantum mechanics. The Danish physicist, Niels Bohr, became the major proponent of the dominant interpretation of quantum mechanics known as the "Copenhagen interpretation." The basic assumptions of this interpretation are the following: firstly, the very act of observing an object changes it. Secondly, in accordance with the principle of quantum uncertainty, it is impossible to determine simultaneously the precise position and velocity of a subatomic particle. Thirdly, all we can ever know is the results of experiments. Quantum mechanics deals only with probabilities, not with certainties. Though he made some of the major contributions to quantum theory, Einstein was vehemently opposed to this new concept of causality. "The dragon's teeth I sewed in my youth", he wrote to his friend Heinrich Zangger, "grew so stately that I am quite frightened." He was not prepared to abandon the concept that an objective world exists independently of any subjective observational process.

Einstein's refusal to accept quantum mechanics led to his increased isolation from the scientific mainstream in his later years. Yet he continued to play a crucial role in the development of modern physics: by providing carefully reasoned opposition to quantum mechanics, he forced its adherents to develop stronger justifications for their theories, which were thereby put on a more secure footing. Experiments carried out since Einstein's death have proved that – in spite of its philosophical absurdities, which defy common sense – quantum mechanics does work and can form the theoretical basis for a vast range of technological applications.

« I find the idea quite intolerable that an electron [...] should choose of its own free will, not only its moment to jump off, but also its direction. In that case, I would rather be a cobbler, or even an employee in a gaming-house, than a physicist. »

↑ From a letter to Max Born, April 29, 1924

→ Albert Einstein and Niels Bohr, Leiden, December 1925
Photo by Paul Ehrenfest

UNIVERSITETETS INSTITUT
FOR
TEORETISK FYSIK

BLEGDAMSVEJ 15 11.April 1949.
COPENHAGEN, DENMARK

Lieber Einstein,

Vielen Dank für Ihre freundlichen Zeilen. Es war für uns alle eine grosse Freude, anlässlich Ihres Geburtstages unseren Gefühlen Ausdruck zu geben. Um in demselben scherzhaften Tone zu sprechen, kann ich nicht umhin, über die bangen Fragen zu sagen, dass es sich meines Erachtens nicht darum handelt, ob wir an einer der physikalischen Beschreibung zugänglichen Realität festhalten sollen oder nicht, sondern darum, den von Ihnen gewiesenen Weg weiter zu verfolgen und die logischen Voraussetzungen für die Beschreibung der Realitäten zu erkennen. In meiner frechen Weise möchte ich sogar sagen, dass niemand -und nicht mal der liebe Gott selber- wissen kann, was ein Wort wie würfeln in diesem Zusammenhang heissen soll.

Mit herzlichen Grüssen

Ihr

Niels Bohr

« Dear Einstein,

Many thanks for your friendly letter. For all of us, it was a great pleasure to express our feelings on the occasion of your birthday. To speak in the same jocular tone, I cannot help saying about the disquieting questions, that to my mind the issue is not whether we should cling to a reality which is accessible to physical description, but rather, we should pursue the path shown by you and discover the logical prerequisites for the description of the realities. In my impertinent manner, I would even go as far as saying that no one – not even the dear Lord himself – can know what a phrase like playing dice means in this context. »

↑↗ Letter from Niels Bohr, April 11, 1949. Bohr thanks Einstein for his friendly reaction to the *Festschrift* published on the occasion of Einstein's seventieth birthday, and alludes to their opposing views on causality. In the late 1920s, Bohr and Einstein were entangled in a controversy about the appropriate interpretations of quantum mechanics which turned out to be one of the most important scientific as well as philosophical debates of the 20th century.

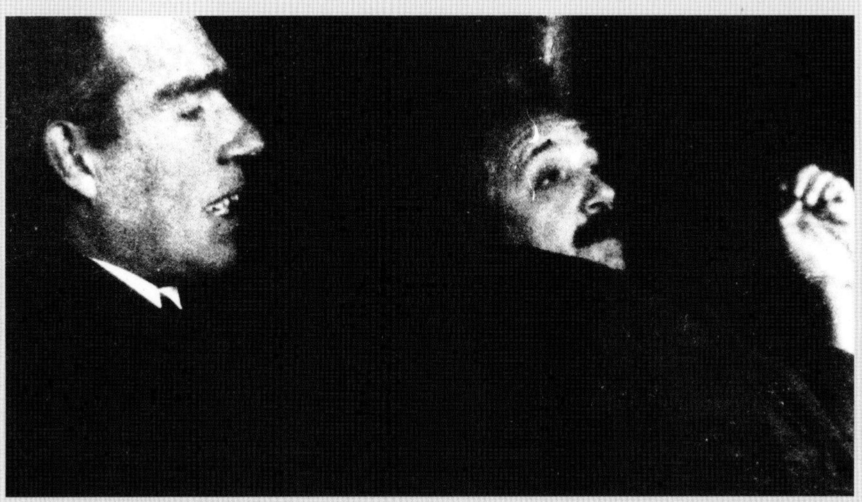

→ Albert Einstein and Niels Bohr, Leiden, December 1925
Photo by Paul Ehrenfest

Prof. Schrödinger
Zürich 6, Huttenstrasse 9

Zürich, am 4. Dezember 1925.

Hochverehrter Herr Professor!

Haben Sie vielen Dank für Ihren freundlichen Brief vom 14. XI., den ich nur deshalb noch nicht beantwortet habe, weil ich Ihnen sogleich die fertige Ausarbeitung (d. h. fertig von meiner Seite) vorlegen wollte, die ich jetzt mit gleicher Post absende.

Sachlich hat sich gegenüber meiner ersten Mitteilung an Sie nur dies geändert, dass man auch mit Beibehaltung des energielosen Zustandsgebietes die gewöhnlichen Gasgesetze bis zu sehr tiefen Temperaturen herab sehr genau gültig bleiben. Die "Entartungstemperatur" wird nur im Verhältnis e:1 grösser und die Entartung erhält den Charakter einer Kondensation, ähnlich wie in Ihrer Theorie der "undulatorischen Moleküle". Gleichwohl lehne ich diese Möglichkeit ab, weil im vorliegenden Fall die letzte Energiestufe makroskopische Grössenordnung bekommt(siehe § 5, Ende).

Ich habe den Autornamen leer gelassen und einige Stellen am Rande rot angestrichen, die rein stilistisch abzuändern wären, wenn Sie mit zeichnen, indem z. B. "ich" durch "der eine von uns" oder durch "wir" zu ersetzen wäre. Daneben werden aber auch Stellen sein, denen Sie vielleicht sachlich nicht ohne weiteres zustimmen, besonders im §1, §6 und §5, Ende, ferner der absolut neutrale Standpunkt, den ich jetzt hinsichtlich der Gewichtszählung (1 oder N!) einnehme. (Nimmt man N! so ist selbstverständlich auch dem abgekühlten Festkörper die Nullpunktsentropie k lg(N!) zuzuschreiben, mit Berufung darauf, dass auch bei der tiefsten Temperatur noch ein, wenn auch noch so kleiner Dampfdruck über dem Körper lagert und dass auf diesem Weg im Lauf der Zeit ein Austausch der Moleküle des Festkörpers sogar wirklich stattfindet.)

Letter from Erwin Schrödinger, December 4, 1925.
Schrödinger's correspondence with Einstein shows the

Kopenhagen 10.6.27.

Hochverehrter, lieber Herr Professor!

Vielen herzlichen Dank für Ihren freundlichen Brief; obwohl ich eigentlich nichts neues weiss, möcht ich doch nocheinmal schreiben, warum ich glaube, dass der Indeterminismus, also die Ungültigkeit der strengen Kausalität, notwendig ist, nicht nur widerspruchsfrei möglich. Wenn ich Ihren Standpunkt richtig verstanden hab, dann meinen Sie, dass zwar alle Experimente so herauskommen würden, wie es die statistische Qu. M. verlangt, dass es aber darüber hinaus später möglich sein werde, über bestimmte Bahnen eines Teilchens zu sprechen. Unter Teilchen meinen Sie dabei nicht etwa ein Wellenpaket nach Schrödinger, sondern einen gegenstand, von bestimmter (von der Geschwindigkeit unabhängiger) „grösse" (d.h. mit bestimmtem, von der Geschwindigkeit unabhängigem Kraftfeld. Mein Haupteinwand ist nun der: Denken Sie an freie Elektronen konstanter, langsamer Geschwindigkeit, so langsam, dass die de Broglie-Wellenlänge sehr gross gegen die Teilchengrösse ist, d.h. die Kraftfelder des Teilchens sollen in Abständen der Grössenordnung der de Broglie-wellenlänge vom Teilchen praktisch Null sein. Solche Elektronen fliegen auf ein Gitter, bei dem der Gitterabstand von der Grössenordnung der genannten

↑ Letter from Werner Heisenberg, June 10, 1927.
Heisenberg's correspondence with Einstein illustrates their fundamental differences of opinion regarding quantum mechanics and causality.

Dialectica 1948

Quanten-Mechanik und Wirklichkeit.

Im Folgenden will ich kurz und elementar darlegen, warum ich die Methode der Quanten-Mechanik nicht für eine im Prinzip befriedigend halte. Ich will aber gleich bemerken, dass ich keineswegs leugnen will, dass diese Theorie einen bedeutenden, in gewissem Sinne sogar endgültigen Fortschritt der physikalischen Erkenntnis darstellt. Ich stelle mir vor, dass diese Theorie in einer späteren etwa so enthalten sein wird, wie die Strahlen-Optik in der Undulations-Optik: Die Beziehungen werden bleiben, die Grundlage aber wird vertieft bezw. durch eine umfassendere ersetzt werden.

I.

Ich denke mir ein freies Teilchen zu einer Zeit durch eine räumlich beschränkte ψ Funktion (im Sinne der Quantenmechanik vollständig) beschrieben. Gemäss einer solchen Darstellung hat das Teilchen weder einen scharf bestimmten Impuls noch einen scharf bestimmten Ort.

In welchem Sinne nun soll ich mir vorstellen, dass diese Beschreibung einen wirklichen individuellen Thatbestand darstellt? Zwei Auffassungen scheinen mir möglich und naheliegend, die wir gegeneinander abwägen wollen:

a) Das (freie) Teilchen hat in Wirklichkeit einen bestimmten Ort und einen bestimmten Impuls, wenn auch nicht beide zugleich in demselben individuellen Falle durch Messung festgestellt werden können. Die ψ Funktion gibt nach dieser Auffassung eine unvollständige Beschreibung eines realen Sachverhaltes.

Diese Auffassung ist nicht die von den Physikern acceptierte. Ihre Annahme würde dazu führen, neben der unvollständigen eine vollständige Beschreibung des Sachverhaltes in die Physik einzuführen und für eine solche Beschreibung Gesetze zu suchen. Damit würde der theoretische Rahmen der Quanten-Mechanik gesprengt.

b) Das Teilchen hat in Wirklichkeit weder einen bestimmten Impuls noch einen bestimmten Ort; die Beschreibung durch die ψ-Funktion ist eine prinzipiell vollständige Beschreibung. Der scharfe Ort des Teilchens, den ich durch eine Orts-Messung erhalte, ist nicht als Ort des Teilchens vor der Messung interpretierbar. Die scharfe Lokalisierung, die bei der Messung zutage tritt, wird nur durch den unvermeidlichen (nicht unwesentlichen) Messungs-Eingriff hervorgebracht. Das Messungsergebnis hängt nicht nur von der realen Teilchen-Situation sondern auch von der prinzipiell unvollständig bekannten Natur des Mess-Mechanismus ab. Analog verhält es sich, wenn der Impuls oder sonst eine das Teilchen betreffende Observable gemessen wird.

« In the following, I want to state briefly and elementarily why I believe the method of quantum mechanics is not a satisfactory one in principle. Yet I want to mention right away that I in no way want to deny that this theory represents a significant, in a sense definitive progress of physical knowledge. I can imagine that this theory will be included in a later one in a similar fashion as radiation optics is included in undulation optics. The relations will remain, yet the foundation will be consolidated or replaced by a more comprehensive one. »

←↑ "Quantum Mechanics and Reality."
Manuscript of an article published in *Dialectica* (1948) in which Einstein justifies his opposition to quantum mechanics, yet acknowledges its importance for the development of modern physics.

→ Albert Einstein and Niels Bohr,
Leiden, December 1925
Photo by Paul Ehrenfest

« We have become Antipodeans in our scientific expectations. You believe in the God who plays dice, and I in complete law and order in a world which objectively exists, and which I, in a wildly speculative way, am trying to capture. I firmly believe, but I hope that someone will discover a more realistic way, or rather a more tangible basis than it has been my lot to find. Even the great initial success of the quantum theory does not make me believe in the fundamental dice-game, although I am well aware that our younger colleagues interpret this as a consequence of senility. No doubt the day will come when we will see whose instinctive attitude was the correct one. »

→ From a letter to Max Born, September 7, 1944.
Repeatedly Einstein stressed he could not believe in a probabilistic physics, a conviction he would express with the metaphor of a God who does not play dice.

UNIFIED FIELD THEORY

By the early 1930s Einstein was planning to divide his time by spending half a year in Berlin and Caputh, and the other half at the newly-founded Institute for Advanced Study at Princeton.
When the Nazis came to power, he found himself in the United States.
Appalled by the news from Germany, he decided not to return to Berlin. Instead he spent the spring and summer of 1933 in Belgium and England, and returned to the United States in October. He took up residence at Princeton, accepting a lifelong appointment at the Institute the following year. Although he officially retired in 1945, he continued to work there until shortly before his death in 1955.

During the last thirty years of his life, Einstein's main scientific interest lay in developing a unified field theory, an attempt to explain both gravity and electromagnetism in one broad mathematical structure. He hoped thereby to fill the troubling gap in quantum theory which is unable to describe the world otherwise than in terms of mere probabilities. Over the years, Einstein proposed unified field theories in various mathematical forms. Einstein himself was usually the first to detect the flaws in them, yet he carried on relentlessly. He published his major attempts in 1923, 1925, 1929, 1931 and 1950.

This quest occupied more of Einstein's years than any other activity. He did not succeed but he was confident that one day someone would. Although it has often been claimed that these were wasted years, it is now believed that Einstein was actually a generation or two ahead of his time.
When Einstein began his quest, the only two forces known to physics were gravity and electromagnetism. Since then, two new nuclear forces have been discovered, the strong and the weak forces. Electromagnetism and the strong and the weak forces can be explained by quantum physics – gravity is the odd one out. Physicists are currently trying to develop a quantum theory of gravity as a first stage towards a theory of everything (TOE) which would encompass all known forces and fields of physics in one set of formulas. The ongoing quest for a theory of everything is Einstein's most significant legacy to science.

→ Einstein with his assistant Peter G. Bergmann at the Institute for Advanced Study, October 2, 1940.
Photo by Lucien Aigner

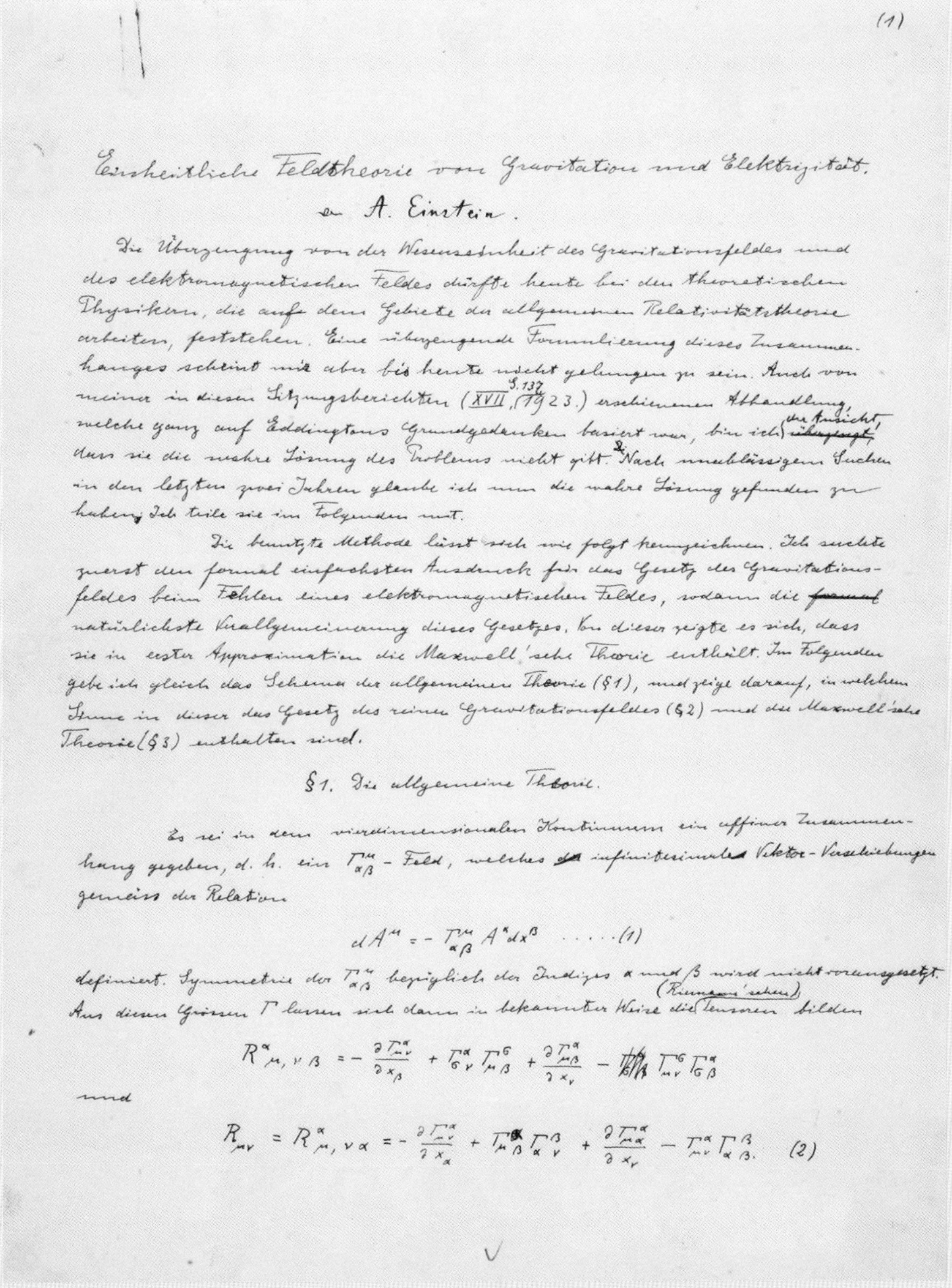

(1)

Einheitliche Feldtheorie von Gravitation und Elektrizität.

von A. Einstein.

Die Überzeugung von der Wesensgleichheit des Gravitationsfeldes und des elektromagnetischen Feldes dürfte heute bei den theoretischen Physikern, die auf dem Gebiete der allgemeinen Relativitätstheorie arbeiten, feststehen. Eine überzeugende Formulierung dieses Zusammenhanges scheint mir aber bis heute nicht gelungen zu sein. Auch von meiner in diesen Sitzungsberichten (XVII, S. 137, 1923.) erschienenen Abhandlung, welche ganz auf Eddingtons Grundgedanken basiert war, bin ich der Ansicht, dass sie die wahre Lösung des Problems nicht gibt. Nach unablässigem Suchen in den letzten zwei Jahren glaube ich nun die wahre Lösung gefunden zu haben. Ich teile sie im Folgenden mit.

Die benutzte Methode lässt sich wie folgt kennzeichnen. Ich suchte zuerst den formal einfachsten Ausdruck für das Gesetz des Gravitationsfeldes beim Fehlen eines elektromagnetischen Feldes, sodann die ~~formal~~ natürlichste Verallgemeinerung dieses Gesetzes. Von dieser zeigte es sich, dass sie in erster Approximation die Maxwell'sche Theorie enthält. Im Folgenden gebe ich gleich das Schema der allgemeinen Theorie (§1), und zeige darauf, in welchem Sinne in dieser das Gesetz des reinen Gravitationsfeldes (§2) und die Maxwell'sche Theorie (§3) enthalten sind.

§1. Die allgemeine Theorie.

Es sei in dem vierdimensionalen Kontinuum ein affiner Zusammenhang gegeben, d. h. ein $\Gamma^{\mu}_{\alpha\beta}$-Feld, welches infinitesimale Vektor-Verschiebungen gemäss der Relation

$$dA^{\mu} = -\Gamma^{\mu}_{\alpha\beta} A^{\alpha} dx^{\beta} \quad \ldots\ldots (1)$$

definiert. Symmetrie der $\Gamma^{\mu}_{\alpha\beta}$ bezüglich der Indizes α und β wird nicht vorausgesetzt. Aus diesen Grössen Γ lassen sich dann in bekannter Weise die (Riemann'schen) Tensoren bilden

$$R^{\alpha}_{\mu,\nu\beta} = -\frac{\partial \Gamma^{\alpha}_{\mu\nu}}{\partial x_{\beta}} + \Gamma^{\alpha}_{\sigma\nu}\Gamma^{\sigma}_{\mu\beta} + \frac{\partial \Gamma^{\alpha}_{\mu\beta}}{\partial x_{\nu}} - \Gamma^{\sigma}_{\mu\nu}\Gamma^{\alpha}_{\sigma\beta}$$

und

$$R_{\mu\nu} = R^{\alpha}_{\mu,\nu\alpha} = -\frac{\partial \Gamma^{\alpha}_{\mu\nu}}{\partial x_{\alpha}} + \Gamma^{\alpha}_{\mu\beta}\Gamma^{\beta}_{\alpha\nu} + \frac{\partial \Gamma^{\alpha}_{\mu\alpha}}{\partial x_{\nu}} - \Gamma^{\alpha}_{\mu\nu}\Gamma^{\beta}_{\alpha\beta}. \quad (2)$$

↑ "Unified Field Theory of Gravitation and Electricity"
Manuscript of an article published in the minutes of the Prussian Academy of Sciences, 1925. One of Einstein's major attempts to develop a theory which would unite all physical forces.

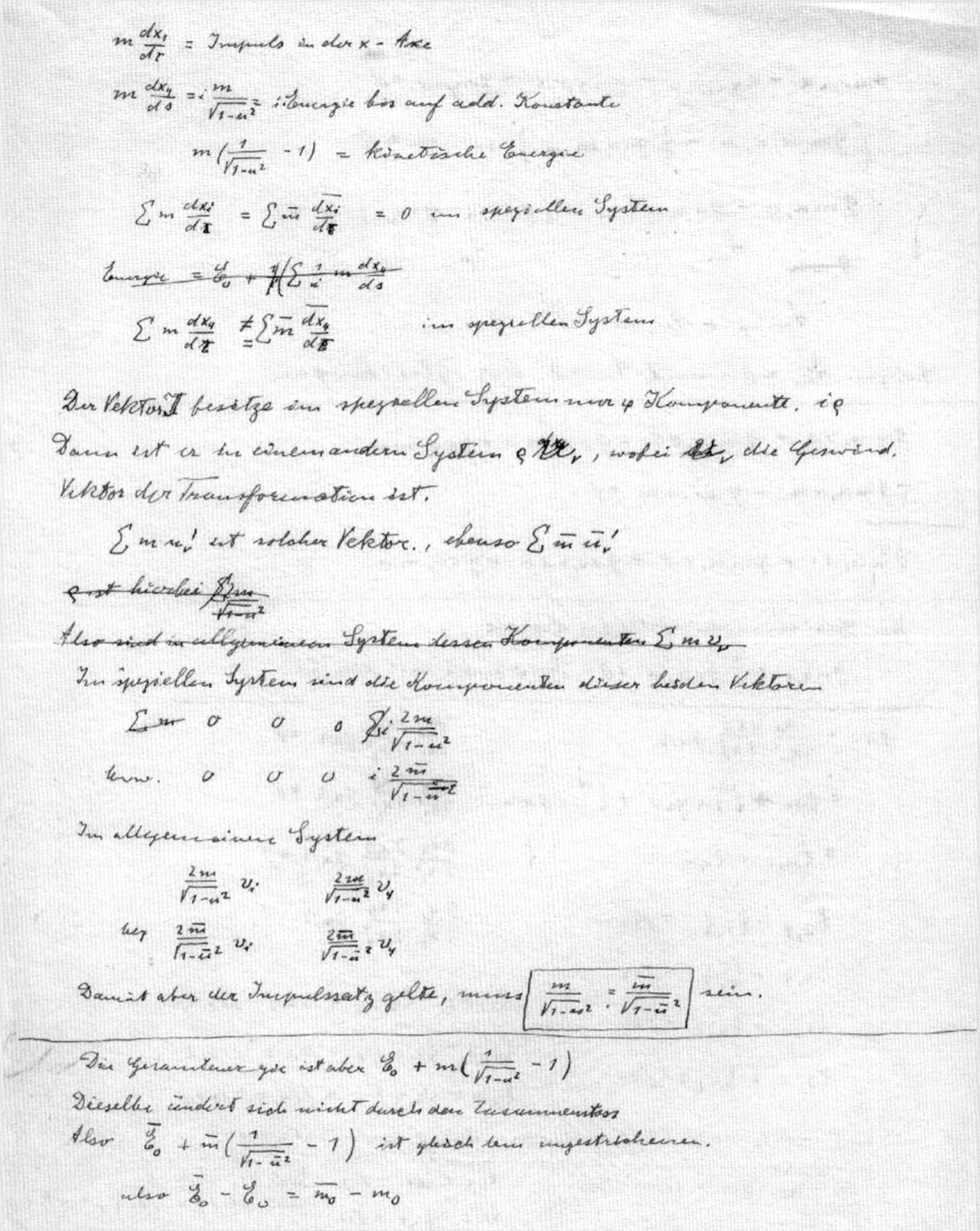
$m \frac{dx_1}{d\tau}$ = Impuls in der x-Axe

$m \frac{dx_4}{ds} = i \frac{m}{\sqrt{1-u^2}}$ = i·Energie bis auf add. Konstante

$m\left(\frac{1}{\sqrt{1-u^2}} - 1\right)$ = kinetische Energie

$\sum m \frac{dx_i}{d\tau} = \sum \bar{m} \frac{dx_i}{d\bar{\tau}} = 0$ im speziellen System

~~Energie $= E_0 + \frac{1}{i}\left(\sum \frac{1}{i} m \frac{dx_4}{ds}\right)$~~

$\sum m \frac{dx_4}{d\tau} \neq = \sum \bar{m} \frac{dx_4}{d\bar{\tau}}$ im speziellen System

Der Vektor T besitze im speziellen System nur 4 Komponente. $i\varphi$

Dann ist er in einem andern System φv_ν, wobei v_ν die Geschwind. Vektor der Transformation ist.

$\sum m u_\nu'$ ist solcher Vektor., ebenso $\sum \bar{m} \bar{u}_\nu'$

~~φ ist hierbei $\sum \frac{m}{\sqrt{1-u^2}}$~~

~~Also sind im allgemeinen System dessen Komponenten $\sum m v_\nu$~~

Im speziellen System sind die Komponenten dieser beiden Vektoren

$\sum m \quad 0 \quad 0 \quad 0 \quad \sum i \frac{2m}{\sqrt{1-u^2}}$

bzw. $\quad 0 \quad 0 \quad 0 \quad i \frac{2\bar{m}}{\sqrt{1-\bar{u}^2}}$

Im allgemeinen System

$\frac{2m}{\sqrt{1-u^2}} v_i \qquad \frac{2m}{\sqrt{1-u^2}} v_4$

bzw $\frac{2\bar{m}}{\sqrt{1-\bar{u}^2}} v_i \qquad \frac{2\bar{m}}{\sqrt{1-\bar{u}^2}} v_4$

Damit aber der Impulssatz gelte, muss $\boxed{\frac{m}{\sqrt{1-u^2}} = \frac{\bar{m}}{\sqrt{1-\bar{u}^2}}}$ sein.

Die Gesamtenergie ist aber $E_0 + m\left(\frac{1}{\sqrt{1-u^2}} - 1\right)$

Dieselbe ändert sich nicht durch den Zusammenstoss

Also $\bar{E}_0 + \bar{m}\left(\frac{1}{\sqrt{1-\bar{u}^2}} - 1\right)$ ist gleich dem ungestrichenen.

also $\bar{E}_0 - E_0 = \bar{m}_0 - m_0$

↑ Over the years, Einstein filled hundreds of pages with calculations, trying to develop a unified field theory. This manuscript stems from the 1950s

↑ Princeton, 1938
Photo by Lotte Jacobi

« The little book Rudi gave me I find extremely appealing. In addition I'm doing science in an easygoing way. Actually it turns out that otherwise I cannot bear it [...]. When I try to refrain from it, life becomes too empty for me. No reading can replace it, not even reading science. »

↑ From a letter to Elsa and her daughters, Cap Polonio, March 7, 1925

THE BRITISH CONNECTION 2

Due to his continental engagements, some long journeys and ill health in the late 1920s, Einstein was not able to accept any invitation to Britain prior to 1930. In May 1931 he would eventually spend several weeks at Christ Church College, Oxford, studying, lecturing sporadically, relaxing, playing music and discussing contemporary issues with colleagues, students and people from all walks of life. At the instigation of the physicist, Frederick Lindemann, professor at Oxford University and director of the Clarendon Laboratory, additional visits as a "Research Student" were offered to Einstein. Going home with yet another honorary degree, Einstein did return to Oxford the following year.
While the 1932 sojourn at Christ Church College may not have been very different from the previous one, by 1933 circumstances had changed. Einstein was now celebrated in Britain mainly as someone who stood up to the Nazi government. In addition to his scientific tasks, Einstein felt challenged by the concern for his persecuted colleagues. He shared this concern with Frederick Lindemann as well as with Commander Oliver Locker Lampson, a member of the British Parliament who, in July 1933, proposed a bill in the House of Commons granting Palestinian citizenship to all "stateless" Jews, amended later by proposing to extend Palestinian nationality to all persecuted Jews.

When after his scheduled visit to England in June 1933, Einstein's Belgian hideout did not seem safe enough any more, Locker Lampson provided a sanctuary near the Norfolk coast. The last month Einstein ever spent in Europe, he was hosted by the Commander in a small wooden cabin not far from Cromer. On October 3rd, he spoke at a mass meeting in London's Royal Albert Hall, and focused on assisting Jewish academics to escape from Nazi persecution. A couple of days later, he boarded a ship in Southampton and left Europe for good.

→ Together with Einstein sixteen English and foreign personalities received honorary degrees at Magdalene College Lodge on 5 June 1930. Among them was Max Planck, here seen together with Einstein in doctor's cap and gown.

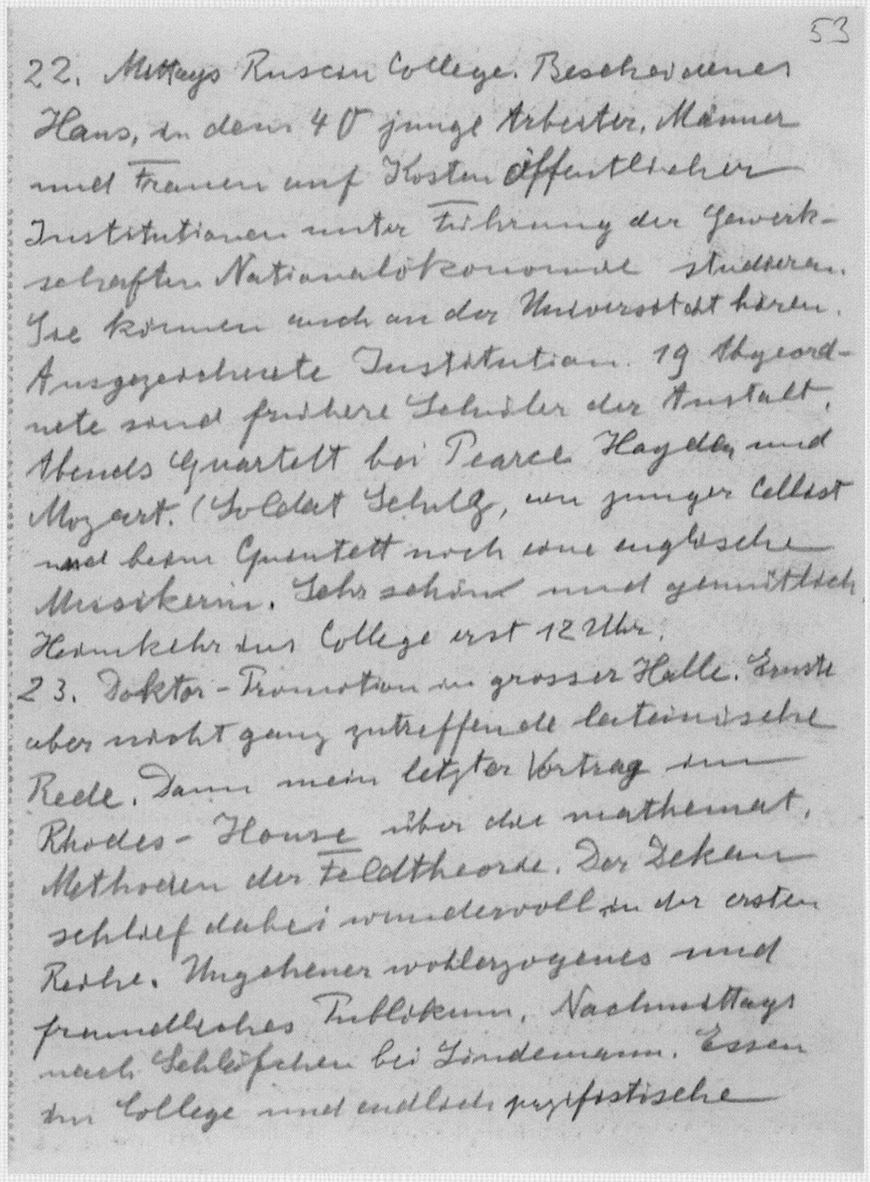
53
22. Mittags Ruskin College. Bescheidenes
Haus, in dem 40 junge Arbeiter, Männer
und Frauen auf Kosten öffentlicher
Institutionen unter Führung der Gewerk-
schaften Nationalökonomie studieren.
Sie können auch an der Universität hören.
Ausgezeichnete Institution. 19 Abgeord-
nete sind frühere Schüler der Anstalt.
Abends Quartett bei Pearce Haydn und
Mozart. (Soldat Schulz, ein junger Cellist
und beim Quintett noch eine englische
Musikerin. Sehr schön und gemütlich.
Heimkehr ins College erst 12 Uhr.
23. Doktor-Promotion in grosser Halle. Ernste
aber nicht ganz zutreffende lateinische
Rede. Dann mein letzter Vortrag im
Rhodes-House über die mathemat.
Methoden der Feldtheorie. Der Dekan
schlief dabei wundervoll in der ersten
Reihe. Ungeheuer wohlerzogenes und
freundliches Publikum. Nachmittags
nach Schläfchen bei Lindemann. Essen
im College und endlich pazifistische

↓→ From Einstein's diary,
May 22/23, 1931

« 22. Noon at Ruskin College. Modest house where 40 young workers, men and women, are studying economics, on scholarships funded by public bodies, principally the unions. They are even allowed to attend university courses. Excellent institution. 19 members of Parliament are former students of this college. In the evening quartet at Pearce's, Haydn and Mozart [...] Very nice and comfortable. Return to the college only at 12 a.m.
23. [Honorary] doctorate ceremony in big hall. Latin speech serious though to be taken with a grain of salt. Then my last lecture at Rhodes House, about mathematical methods of the field theory during which the Dean, delightfully, was sleeping in the front row. Tremendously well-mannered and friendly audience. ... »

→ Einstein and Oliver Locker Lampson in front of the cabin at Roughton Heath near Cromer that sheltered Einstein in September 1933. Indoors a piano was at Einstein's disposal, outdoors armed guards watched over the scientist.

→↓ From a letter to Elsa, Cromer/Norfolk, September 10, 1933

« […] I'm living here like a hermit; I just don't have to munch roots and herbs. I feel fortunate with this quiet life, and, to my satisfaction, I observe that I am a pleasant companion to myself. »

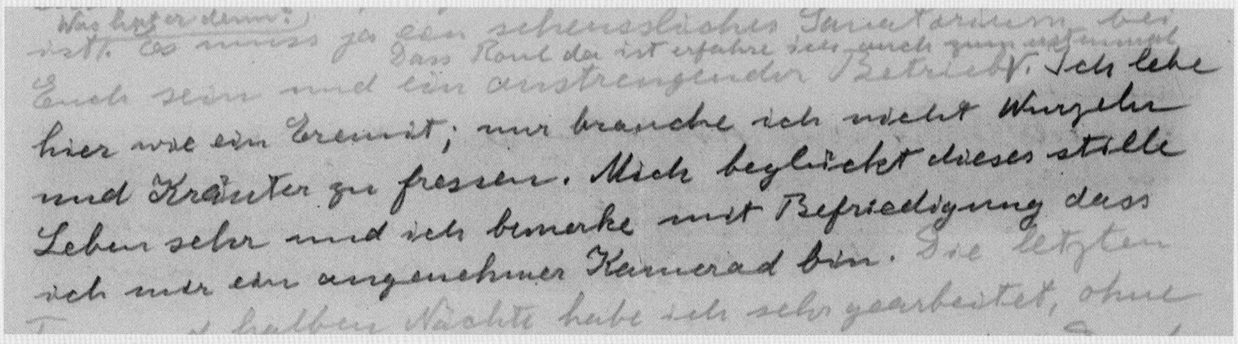

ist. Es muss ja ein scheussliches Sanatorium bei
Dass Raoul da ist erfahre ich auch zum erstenmal
Euch sein und ein anstrengender Betrieb. Ich lebe
hier wie ein Eremit; nur brauche ich nicht Wurzeln
und Kräuter zu fressen. Mich beglückt dieses stille
Leben sehr und ich bemerke mit Befriedigung dass
ich mir ein angenehmer Kamerad bin. Die letzten
halben Nächte habe ich sehr gearbeitet, ohne

↓→ Waiting for his turn, Einstein is consulting here with O. Locker Lampson. Next to him sits Ernest Rutherford, known as the "father of nuclear physics." After the mass rally for the Refugee Assistance Fund Einstein's wife Elsa commented: "Albert was immensely successful at the Albert Hall. It is said that, due to his speech, almost 100.000 Marks were collected. Nobody else would have accomplished such a feat."
Royal Albert Hall, London, October 3, 1933

« I am glad you have given me an opportunity of expressing to you my deep sense of gratitude as a man, a good European and a Jew. Through your well-organized program of relief you have rendered great service, not only to those scholars who have been the innocent victims of persecution, but to all of humanity and of science. You have shown that you, and the British people as a whole, have remained faithful to the tradition of tolerance and justice which your country has proudly upheld for centuries.
It is precisely in times of economic distress, such as we experience everywhere today, that we may recognize the effectiveness of the vital moral force of a people. Let us hope that, at some future time, when Europe is politically and economically united, the historian rendering judgment will be able to say that, in our own days, the liberty and honor of this continent were saved by the nations of Western Europe; that they stood fast in bitter times against the forces of hatred and oppression; that they successfully defended that which has brought us every advance in knowledge and invention: the freedom of the individual without which no self-respecting individual finds life worth living. »

THE SCIENTIST IN SOCIETY

One of the main incentives for Einstein to embark on a career in science was the independence he believed it offered. Einstein viewed scientific research as a pure quest for knowledge and truth. He was firmly convinced of the inalienable right of the scientist to think, investigate, and act independently. Scientists therefore must have unimpeded access to all the information they require and must be free to discuss work in progress with their colleagues without any restrictions. To his mind, neither the state nor society had the right to interfere with the scientist's freedom of inquiry and teaching.

During his lifetime, Einstein perceived a growing threat to the freedom of scientists: first in Europe in the wake of the rise of Nazism and subsequently in the U.S. as a result of the Cold War and McCarthyism. In reaction to these dangers, Einstein maintained that scientists are not merely experts working in a vacuum – they also have some major social responsibilities.

Alarmed by the reproaches made toward him after the American atom bomb hit Japanese cities, he reasoned that scientists are obliged to anticipate the consequences of their work, holding that if the fruits of their labors are incompatible with their ethical values, they must refuse to participate, even at the risk of losing their jobs.

Unambiguously, he pointed out that scientists must work towards increasing society's awareness of the implications of scientific discoveries. Given that technological applications of scientific theories have the potential to either improve the plight of humankind or to threaten its very existence. Einstein held that it is up to society to decide which option it prefers.

« We live in a time of moral decay. Reverence for life and respect for truth has been deteriorating. The blatant idol of brute force imposes itself everywhere. Those whose obligation it is to guard our spiritual heritage have yielded to weary skepticism. They stand idly by watching our moral impoverishment. [...]
Monde is a solitary voice of humanity, seeking to rouse the dormant conscience of the indolent and exposing, honestly and fearlessly, the origin and evil implications of recent developments in the world. »

→ Einstein composed these lines in 1932 for the weekly *Monde*, published by Henri Barbusse. It was the pacifist ideals which connected Einstein to the French author, although he did not share his communist point of view.

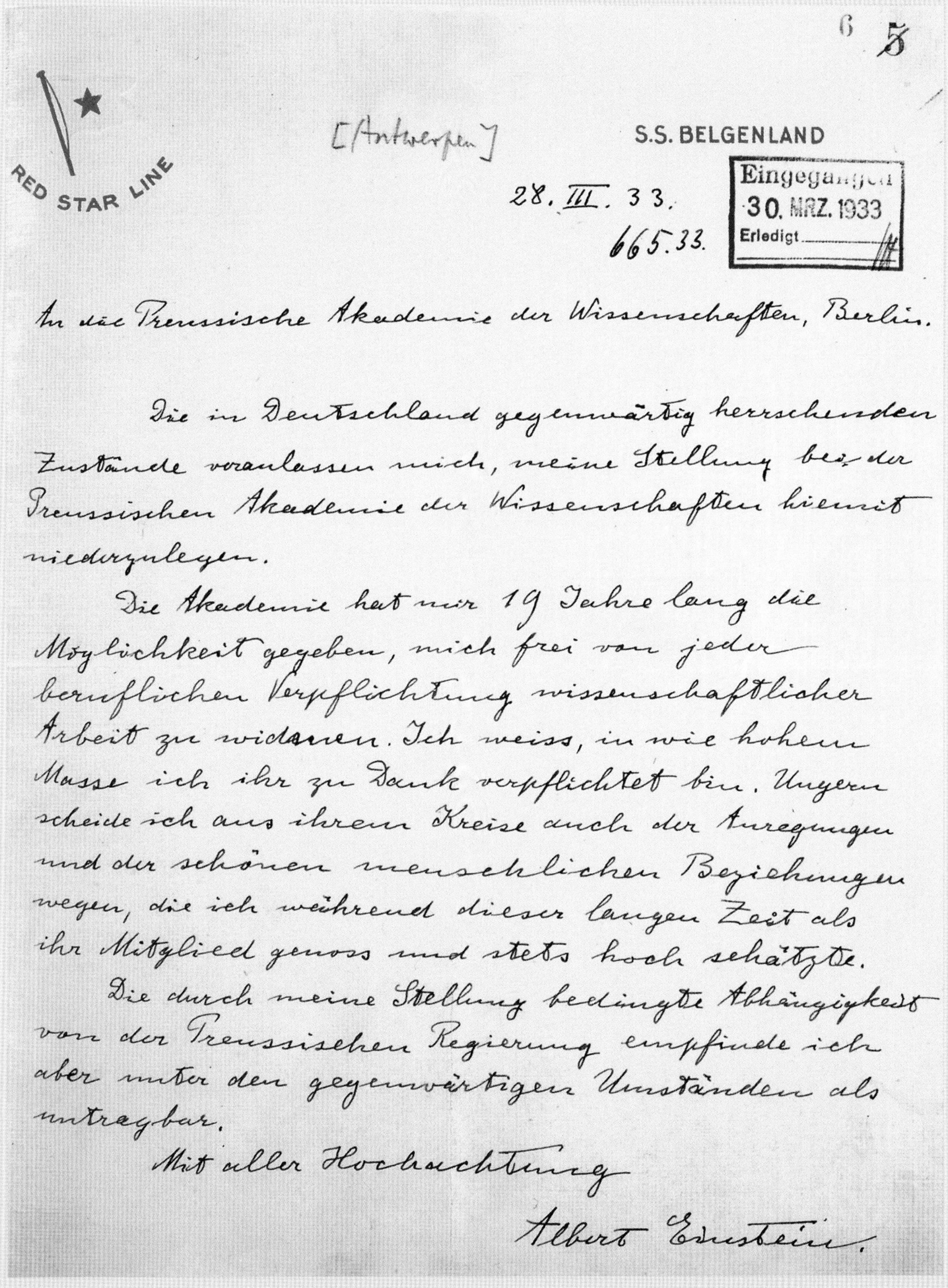

RED STAR LINE

6 5

[Antwerpen]

S.S. BELGENLAND

28. III. 33.

Eingegangen
30. MÄRZ 1933
Erledigt

665.33.

An die Preussische Akademie der Wissenschaften, Berlin.

Die in Deutschland gegenwärtig herrschenden Zustände veranlassen mich, meine Stellung bei der Preussischen Akademie der Wissenschaften hiemit niederzulegen.

Die Akademie hat mir 19 Jahre lang die Möglichkeit gegeben, mich frei von jeder beruflichen Verpflichtung wissenschaftlicher Arbeit zu widmen. Ich weiss, in wie hohem Masse ich ihr zu Dank verpflichtet bin. Ungern scheide ich aus ihrem Kreise auch der Anregungen und der schönen menschlichen Beziehungen wegen, die ich während dieser langen Zeit als ihr Mitglied genoss und stets hoch schätzte.

Die durch meine Stellung bedingte Abhängigkeit von der Preussischen Regierung empfinde ich aber unter den gegenwärtigen Umständen als untragbar.

Mit aller Hochachtung

Albert Einstein.

↑↗ Still on his way back to Europe, Einstein composed this letter of resignation from the Prussian Academy of Sciences, thus anticipating his dismissal by the National Socialists, March 28, 1933

« To the Prussian Academy of Sciences

The conditions that currently prevail in Germany prompt me to herewith resign from my position at the Prussian Academy of Sciences.
For 19 years, the Academy offered me the opportunity to attend to my scientific work free of any professional obligations. I know to what great extent I am indebted to it.
Reluctantly, I'm retiring from its circle where over such a long period of time as a member I enjoyed and valued the stimulation and fine human relations.
Yet under the current conditions I consider unbearable my dependency on the Prussian government which results from my position.
Yours respectfully

Albert Einstein. »

s.Einstein on Peace, p 122, Ch.4 "Friede" p 138 16. Febr. 1931

Rede an die Studenten in Pasadena! (Cal. Tech)

Liebe junge Freunde!

Ich freue mich, Sie vor mir zu sehen, eine blühende Schar junger Menschen, die sich die Technik zum Lebensberuf erkoren haben.

(Ich könnte ein Jubellied singen mit dem Refrain: Wie herrlich weit haben wirs gebracht, und Ihr werdet es noch ungeheuer viel weiter bringen. Sind wir doch im Jahrhundert und dazu im Vaterlande der Technik.

Aber es liegt mir ferne so zu sprechen.) Vielmehr fällt mir dabei jener Mann ein, der eine nicht sehr anziehende Frau geheiratet hat und gefragt wird, ob er glücklich sei. Er antwortete nämlich so: "Wenn ich die Wahrheit sagen wollte, müsste ich lügen".

So geht es auch mir. Seht Euch einmal einen recht unzivilisierten Indianer daraufhin an, ob sein Erleben weniger reich und froh sei als das des zivilisierten Durchschnittsmenschen! Ich glaube kaum. Es liegt ein tiefer Sinn darin, dass die Jugend aller zivilisierten Länder mit Vorliebe "Indianer spielt".

(Warum beglückt uns so wenig die herrliche, das Leben erleichternde Arbeit ersparende Technick? Die einfache Antwort lautet: weil wir noch nicht gelernt haben, einen vernünftigen Gebrauch von ihr zu machen.

Im Kriege dient sie dazu, dass wir uns gegenseitig vergiften oder verstümmeln. Im Frieden hat sie unser Leben hastig und unsicher gestaltet. Statt uns weitgehend von geisttötender Arbeit zu befreien, hat sie die Menschen zu Sklaven der Maschine gemacht, die meist mit Unlust ihr eintöniges, langes Tagewerk vollbringen und stets um ihr armseliges Brot zittern müssen.

Ein hässliches Lied singt uns der alte Mann, werdet Ihr denken. Ich tue es aber in einer guten Absicht, indem ich Euch eine Konsequenz nahelegen möchte.

Es genügt nicht, dass Ihr etwas von Technik verstehet, wenn Eure Arbeit den Menschen einst zum Segen gereichen soll. Die Sorge um die Menschen und ihr Schicksal muss stets das Hauptinteresse allen technischen Strebens bilden, die grossen ungelösten Fragen der Organisation der Arbeit und der Güterverteilung, damit die Erzeugnisse unseres Geistes dem Menschengeschlecht zum Segen gereichen und nicht zum Fluche.

Vergesst dies nie über Euren Zeichnungen und Gleichungen.

« Concern for man himself and his fate must always form the chief interest for all technical endeavors, concern for the great unsolved problems of the organization of labor and the distribution of goods – in order that the creations of our mind shall be a blessing and not a curse for mankind. Never forget this in the midst of your diagrams and equations. »

←↑ From a speech held at the California Institute of Technology, Pasadena, February 16, 1931

« Thus the man of science, as we can observe with our own eyes, suffers a truly tragic fate. In his sincere attempt to achieve clarity and inner independence, he has succeeded, by his sheer super-human efforts, in fashioning the tools which will not only enslave him but also destroy him from within. He cannot escape being muzzled by those who wield political power. He also realizes that mankind can be saved only if a supranational system, based on law, is created to eliminate the methods of brute force. However, the man of science has retrogressed to such an extent that he accepts as inevitable the slavery inflicted upon him by national states. He even degrades himself to such an extent that he obediently lends his talents to help perfect the means destined for the general destruction of mankind. If today's man of science could find the time and the courage to reflect calmly and critically about his plight and the tasks before him, and if he would then act accordingly, the possibilities for a reasonable and satisfactory solution of the present dangerous international situation would be considerably improved. »

→ Well before 1945, Einstein began to reflect on the moral responsibility of the scientist. The atomic bomb gave this issue a new immediacy.
In October 1950, Einstein drafted a long message "On the Moral Obligation of the Scientist," to the "Società Italiana per il Progresso delle Scienze," from which these lines are extracted.

Wien im September 1932.

Lieber Herr Einstein!

Als ich hörte, dass Sie die Absicht haben, mich

zum Gedankenaustausch über ein Thema aufzufordern,

Ihr Interesse schenken und das Ihnen auch des Inte

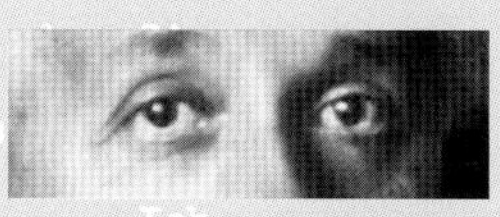

Ich

Sie würden ein Problem

der Physiker

der Psycholog,

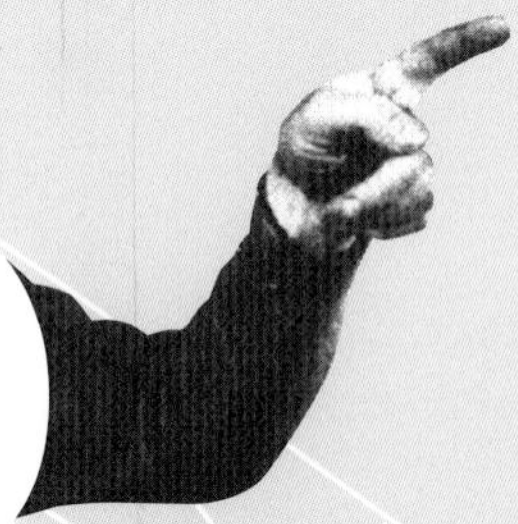

If Einstein Were Young Again,
He Says, He'd Become a Plumber

des Krieges

3

Polarforscher Fridtjof Nansen

das

Problem der Kriegsverhütung

EINSTEIN'S POLITICAL ACTIVITIES

« I myself have never hesitated to express my opinions freely; I have considered it my duty to do so. However, the voice of an individual is powerless against the shouting of the masses – this has always been so. »

From a letter to A. J. Muste, January 23, 1950

THE RADICAL PACIFIST 1914-1933

Starting with his Berlin years, Einstein devoted increasingly more of his time and energy to political causes close to his heart. Driven by an ardent humanism he used his moral authority to foster peace, freedom and social justice.

As a pupil, Einstein had felt repelled by the authoritarianism and militarism he experienced in German schools. The virulent nationalism and brutality of the First World War that he witnessed after his return to Germany in 1914 served to confirm his pacifist and internationalist convictions. When, in the third month of the war, 93 prominent German scientists and artists – among them several of Einstein's colleagues – publicly hailed German militarism, claiming that Germany's culture and military tradition were one and the same, Einstein's first overt political act was the signing of a counter-manifesto calling for a just peace and a "supranational" organization to prevent future wars. Even though this "Manifesto to the Europeans" was not published in wartime Germany, and even though Einstein confined himself to share his opposition to the war mainly with friends and in private letters, many of his colleagues saw his pacifist views as a provocation. This provocation, however, was attenuated by a jester's license granted to the neutral foreigner and notorious non-conformist Einstein.
Following the war and the abolition of the German monarchy, Einstein became, somewhat unintentionally, a national asset and, abroad, an unofficial spokesman for the democratic Weimar Republic.

In the early 1920s, together with Marie Curie, Henri Bergson and other outstanding intellectuals, he took an active role in the Committee for Intellectual Cooperation of the League of Nations which fostered understanding within the international scientific community. As a leading member of the German League for Human Rights he spoke out against the spread of fascism and in defense of democracy. And in the second half of the 1920s, the international anti-war movement found in Einstein one of its most eminent advocates.
In 1932, at the suggestion of the League of Nations' International Institute of Intellectual Cooperation, Einstein invited Sigmund Freud to a public correspondence on how humanity could be spared the continuing menace of war.
The Nazi rise to power, in the following year, brought about a substantial change in Einstein's position. Having endorsed conscientious objection as long as he was convinced that broad-based individual refusal would avert any war, Einstein now felt compelled to favor military preparedness by the European democracies against the threat of Nazism.

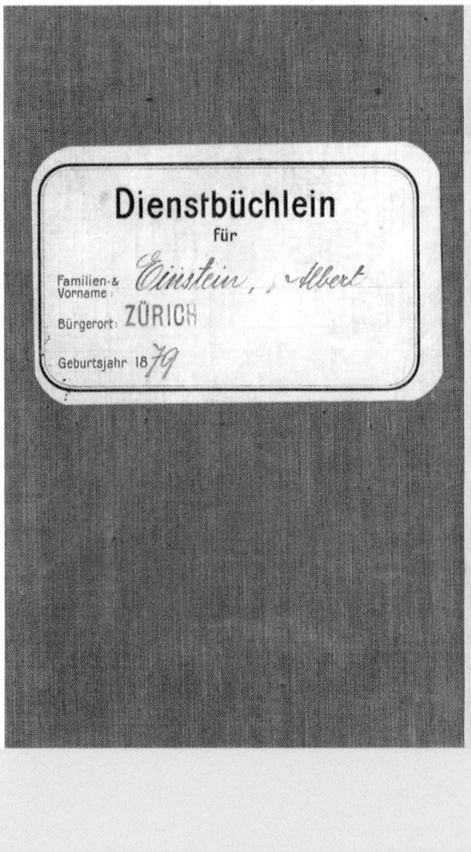

Dienstbüchlein
für
Familien- & Vorname: Einstein, Albert
Bürgerort: ZÜRICH
Geburtsjahr 1879

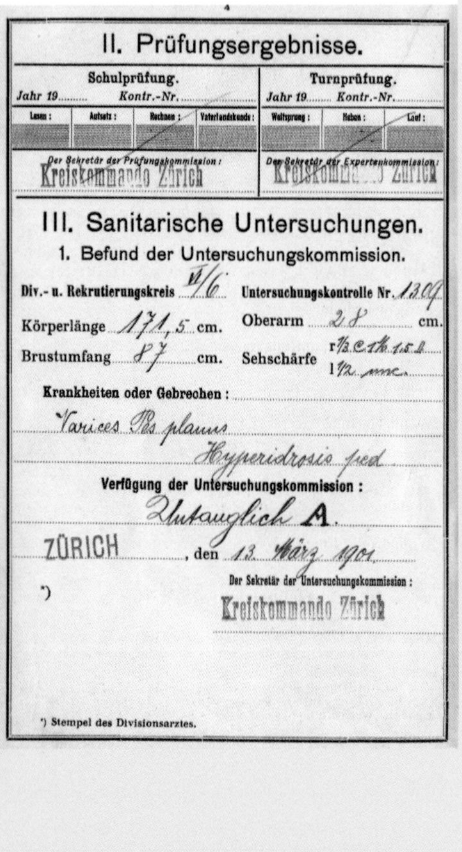

II. Prüfungsergebnisse.

Schulprüfung. Jahr 19...... Kontr.-Nr.				Turnprüfung. Jahr 19...... Kontr.-Nr.		
Lesen:	Aufsatz:	Rechnen:	Vaterlandskunde:	Weitsprung:	Heben:	Lauf:
Der Sekretär der Prüfungskommission: Kreiskommando Zürich				Der Sekretär der Expertenkommission: Kreiskommando Zürich		

III. Sanitarische Untersuchungen.
1. Befund der Untersuchungskommission.

Div.- u. Rekrutierungskreis VI/6 Untersuchungskontrolle Nr. 1309
Körperlänge 171,5 cm. Oberarm 28 cm.
Brustumfang 87 cm. Sehschärfe r 1/3 c 1.5 / l 1/2

Krankheiten oder Gebrechen:
Varices Pes planus
Hyperidrosis ped.

Verfügung der Untersuchungskommission:
Untauglich A.

ZÜRICH, den 13. März 1901.
Der Sekretär der Untersuchungskommission:
*) Kreiskommando Zürich

*) Stempel des Divisionsarztes.

→ Like every Swiss citizen Einstein was called up to the army and received his "Dienstbüchlein" (Army registration booklet). Would he have refused to serve if the army had not exempted him due to "flat and sweaty feet and varicose veins"?

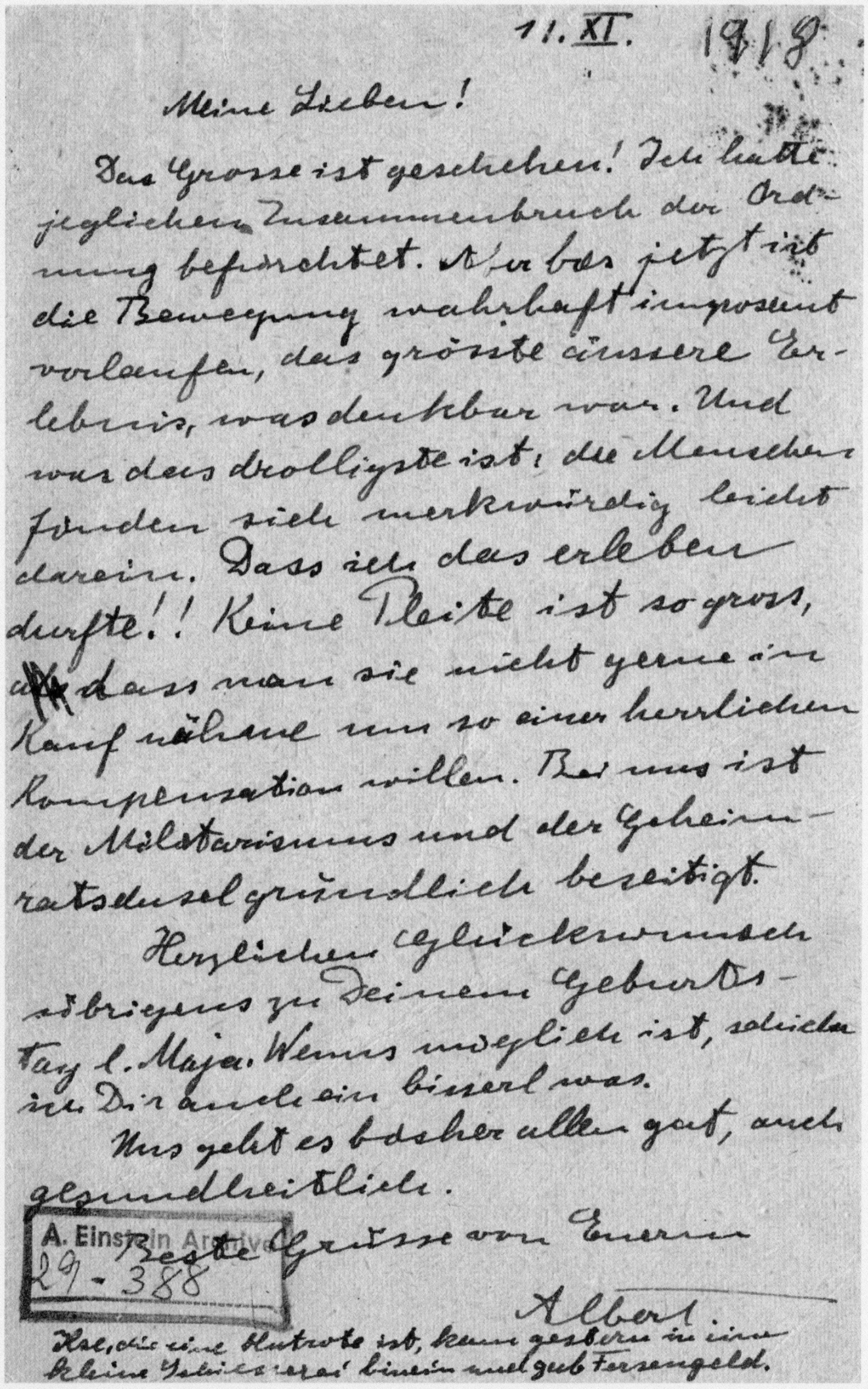

11. XI. 1918

Meine Lieben!

Das Grosse ist geschehen! Ich hatte jeglichen Zusammenbruch der Ordnung befürchtet. Aber bis jetzt ist die Bewegung wahrhaft imposant verlaufen, das grösste äussere Erlebnis, was denkbar war. Und was das drolligste ist: die Menschen finden sich merkwürdig leicht darein. Dass ich das erleben durfte!! Keine Pleite ist so gross, dass man sie nicht gerne in Kauf nähme um so einer herrlichen Kompensation willen. Bei uns ist der Militarismus und der Geheimratsdusel gründlich beseitigt.

Herzlichen Glückwunsch übrigens zu Deinem Geburtstag l. Maja. Wenns möglich ist, schicke ich Dir auch ein bisserl was.

Uns geht es bisher allen gut, auch gesundheitlich.

Beste Grüsse von Eurem

Albert

Ilse, die eine Blutrote ist, kam gestern in eine kleine Schiesserei hinein und gab Fersengeld.

↑→ On November 9, 1918, Einstein marked in his notebook "[Lecture] cancelled due to revolution." Two days later, full of enthusiasm he reported to his sister and brother-in-law on the overthrow of the government in Berlin. Postcard to Paul and Maja Winteler, November 11, 1918

« The great event has taken place! I had feared a complete breakdown of the order. But up to now the action has been taking a truly impressive course, the greatest public experience conceivable. And the funniest thing of all is: people are adjusting themselves remarkably well to it. That I could live to see this!! No flop is too great not to be gladly risked for such magnificent compensation. Where we are, militarism and the foolish faith in illusory authorities has been thoroughly obliterated. […]
Yesterday, Ilse who is a sanguineous red one, got into a little shoot-out and turned tail and ran. »

Genossen und Genossinnen!

Gestatten Sie einem alten Demokraten, der nicht hat umlernen müssen, einige wenige Worte.

Unser aller Ziel ist die Demokratie, d. i. Herrschaft des Volkes. Sie ist nur möglich, wenn der einzelne zwei Dinge heilig hält, nämlich

den Glauben an das gesunde Urteil und den gesunden Willen des Volkes

die willige Unterordnung unter den ~~gesun~~ ~~Beschluss erhobenen~~ durch Abstimmung und Wahl bekundeten Volkswillen, auch wenn ~~dieser~~ ~~nicht~~ Volkswille oder Urteil mit dem eigenen persönlichen Willen im Widerspruch ist.

Wie gelangen wir zu diesem Ziel? Was ist schon erreicht? Was muss ~~sich~~ noch geschehen?

Die alte Klassenherrschaft ist beseitigt. Sie fiel durch die eigenen Sünden und durch die befreiende That der Soldaten. Der von ~~ihnen~~ diesen rasch gewählte Soldatenrat ~~kann~~ muss vorläufig im Verein mit dem Arbeiterrat als Organ des Volkswillens aufgefasst werden. Wir sind diesen Behörden also in dieser kritischen Stunde unbedingten Gehorsam schuldig und müssen sie mit allen Kräften stützen~~, mögen wir nun im Einzelnen deren Entschlüsse billigen oder nicht~~.

Andererseits müssen alle wahren Demokraten

←↓ Shortly after the revolution, Einstein made his first known political appearance in public. This speech was given on November 13, 1918, to the New Fatherland League.

« Comrades!

Speaking as an old-time believer in democracy, one who is not a recent convert, may I be permitted a few words: Our common goal is democracy, the rule of the people. It can be achieved only if the individual holds two things sacred:
First, willing subordination to the will of the people, as expressed at the polls, even when the majority is at odds with one's own personal desires and judgments.
How can we achieve this goal? What has been attained so far? What must still be done?
The old society of class rule has been abolished. It fell of its own sins and by the liberating acts of the soldiers. The councils which the soldiers swiftly elected, acting in concert with the worker's councils, must be accepted for the time being as the organs of the popular will. In this critical hour we owe them our unconditional obedience and must support them with all our power.
Secondly, all true democrats must stand guard lest the old class tyranny of the right be replaced by a new class tyranny of the left. Do not be lured by feelings of vengeance to the fateful view that violence must be fought with violence, that a dictatorship of the proletariat is temporarily needed in order to hammer the concept of freedom into the heads of our fellow countrymen. Force breeds only bitterness, hatred and reaction.
We must, therefore, unconditionally demand of the present dictatorial government [...] that, irrespective of party interests, it immediately prepare for the election of a constituent assembly [...].
Our present social democratic leaders deserve our wholehearted support.
Confident of the power of their ideals, they have already gone on record in favor of a constituent assembly.
[...] »

→ The revolutionary student council formed at the university had deposed and locked up the Rector and some of the other dignitaries. Einstein who, due to his left-wing political views, was believed to have some influence with these students, was asked to negotiate with the council and to bring about the release of the detainees. Trusting in the triumph of reason, together with his colleagues Max Born and Max Wertheimer, a psychologist, Einstein set out for the Chancellor's palace and met indeed with success. They left, as Max Born reports, in high spirits, feeling that they had taken part in a historical event, and convinced that democracy had ultimately won.
From a letter to Max Born, September 7, 1944

« Do you still remember the occasion some twenty-five years ago when we went together by tram to the Reichstag building, convinced that we could effectively help to turn the people there into honest democrats? How naïve we were, for all our forty years. I have to laugh when I think of it. We neither of us realized that the spinal cord plays a far more important role than the brain itself, and how much stronger its hold is. I have to recall this now, to prevent me from repeating the tragic mistakes of those days. We really should not be surprised that scientists (the vast majority of them) are no exception to this rule. »

←In summer 1913, Marie Curie and her daughters, including their governess, and Albert Einstein and his elder son met for hiking vacations in the Swiss Alps.
The picture shows, in the front row from the left:
the governess Miss Nanley, Eve Curie, Hans Albert Einstein. Behind from the left: Albert Einstein, Marie Curie, Irène Curie.

The amicable relationship Einstein maintained with Marie Curie, was based upon a deep respect between two colleagues. After a fleeting encounter in Geneva, in 1909, it was not until two years later, on the occasion of the first Solvay Congress in Brussels, that they became acquainted with one another. The *grande dame* of French nuclear physics was so highly impressed by the young, unknown colleague's "clarity of mind, breadth of presentation, and depth of knowledge," that, when asked for her opinion shortly after the meeting, she recommended Einstein in exceptionally favorable words.
The scientific discussions Marie Curie and Einstein had while walking through the Engadin in 1913, may have deepened their relationship. With the start of the 1920s, politics became an additional issue of common interest, when both, Curie and Einstein, engaged in committee work for the League of Nations.

« [...]
The Commission from which you resigned understands the necessity of international intellectual collaboration and has already made appropriate efforts.
[…]
I willingly concede to you that the League of Nations is not perfect. It had no chance to be so, for human beings are imperfect.
But […] it is the first attempt toward international understanding without which civilization is threatened to vanish.
[…]
Europe seems to me like an organism recovering from a severe illness and in need of eliminating much poison.
[…]
Look at what can be gained through education: A physician knows that he has to attend to a sick person regardless of his nationality. Doesn't that prove that solidarity can and has to be taught and that men are able to recognize it across national boundaries even during the war? »

←↓ From Marie Curie's letter, January 6, 1924

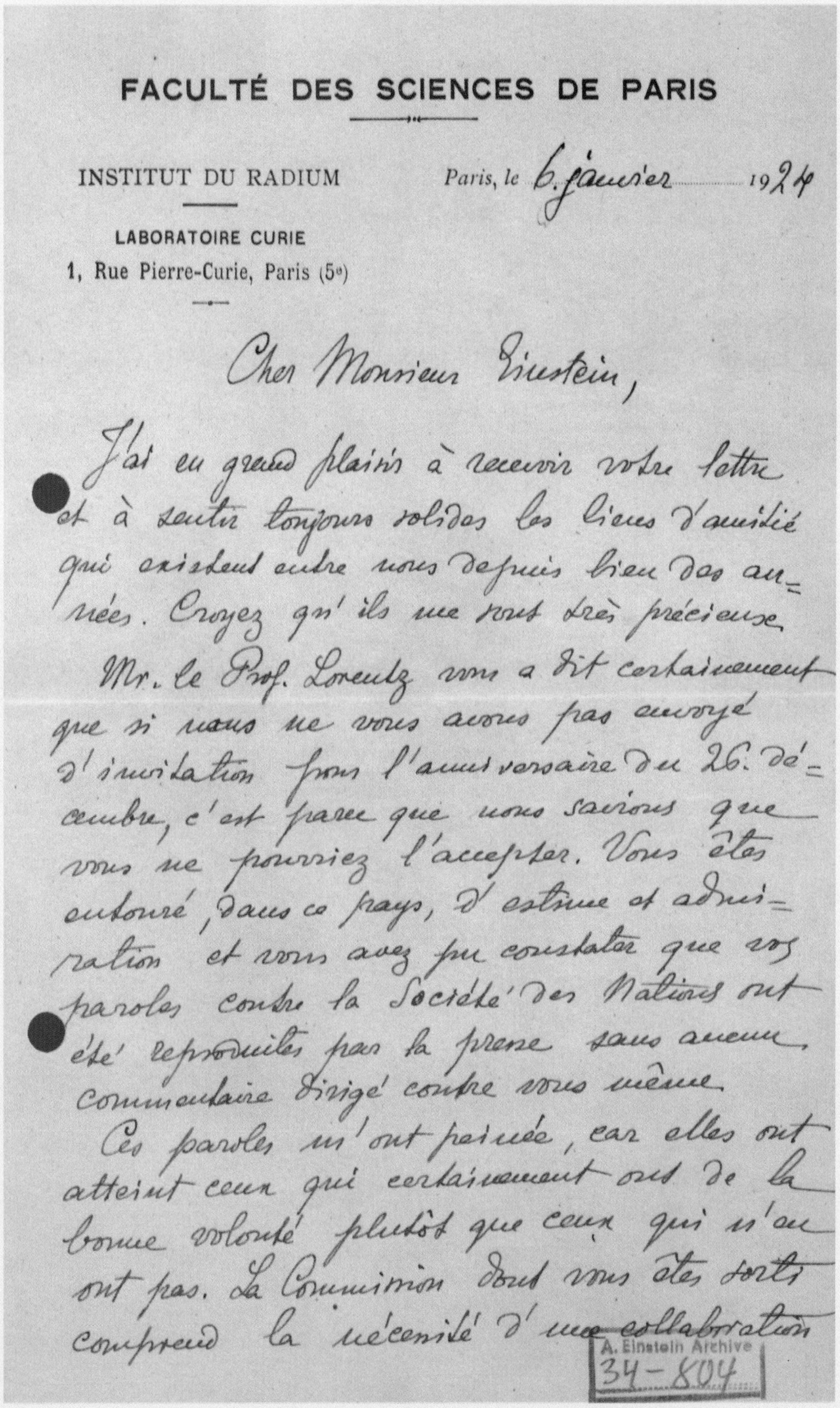
FACULTÉ DES SCIENCES DE PARIS

INSTITUT DU RADIUM — Paris, le 6 janvier 1924

LABORATOIRE CURIE
1, Rue Pierre-Curie, Paris (5e)

Cher Monsieur Einstein,

J'ai eu grand plaisir à recevoir votre lettre et à sentir toujours solides les liens d'amitié qui existent entre nous depuis bien des années. Croyez qu'ils me sont très précieux.

Mr. le Prof. Lorentz vous a dit certainement que si nous ne vous avons pas envoyé d'invitation pour l'anniversaire du 26. décembre, c'est parce que nous savions que vous ne pourriez l'accepter. Vous êtes entouré, dans ce pays, d'estime et admiration et vous avez pu constater que vos paroles contre la Société des Nations ont été reproduites par la presse sans aucun commentaire dirigé contre vous même.

Ces paroles m'ont peinée, car elles ont atteint ceux qui certainement ont de la bonne volonté plutôt que ceux qui n'en ont pas. La Commission dont vous êtes sorti comprend la nécessité d'une collaboration

A. Einstein Archive
34-804

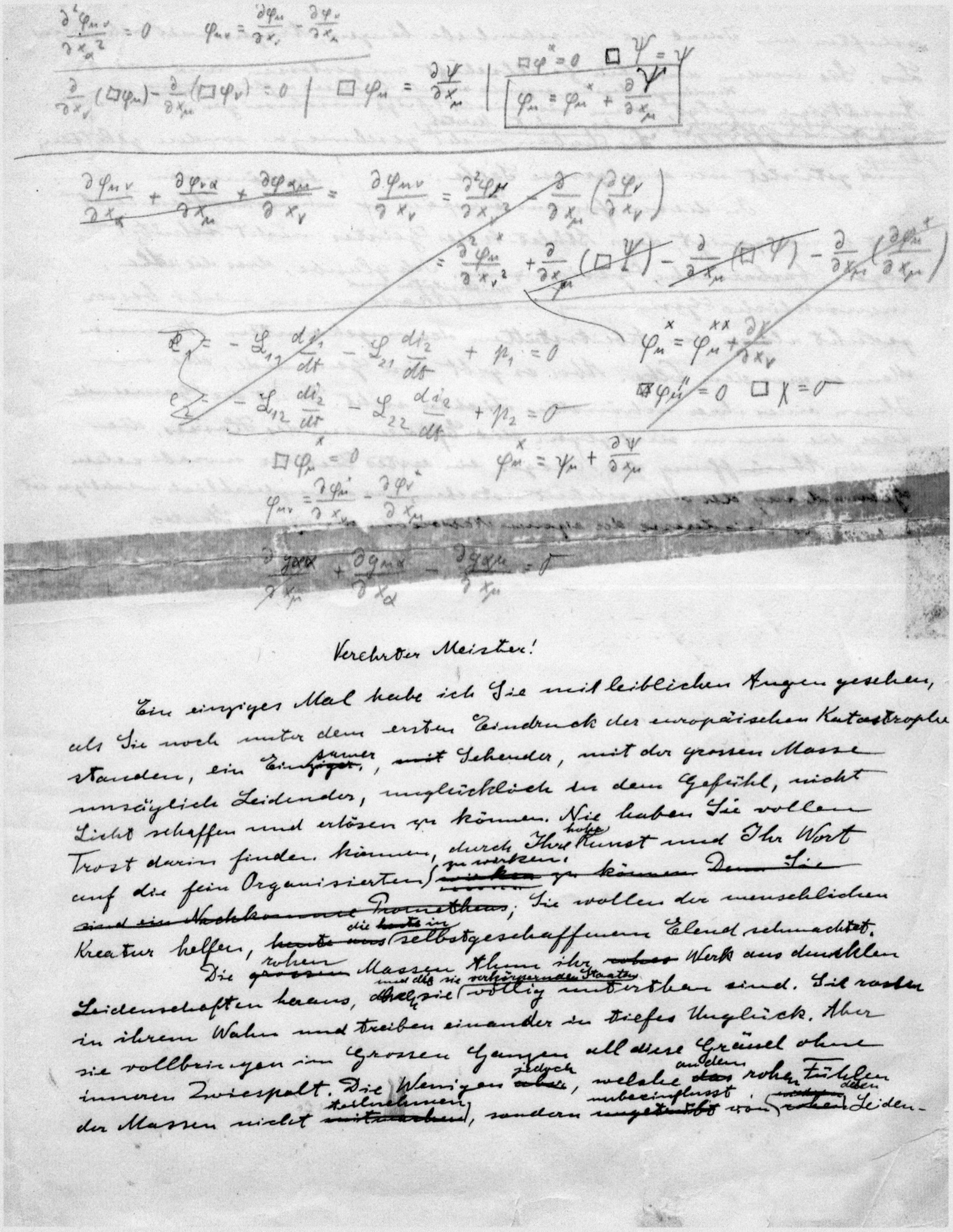
Verehrter Meister!

Ein einziges Mal habe ich Sie mit leiblichen Augen gesehen,
als Sie noch unter dem ersten Eindruck der europäischen Katastrophe
standen, ein einsamer, Sehender, mit der grossen Masse
unsäglich Leidender, unglücklich in dem Gefühl, nicht
Licht schaffen und erlösen zu können. Nie haben Sie vollen
Trost darin finden können, durch Ihre hohe Kunst und Ihr Wort
auf die fein Organisierten zu wirken;
Sie wollen der menschlichen
Kreatur helfen, die in selbstgeschaffenem Elend schmachtet.
Die rohen Massen ahnen ihr Werk aus dunklen
Leidenschaften heraus, und die sie verkörpernden Staaten, die sie völlig unterthan sind. Sie rasen
in ihrem Wahn und treiben einander in tiefes Unglück. Aber
sie vollbringen im Grossen Ganzen all diese Gräuel ohne
inneren Zwiespalt. Die Wenigen jedoch, welche an den rohen Fühlen
der Massen nicht teilnehmen, sondern unbeeinflusst von deren Leiden-

↑↗ Draft of Einstein's contribution to the "Liber Amicorum" to be published on the occasion of Romain Rolland's 60th birthday on January 29, 1926. With Rolland, Einstein shared the passionate commitment to peace.

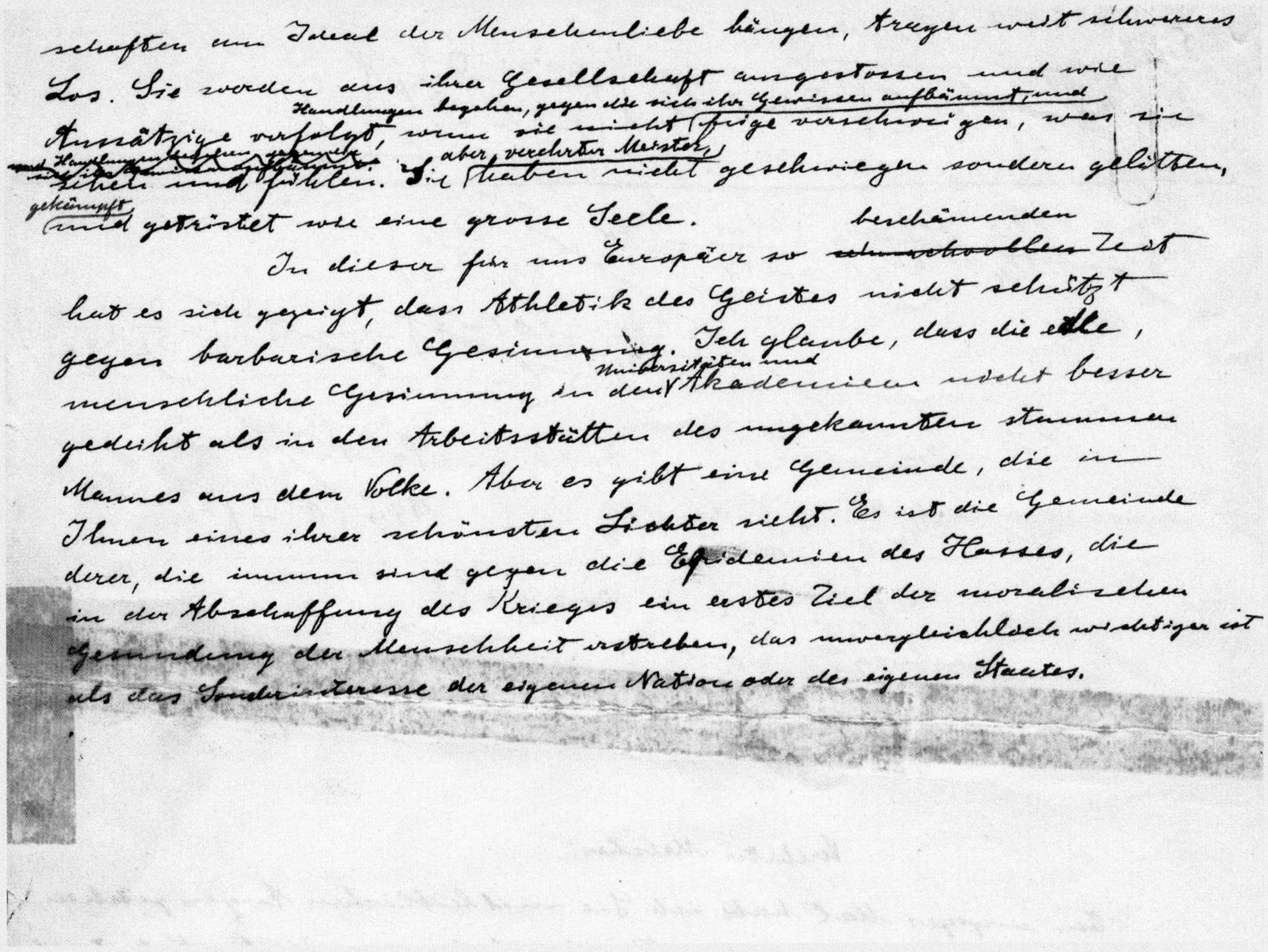

schaften am Ideal der Menschenliebe hängen, tragen weit schweres Los. Sie werden aus ihrer Gesellschaft ausgestossen und wie Aussätzige verfolgt, wenn sie nicht Handlungen begehen, gegen die sich ihr Gewissen aufbäumt, und feige verschweigen, was sie sehen und fühlen. Sie aber, verehrter Meister, haben nicht geschwiegen sondern gelitten, gekämpft und getröstet wie eine grosse Seele.

In dieser für uns Europäer so beschämenden Zeit hat es sich gezeigt, dass Athletik des Geistes nicht schützt gegen barbarische Gesinnung. Ich glaube, dass die edle, menschliche Gesinnung in den Universitäten und Akademien nicht besser gedeiht als in den Arbeitsstätten des ungekannten stummen Mannes aus dem Volke. Aber es gibt eine Gemeinde, die in Ihnen eines ihrer schönsten Lichter sieht. Es ist die Gemeinde derer, die immun sind gegen die Epidemien des Hasses, die in der Abschaffung des Krieges ein erstes Ziel der moralischen Gesundung der Menschheit erstreben, das unvergleichlich wichtiger ist als das Sonderinteresse der eigenen Nation oder des eigenen Staates.

« Revered Master!

Only once did I see you in the flesh: you were still shaken by the initial impact of the European crisis, a lonely visionary immensely suffering with the tortured masses, frustrated by your inability to bring them light and deliverance. You were never fully satisfied to use your rare creative talent to communicate only with the finer spirits; you long to help all human beings who are victims of self-inflicted misery.

[...]

This age which has so deeply shamed us Europeans has made it obvious that even noble minds may fall prey to barbaric attitudes. I do not believe that human nobleness flourishes any better in the universities and academies than in the shops of the unknown, silent, common man.

There is one community, however, that counts you among its most illustrious luminaries. It is the community of those who are immune of the pestilence of hate, who seek to abolish war as the first step toward the moral regeneration of mankind and who view this task as incomparably more important than the special interests of their own particular nation or state. »

↑ Einstein and Rabindranath Tagore, Bengali poet and philosopher, Berlin, Summer 1930.
Between 1926 and 1930, Einstein and Tagore met several times. Their discussions, covering philosophical questions and contemporary issues, although being "a complete disaster because of difficulties in communication," as Einstein admitted to Romain Rolland, did get public attention.

→ From a manifesto against conscription and the military training of youth, signed by Tagore and Einstein, as well as Upton Sinclair, Sigmund Freud, Bertrand Russell and many other international intellectuals.

« Military training is the education of the mind and body in the technique of killing. It is education for war. It is the perpetuation of the war mentality. It thwarts the growth of man's will for peace. [...]
Let the peoples of all countries adopt as their goal:
NO MORE MILITARIZATION!
NO MORE CONSCRIPTION!
EDUCATION FOR HUMANITY AND PEACE! »

→ From a letter to his secretary, Helen Dukas, Cromer, September 1933

« The Anti-Militarists now descend upon me as upon a wicked apostate. These guys have blinders and do not want to admit their expulsion from 'paradise.' »

EINSTEIN TAKES UP THE SWORD

↑ Cartoon by Charles Raymond Macauley, Published in *The Brooklyn Eagle*, 1933

« My abhorrence of militarism and war is as great as yours. Until about 1933 I advocated conscientious objection. But with the rise of Fascism I recognized that one could not maintain such a point of view except at the risk of allowing the whole world to fall into the hands of the most terrible enemies of mankind. Organized power can be opposed only by organized power. Much as I regret this, there is no other way. »

↓↑ From a letter to Robert Fowlkes, July 14, 1941

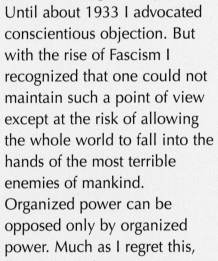

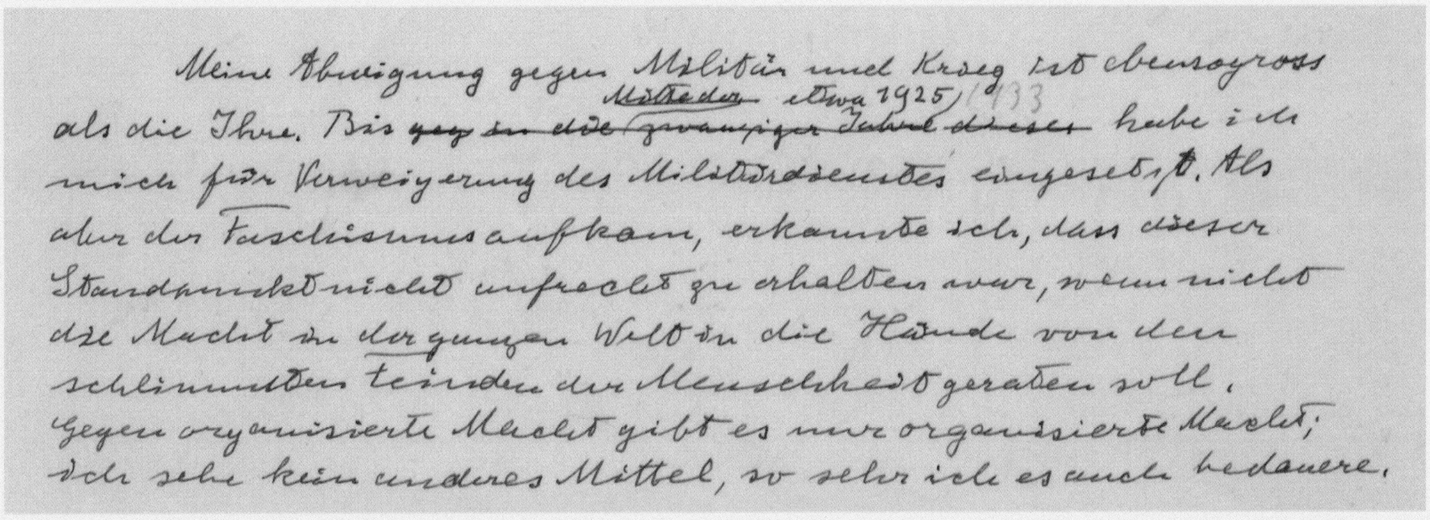

Meine Abneigung gegen Militär und Krieg ist ebensogross als die Ihre. Bis ~~gegen die zwanziger Jahre dieses~~ Mitte der etwa 1925 / 1933 habe ich mich für Verweigerung des Militärdienstes eingesetzt. Als aber der Faschismus aufkam, erkannte ich, dass dieser Standpunkt nicht aufrecht zu erhalten war, wenn nicht die Macht in der ganzen Welt in die Hände von den schlimmsten Feinden der Menschheit geraten soll. Gegen organisierte Macht gibt es nur organisierte Macht; ich sehe kein anderes Mittel, so sehr ich es auch bedauere.

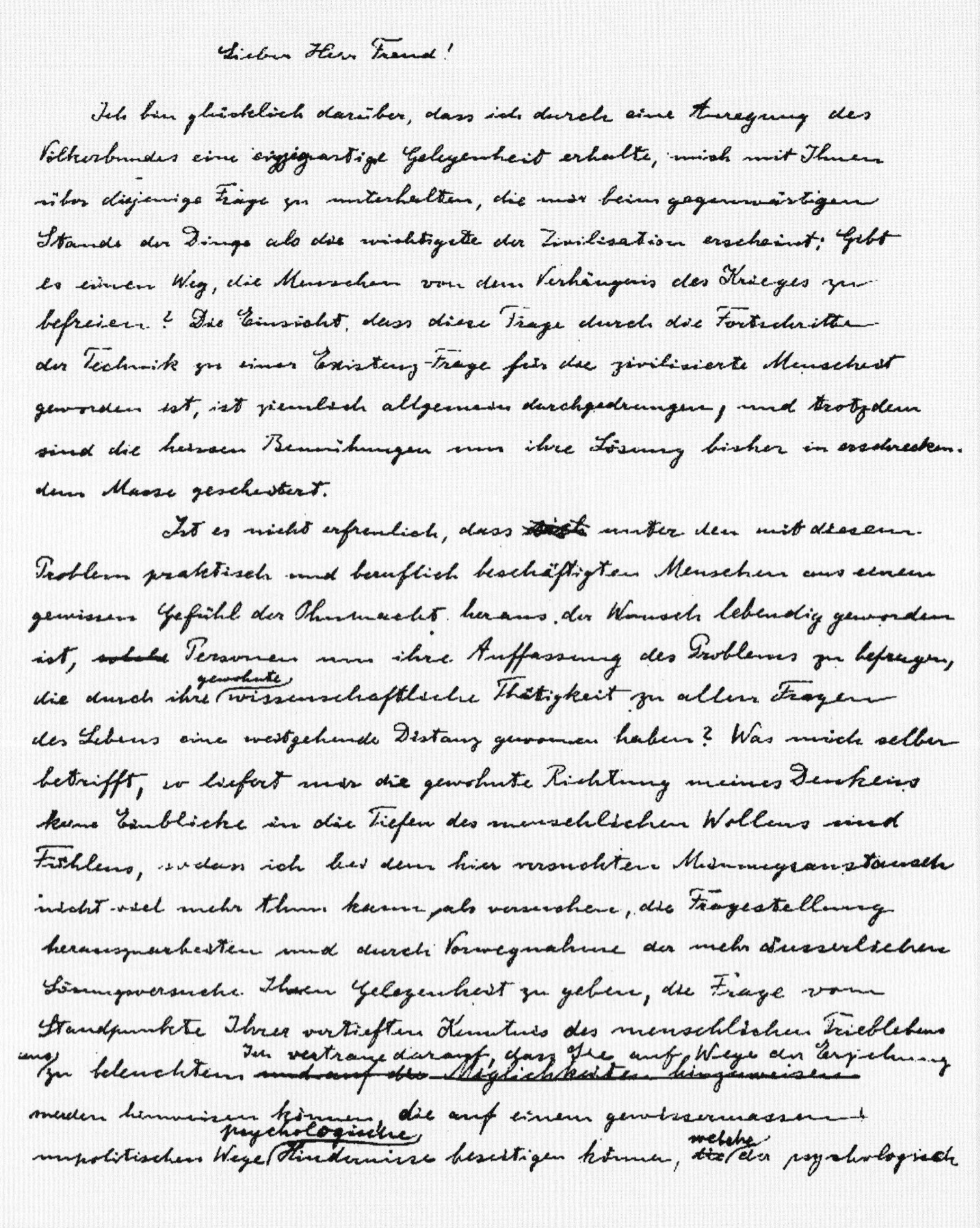

Lieber Herr Freud!

Ich bin glücklich darüber, dass ich durch eine Anregung des Völkerbundes eine einzigartige Gelegenheit erhalte, mich mit Ihnen über diejenige Frage zu unterhalten, die mir beim gegenwärtigen Stande der Dinge als die wichtigste der Zivilisation erscheint: Gibt es einen Weg, die Menschen von dem Verhängnis des Krieges zu befreien? Die Einsicht, dass diese Frage durch die Fortschritte der Technik zu einer Existenz-Frage für die zivilisierte Menschheit geworden ist, ist ziemlich allgemein durchgedrungen, und trotzdem sind die heissen Bemühungen um ihre Lösung bisher in erschreckendem Masse gescheitert.

Ist es nicht erfreulich, dass ~~sich~~ unter den mit diesem Problem praktisch und beruflich beschäftigten Menschen aus einem gewissen Gefühl der Ohnmacht heraus der Wunsch lebendig geworden ist, ~~solche~~ Personen um ihre Auffassung des Problems zu befragen, die durch ihre gewohnte wissenschaftliche Thätigkeit zu allen Fragen des Lebens eine weitgehende Distanz gewonnen haben? Was mich selber betrifft, so liefert mir die gewohnte Richtung meines Denkens keine Einblicke in die Tiefen des menschlichen Wollens und Fühlens, sodass ich bei dem hier versuchten Meinungsaustausch nicht viel mehr thun kann, als versuchen, die Fragestellung herauszuarbeiten und durch Vorwegnahme der mehr äusserlichen Lösungsversuche Ihnen Gelegenheit zu geben, die Frage vom Standpunkte Ihrer vertieften Kenntnis des menschlichen Trieblebens zu beleuchten. ~~und auf die Möglichkeiten hinzuweisen~~ Ich vertraue darauf, dass Sie auf Wege der Erziehung werden hinweisen können, die auf einem gewissermassen unpolitischen Wege psychologische Hindernisse beseitigen können, ~~die~~ welche der psychologisch

↑↗ Letter to Sigmund Freud, July 30, 1932

The Committee for Intellectual Cooperation of the League of Nations suggested to Einstein to choose a subject and a correspondent for his contribution to a series of books dealing with current problems. Einstein consented and picked another famous Jew as his partner. The exchange of letters between Einstein and Freud on the causes of war and violence and on possible solutions, was published in English in 1933 under the title, *Why War?*

« The road to international security demands the unconditional renunciation by all nations of part of their freedom of action and sovereignty. I doubt that there is another way to international security. The desire for power makes the ruling party of a nation resist any limitation of its rights to sovereignty. How is it possible that this group, such a small minority, can make subservient to its desires the masses of the people who by a war stand only to lose and to suffer? (In speaking of the masses, I do not exclude soldiers of every rank who have chosen war as their profession, in the belief that they are serving to defend the most precious possessions of their race, and that attack is often the best method of defense.) The immediate answer is: the minority, the ruling class, is in possession of the schools, the church and the press. By these means it rules and guides the feelings of the majority of the people and bends them to compliance. »

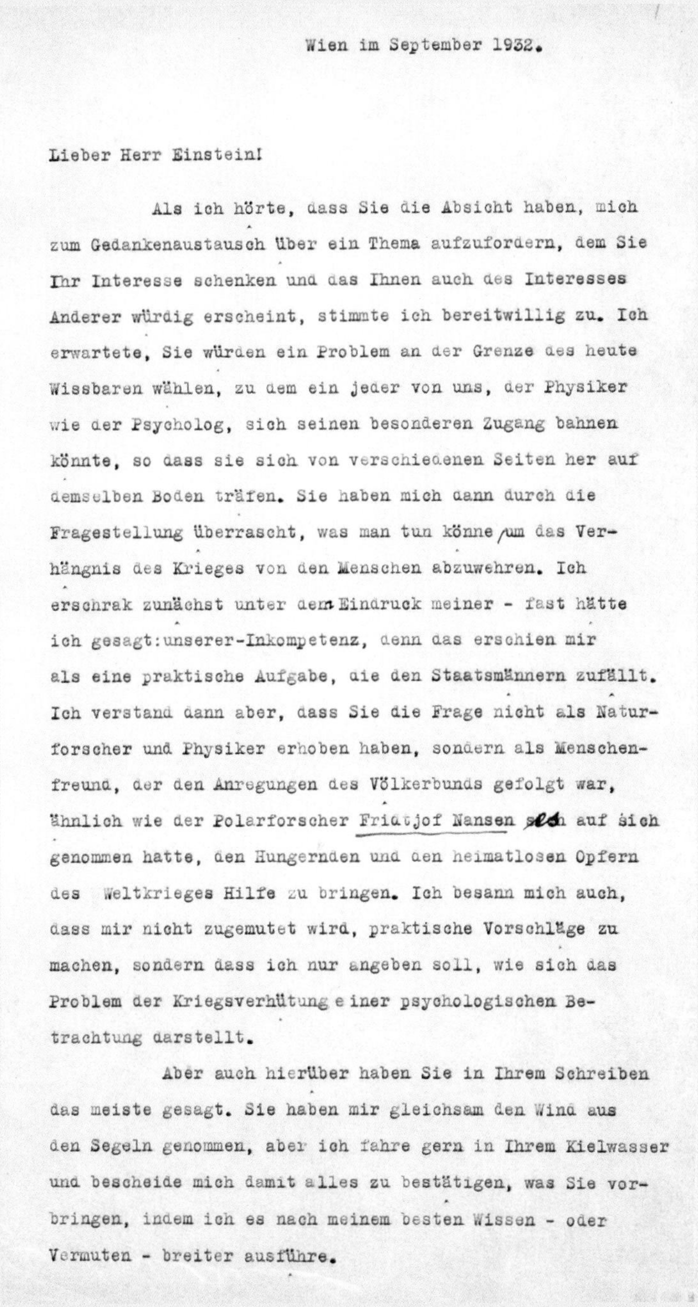

Wien im September 1932.

Lieber Herr Einstein!

Als ich hörte, dass Sie die Absicht haben, mich zum Gedankenaustausch über ein Thema aufzufordern, dem Sie Ihr Interesse schenken und das Ihnen auch des Interesses Anderer würdig erscheint, stimmte ich bereitwillig zu. Ich erwartete, Sie würden ein Problem an der Grenze des heute Wissbaren wählen, zu dem ein jeder von uns, der Physiker wie der Psycholog, sich seinen besonderen Zugang bahnen könnte, so dass sie sich von verschiedenen Seiten her auf demselben Boden träfen. Sie haben mich dann durch die Fragestellung überrascht, was man tun könne, um das Verhängnis des Krieges von den Menschen abzuwehren. Ich erschrak zunächst unter dem Eindruck meiner - fast hätte ich gesagt: unserer-Inkompetenz, denn das erschien mir als eine praktische Aufgabe, die den Staatsmännern zufällt. Ich verstand dann aber, dass Sie die Frage nicht als Naturforscher und Physiker erhoben haben, sondern als Menschenfreund, der den Anregungen des Völkerbunds gefolgt war, ähnlich wie der Polarforscher Fridtjof Nansen es auf sich genommen hatte, den Hungernden und den heimatlosen Opfern des Weltkrieges Hilfe zu bringen. Ich besann mich auch, dass mir nicht zugemutet wird, praktische Vorschläge zu machen, sondern dass ich nur angeben soll, wie sich das Problem der Kriegsverhütung einer psychologischen Betrachtung darstellt.

Aber auch hierüber haben Sie in Ihrem Schreiben das meiste gesagt. Sie haben mir gleichsam den Wind aus den Segeln genommen, aber ich fahre gern in Ihrem Kielwasser und bescheide mich damit alles zu bestätigen, was Sie vorbringen, indem ich es nach meinem besten Wissen - oder Vermuten - breiter ausführe.

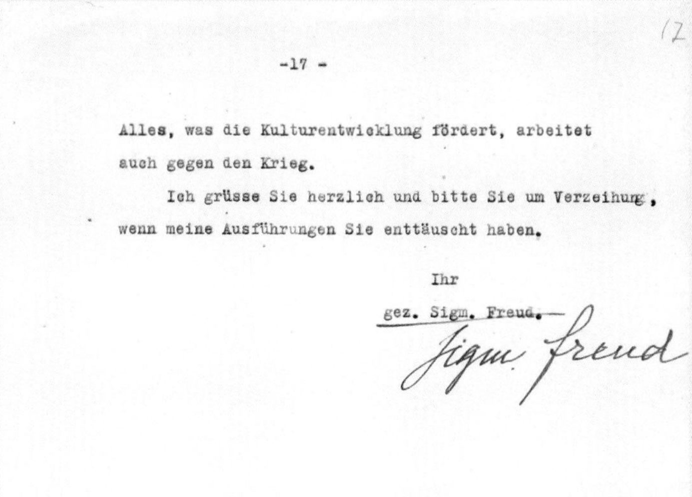

-17 -

Alles, was die Kulturentwicklung fördert, arbeitet auch gegen den Krieg.

Ich grüsse Sie herzlich und bitte Sie um Verzeihung, wenn meine Ausführungen Sie enttäuscht haben.

Ihr

gez. Sigm. Freud.

Sigm. Freud

↑↗ From Sigmund Freud's reply, September 1932

« Now war is in the crassest opposition to the psychical attitude imposed on us by the cultural process, and for that reason we must rebel against it; we simply cannot any longer put up with it. This is not merely an intellectual and emotional repudiation; we pacifists have a constitutional intolerance of war, an idiosyncrasy magnified, as it were, to the highest degree. It seems, indeed, as though the aesthetic humiliation caused by war plays a scarcely smaller part in our rebellion than do its cruelties.

And how long shall we have to wait before the rest of mankind become pacifists too? There is no telling. But it may not be utopian to hope that these two factors, the cultural attitude and the justified dread of the consequences of a future war, may result within a measurable time in putting an end to the waging of war. By what paths or by what side-tracks this will come about we cannot guess. But one thing we *can* say; whatever fosters the growth of culture works at the same time against war. »

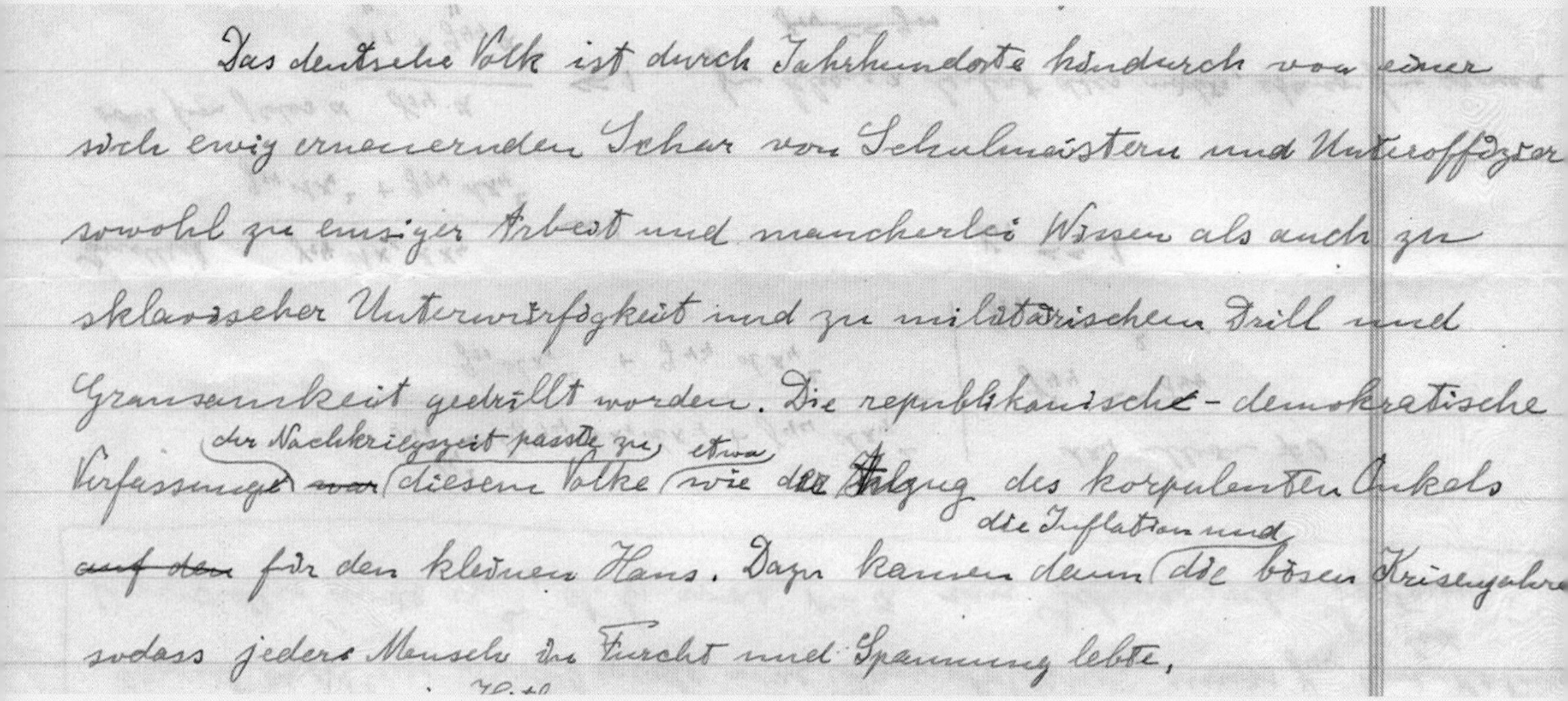
Das deutsche Volk ist durch Jahrhunderte hindurch von einer sich ewig erneuernden Schar von Schulmeistern und Unteroffizieren sowohl zu emsiger Arbeit und mancherlei Wissen als auch zu sklavischer Unterwürfigkeit und zu militärischem Drill und Grausamkeit gedrillt worden. Die republikanisch-demokratische Verfassung der Nachkriegszeit passte zu ~~war~~ diesem Volke etwa wie der Anzug des korpulenten Onkels ~~auf den~~ für den kleinen Hans. Dazu kamen dann die Inflation und die bösen Krisenjahre sodass jeder Mensch in Furcht und Spannung lebte,

↑↘ A not too flattering description of the Germans, 1935

« Through the centuries the German people have been drilled by a continual self-perpetuating band of schoolmasters and sergeants to arduous work and to some knowledge, as well as to slavish submissiveness, military obedience and savageness. The republican-democratic constitution of the post-war period did fit this people almost like the suit of the corpulent uncle fits little Johnny. »

« As long as I have any choice, I will only stay in a country where political liberty, tolerance, and equality of all citizens before the law prevail. Political liberty implies the freedom to express one's political opinions orally and in writing; tolerance implies respect for any and every individual opinion. These conditions are not maintained in Germany at the present time. »

↑ From "Manifesto"
March 1933

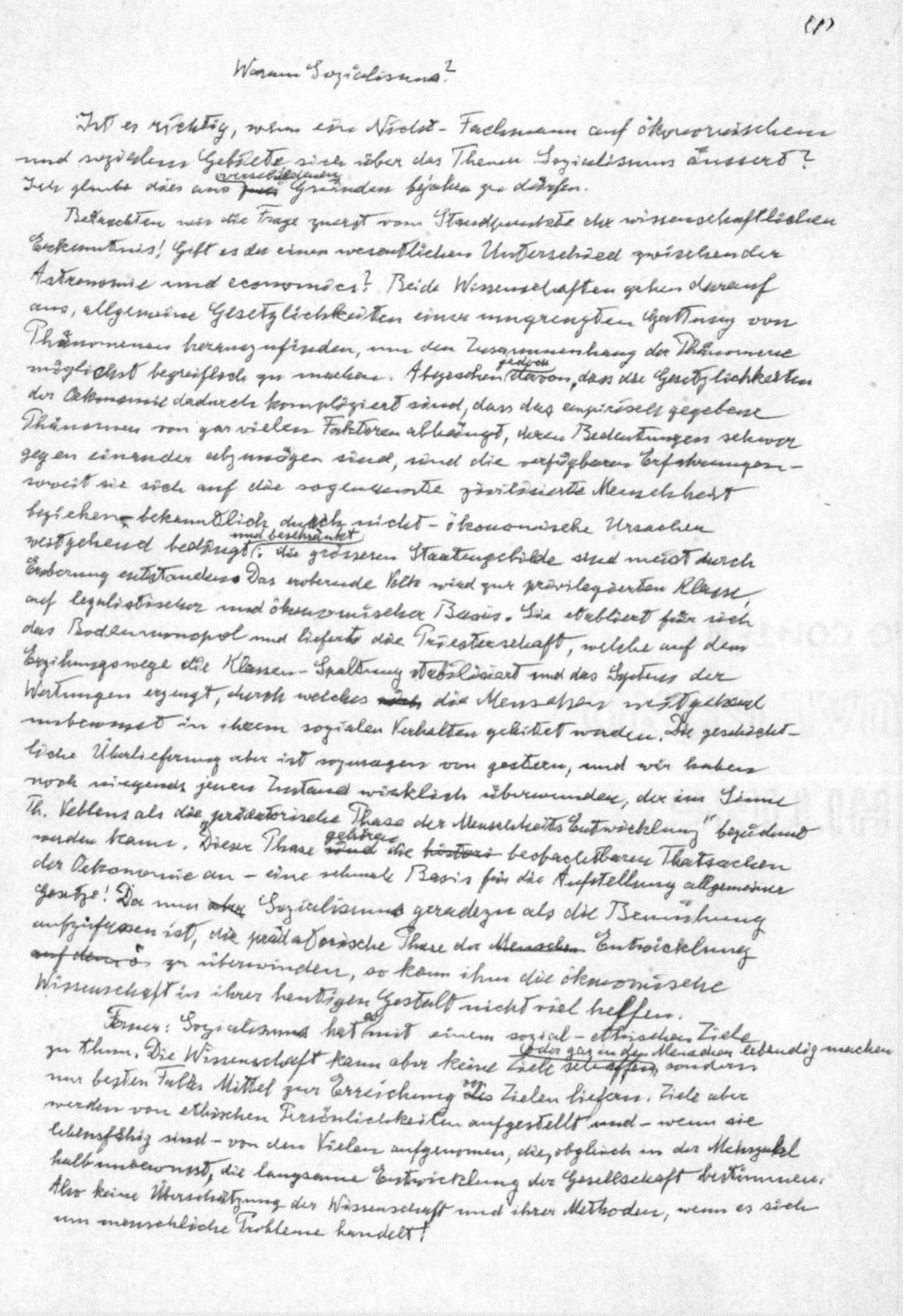

(1)

Warum Sozialismus?

Ist es richtig, wenn ein Nicht-Fachmann auf ökonomischen und sozialen Gebiete sich über das Thema Sozialismus äussert? Ich glaube dies aus verschiedenen Gründen bejahen zu dürfen.

Betrachten wir die Frage zuerst vom Standpunkte der wissenschaftlichen Erkenntnis! Gibt es da einen wesentlichen Unterschied zwischen der Astronomie und economics? Beide Wissenschaften gehen darauf aus, allgemeine Gesetzlichkeiten einer umgrenzten Gattung von Phänomenen herauszufinden, um den Zusammenhang der Phänomene möglichst begreiflich zu machen. Abgesehen jedoch davon, dass die Gesetzlichkeiten der Oekonomie dadurch kompliziert sind, dass das empirisch gegebene Phänomen von gar vielen Faktoren abhängt, deren Bedeutungen schwer gegen einander abzuwägen sind, sind die verfügbaren Erfahrungen – soweit sie sich auf die sogenannte zivilisierte Menschheit beziehen – bekanntlich durch nicht-ökonomische Ursachen weitgehend bedingt und beschränkt: die grösseren Staatengebilde sind meist durch Eroberung entstanden. Das erobernde Volk wird zur privilegierten Klasse, auf legalistischer und ökonomischer Basis. Sie etabliert für sich das Bodenmonopol und liefert die Priesterschaft, welche auf dem Erziehungswege die Klassen-Spaltung stabilisiert und das System der Wertungen erzeugt, durch welches die Menschen weitgehend unbewusst in ihrem sozialen Verhalten geleitet werden. Die geschichtliche Überlieferung aber ist sozusagen von gestern, und wir haben noch nirgends jenen Zustand wirklich überwunden, der im Sinne Th. Veblens als die "prädatorische Phase der Menschheits-Entwicklung" bezeichnet werden kann. Dieser Phase gehören die beobachtbaren Thatsachen der Oekonomie an – eine schmale Basis für die Aufstellung allgemeiner Gesetze! Da nun Sozialismus geradezu als die Bemühung aufzufassen ist, die prädatorische Phase der Entwicklung zu überwinden, so kann ihm die ökonomische Wissenschaft in ihrer heutigen Gestalt nicht viel helfen.

Ferner: Sozialismus hat es mit einem sozial-ethischen Ziele zu thun. Die Wissenschaft kann aber keine Ziele schaffen oder gar in den Menschen lebendig machen, sondern nur besten Falles Mittel zur Erreichung von Zielen liefern. Ziele aber werden von ethischen Persönlichkeiten aufgestellt und – wenn sie lebensfähig sind – von den Vielen aufgenommen, die, obgleich in der Mehrzahl halbunbewusst, die langsame Entwicklung der Gesellschaft bestimmen. Also keine Überschätzung der Wissenschaft und ihrer Methoden, wenn es sich um menschliche Probleme handelt!

↑↗ From the draft of "Why Socialism?"
This article, composed at the suggestion of the new socialist magazine's editor, was published in the first edition of the *Monthly Review* in May, 1949. In it Einstein expresses his criticism of capitalism and Soviet communism and his support for ethical socialism.

« This crippling of individuals I consider the worst evil of "capitalism." Our whole educational system suffers from this evil. An exaggerated competitive attitude is inculcated into the young individual, who is trained to worship acquisitive success as a preparation for his future career.
I am convinced there is only one way to eliminate these grave evils, namely through the establishment of a socialist economy, accompanied by an educational system which would be oriented toward social goals. In such an economy, the means of production are owned by society itself and are utilized in a planned fashion [...]
Nevertheless, a planned economy is not yet socialism. A planned economy as such may be accompanied by the complete enslavement of the individual. The achievement of socialism requires the solution of some extremely difficult socio-political problems: how is it possible, in view of the far-reaching centralization of political and economic power, to prevent bureaucracy from becoming all-powerful and overweening? How can the rights of the individual be protected and therewith a democratic counterweight to the power of bureaucracy be assured? »

EINSTEIN'S SOCIAL AND ECONOMIC VIEWS

A pacifist in political affairs, Einstein was a committed socialist on social and economic issues. To him the purpose of socialism, as he put it in "Why Socialism?" in 1949, was to overcome what Thorstein Veblen called the predatory phase of human development characterized by conquest, subjugation and exploitation of entire societies as well as single individuals.
In his opinion, a capitalist economy renders society vulnerable to severe cycles of economic depression with devastating social consequences. Einstein, therefore, supported a moderately planned economy to control the excesses of both capitalism and Soviet communism.

As a precondition and integral part of the ideal society Einstein considered an educational system that offers equal opportunities to everyone and fosters democratic values. From its schools would emerge the creative and independently thinking and reasoning individuals no just society can do without.

→ Princeton, mid-1940s.
Photo by Hermann Landshoff

« The obsession to possess the Beautiful is the first step from the Barbarian to the more civilized man. He can be compared to the child who does not sufficiently appreciate the sight of the butterfly but has to grab at it or even put it into his mouth in order to get the particular satisfaction he desires. »

↑ Did Einstein who hardly cared about possessions consider himself one of the less civilized men?
From his travel diary to South-America, April 27, 1925

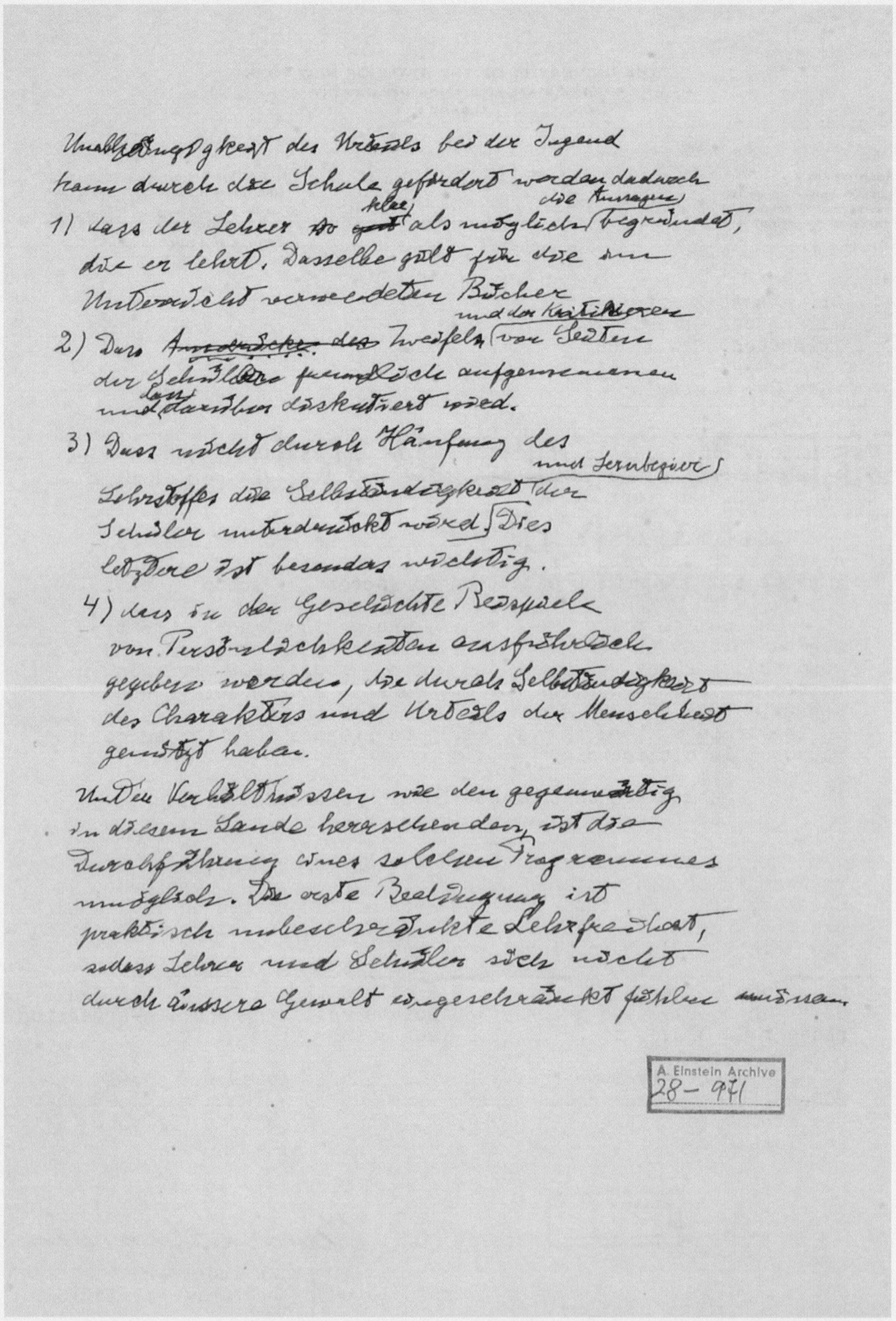
Unabhängigkeit des Urteils bei der Jugend
kann durch die Schule gefördert werden dadurch
1) dass der Lehrer ~~so gut~~ klar als möglich die Aussagen begründet,
die er lehrt. Dasselbe gilt für die im
Unterricht verwendeten Bücher
2) Dass ~~Ansichten des~~ Zweifel und der Kritik von Seiten
der Schüler freundlich aufgenommen
und dass darüber diskutiert wird.
3) Dass nicht durch Häufung des
Lehrstoffes die Selbständigkeit und Lernbegier der
Schüler unterdrückt wird. Dies
letztere ist besonders wichtig.
4) dass in der Geschichte Beispiele
von Persönlichkeiten ausführlich
gegeben werden, die durch Selbständigkeit
des Charakters und Urteils der Menschheit
genützt haben.
Unter Verhältnissen wie den gegenwärtig
in diesem Lande herrschenden, ist die
Durchführung eines solchen Programmes
unmöglich. Die erste Bedingung ist
praktisch unbeschränkte Lehrfreiheit,
sodass Lehrer und Schüler sich nicht
durch äussere Gewalt eingeschränkt fühlen ~~müssen~~.

A. Einstein Archive 28-971

↑ Draft of Einstein's answer to the question "How can the schools develop in youth the ability to face and solve problems objectively?" published in *Schools in Action*, a magazine of the New York State Education Department, in September 1953

« The basic prerequisite for the ability to face and solve problems objectively is independence of judgment.
Schools can assist in developing this faculty in the following ways:
1) The teacher should – as far as possible – present substantiated arguments for his assertions. This applies as well to the books used in school work.
2) Doubts and critical comments on the part of the students should be accepted in a friendly spirit and should be discussed in class.
3) Accumulation of material should not stifle the students' independence and their zest for learning. This latter point is particularly important.
4) In teaching history such personalities should be discussed extensively who benefitted mankind through independence of character and judgment.
Under conditions such as they presently prevail in this country the realization of such a program is impossible. Its most important prerequisite is virtually unlimited freedom of teaching so that teachers and students do not feel constrained by external pressure. »

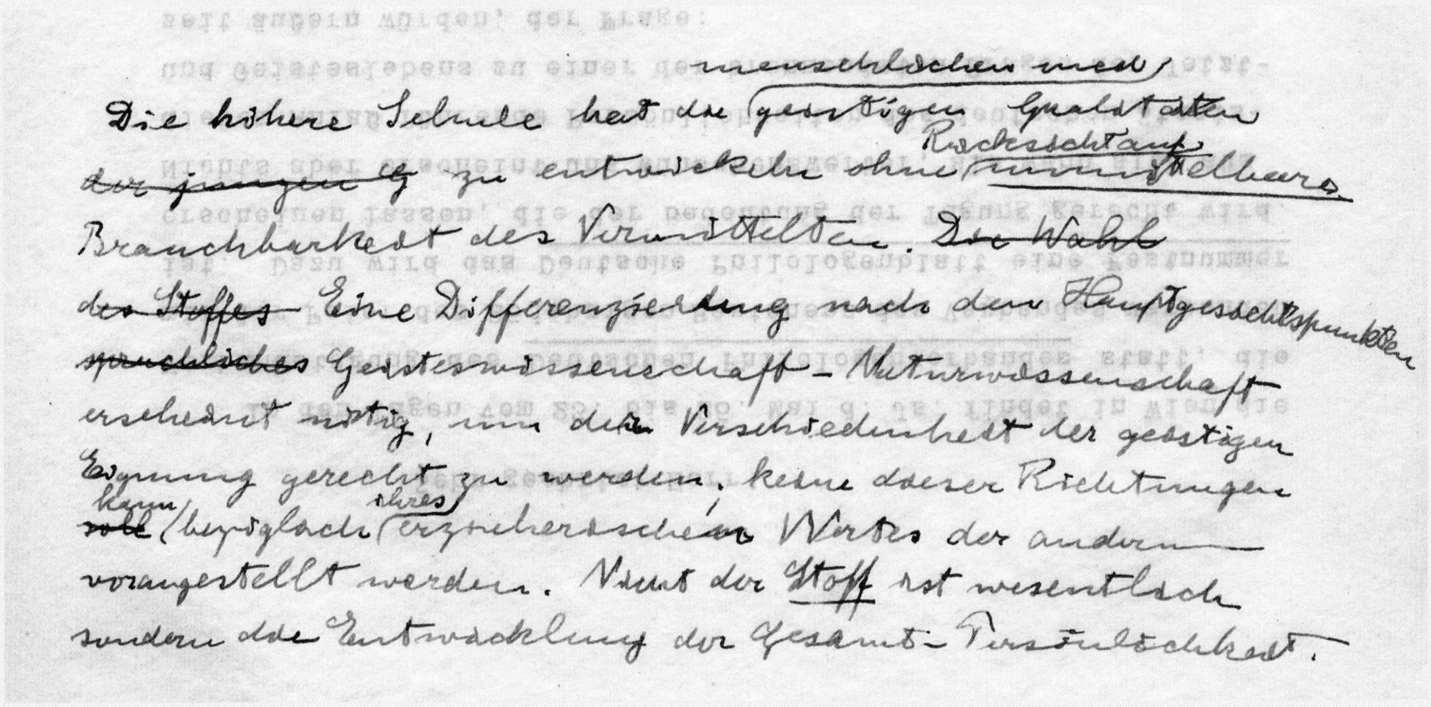
Die höhere Schule hat die geistigen menschlichen und Qualitäten ~~der jungen~~ zu entwickeln ohne Rücksicht auf ~~unmittelbare~~ Brauchbarkeit des Vermittelten. ~~Die Wahl des Stoffes~~ Eine Differenzierung nach den Hauptgesichtspunkten ~~sprachliches~~ Geisteswissenschaft – Naturwissenschaft erscheint nötig, um der Verschiedenheit der geistigen Eignung gerecht zu werden. Keine dieser Richtungen kann ~~soll~~ bezüglich ihres erzieherischen Wertes der andern vorangestellt werden. Nicht der Stoff ist wesentlich sondern die Entwicklung der Gesamt-Persönlichkeit.

↑ Einstein's contribution to the *Festschrift des Deutschen Philologenverbandes*, April 1929

→ From *Education for Independent Thought*, 1952

« Overemphasis on the competitive system and premature specialization on the ground of immediate usefulness kill the spirit on which all cultural life depends, specialized knowledge included. - It is also vital to a valuable education that independent critical thinking be developed in the young human being, a development that is greatly jeopardized by overburdening him with too much and with too varied subjects [...]. Overburdening necessarily leads to superficiality. Teaching should be such that what is offered is perceived as a valuable gift and not as a hard duty. »

4

PALESTINE ZIONIST EXECUTIVE
EMBASSY OF ISRAEL
WASHINGTON, D.C.
שגרירות ישראל
ושינגטון
November 17, 1952
Dear Professor Einstein:

EINSTEIN'S JEWISH IDENTITY

« The pursuit of knowledge for its own sake, an almost fanatical love of justice, and the desire for personal independence – these are the features of the Jewish tradition which make me thank the stars that I belong to it. »

From *Jewish Ideals*, 1925

EINSTEIN THE JEW

Born into one of those secular Jewish families whose only religion was the humanist ideal of *Bildung* and whose actual house of worship was the opera or the concert hall, as Amos Elon described it, Einstein nevertheless became aware of his Jewish identity from early childhood.
Throughout his life, he felt a close affinity with, and commitment to, the Jewish people.
Yet his solidarity did not apply to any institutionalized religion, but rather to a community with a shared past and common ethical values.
For him the main values of Judaism were intellectual endeavors and the pursuit of social justice.
Like Spinoza, to whom he often referred, Einstein did not believe in a personal god, but held, with awe and reverence, that the divine reveals itself in the physical universe.

↓↗ Incomplete draft of an address to unknown audience, probably around 1934

« Doubly I feel connected with you, namely as Jews and those of a particular community of fate.
I don't say as 'German Jews,' since such a thing as this does not exist for me. We Jews should have eventually learnt not to separate ourselves according to the country where we last resided or according to the language of the country where we were brought up. Our particular tradition is not only a religious one but embraces an approach to all aspects of life which has gradually developed over thousands of years. To be a Jew means to live in this particular tradition and to be loyal to it. To be a Jew means not to base the struggle of life on violence, but on understanding, empathy and mutual aid. »

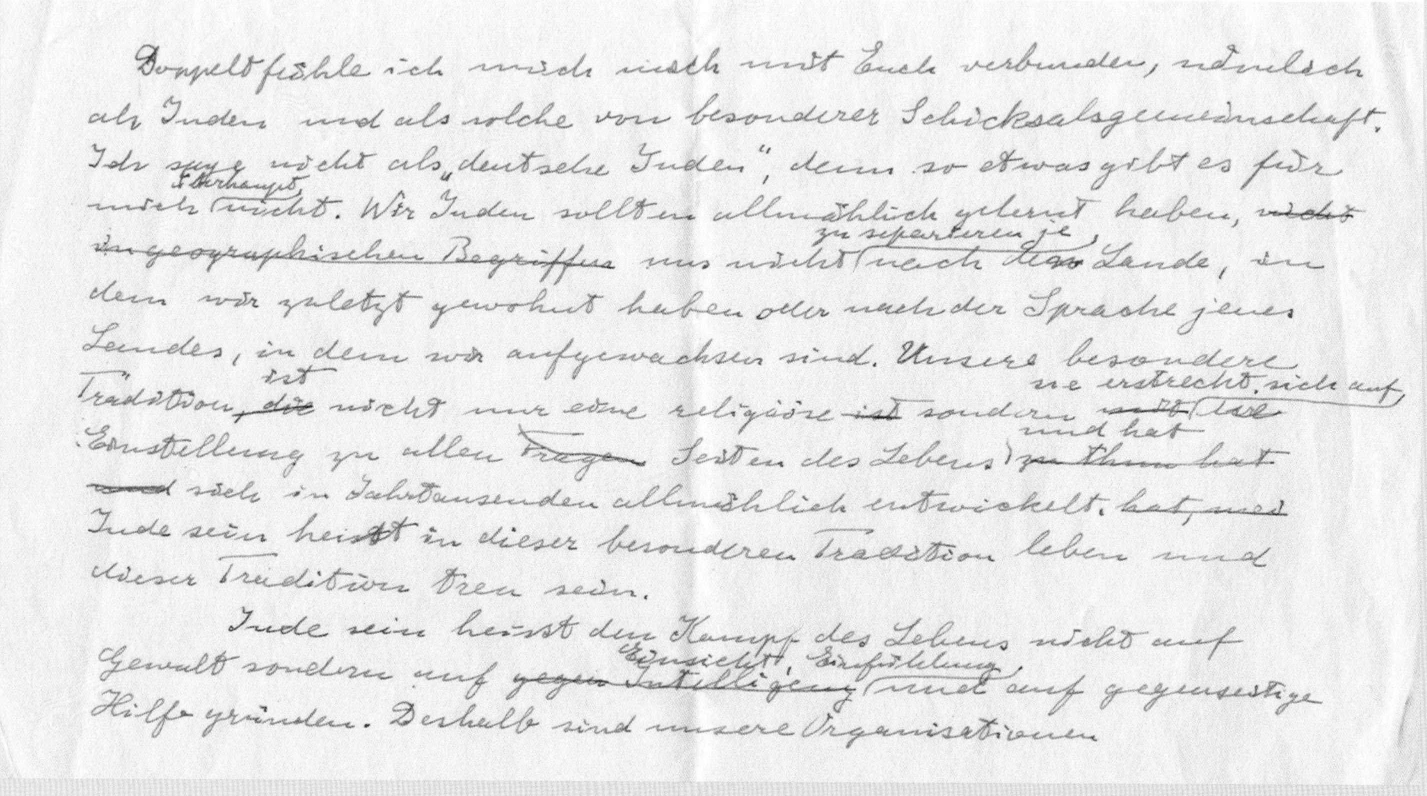
Doppelt fühle ich mich mit Euch verbunden, nämlich als Juden und als solche von besonderer Schicksalsgemeinschaft. Ich sage nicht als „deutsche Juden", denn so etwas gibt es für mich überhaupt nicht. Wir Juden sollten allmählich gelernt haben, uns nicht zu separieren je nach Lande, in dem wir zuletzt gewohnt haben oder nach der Sprache jenes Landes, in dem wir aufgewachsen sind. Unsere besondere Tradition ist nicht nur eine religiöse sondern sie erstreckt sich auf alle Seiten des Lebens und hat sich in Jahrtausenden allmählich entwickelt. Jude sein heisst in dieser besonderen Tradition leben und dieser Tradition treu sein.

Jude sein heisst den Kampf des Lebens nicht auf Gewalt sondern auf Einsicht, Einfühlung und auf gegenseitige Hilfe gründen. Deshalb sind unsere Organisationen

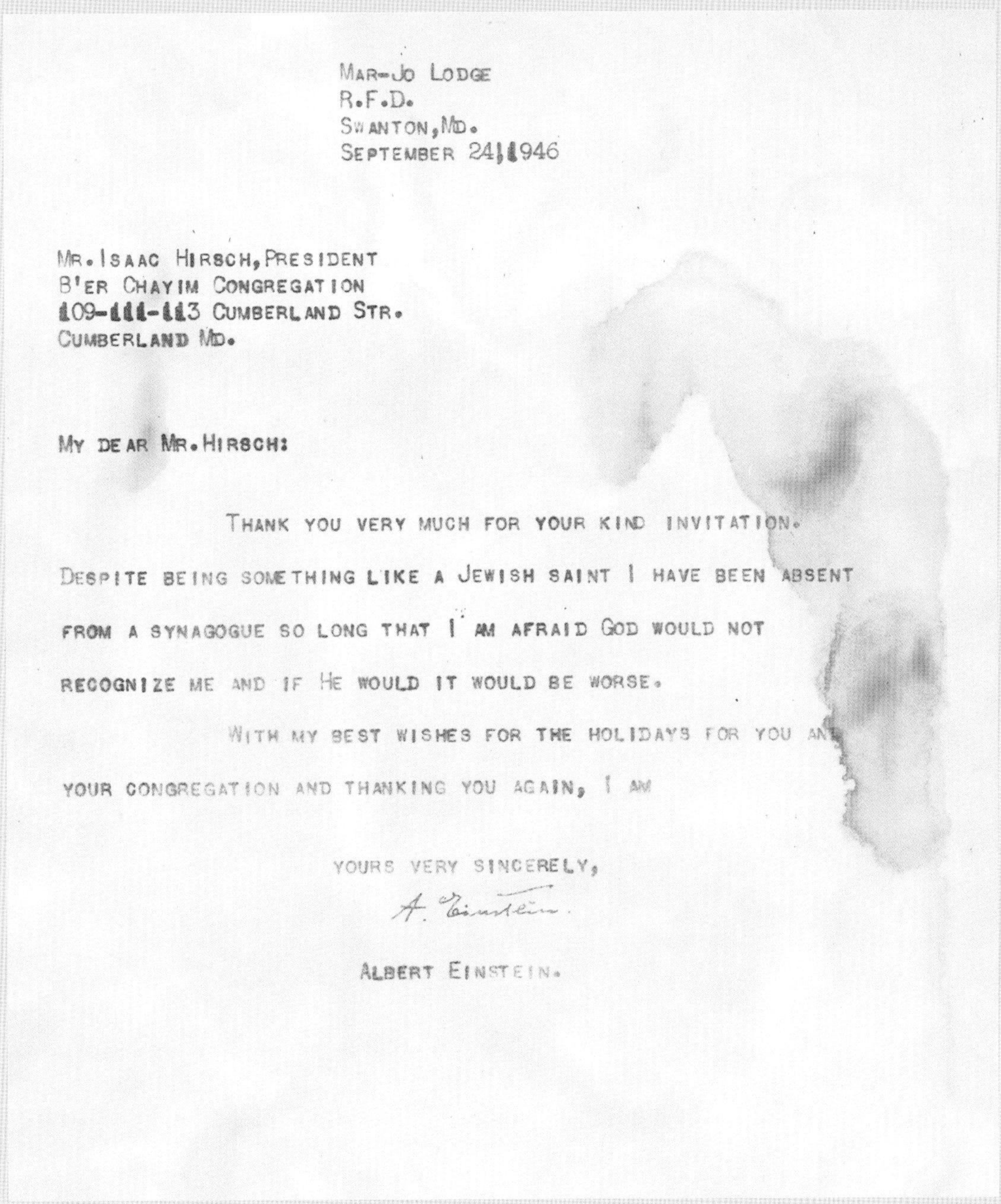

MAR-JO LODGE
R.F.D.
SWANTON, MD.
SEPTEMBER 24, 1946

MR. ISAAC HIRSCH, PRESIDENT
B'ER CHAYIM CONGREGATION
109-111-113 CUMBERLAND STR.
CUMBERLAND MD.

MY DEAR MR. HIRSCH:

THANK YOU VERY MUCH FOR YOUR KIND INVITATION. DESPITE BEING SOMETHING LIKE A JEWISH SAINT I HAVE BEEN ABSENT FROM A SYNAGOGUE SO LONG THAT I AM AFRAID GOD WOULD NOT RECOGNIZE ME AND IF HE WOULD IT WOULD BE WORSE.

WITH MY BEST WISHES FOR THE HOLIDAYS FOR YOU AND YOUR CONGREGATION AND THANKING YOU AGAIN, I AM

YOURS VERY SINCERELY,

A. Einstein.

ALBERT EINSTEIN.

← Reply to an invitation for the High Holidays service, September 24, 1946

« Not only don't I believe in a personal God, but I consider such a belief downright naïve.
On the other hand it seems to me that the mere non-belief in a personal God does not yet represent much of a philosophy either.

→ From a letter to V.T. Aaltonen, May 7, 1952

The human situation is such that we have just enough mind to grasp, with some effort, a small part of the harmony of the structural coherence of the universe. Serious effort to that end fills man with a humility that is at least akin to a religious sentiment. Therefore you may consider me a religious un-believer. »

↑ Albert Einstein with Maurice Schwartz and the actors of the Yiddish Art Theater after the performance of I.J.Singer's *Yoshe Kalb*, Princeton 1934

« Your presentation of 'Yoshe Kalb' made one of the greatest impressions ever on me, in the dramatic arts. The tragedy of the hero is actually the tragedy of the Jewish people, the tragedy of its best sons. The whole is immersed in humor, and reflects in a very unique way the multifaceted ethnic soul. Such an art requires devotion, with no criticism. »

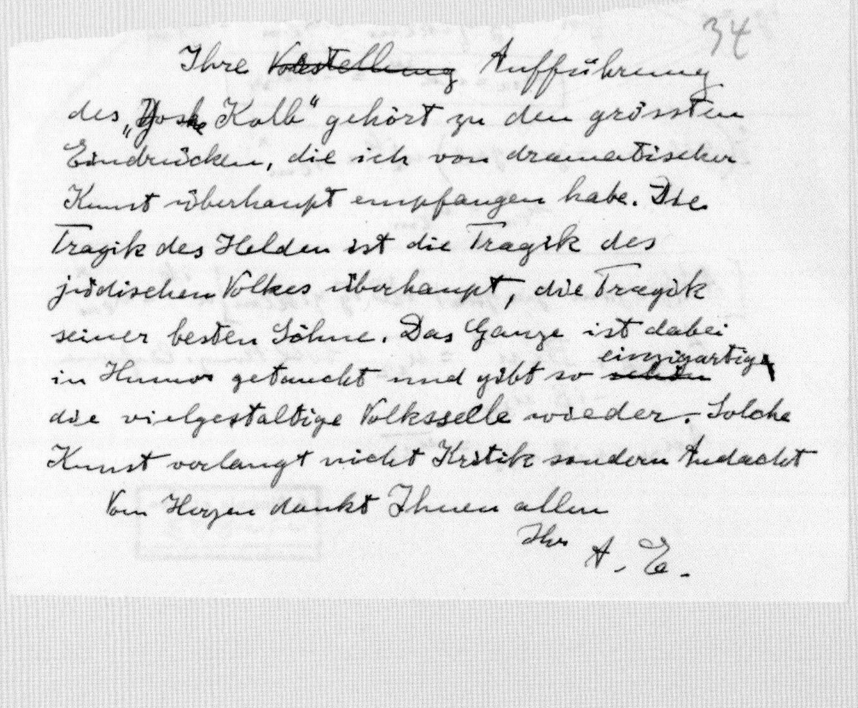
34

Ihre ~~Vorstellung~~ Aufführung
des „Yoshe Kalb" gehört zu den grössten
Eindrücken, die ich von dramatischer
Kunst überhaupt empfangen habe. Die
Tragik des Helden ist die Tragik des
jüdischen Volkes überhaupt, die Tragik
seiner besten Söhne. Das Ganze ist dabei
in Humor getaucht und gibt so ~~schön~~ einzigartig
die vielgestaltige Volksseele wieder. Solche
Kunst verlangt nicht Kritik sondern Andacht
Von Herzen dankt Ihnen allen
Ihr A. E.

↑↗ Draft of a letter to Maurice Schwartz and the Yiddish Art Theater, 1934

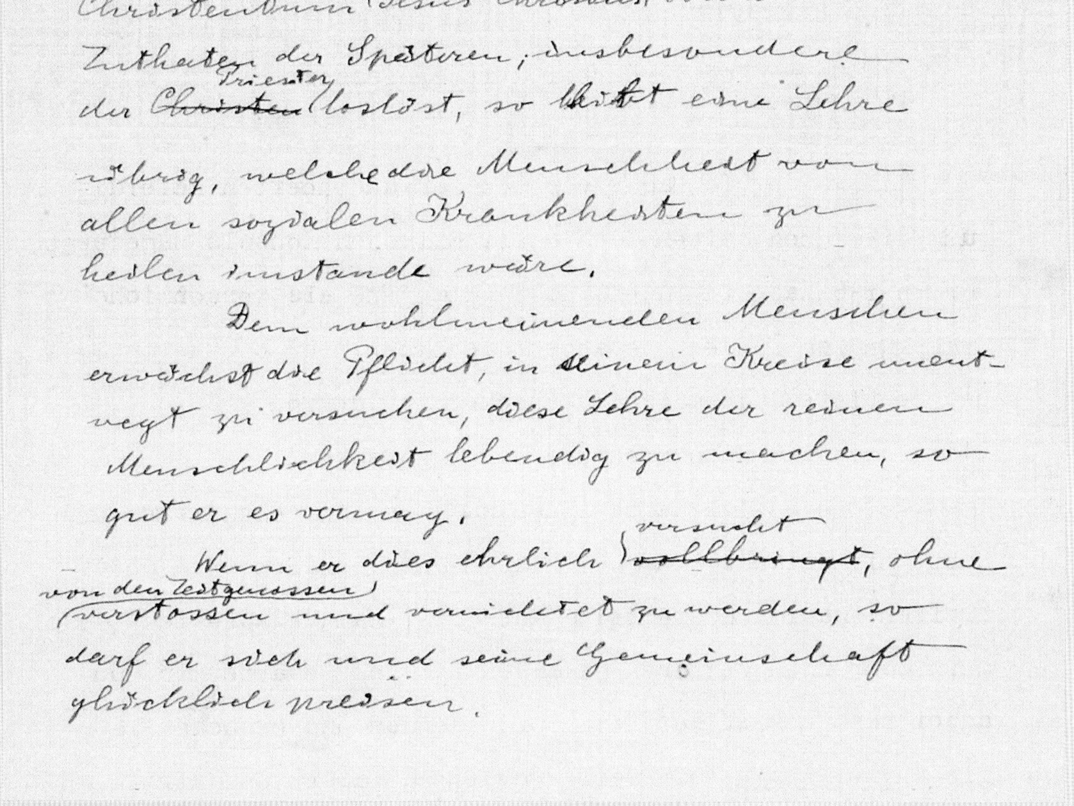

71

Christentum und Judentum

Wenn man das Judentum der Propheten und das Christentum wie es Jesus Christus gelehrt hat, von allen Zuthaten der Späteren, insbesondere der ~~Christen~~ Priester loslöst, so bleibt eine Lehre übrig, welche die Menschheit von allen sozialen Krankheiten zu heilen imstande wäre.

Dem wohlmeinenden Menschen erwächst die Pflicht, in seinem Kreise unentwegt zu versuchen, diese Lehre der reinen Menschlichkeit lebendig zu machen, so gut er es vermag.

Wenn er dies ehrlich versucht ~~vollbringt~~, ohne von den Zeitgenossen verstossen und vernichtet zu werden, so darf er sich und seine Gemeinschaft glücklich preisen.

↑↗ "Christianity and Judaism," statement for the Rumanian Jewish journal *Renasterea Noastra*, January 1933

« If one purges the Judaism of the prophets and Christianity as Jesus Christ taught it of all subsequent additions, especially those of the priests, one is left with a teaching which is capable of curing all the social ills of humanity.
It is the duty of every man of good will to strive steadfastly in his own little world to make this teaching of pure humanity a living force, so far as he can. If he makes an honest attempt in this direction without being crushed and trampled underfoot by his contemporaries, he may consider himself and the community to which he belongs lucky. »

↓↘ In a letter to Einstein, Gerald M. Donahue had argued that Jews were first and foremost citizens of their countries. Einstein dissents and, in his reply of April 3, 1935, expresses his own views on ethnic and cultural diversity and national conflicts.

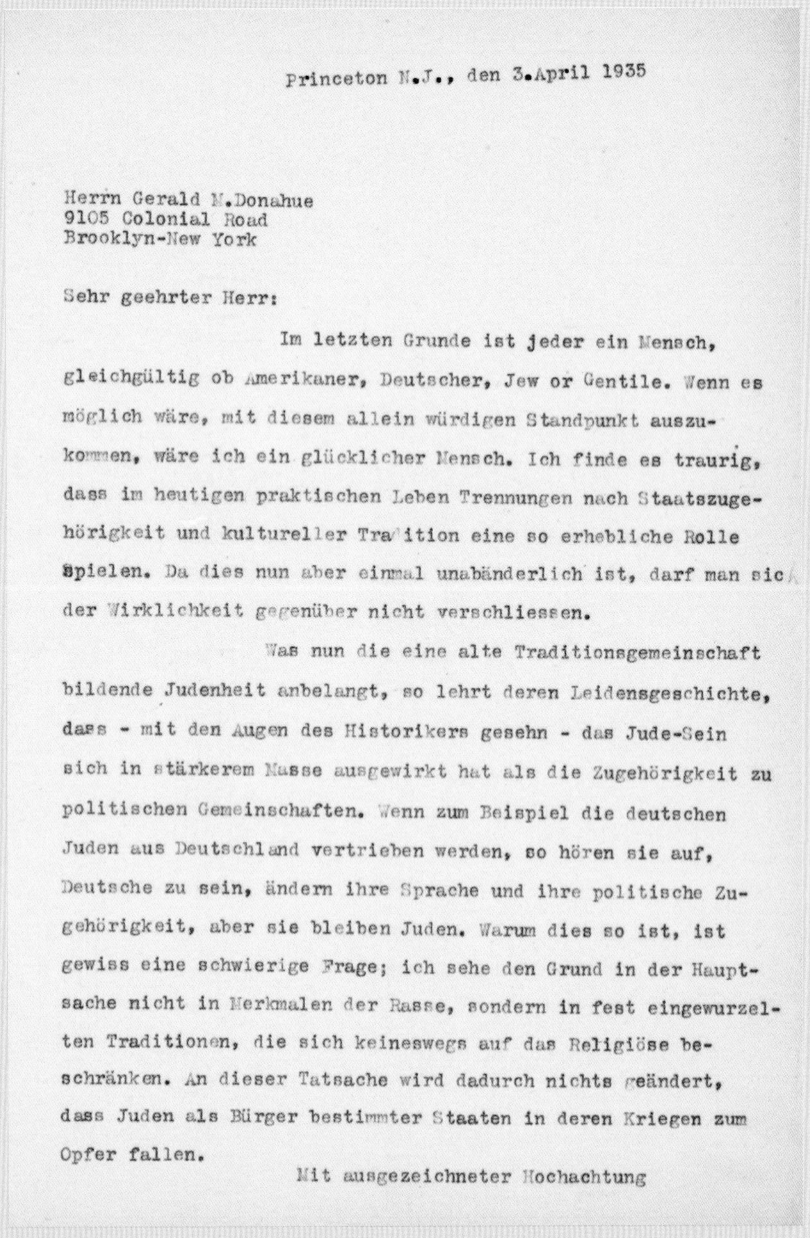

Princeton N.J., den 3.April 1935

Herrn Gerald M.Donahue
9105 Colonial Road
Brooklyn-New York

Sehr geehrter Herr:

Im letzten Grunde ist jeder ein Mensch, gleichgültig ob Amerikaner, Deutscher, Jew or Gentile. Wenn es möglich wäre, mit diesem allein würdigen Standpunkt auszukommen, wäre ich ein glücklicher Mensch. Ich finde es traurig, dass im heutigen praktischen Leben Trennungen nach Staatszugehörigkeit und kultureller Tradition eine so erhebliche Rolle spielen. Da dies nun aber einmal unabänderlich ist, darf man sic der Wirklichkeit gegenüber nicht verschliessen.

Was nun die eine alte Traditionsgemeinschaft bildende Judenheit anbelangt, so lehrt deren Leidensgeschichte, dass - mit den Augen des Historikers gesehn - das Jude-Sein sich in stärkerem Masse ausgewirkt hat als die Zugehörigkeit zu politischen Gemeinschaften. Wenn zum Beispiel die deutschen Juden aus Deutschland vertrieben werden, so hören sie auf, Deutsche zu sein, ändern ihre Sprache und ihre politische Zugehörigkeit, aber sie bleiben Juden. Warum dies so ist, ist gewiss eine schwierige Frage; ich sehe den Grund in der Hauptsache nicht in Merkmalen der Rasse, sondern in fest eingewurzelten Traditionen, die sich keineswegs auf das Religiöse beschränken. An dieser Tatsache wird dadurch nichts geändert, dass Juden als Bürger bestimmter Staaten in deren Kriegen zum Opfer fallen.

Mit ausgezeichneter Hochachtung

« The bond that has united the Jews for thousands of years and that unites them today is, above all, the democratic ideal of social justice, coupled with the ideal of mutual aid and tolerance among all men. Even the most ancient religious scriptures of the Jews are steeped in these social ideals, which have powerfully affected Christianity and Mohammedanism and have had a benign influence upon the social structure of a great part of mankind. Personalities such as Moses, Spinoza, and Karl Marx, dissimilar as they may be, all lived and sacrificed themselves for the ideal of social justice; and it was the tradition of their forefathers that led them on this thorny path. »

« In the last analysis, everyone is a human being, irrespective of whether he is an American or a German, a Jew or a Gentile. If it were possible to manage with this point of view, which is the only dignified one, I would be a happy man. I find it very sad that divisions according to citizenship and cultural tradition should play so great a role in modern practical life. But since this cannot be changed, one should not close one's eyes to reality. »

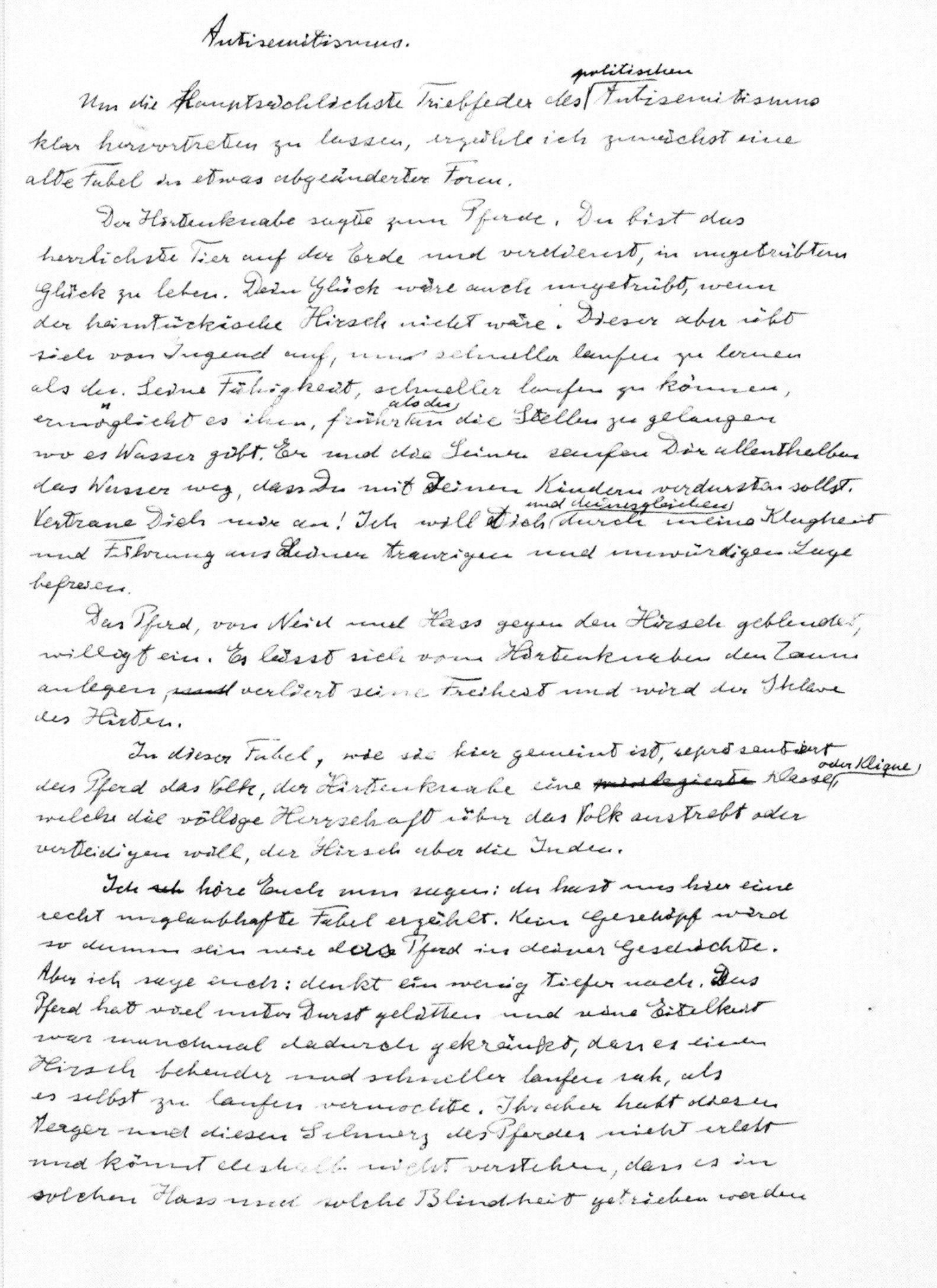

Antisemitismus.

Um die Hauptsächlichste Triebfeder des politischen Antisemitismus klar hervortreten zu lassen, erzähle ich zunächst eine alte Fabel in etwas abgeänderter Form.

Der Hirtenknabe sagte zum Pferde: Du bist das herrlichste Tier auf der Erde und verdienst, in ungetrübtem Glück zu leben. Dein Glück wäre auch ungetrübt, wenn der heimtückische Hirsch nicht wäre. Dieser aber übt sich von Jugend auf, um schneller laufen zu lernen als du. Seine Fähigkeit, schneller laufen zu können, ermöglicht es ihm, früher als du an die Stellen zu gelangen wo es Wasser gibt. Er und die Seinen saufen Dir allenthalben das Wasser weg, dass Du mit Deinen Kindern verdursten sollst. Vertraue Dich mir an! Ich will Dich und deinesgleichen durch meine Klugheit und Führung aus Deiner traurigen und unwürdigen Lage befreien.

Das Pferd, vom Neid und Hass gegen den Hirsch geblendet, willigt ein. Es lässt sich vom Hirtenknaben den Zaum anlegen, ~~und~~ verliert seine Freiheit und wird der Sklave des Hirten.

In dieser Fabel, wie sie hier gemeint ist, repräsentiert das Pferd das Volk, der Hirtenknabe eine ~~privilegierte~~ Klasse oder Klique, welche die völlige Herrschaft über das Volk anstrebt oder verteidigen will, der Hirsch aber die Juden.

Ich ~~ich~~ höre Euch nun sagen: du hast uns hier eine recht unglaubhafte Fabel erzählt. Kein Geschöpf wird so dumm sein wie das Pferd in deiner Geschichte. Aber ich sage euch: denkt ein wenig tiefer nach. Das Pferd hat viel unter Durst gelitten und seine Eitelkeit war manchmal dadurch gekränkt, dass es einen Hirsch behender und schneller laufen sah, als es selbst zu laufen vermochte. Ihr aber habt diesen Ärger und diesen Schmerz des Pferdes nicht erlebt und könnt deshalb nicht verstehen, dass es in solchen Hass und solche Blindheit getrieben werden

↖↑↗ Struck by what became known in the U.S. about the pogrom of November 9, 1938 in Germany, Einstein composed this essay, which was published the same month in *Collier's Weekly*, under the title "Why Do They Hate the Jews?" In this text he defines the social characteristics of the Jewish people and affirms his belief in humanistic Judaism.

« Why Do They Hate The Jews?
[...]
The crimes with which the Jews have been charged in the course of the history – crimes which were to justify the atrocities perpetrated against them – have changed in rapid succession. They were supposed to have poisoned wells. They were said to have murdered children for ritual purposes. They were falsely charged with a systematic attempt at the economic domination and exploitation of all mankind. Pseudo-scientific books were written to brand them as an inferior, dangerous race. They were reputed to foment wars and revolutions for their own selfish purposes. They were presented at once as dangerous innovators and as enemies of true progress. They were charged with falsifying the culture of nations by penetrating the national life under the guise of becoming assimilated. In the same breath they were accused of being so stubbornly inflexible that it was impossible for them to fit into any society.
Almost beyond imagination were the charges brought against them, charges known to their instigators to be untrue all the while, but which time and again influenced the masses. In times of unrest and turmoil the masses are inclined to hatred and cruelty, whereas in times of peace these traits of human nature emerge but stealthily. »

EINSTEIN AND JEWISH NATIONALISM

Even though Einstein had socialized with some Zionists during his sojourn in Prague in 1911/12, he did not display an overt interest in Jewish affairs prior to his move to Berlin in 1914.
As no more than a quixotic anachronism did Einstein consider the Zionist ideas that those Prague Jewish intellectuals were "infested with." Yet the complex circumstances of the Jewish community there, caught between the increasingly fervent nationalistic movements of both their German and Czech neighbors, may have heightened Einstein's awareness of the Jews' precarious situation in Central and Eastern Europe. Hence he refused to follow an invitation from the Imperial Academy of Sciences in St. Petersburg in 1914 "to a country where my tribesmen are so brutally persecuted."

His exposure to German anti-Semitism directed against Eastern European Jewish immigrants during and after the First World War made him reassess the place of Jews in German society. He came to reject Jewish attempts at total assimilation and to believe that Jewish self-confidence could be restored through a cultural renaissance.
Some years later, when he encountered assimilationist groups among U.S. Jewry, he warned them not to follow what he perceived as the negative example of German Jewry.

Despite his distaste for every form of nationalism, he was poised to adopt a cultural and non-political definition of Jewish nationalism, akin to that espoused by Ahad Ha-am. Therefore, the cultural aspects of German Zionism greatly appealed to him.
Einstein, though, was rather scrupulous about the Jewish causes to which he was willing to lend his name. He was particularly interested in the education of Jewish youth, the strengthening of Jewish social solidarity and the consolidation of the Jewish community in Palestine.

For Einstein, the Jewish homeland in Palestine, promised by the Balfour Declaration of 1917, represented first and foremost a spiritual center, a model society. Impressed by the idealism of farmers and workmen he had observed in Palestine in 1923, he supported the colonization efforts to provide a refuge for Eastern European Jews, but regarded the settlement of Palestine mainly as an instrument for enhancing the cultural identity and social cohesion of Western Jewry.
Einstein did not see either any moral justification or practical possibility for realizing Zionism in the absence of cooperation with the Arab population. Therefore, already in 1929 he urged for a solution of the Arab-Jewish conflict in Palestine based on mutual understanding and consent. Until the summer of 1947, he advocated a bi-national solution in Palestine. In the light of the war of 1948, he resigned himself to the actual solution involving partition.
Once the State of Israel had become a reality, Einstein followed its development with sympathetic interest, yet remained highly critical of its political leadership. He warned of the pitfalls of narrow nationalism inherent in statehood. In his view, Israel's treatment of its Arab minority would be the test of its moral integrity.

« I cannot understand how – by sponsoring the Biro Bidjan Project – I should have done any wrong to the cause of Palestine. I ardently hope that God will protect all the chickens in Palestine and in Biro Bidjan together with their promoters. »

↑ In view of the urgency of the matter, Einstein supported colonization projects in Latin America and East Asia, in addition to the colonization of Palestine. A letter to the chairman of the American Jewish Farmers' Committee of September 6, 1947 attests that a conflict of interest with the Zionists was not always avoidable.

↑ Einstein addresses the Conference of Jewish Students in Germany, mid-1920s

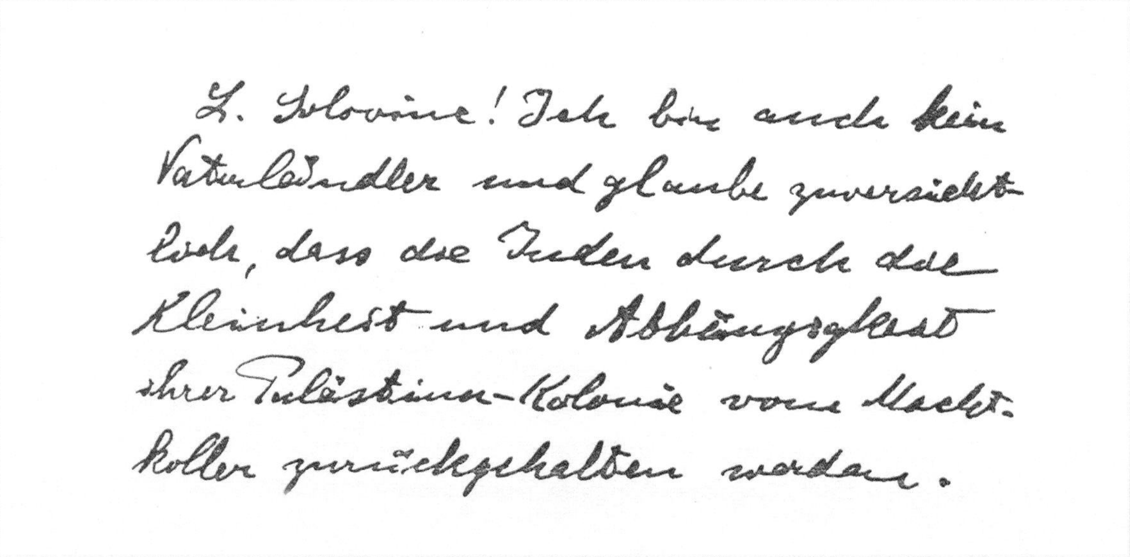
L. Solovine! Ich bin auch kein Vaterländler und glaube zuversichtlich, dass die Juden durch die Kleinheit und Abhängigkeit ihrer Palästina-Kolonie vom Macht-koller zurückgehalten werden.

↑→ From a letter to Maurice Solovine, March 16, 1921

« I am no jingo either and confident that the smallness and dependency of their Palestinian colony will deter the Jews from evolving any craving for power. »

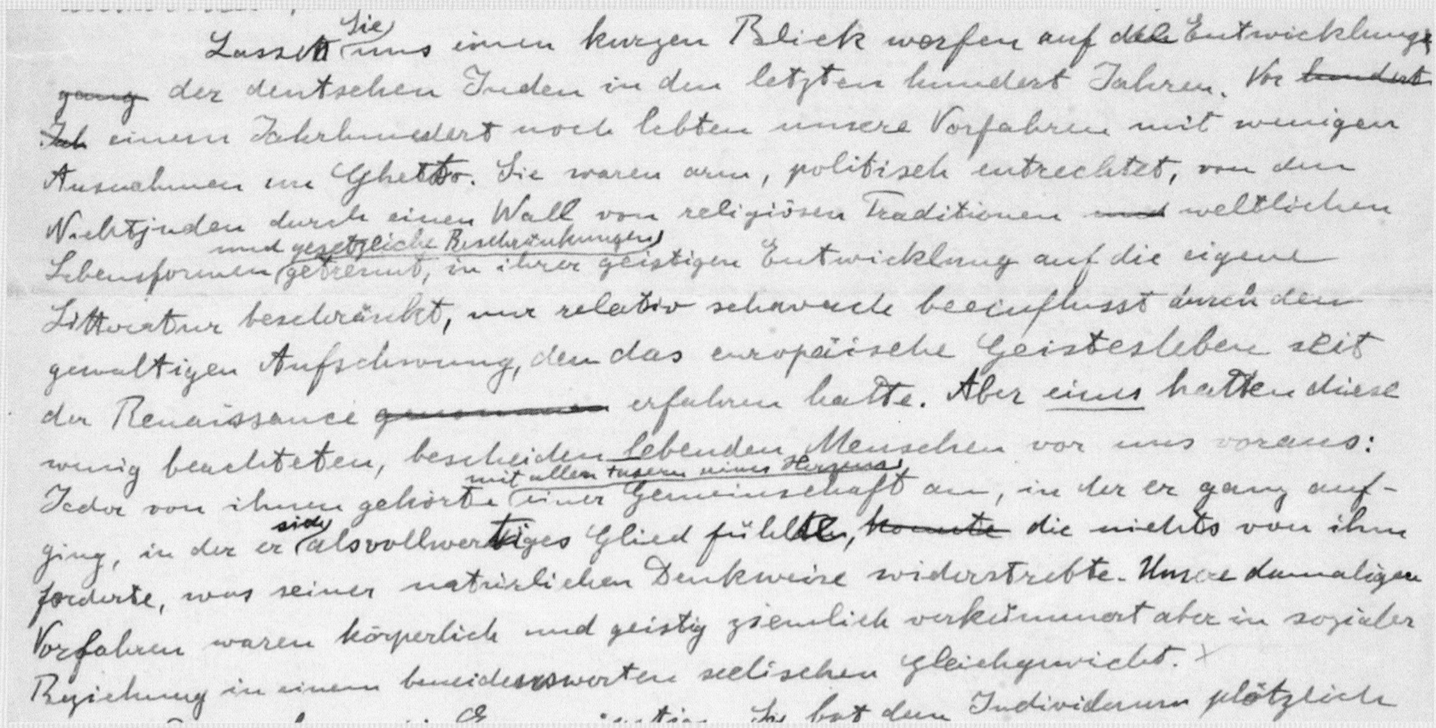

Lasst Sie uns einen kurzen Blick werfen auf die Entwicklung
der deutschen Juden in den letzten hundert Jahren. Vor
einem Jahrhundert noch lebten unsere Vorfahren mit wenigen
Ausnahmen im Ghetto. Sie waren arm, politisch entrechtet, von den
Nichtjuden durch einen Wall von religiösen Traditionen weltlichen
Lebensformen und gesetzliche Beschränkungen getrennt, in ihrer geistigen Entwicklung auf die eigene
Litteratur beschränkt, nur relativ schwach beeinflusst durch den
gewaltigen Aufschwung, den das europäische Geistesleben seit
der Renaissance erfahren hatte. Aber eines hatten diese
wenig beachteten, bescheiden lebenden Menschen vor uns voraus:
Jeder von ihnen gehörte mit allen Fasern seines Herzens einer Gemeinschaft an, in der er ganz auf-
ging, in der er sich als vollwertiges Glied fühlte, die nichts von ihm
forderte, was seiner natürlichen Denkweise widerstrebte. Unsere damaligen
Vorfahren waren körperlich und geistig ziemlich verkümmert aber in sozialer
Beziehung in einem beneidenswerten seelischen Gleichgewicht. ×

↑↓ From a speech to U.S. Zionists,
New York, April 1921

« Palestine is for us Jews not a mere matter of charity or colonization: it is a problem of paramount importance for the Jewish people. Palestine is first and foremost not a refuge for east European Jews, but the incarnation of a re-awakening sense of national solidarity for all Jews.[…]

A century ago, our forefathers, with few exceptions, lived in the ghetto. They were poor, without political rights, separated from the Gentiles by a barrier of religious traditions, habits of life and legal restrictions; their intellectual development was restricted to their own literature, and they had remained almost unaffected by the mighty advance of the European intellect which dates from the Renaissance. And yet, these obscure, humble people had one great advantage over us: each of them belonged in every fiber of his being to a community in which he was completely absorbed, in which he felt himself a fully privileged member, and which demanded nothing of him that was contrary to his natural habit of thought. Our forefathers in those days were pretty poor specimens intellectually and physically, but socially speaking they enjoyed an enviable spiritual equilibrium. […]

We Jews [must] become once more conscious of our existence as a nation and regain the self-respect which we require for a prosperous existence. We must learn once more to enthusiastically declare our loyalty to our ancestry and our history; we must once more take upon ourselves, as a nation, cultural tasks of a kind calculated to strengthen our feeling of solidarity. It is not sufficient for us to participate as individuals in the cultural development of mankind: we must also set our hands to such tasks which can only be accomplished by national communities. In this way and in this way only can the Jewish people regain its social health. »

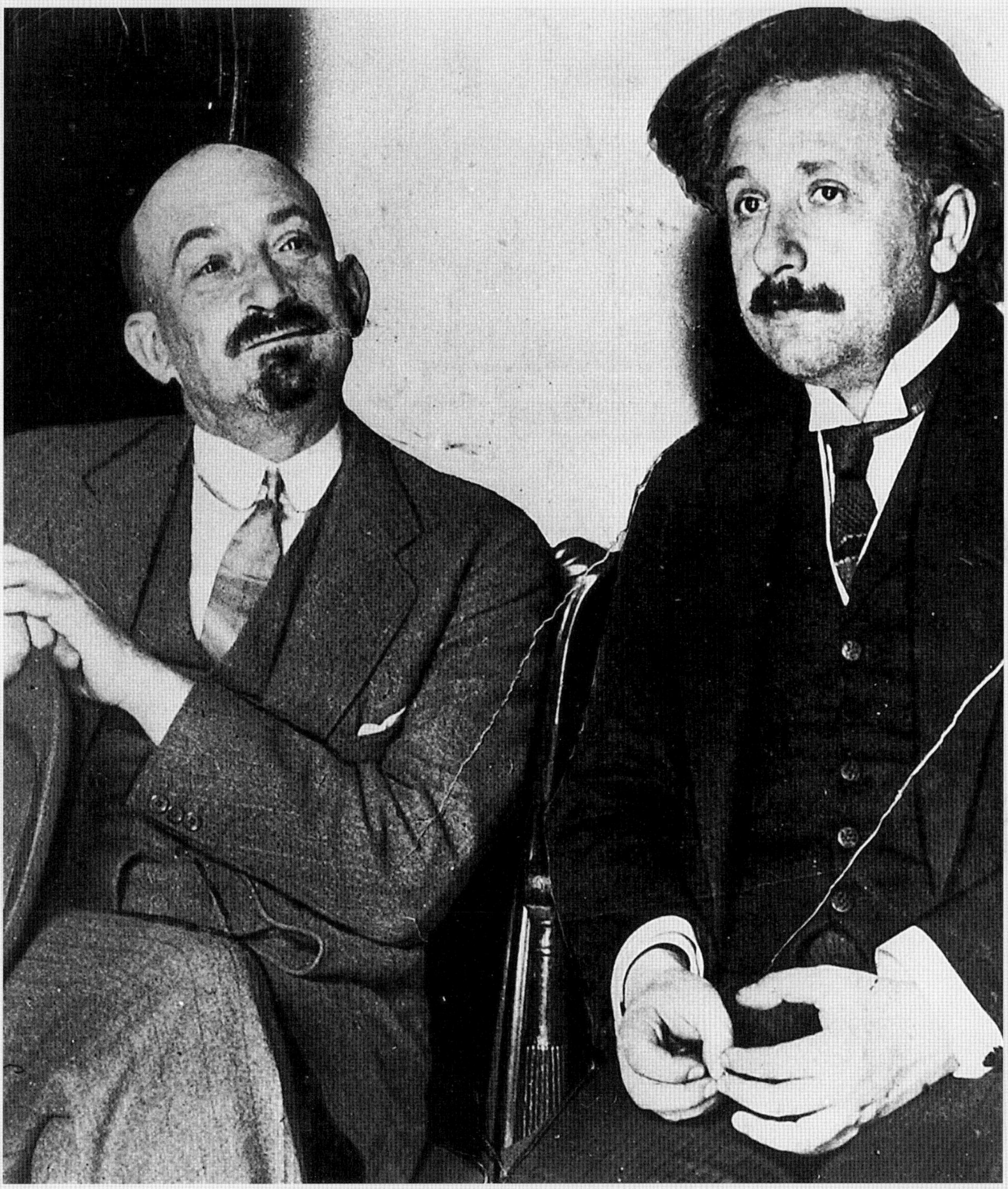

↑ Albert Einstein and Chaim Weizmann on fundraising tour for The Hebrew University in Jerusalem, New York, April 1921

↑ On February 6, 1923, Einstein and his wife paid a visit to the British High Commissioner Herbert Samuel, at his residence at Augusta Victoria Hospital, Jerusalem.
Front row includes, left to right: Elsa Einstein, Herbert Samuel, Lady Beatrice Samuel, Einstein, and Father Dhorme
Back row includes, left to right: Father Sertillange, Norman Bentwich, Ernest T. Richmond, Mrs. Richmond and Father Orfali
Photo by Father Carrière.

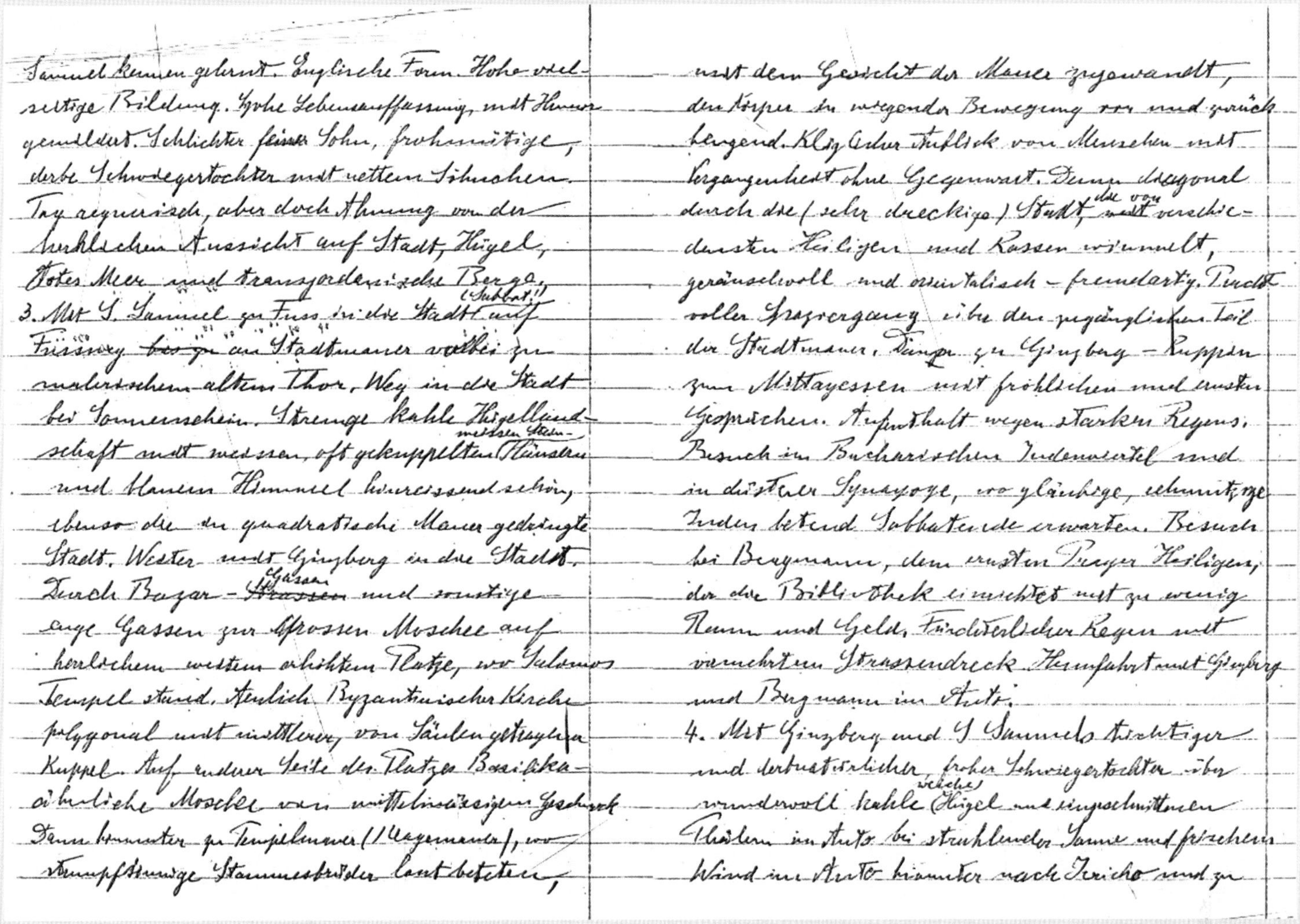

Samuel kennen gelernt. Englische Form. Hohe vielseitige Bildung. Hohe Lebensauffassung, mit Humor gemildert. Schlichter feiner Sohn, frohmütige, derbe Schwiegertochter mit nettem Söhnchen. Tag regnerisch, aber doch Ahnung von der herrlichen Aussicht auf Stadt, Hügel, Totes Meer und transjordanische Berge. 3. Mit S. Samuel zu Fuss in die Stadt (Sabbat!) auf Fussweg an Stadtmauer vorbei zu malerischem alten Thor. Weg in die Stadt bei Sonnenschein. Strenge kahle Hügellandschaft mit weissen, oft gekuppelten Steinhäusern und blauem Himmel hinreissend schön, ebenso die in quadratische Mauer gedrängte Stadt. Weiter mit Ginzberg in die Stadt. Durch Bazar-Gassen und sonstige enge Gassen zur grossen Moschee auf herrlichem weitem erhöhten Platze, wo Salomos Tempel stand. Ähnlich Byzantinischer Kirche polygonal mit mittlerer, von Säulen getragener Kuppel. Auf anderer Seite des Platzes Basilika-ähnliche Moschee von mittelmässigem Geschmack. Dann hinunter zu Tempelmauer (Klagemauer), wo stumpfsinnige Stammesbrüder laut beteten, mit dem Gesicht der Mauer zugewandt, den Körper in wiegender Bewegung vor und zurück beugend. Kläglicher Anblick von Menschen mit Vergangenheit ohne Gegenwart. Dann diagonal durch die (sehr dreckige) Stadt, die von verschiedensten Heiligen und Rassen wimmelt, geräuschvoll und orientalisch – fremdartig. Prächtiger Spaziergang über den zugänglichen Teil der Stadtmauer. Dann zu Ginzberg – Ruppin zum Mittagessen mit fröhlichen und ernsten Gesprächen. Aufenthalt wegen starken Regens. Besuch im Bucharischen Judenviertel und in düsterer Synagoge, wo gläubige, schmutzige Juden betend Sabbatende erwarten. Besuch bei Bergmann, dem ernsten Prager Heiligen, der die Bibliothek einrichtet mit zu wenig Raum und Geld. Fürchterlicher Regen mit vermehrtem Strassendreck. Heimfahrt mit Ginzberg und Bergmann im Auto. 4. Mit Ginzberg und S. Samuels tüchtiger und derbtatkräftiger, froher Schwiegertochter über wundervoll kahle Hügel welche eingeschnittenen Tälern im Auto bei strahlender Sonne und frischem Wind im Auto hinunter nach Jericho und zu

↑↗ Einstein's impressions of Jerusalem during his only visit to Palestine. From his travel diary, February 3, 1923

« Went with Sir Herbert Samuel on foot into the city (Sabbath!), walked on path past city walls to picturesque, old gate. Path into the city bathed in sunshine. Hard, barren hilly landscape with white, stone houses, mostly dome-topped, and blue sky, breathtakingly beautiful, as is the city squeezed into the square walls. Continued into the city with Ginzberg.* Through the bazaar and other narrow alleys to the large mosque on a splendidly wide, raised square where Solomon's temple stood. Resembles Byzantine church, polygonal, with a central dome supported by columns. On the other side of the square a basilica-like mosque of mediocre taste. Then down to the temple wall (Wailing Wall) where dull-minded fellow Jews prayed out loud, their faces turned to the wall, bending their bodies backwards and forwards in a rocking movement. Pitiful sight of people with a past but no present. Then zig-zag through the (very dirty) city, swarming with all kinds of holy men and members of various races, noisy and strangely oriental. »

* Shlomo Ginzberg-Ginossar, son of Ahad Ha-am, accompanied Einstein throughout his visit to Palestine.

↑ Reception for Einstein at the Municipality of Tel Aviv at which he was made an honorary citizen of the city, February 8, 1923. Front row includes Elsa and Albert Einstein with Mayor Meir Dizengoff and A.L. Esterman.
Second row includes Avraham Mibashan, Yehuda Grazovsky, Bezalel Jaffe, Ahad Ha-am, Yosef Zeidner, Theodor Zlocisti, David Ijmojic, Shmuel Tulkovsky and Benzion Mossinson.

↓→ In this letter to Chaim Weizmann of November 25, 1929, like on many other occasions, Einstein advocates reconciliation with the Arab population of Palestine.

« If we do not succeed in finding the path of honest cooperation and coming to terms with the Arabs, we will not have learned anything from our two thousand year old ordeal and will deserve the fate which will beset us. »

Herrn Professor Dr.Weizmann
London W.14
Oakwood,16,Addison Crescent

Lieber Herr Weizmann!

Ich danke Ihnen bestens für Ihren Brief und kann mir denken,dass Sie von schweren Sorgen erfüllt sind. Gleichzeitig aber muss ich Ihnen offen sagen,dass mich die Haltung unserer leitenden Männer beunruhigt. Neulich hat Brodetzki in einem Agency-Vortrag mit jener Aeusserlichkeit und Oberflächlichkeit wieder das arabische Problem behandelt,die den gegenwärtigen Zustand der Dinge herbeigeführt hat. Das wirtschaftliche und psychologische Problem der jüdisch-arabischen Symbiose wurde überhaupt nicht berührt,sondern der Konflikt als Episode behandelt. Dies war umso unangebrachter,als die vernünftigeren Zuhörer von der Unaufrichtigkeit einer solchen Betrachtungsweise voll überzeugt sein werden. Ich sende Ihnen hier einen Brief von Hugo Bergmann,der nach meiner Ueberzeugung das Wesentliche trifft. Wenn wir den Weg ehrlicher Kooperation und ehrlichen Paktierens mit den Arabern nicht finden werden,so haben wir auf unserem zweitausendjährigen Leidensweg nichts gelernt und verdienen das Schicksal,das uns treffen wird.Insbesondere müssen wir uns nach meiner Meinung davor hüten,uns zuviel

2. Ofr   28.1.30   25. Jan. 1930

An die Redaction des "Falastin"

Sehr geehrte Redaction,

Meine Aufmerksamkeit wurde auf einen Artikel "Relativität und Propaganda" gelenkt, den Sie in Ihrer englischen Ausgabe vom 19. Oktober veröffentlicht haben. Ich will davon absehen, dass Sie in diesem Artikel neben manchem Schmeichelhaften auch manches Unschmeichelhafte über mich sagen, und ich will auch Ihre verletzenden Bemerkungen über den Charakter des jüdischen ~~xxxxxxx~~ Volkes nicht zu schwer nehmen. Leider ist es ja eine Gewohnheit streitender Völker geworden, das andere Volk ungebührlich herabzusetzen.

Auf das Vergangene will ich hier nicht eingehen. Was ich darüber zu sagen habe, habe ich in meinem Brief an den "Manchester Guardian" gesagt, mit dem Sie sich in Ihrem Artikel beschäftigen. Aber Ihr Artikel gibt mir Anlass, ein paar Worte über die Zukunft zu sagen, wie ich sie sehe. Sie bezweifeln meine Worte, dass die Juden mit der arabischen Bevölkerung Palästinas nur freundliche Beziehungen zu haben wünschen. Wer wie ich seit Jahrzehnten die Ueberzeugung vertritt, dass die zukünftige Menschheit auf einer innigen Gemeinschaft der Nationen aufgebaut sein muss und dass der aggressive Nationalismus~~, xxxxxxxxxx~~ überwunden werden muss, der kann auch die Zukunft Palästinas nur in der Form einer friedlichen Kooperation der beiden dort beheimateten Völker sehen. Darum hätte ich erwartet, dass das grosse arabische Volk die jüdische Notwendigkeit, in der alten Heimat des Judentums sein nationales Heim wieder aufzubauen, besser würdigt und dass gemeinsam Mittel und Wege gefunden werden, um ~~xx~~ eine ausgedehnte jüdische Siedlung im Lande zu ermöglichen. Ich bin überzeugt, dass durch das liebevolle Interesse, das die gesamte Juden-

« [...]
One who, like myself, has cherished for many years the conviction that the humanity of the future must be built up on an intimate community of the nations, and that aggressive nationalism must be conquered, can see a future for Palestine only on the basis of peaceful cooperation between the two peoples that are at home in the country.

For this reason I should have expected that the great Arab people will show a truer appreciation of the need which the Jews feel to re-build their national home in the ancient seat of Judaism; I should have expected that by common effort ways and means would be found to render possible an extensive Jewish settlement in the country. I am convinced that the devotion of the Jewish people to Palestine will benefit all the inhabitants of the country, not only materially, but also culturally and nationally.

I believe that the Arab renaissance in the vast expanse of territory now occupied by the Arabs stands only to gain from Jewish sympathy. I should welcome the creation of an opportunity for absolutely free and frank discussions of these possibilities, for I believe that the two great Semitic peoples, each of which has in its way contributed something of lasting value to the civilization of the West, may have a great future in common, and that instead of facing each other with barren enmity and mutual distrust, they should support each other's national and cultural endeavours, and should seek the possibility of sympathetic cooperation. I think that those who are not actively engaged in politics, should above all contribute to the creation of this atmosphere of confidence.

I deplore the tragic events of last August not only because they revealed human nature in its lowest aspects, but also because they have estranged the two peoples and have made it temporarily more difficult for them to approach one another. But come together they must, in spite of all. »

↖↗ In the aftermath of the 1929 pogrom against the Jews of Hebron, Einstein wrote this letter to Azmi El-Nashashibi, the editor of the Palestinian Arab newspaper *Falastin*, January 28, 1930

EINSTEIN AND THE HOLOCAUST

Einstein had escaped from Germany under particularly favorable conditions and the United States welcomed him largely with open arms. Thus, he considered it his obligation to come to the aid of countless less favored Jewish and political refugees.

Einstein was particularly concerned with the plight of Jewish intellectuals from Germany and Austria and supported the concept to establish special universities to accommodate them.

Innumerable cries for help reached Einstein during the years the Nazis ruled a large part of Europe. Petitions came from relatives, near and far, from former colleagues and acquaintances and from relatives of these colleagues and acquaintances, and also from complete strangers. Those who could not refer to any personal connection at least appealed to Einstein's reputation as a large-hearted advocate of his tribesmen.
The missives contained stirring reports, photographs of imperiled children, elaborate curricula vitae and desperate calls for help; all were fraught with the hope that Einstein might bear an influence on the authorities which matched his public image as a world-renowned genius.

Einstein issued affidavits until the authorities did not accept his affidavits any more; he sent smaller and larger sums of money to needy people, mediated between petitioners, relief organizations and possible employers, and even "adopted" some "remote relatives" who could hardly draw upon an authentic family relationship in order to facilitate their immigration.

All in all, however, Einstein felt rather at a loss with the immense number of those who were seeking help.

When the full dimension of the Holocaust became known, Einstein was deeply affected. Shaken by the extent of man's inhumanity to man, he never felt up to reconciling with Germany again.

↓ With his secretary, Helen Dukas, October 2, 1940
Photo by Lucien Aigner

By the summer of 1938 Einstein had already received so many cries for help that he could tell friends:

« [I'm running a] broker's office for persecuted people and intellectual eccentrics, and I can assure you that it is an enormously swinging business. »

↑ From a letter to the widow of Paul Ehrenfest, Tatiana, August 4, 1938

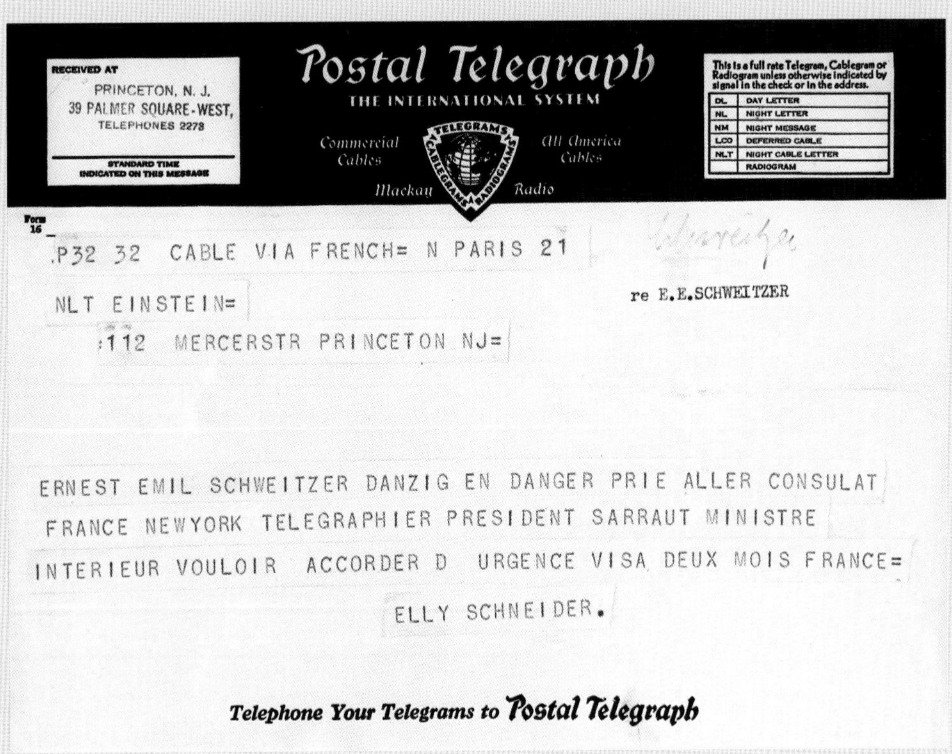

RECEIVED AT PRINCETON, N. J. 39 PALMER SQUARE-WEST, TELEPHONES 2278

STANDARD TIME INDICATED ON THIS MESSAGE

Postal Telegraph
THE INTERNATIONAL SYSTEM
Commercial Cables · All America Cables · Mackay Radio

This is a full rate Telegram, Cablegram or Radiogram unless otherwise indicated by signal in the check or in the address.

DL	DAY LETTER
NL	NIGHT LETTER
NM	NIGHT MESSAGE
LCO	DEFERRED CABLE
NLT	NIGHT CABLE LETTER
	RADIOGRAM

Form 16

.P32 32 CABLE VIA FRENCH= N PARIS 21

NLT EINSTEIN=
:112 MERCERSTR PRINCETON NJ=

re E.E.SCHWEITZER

ERNEST EMIL SCHWEITZER DANZIG EN DANGER PRIE ALLER CONSULAT FRANCE NEWYORK TELEGRAPHIER PRESIDENT SARRAUT MINISTRE INTERIEUR VOULOIR ACCORDER D URGENCE VISA DEUX MOIS FRANCE=
ELLY SCHNEIDER.

Telephone Your Telegrams to Postal Telegraph

« Ernest Emil Schweitzer Danzig in danger please go consulat France New York cable president Sarraut minister interior grant urgently visa two months France = Elly Schneider »

↖↑ Telegram from Elly von Schneider-Glend, April 1939.
The sender was a friend of Einstein's stepdaughters and, in a certain way, a member of the family. Soon after the Nazis came into power, she fled first to Switzerland, then settled in France. Ernst Emil Schweitzer, a well-known lawyer in Berlin and member of the League for Human Rights, lost his license in 1933, yet was apparently able to practice law in the Free City of Danzig until 1939.

« Request urgently residence permit required by Mr. Schweitzer Danzig motivation: imminent danger of death for political reasons Professor Einstein Princeton »

↑→ Message to be sent to the French Minister of Interior, Albert Sarraut. Einstein drafted the German text, along with his sister Maja's translation below.

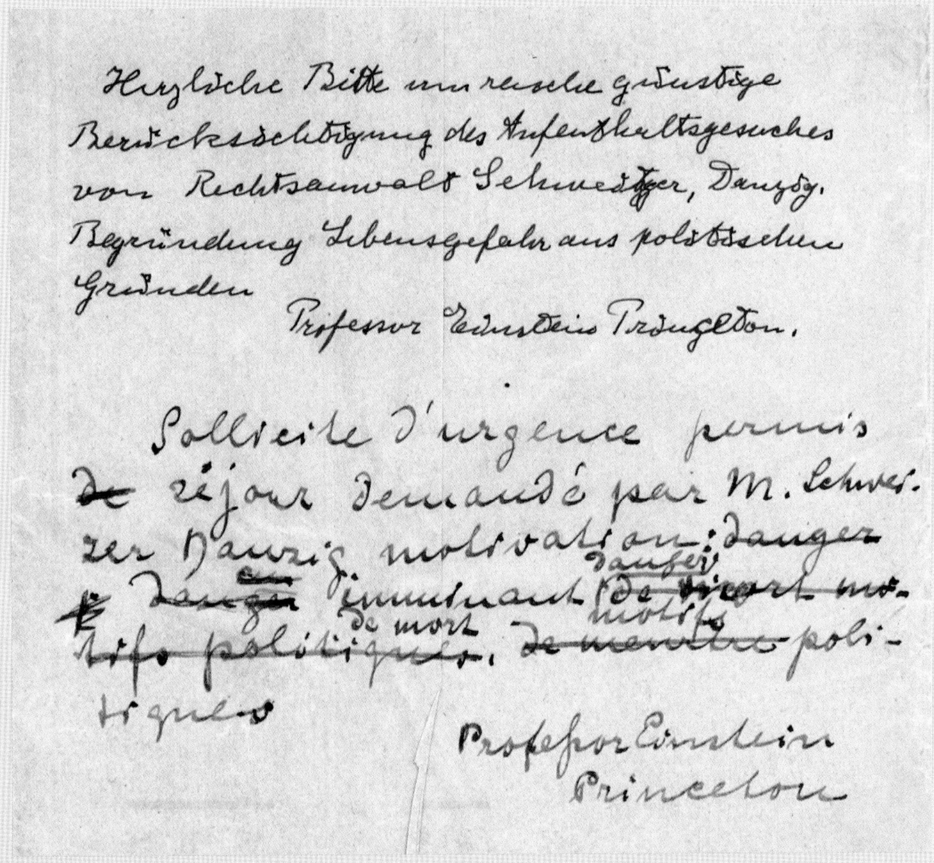

Herzliche Bitte um rasche günstige Berücksichtigung des Aufenthaltsgesuches von Rechtsanwalt Schweitzer, Danzig. Begründung Lebensgefahr aus politischen Gründen
Professor Einstein Princeton.

Sollicite d'urgence permis ~~de~~ séjour demandé par M. Schweitzer Danzig motivation: ~~danger~~ ~~danger~~ imminent ~~de mort~~ danger de mort ~~pour motifs politiques~~ ~~de manière~~ motifs politiques
Professor Einstein
Princeton

MINISTÈRE DE L'INTÉRIEUR
CABINET DU MINISTRE

LE CHEF DU CABINET

Paris, le 22 Avril
1939.

Monsieur le Professeur,

Vous avez bien voulu appeler par votre télégramme du 21 Avril l'attention de M.le Président Albert SARRAUT, Ministre de l'Intérieur, sur une demande d'entrée en France, formulé par M. Ernest SCHWEITZER, demeurant à Danzig.

Le Président me prie de vous faire connaître qu'il a immédiatement adressé au Ministère des Affaires Etrangères un avis favorable à l'entrée en France de M. SCHWEITZER.

Veuillez agréer, Monsieur le Professeur, l'assurance de ma haute considération.

Le Chef Adjoint du Cabinet

Monsieur le Professeur EINSTEIN,
112, Mercerstr. Princeton
New Jersey.
U.S.A.

↑→ Reply from the French Ministry of Interior, April 22, 1939.
Einstein's name opened the floodgates even in France.

« ... In your telegram of April 21 you kindly called the attention of President Albert Sarraut, the Minister of Interior, to a request by Ernst Schweitzer, Danzig, to enter France. The President asks me to convey to you that he has immediately sent a note to the Ministry of Foreign Affairs favoring Mr. Schweitzer's entrance to France... »

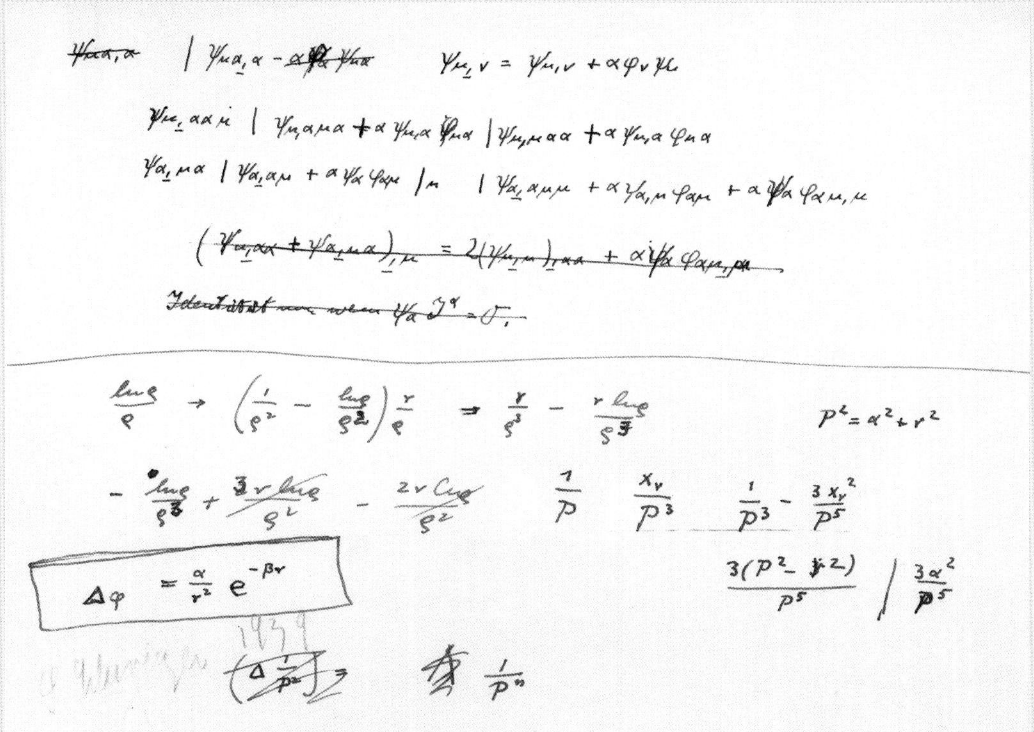
Herr Schweizer ist einer jener Tapferen ~~und rüstigen~~ Emigranten, die durch Änderung ihres Berufes und persönliche Tüchtigkeit sich erfolgreich in die Wirtschaft dieses Landes eingegliedert haben. Er hat aber auch ungeachtet der Schwere des eigenen Lebenskampfes einen Teil seiner Kraft eingesetzt, um ~~Landsleuten~~ uns den gegenwärtigen Lebensgefahr zu retten.

Ich bitte diejenigen amerikanischen Juden, an die er sich wendet, ihm in seinem Hilfswerk beizustehen. Ihr müsst bedenken, dass jüdische Solidarität ~~die~~ einzige ~~für~~ wirklich dauernd zuverlässige Notanker ist, auf den wir Juden in Zeiten bitterer Not bauen können. Ihr wisst auch, dass durch organisierte Hilfeleistung für die Einwanderer dafür gesorgt ist, dass Ihr ohne Gefährdung eures eigenen ökonomischen Gleichgewichts Affidavits geben könnt. Dies zu thun ist heute die Pflicht jedes aufrechten Juden in diesem Lande, der über nachweisbares Einkommen von dem gesetzlich erforderlichen Betrage verfügt.

A. E.

↑↗ Undated draft of a letter of recommendation.
Is the Mr. Schweizer, introduced here, the lawyer on behalf of whom Einstein intervened with the French authorities, when France was still a harbor of refuge? Yet even if the immigrant to the U.S., Mr. Schweizer, is only a namesake of M. Schweitzer, this draft gives evidence of Einstein's generous efforts in support of the refugees.

« Mr. Schweizer is one of those courageous emigrants who, by change of profession and personal competence, have succeeded in integrating into the economy of this country. In spite of the hardships of his own struggle for life, he invested a part of his energy to save his fellow-countrymen from the present deadly peril.
I request those American Jews to whom he turns, to provide him with assistance for his aid work.
You have to keep in mind that Jewish solidarity is the only really constantly reliable emergency anchor that we Jews can depend on in times of bitter distress. You also know that due to organized aid for immigrants, you can give affidavits without jeopardizing your financial equilibrium. To do that is today the obligation of every honest Jew in this country whose disposable attestable income reaches the legally required sum. »

→ Albert Einstein, Princeton, April 1940.

« Today's solemn meeting has deep significance. Few years separate us from the most horrible mass crime that modern history has to relate; a crime committed not by a fanatical mob, but in cold calculation by the government of a powerful nation. The plight of the surviving victims of German persecution bears witness to the degree to which the moral conscience of mankind has weakened.
Today's meeting shows that not all men are prepared to accept the Horror in silence. This meeting is inspired by the will to secure the dignity and the natural rights of individual man. It stands for the idea that a tolerable existence for man – and even his bare existence – is tied to our adherence to the external moral demands.
For this stand I wish to express my appreciation and thanks as a human being and as a Jew. »

↑ Message on the dedication of Riverside Drive Memorial to the Victims of the Holocaust, New York, October 19, 1947

→ As the successor of the Kaiser-Wilhelm-Gesellschaft, where Einstein had been a member until 1933, the Max-Planck-Gesellschaft was founded in 1948. Its president, Otto Hahn, one of the very few German colleagues Einstein still held in high esteem for his integrity, invited him to join the new society as a foreign scientific member. Einstein, however, did not wish to follow the example of many more conciliatory former colleagues and rejected the proposal. From his letter to Otto Hahn, January 28, 1949

« [...]
The crimes the Germans committed are actually the most heinous deeds that the history of the so-called civilized nations has ever exhibited. The attitude of the German intellectuals – viewed as a class – was not any better than that of the mob.
There isn't even any evidence of remorse and of an honest intention to restitute what might, after the gigantic murdering, still be restituted. Under these conditions, I feel an irresistible aversion against being involved with anything that represents a part of Germany's public life, and I feel it simply due to a need for cleanliness.
[...] »

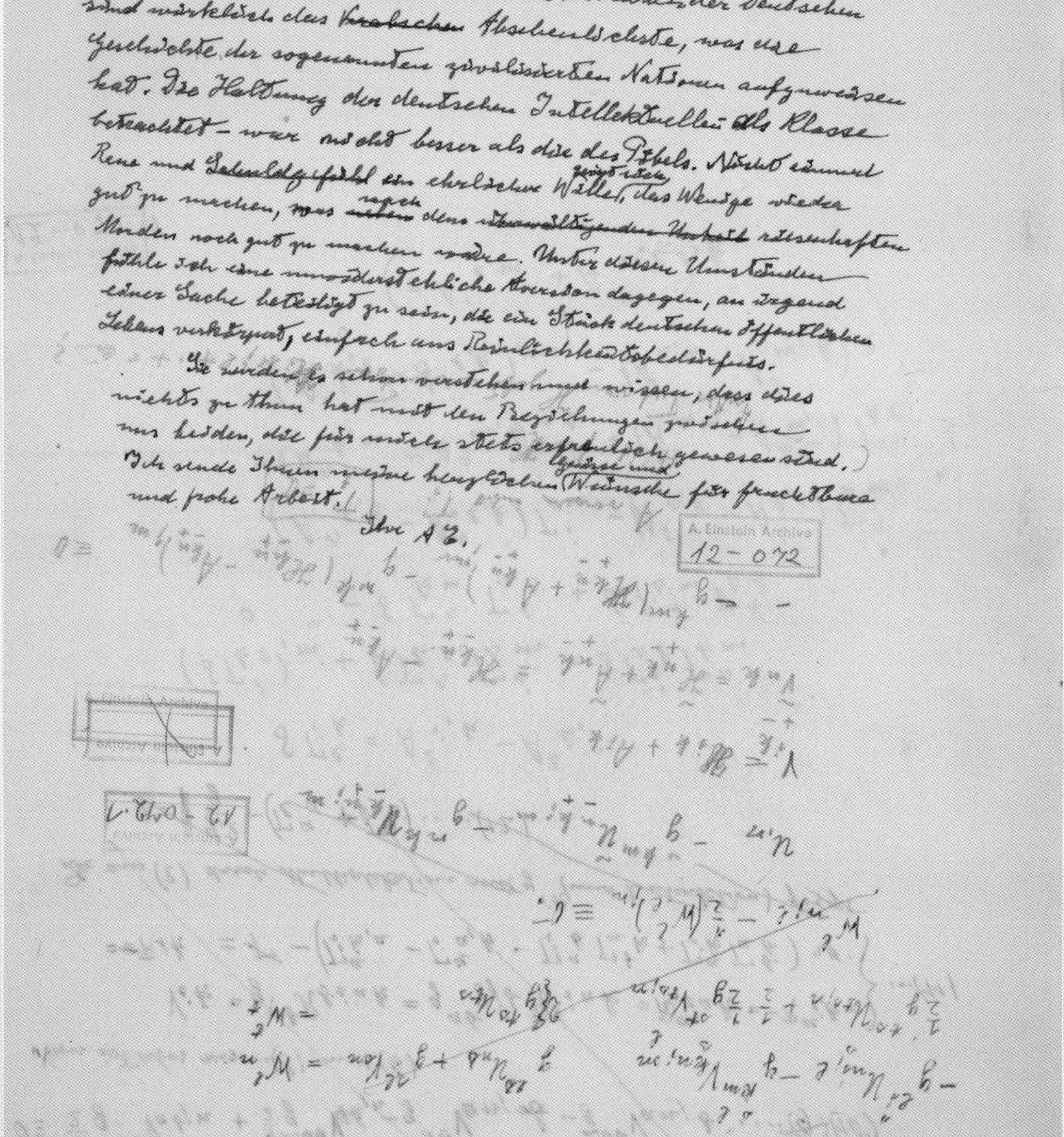

28. Jan. 1949

Lieber Herr Hahn!

Ich empfinde es schmerzlich, dass ich gerade Ihnen, d. h. einem der Wenigen, die aufrecht geblieben sind und Ihr Bestes taten während dieser bösen Jahre, eine Absage senden muss. Aber es geht nicht anders. Die Verbrechen der Deutschen sind wirklich das ~~krassesten~~ Abscheulichste, was die Geschichte der sogenannten zivilisierten Nationen aufzuweisen hat. Die Haltung der deutschen Intellektuellen – als Klasse betrachtet – war nicht besser als die des Pöbels. Nicht einmal Reue und ~~Schuldgefühl~~ ein ehrlicher Wille zeigt sich, das Wenige wieder gut zu machen, was ~~neben~~ nach dem ~~überwältigenden Unheil~~ riesenhaften Morden noch gut zu machen wäre. Unter diesen Umständen fühle ich eine unwiderstehliche Aversion dagegen, an irgend einer Sache beteiligt zu sein, die ein Stück deutschen öffentlichen Lebens verkörpert, einfach aus Reinlichkeitsbedürfnis.

Sie werden es schon verstehen und wissen, dass dies nichts zu thun hat mit den Beziehungen zwischen uns beiden, die für mich stets erfreulich gewesen sind.

Ich sende Ihnen meine herzlichen Grüsse und Wünsche für fruchtbare und frohe Arbeit.

Ihr A. E.

EINSTEIN AND THE PRESIDENCY OF ISRAEL

Upon the death of Chaim Weizmann, the first President of Israel, in November 1952, Einstein, the most famous Jew of the time, was proposed as his successor.
The editor-in-chief of the Hebrew daily, *Ma'ariv*, Azriel Carlebach, initiated a public campaign urging that the Israeli government offer the presidency of the state to Albert Einstein.
This proposal was taken up by Prime Minister David Ben-Gurion. To his aide, Yitzhak Navon, however, the Prime Minister expressed his skepticism: "Tell me what to do if he says yes! If he accepts, we are in for trouble."

Hearing rumors of the offer, members of the Einstein household jokingly started to appoint ministers. Yet before the official approach was made by Abba Eban, Israel's Ambassador to the US., Einstein had already made up his mind. Although he felt deeply moved by the offer, he declined with sincere regret.

↓ David Ben-Gurion, Prime Minister of Israel, visits Einstein in Princeton, May 13, 1951

EMBASSY OF ISRAEL
WASHINGTON, D.C.

שגרירות ישראל
וושינגטון

November 17, 1952

Dear Professor Einstein:

The bearer of this letter is Mr. David Goitein of Jerusalem who is now serving as Minister at our Embassy in Washington. He is bringing you the question which Prime Minister Ben Gurion asked me to convey to you, namely, whether you would accept the Presidency of Israel if it were offered you by a vote of the Knesset. Acceptance would entail moving to Israel and taking its citizenship. The Prime Minister assures me that in such circumstances complete facility and freedom to pursue your great scientific work would be afforded by a government and people who are fully conscious of the supreme significance of your labors.

Mr. Coitein will be able to give you any information that you may desire on the implications of the Prime Minister's question.

Whatever your inclination or decision may be, I should be deeply grateful for an opportunity to speak with you again within the next day or two at any place convenient for you. I understand the anxieties and doubts which you expressed to me this evening. On the other hand, whatever your answer, I am anxious for you to feel that the Prime Minister's question embodies the deepest respect which the Jewish people can repose in any of its sons. To this element of personal regard, we add the sentiment that Israel is a small State in its physical dimensions, but can rise to the level of greatness in the measure that it exemplifies the most elevated spiritual and intellectual traditions which the Jewish people has established through its best minds and hearts both in antiquity and in modern times. Our first President, as you know, taught us to see our destiny in these great perspectives, as you yourself have often exhorted us to do.

Therefore, whatever your response to this question, I hope that you will think generously of those who have asked it, and will commend the high purposes and motives which prompted them to think of you at this solemn hour in our people's history.

With cordial personal wishes,

Yours respectfully,

Abba Eban

Abba Eban

Professor Albert Einstein
Princeton, N.J.

↑ The official offer of the presidency of the State of Israel.
Letter from Abba Eban, Israeli ambassador to the United States, November 17, 1952

↓→ Draft of Einstein's response to the offer of the Israeli presidency, November 18, 1952

« I am deeply moved by the offer from our State of Israel, and at once saddened and ashamed that I cannot accept it. All my life I have dealt with objective matters, hence I lack both the natural aptitude and the experience to deal properly with people and to exercise official functions. For these reasons alone I should be unsuited to fulfill the duties of that high office, even if advancing age was not making increasing inroads on my strength.
I am the more distressed over these circumstances because my relationship to the Jewish people has become my strongest human bond, ever since I became fully aware of our precarious situation among the nations of the world. »

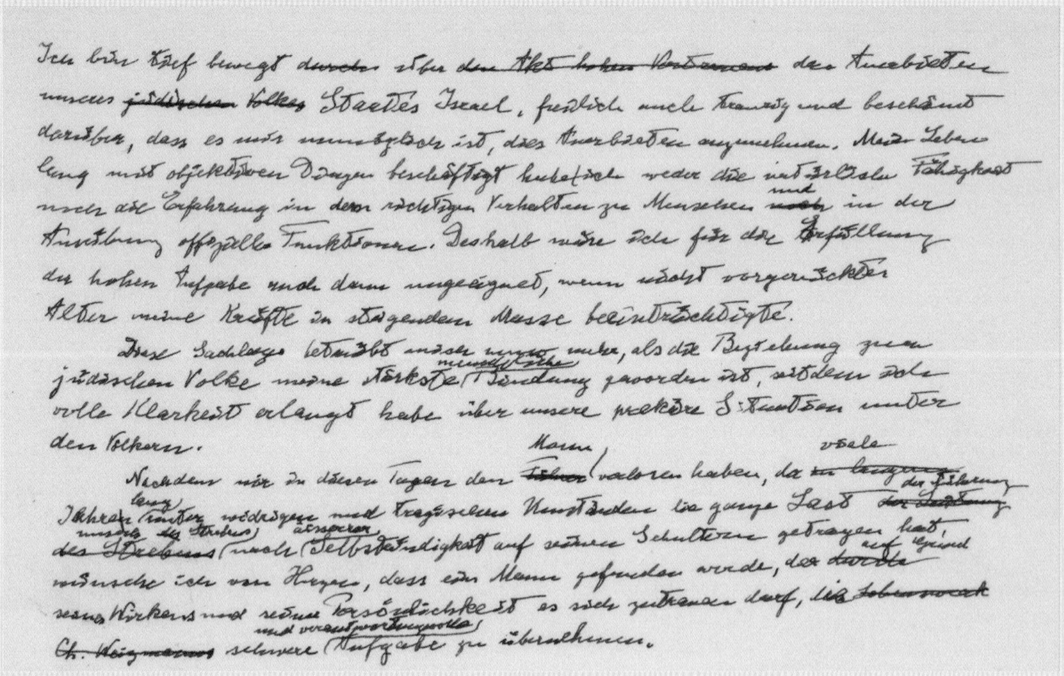
Ich bin tief bewegt durch das Anerbieten unseres Staates Israel, freilich auch traurig und beschämt darüber, dass es mir unmöglich ist, das Anerbieten anzunehmen. Mein Leben lang mit objektiven Dingen beschäftigt habe ich weder die natürliche Fähigkeit noch die Erfahrung im richtigen Verhalten zu Menschen und in der Ausübung offizieller Funktionen. Deshalb wäre ich für die Erfüllung der hohen Aufgabe auch dann ungeeignet, wenn nicht vorgerückter Alter meine Kräfte in steigendem Masse beeinträchtigte.
Diese Sachlage betrübt mich umso mehr, als die Beziehung zum jüdischen Volke meine stärkste menschliche Bindung geworden ist, seitdem ich volle Klarheit erlangt habe über unsere prekäre Situation unter den Völkern.
Nachdem wir in diesen Tagen den Mann verloren haben, der viele Jahre lang unter widrigen und tragischen Umständen die ganze Last der Führung unseres Strebens nach Selbständigkeit auf seinen Schultern getragen hat, wünsche ich von Herzen, dass ein Mann gefunden werde, der auf Grund seines Wirkens und seiner Persönlichkeit es sich zutrauen darf, die schwere und verantwortungsvolle Aufgabe zu übernehmen.

↓→ In his letter to Azriel Carlebach, editor-in-chief of the popular daily *Ma'ariv*, Einstein reveals reasons for rejecting the post of Israeli president not included in his official response. November 21, 1952

« [...]
You may imagine how difficult I found it to decline the offer, moving as it was, and coming from our own people. [...]
What I said in [my formal answer to the Israeli embassy in Washington] accurately reflects my thoughts and feelings. There is no doubt that I would not have been able to cope with the task awaiting me there, even though the position has a mainly ceremonial character. My name alone cannot compensate for this deficiency.
Also, I have taken into consideration what a strained situation would arise when the government or the parliament makes decisions which might put me into a moral conflict, all the more so as the moral responsibility is not relieved by the fact that, actually, one has no influence on the course of events. I have the highest respect for the great energy you have devoted to this cause, and I am grateful for the confidence revealed by your action. Yet I am convinced as well, that I should have done a disservice to the important matter, had I responded to the tempting and honorable call. [...]

den 21.November 1952

Herrn
Dr.Azriel Carlebach, Chef-Redakteur
MAARIV
Tel-Aviv, Israel.

Sehr geehrter Herr Dr.Carlebach:

Ich schreibe Ihnen deutsch, einmal weil es mir leichter ist, ferner weil Sie Ihren Ursprung dadurch genügend manifestiert haben, dass Sie sich als Doktor bezeichnen.

Als einem hausväterischen Kleinbürger hat die Länge Ihres Cabels einen geradezu niederschmetternden Eindruck auf mich gemacht. Es kam aber post festum an, indem ich infolge einer Indiskretion zu frühzeitig gezwungen wurde, zu der Angelegenheit Stellung zu nehmen.

Sie können sich denken, wie schwer es mir wurde, ein so rührendes Angebot, das von den Eigenen kommt, abzulehnen. Aus der J.T.A. sehe ich, dass meine wirkliche Antwort (die vor Eintreffen Ihres Cabels bereits an unsere Botschaft in Washington abgegangen war) dem Wortlaute nach bekannt ist. Das dort Gesagte ist genau der Ausdruck meines Fühlens und Denkens. Es ist kein Zweifel, dass ich der Aufgabe, die mich dort erwartet hätte, nicht gewachsen gewesen wäre, obschon das Amt in der Hauptsache nur dekorativen Character hat. Mein Name allein kann diese Schwächen nicht ausgleichen.

Ich habe auch daran gedacht, was für eine schwierige Situation entstünde, wenn die Regierung, bezw. das Parlament Dinge beschliessen würde, die mich in einen Gewissenskonflikt bringen würden, zumal die moralische Verantwortung nicht durch die Tatsache aufgehoben wird, dass man de facto keinen Einfluss auf die Ereignisse hat. - Ich habe alle Hochachtung vor der grossen Energie, die Sie dieser Sache gewidmet haben und bin dankbar für das Vertrauen, das aus Ihrer Handlungsweise spricht. Ich bin aber auch davon überzeugt, dass ich der grossen Sache einen schlechten Dienst geleistet hätte, wenn ich dem ehrenvollen und verführerischen Rufe gefolgt wäre.

Herzlich grüsst Sie

Ihr

Albert Einstein.

P.S.
Inwieweit es angezeigt ist, von Ihrem Telegram und dieser meiner Antwort öffentlichen Gebrauch zu machen, kann ich von hier aus nicht beurteilen. Ich überlasse die Entscheidung hierüber Ihrem Takt und Ihrer Erfahrung.

EINSTEIN AND THE HEBREW UNIVERSITY IN JERUSALEM

Due to his concern for the plight of young Jewish academics and students who faced restriction quotas at Eastern European universities, Einstein became involved with the project to set up a Jewish university in Jerusalem. It was this cause that first stirred Einstein's interest in the Zionist movement shortly after the First World War.

Beginning in 1919, Einstein played a major role in discussions concerning the establishment of The Hebrew University. The main purpose of his first trip to the U.S. in 1921 was to raise funds for the university's planned medical faculty.

During his only visit to Palestine in 1923, he gave the university's inaugural scientific lecture on Mount Scopus, where The Hebrew University would eventually open its doors two years later. That same year he edited the university's first scientific publication. From the 1920s onwards, Einstein also played a central role in the development of the Jewish National & University Library: he allowed his name to be used for fund-raising and donated hundreds of books and periodicals to the library.
Upon its opening in 1925, The Hebrew University received the original manuscript of Einstein's general theory of relativity.

Einstein also served as a member of The Hebrew University's first Board of Governors and as Chairman of its first Academic Council. However, major differences of opinion developed between Einstein and the Chancellor, J.L. Magnes, concerning the running of the university. Einstein was opposed to the influence of American philanthropists on the handling of academic affairs and not willing to compromise on academic standards. He advocated a German model whereby the academics would have the decisive say. In 1928, he resigned from his official posts at the university, yet remained closely involved in its affairs. When, in 1935, Einstein's views were adopted by the university, he resumed his official ties.
During the several decades of his affiliation with the university, he repeatedly stressed the institution's social and cultural importance for Israel and the Jewish people. As a lasting expression of this special association, he bequeathed his personal papers and literary estate to the university in his Last Will and Testament.

→ Einstein and his colleague and friend, chemist Fritz Haber, Berlin, July 1, 1914

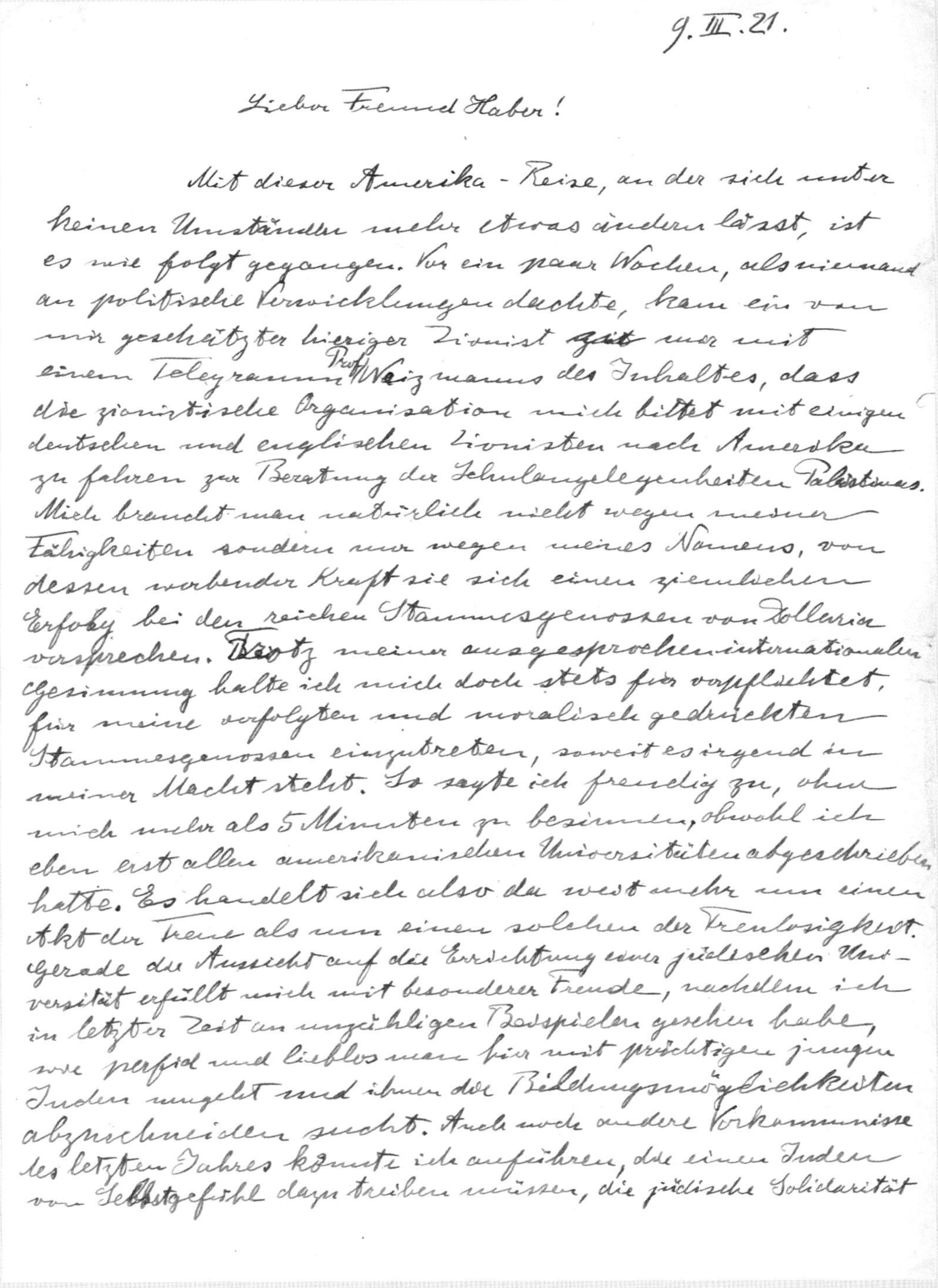

9. III. 21.

Lieber Freund Haber!

Mit dieser Amerika-Reise, an der sich unter keinen Umständen mehr etwas ändern lässt, ist es wie folgt gegangen. Vor ein paar Wochen, als niemand an politische Verwicklungen dachte, kam ein von mir geschätzter hiesiger Zionist ~~zu~~ mir mit einem Telegramm Prof. Weizmanns des Inhaltes, dass die zionistische Organisation mich bittet mit einigen deutschen und englischen Zionisten nach Amerika zu fahren zur Beratung der Schulangelegenheiten Palästinas. Mich braucht man natürlich nicht wegen meiner Fähigkeiten sondern nur wegen meines Namens, von dessen werbender Kraft sie sich einen ziemlichen Erfolg bei den reichen Stammesgenossen von Dollaria versprechen. Trotz meiner ausgesprochen internationalen Gesinnung halte ich mich doch stets für verpflichtet, für meine verfolgten und moralisch gedrückten Stammesgenossen einzutreten, soweit es irgend in meiner Macht steht. So sagte ich freudig zu, ohne mich mehr als 5 Minuten zu besinnen, obwohl ich eben erst allen amerikanischen Universitäten abgeschrieben hatte. Es handelt sich also da weit mehr um einen Akt der Treue als um einen solchen der Treulosigkeit. Gerade die Aussicht auf die Errichtung einer jüdischen Universität erfüllt mich mit besonderer Freude, nachdem ich in letzter Zeit an unzähligen Beispielen gesehen habe, wie perfid und lieblos man hier mit prächtigen jungen Juden umgeht und ihnen die Bildungsmöglichkeiten abzuschneiden sucht. Auch noch andere Vorkommnisse des letzten Jahres könnte ich anführen, die einen Juden von Selbstgefühl dazu treiben müssen, die jüdische Solidarität

↑↗ From a letter to Fritz Haber, March 9, 1921

« A couple of weeks ago […] a local Zionist whom I appreciate approached me with a telegram from Prof. Weizmann informing me that the Zionist Organization requests I join some German and English Zionists on their trip to America on behalf of Palestinian school issues. They certainly do not need me for my competence but only for my name, whose publicity impact, they reckon, will bring success with the rich members of the tribe of Dollaria. Despite my outspoken internationalist position, I always feel obliged to stand up, as much as possible, for my persecuted and morally oppressed tribesmen. […] Especially the prospect of the establishment of a Jewish University fills me with particular joy, since I have seen how perfidiously and heartlessly they are dealing here with fine young Jews and are attempting to cut them off from getting an education. »

294 THE NEW PALESTINE March 27, 1925

The Mission of Our University

By ALBERT EINSTEIN

THE opening of our Hebrew University on Mount Scopus, at Jerusalem, is an event which should not only fill us with just pride, but should also inspire us to serious reflection.

A University is a place where the universality of the human spirit manifests itself. Science and investigation recognize as their aim the truth only. It is natural, therefore, that institutions which serve the interests of science should be a factor making for the union of nations and men. Unfortunately, the universities of Europe today are for the most part the nurseries of chauvinism and of a blind intolerance of all things foreign to the particular nation or race, of all things bearing the stamp of a different individuality. Under this regime the Jews are the principal sufferers, not only because they are thwarted in their desire for free participation and in their striving for education, but also because most Jews find themselves particularly cramped in this spirit of narrow nationalism. On this occasion of the birth of our University, I should like to express the hope that our University will always be free from this evil, that teachers and students will always preserve the consciousness that they serve their people best when they maintain its union with humanity and with the highest human values.

Jewish nationalism is today a necessity because only through a consolidation of our national life can we eliminate those conflicts from which the Jews suffer today. May the time soon come when this nationalism will have become so thoroughly a matter of course that it will no longer be necessary for us to give it special emphasis. Our affiliation with our past and with the present-day achievements of our people inspires us with assurance and pride *vis-à-vis* the entire world. But our educational institutions in particular must regard it as one of their noblest tasks to keep our people free from nationalistic obscurantism and aggressive intolerance.

Our University is still a modest undertaking. It is quite the correct policy to begin with a number of research institutes, and the University will develop naturally and organically. I am convinced that this development will make rapid progress and that in the course of time this institution will demonstrate with the greatest clearness the achievements of which the Jewish spirit is capable.

A special task devolves upon the University in the spiritual direction and education of the laboring sections of our people in the land. In Palestine it is not our aim to create another people of city dwellers leading the same life as in the European cities and possessing the European bourgeois standards and conceptions. We aim at creating a people of workers, at creating the Jewish village in the first place, and we desire that the treasures of culture should be accessible to our laboring class, especially since, as we know, Jews, in all circumstances, place education above all things. In this connection it devolves upon the University to create something unique in order to serve the specific needs of the forms of life developed by our people in Palestine.

All of us desire to cooperate in order that the University may accomplish its mission. May the realization of the significance of this cause penetrate among the large masses of Jewry. Then our University will develop speedily into a great spiritual center which will evoke the respect of cultured mankind the world over.

← In this article, published on the occasion of the opening of The Hebrew University, Einstein affirms the universalism of scientific work and warns against narrow-minded nationalism. *The New Palestine*, March 27, 1925

↑ Arriving in the United States on April 2, 1921:
Benzion Mossinson, Albert Einstein,
Chaim Weizmann and Menahem Ussishkin.

The
PALESTINE ZIONIST EXECUTIVE
Request the pleasure of your
company at a lecture to be given
by Prof.
ALBERT EINSTEIN
on
"The Theory of Relativity"
At the Hebrew University House,
Mount Scopus,
On Wednesdy Feb. 7th at 4.30 p.m.

حضرة افاضل
الادارة الصهيونية تدعو حضرتكم للحضور
الى المحاضرة التى سيلقيها
« البروفسور البرت آينشتين »
في موضوع :
« شريعة التناسب »
وستلقى المحاضرة يوم الاربعاء ٧ شباط
سنة ١٩٢٣ الساعة ٤ ونصف بعد الظهر
بعمارة الكلية الاسرائيلية على جبل الطور

ההנהלה הציונית בארץ־ישראל
מזמינה את כב׳ להרצאה
של הפרופסור
אלברט אינשטין
על הנושא:
"תורת היחסיות"
ההרצאה תהיה ביום הרביעי בשעה ארבע וחצי אחה"צ
בבית המכללה העברית שעל "הר הצופים".

↑ Invitation to Einstein's lecture at the site of
The Hebrew University to-be, February 7, 1923

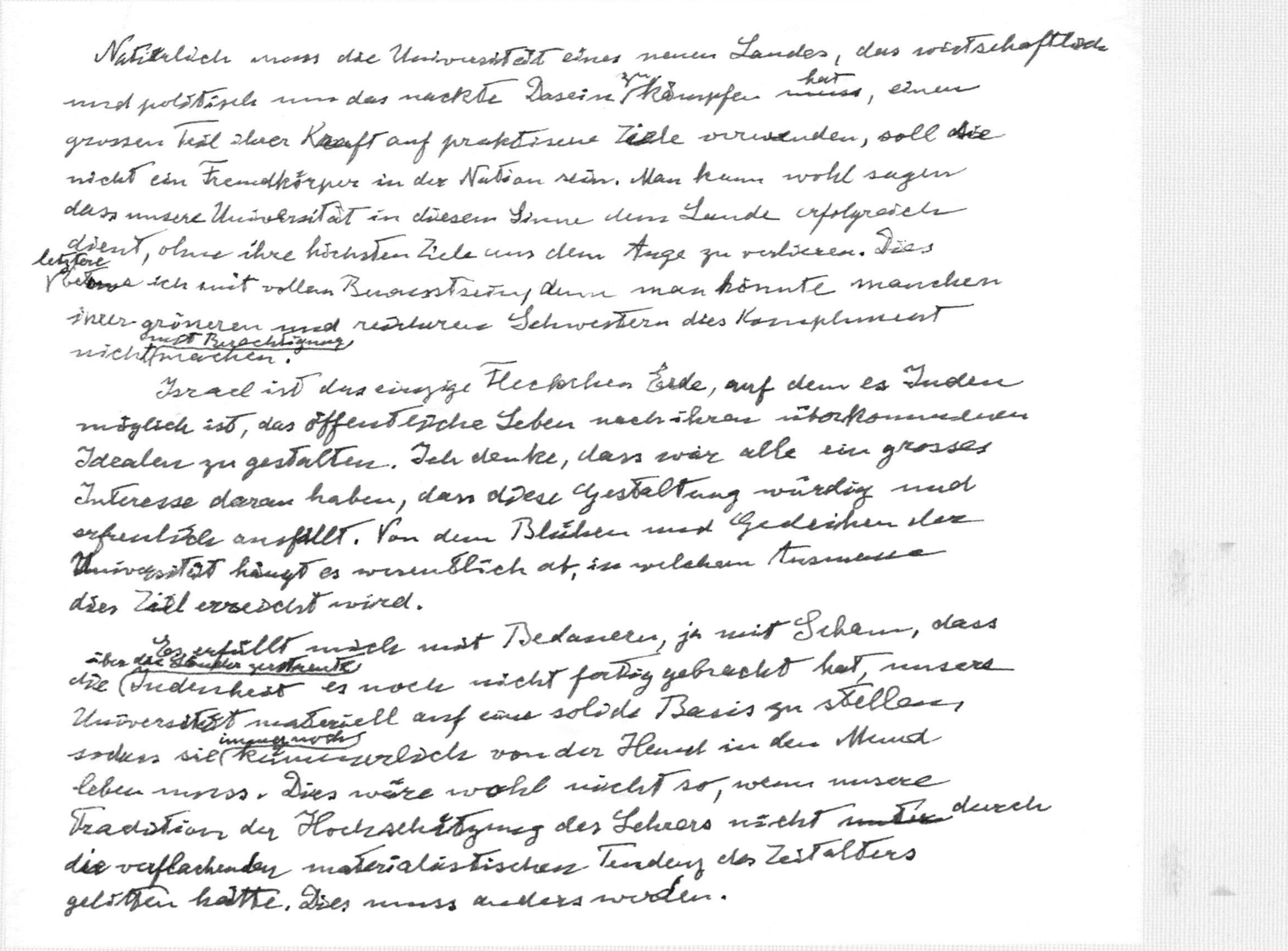

Natürlich muss die Universität eines neuen Landes, das wirtschaftlich und politisch um das nackte Dasein zu kämpfen hat, einen grossen Teil ihrer Kraft auf praktische Ziele verwenden, soll sie nicht ein Fremdkörper in der Nation sein. Man kann wohl sagen dass unsere Universität in diesem Sinne dem Lande erfolgreich dient, ohne ihre höchsten Ziele aus dem Auge zu verlieren. Dies letztere betone ich mit vollem Bewusstsein, denn man könnte manchen ihrer grösseren und reicheren Schwestern dies Kompliment mit Berechtigung nicht machen.

Israel ist das einzige Fleckchen Erde, auf dem es Juden möglich ist, das öffentliche Leben nach ihren überkommenen Idealen zu gestalten. Ich denke, dass wir alle ein grosses Interesse daran haben, dass diese Gestaltung würdig und erfreulich ausfällt. Von dem Blühen und Gedeihen der Universität hängt es wesentlich ab, in welchem Ausmasse dies Ziel erreicht wird.

Es erfüllt mich mit Bedauern, ja mit Scham, dass die über die Länder zerstreute Judenheit es noch nicht fertig gebracht hat, unsere Universität materiell auf eine solide Basis zu stellen, sodass sie immer noch kümmerlich von der Hand in den Mund leben muss. Dies wäre wohl nicht so, wenn unsere Tradition der Hochschätzung des Lehrers nicht durch die verflachenden materialistischen Tendenz des Zeitalters gelitten hätte. Dies muss anders werden.

↑→ From a draft of a message to the Friends of The Hebrew University, September 19, 1954

« [...]
Israel is the only place on earth where Jews have the possibility to shape public life according to their traditional ideals. I think we all are greatly concerned that its final shape will be worthy and gratifying. To what extent this goal will be reached depends significantly on the growth and development of the university.
[...] »

↖ Einstein receives an honorary degree from The Hebrew University, at his office at the Institute for Advanced Study, Princeton, 1951 (with Leo Schwartz and High Salpeter of the American Friends of the Hebrew University)
Photo by Edward H. Zwerin

← Einstein with Eliahu Elath, Israel's ambassador to the U.S., May 1950. Elath served as President of The Hebrew University from 1962 to 1968
Photo by Edward H. Zwerin

5

EINSTEIN AND THE UNITED STATES

« It is now two months that I have been in this country of contradictions and surprises, where one alternates between admiration and headshaking. One realizes that one is attached to old Europe with its hardships and heartaches ... »

To Queen Elisabeth of Belgium, February 9, 1931

ON AMERICA

Like many European intellectuals', Einstein's attitude towards the United States was a mixture of admiration, irreverence and, at times, bewilderment.

Some controversial statements, reflecting his perplexity, and meant to be quickly dropped jokes rather than mature judgments, were published without Einstein's consent upon his return from his first trip to the U.S. in 1921.

This trip was a sort of triumphal procession through a country where the lionized Einstein may indeed have received the impression, as the newspapers quoted, that the Americans are so unusually bored and suffering from spiritual poverty, that they are "happy when they are given something to play with and which they can revere," as was the case with the "Einstein-craze."

After those statements had provoked fierce public criticism, Einstein hastened to rectify some flagrant distortions and stressed the warmth and cordiality, the impartiality and the team spirit he had encountered among the Americans.

↓ The "Einstein craze": thousands cheered as his motorcade drove to City Hall where he was welcomed by Mayor James J. Hylan. New York, April 4, 1921

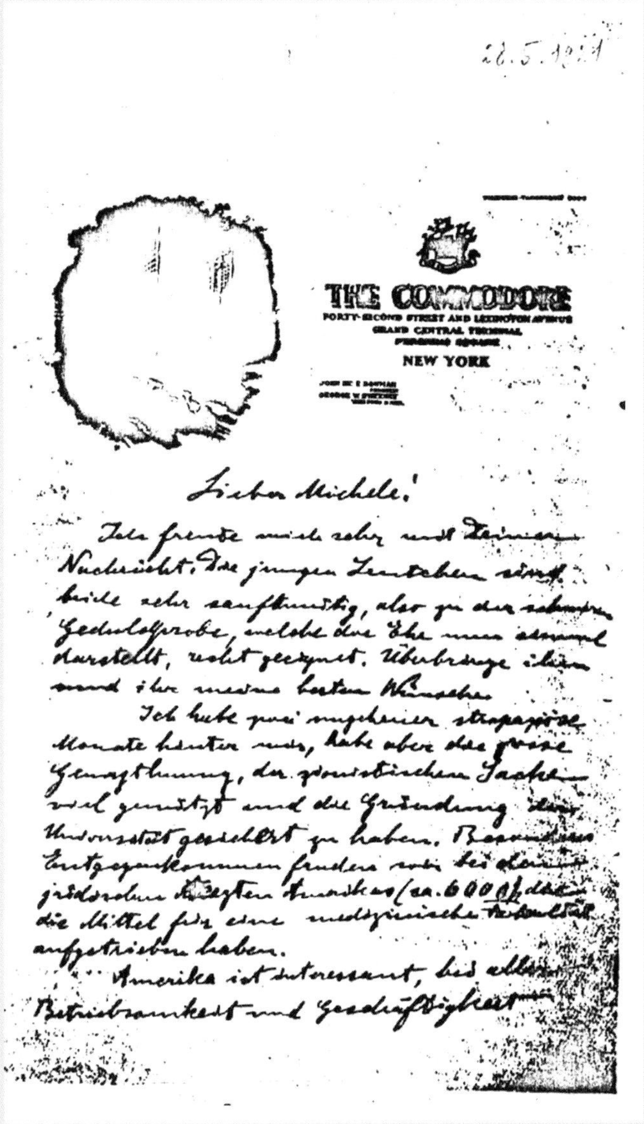

28.5.1921

THE COMMODORE
FORTY-SECOND STREET AND LEXINGTON AVENUE
GRAND CENTRAL TERMINAL
NEW YORK

Lieber Michele!

Ich freute mich sehr mit Deiner Nachricht. Die jungen Leutchen sind beide sehr sanftmütig, aber zu der schweren Geduldsprobe, welche die Ehe nun einmal darstellt, nicht geeignet. Überbringe ihnen und ihr meine besten Wünsche.

Ich habe zwei ungeheuer strapaziöse Monate hinter mir, habe aber die grosse Genugthuung, der zionistischen Sache viel genützt und die Gründung der Universität gesichert zu haben. Besonderes Entgegenkommen fanden wir bei den jüdischen Ärzten Amerikas (ca. 6000), die die Mittel für eine medizinische Fakultät aufgetrieben haben.

Amerika ist interessant, bei aller Betriebsamkeit und Geschäftigkeit

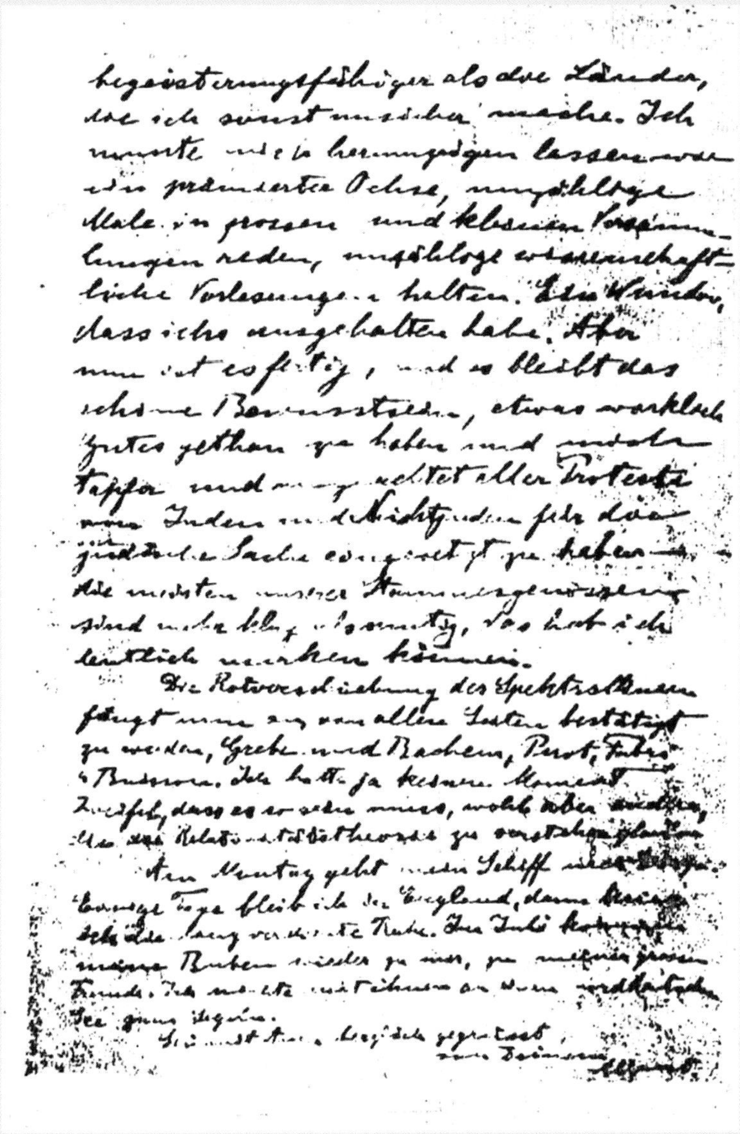

begeisterungsfähiger als die Länder, die ich sonst unsicher mache. Ich musste mich herumzeigen lassen wie ein prämierter Ochse, unzählige Male in grossen und kleinen Versammlungen reden, unzählige wissenschaftliche Vorlesungen halten. Ein Wunder, dass ichs ausgehalten habe. Aber nun ist es fertig, und es bleibt das schöne Bewusstsein, etwas wirklich Gutes gethan zu haben und mich tapfer und ungeachtet aller Proteste von Juden und Nichtjuden für die jüdische Sache eingesetzt zu haben. Die meisten unserer Stammesgenossen sind mehr klug als mutig, das habe ich deutlich merken können.

Die Rotverschiebung der Spektrallinien fängt nun an von allen Seiten bestätigt zu werden, Grebe und Bachem, Perot, Fabry & Buisson. Ich hatte ja keinen Moment Zweifel, dass es so sein muss, wohl aber andere, die die Relativitätstheorie zu verstehen glauben.

Am Montag geht mein Schiff nach England. Einige Tage bleibe ich in England, dann [illegible] die lang ersehnte Ruhe. Im Juli kommen meine Buben wieder zu mir, zu meiner grossen Freude. Ich möchte mit ihnen an einem nordischen See ganz [illegible].

Sei mit Anna herzlich gegrüsst von Deinem Albert.

↑→ Letter to Michele Besso, May 28, 1921

« […]
America is interesting – for all its bustling activity it is more capable of enthusiasm than the other countries that I'm usually haunting. I had to let myself be shown around like a prize-winning ox, talk at countless large and small assemblies, hold innumerable scientific lectures. It's a miracle I could stand it all. But now it's over and what remains is the pleasant awareness that I've accomplished something really worthwhile, and that I fought bravely for the Jewish cause in spite of all the protests from Jews and Gentiles
[…] »

In 1931, in a speech given toward the end of his first stay in California, Einstein expressed his high regard for America's democratic system, its scientific institutions and technology, and its optimism, philanthropy, and organizational capabilities. Yet he was critical of what he perceived as the materialism and conformism of American society, the commercialism of its culture, and its political isolationism.
Two years later, Einstein took up residence in Princeton as a refugee from Germany.
By March 1934, Congress proposed to grant him citizenship, but he rejected any preferential treatment. Only in the following year did Einstein decide to settle permanently in America and apply for citizenship. After the customary qualifying period, on October 1, 1940, Einstein became an American citizen.

During World War II, the FBI considered Einstein a risk to national security and objected to his receiving information on the progress of the atomic bomb project. Nevertheless, the U.S. Navy asked Einstein to carry out some work for them on high explosives.
Following the war, Einstein determinedly expressed his criticism of America's official policies, of its role in the nuclear arms race, the separation between white and black citizens, as well as between Jews and Gentiles, and he warned of the dangers to democracy of McCarthyism and of unrestrained capitalism.

↙↓ A long letter by Harvard Law Professor Felix Frankfurter, commenting on Einstein's first visit to the United States and anticipating another visit which, however, took place only a decade after July 1, 1921.

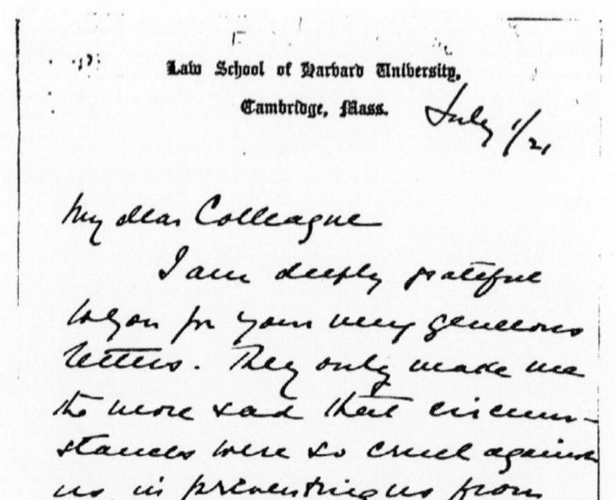

Law School of Harvard University,
Cambridge, Mass. July 1/21

My dear Colleague

I am deeply grateful to you for your very generous letters. They only make me the more sad that circumstances were so cruel against us, in preventing us from having a real talk, and [illegible], during your visit. What is past is past. But I am abidingly grateful for the complete candor and heartiness of your letters. It would have been too cruel were it left otherwise between us -

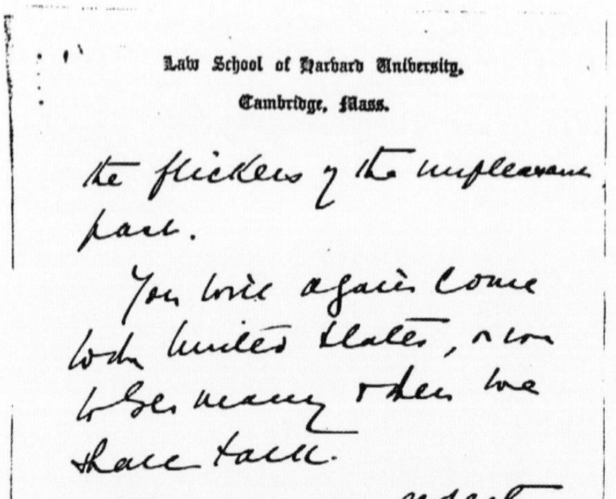

Law School of Harvard University,
Cambridge, Mass.

the flickers of the unpleasant past.

You will again come to the United States, and to Germany, and then we shall talk.

Please give my respects to Frau Einstein.

With high regard

Very sincerely

Felix Frankfurter

→ Letter from Robert A. Millikan informing Einstein of his election to the National Academy of Sciences, May 22, 1922

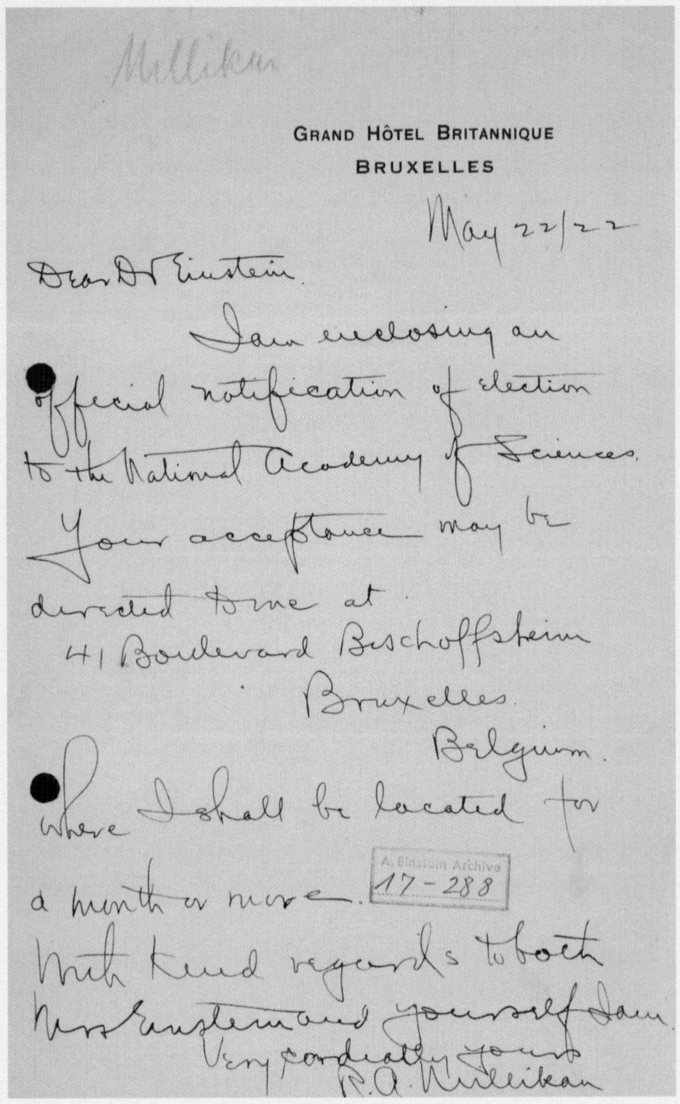

Millikan

GRAND HÔTEL BRITANNIQUE
BRUXELLES

May 22/22

Dear Dr Einstein.

I am enclosing an official notification of election to the National Academy of Sciences. Your acceptance may be directed to me at
41 Boulevard Bischoffsheim
Bruxelles.
Belgium.
where I shall be located for a month or more.

With kind regards to both Mrs Einstein and yourself I am
Very cordially yours
R. A. Millikan

A. Einstein Archive
17-288

↓ Honorary diploma of the National Academy of Sciences of the United States of America stating that Einstein has been elected a foreign associate of the Academy, April 26, 1922

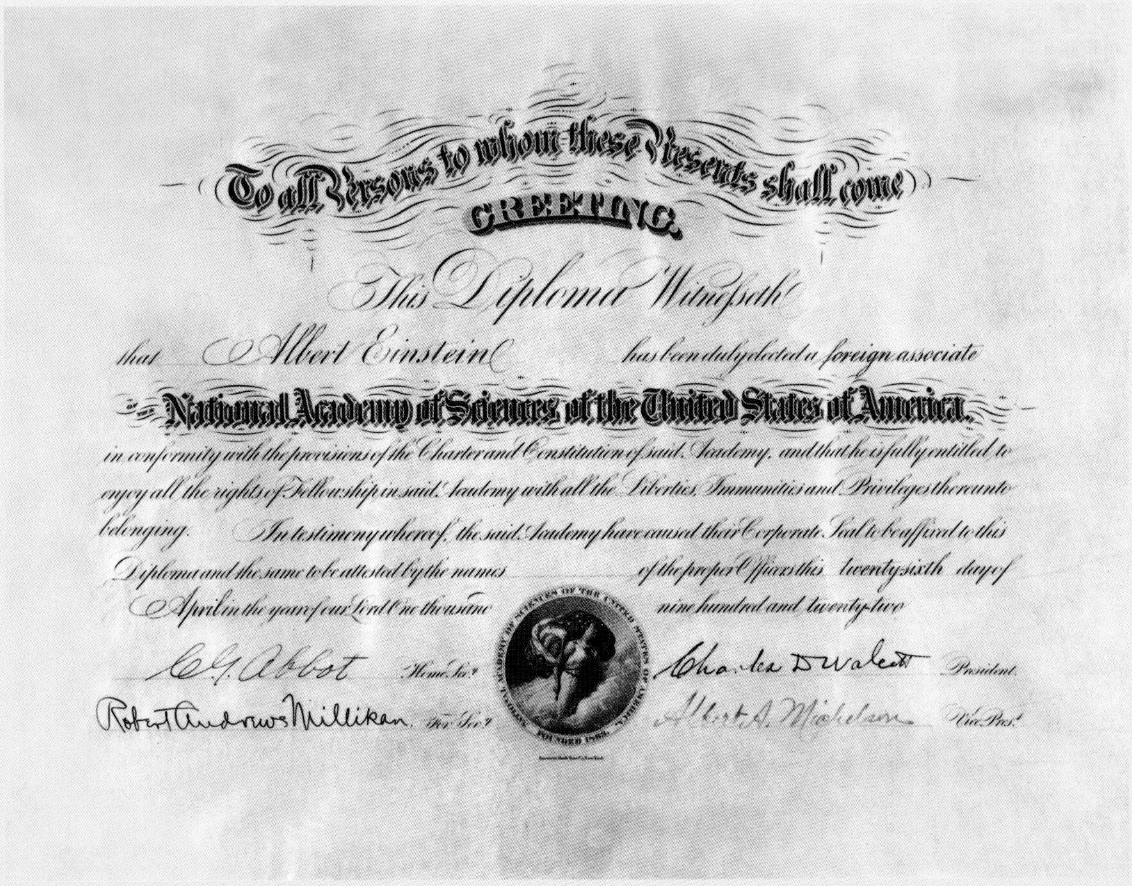

To all Persons to whom these Presents shall come
GREETING.

This Diploma Witnesseth

that Albert Einstein has been duly elected a foreign associate of the National Academy of Sciences of the United States of America, in conformity with the provisions of the Charter and Constitution of said Academy, and that he is fully entitled to enjoy all the rights of Fellowship in said Academy with all the Liberties, Immunities and Privileges thereunto belonging. In testimony whereof, the said Academy have caused their Corporate Seal to be affixed to this Diploma and the same to be attested by the names of the proper Officers this twenty sixth day of April in the year of our Lord One thousand nine hundred and twenty-two

C. G. Abbot Home Sec.y
Charles D. Walcott President
Robert Andrews Millikan For. Sec.y
Albert A. Michelson Vice Pres.t

AT THE CALIFORNIA INSTITUTE OF TECHNOLOGY

Einstein spent the winter semesters of three consecutive years – from 1930/31 to 1932/33 – at the California Institute of Technology in Pasadena. When he arrived for the first time in December 1930, he was immediately struck by the unfamiliar landscape, so different from the Central European countryside. The travel diaries he kept during his recurring sojourns in California reveal that he fully enjoyed spending the winter months there.

The invitation to serve as a visiting professor was made by Robert A. Millikan, the first president of Caltech, who in 1916 had provided an experimental verification of Einstein's equation of the photoelectric effect. It gave Einstein the opportunity to meet an impressive community of theoretical physicists.
Among them was Albert A. Michelson, known for the Michelson-Morley experiment of 1887, which attempted to measure the relative motion of the earth through a hypothetical ether, and thus preceded Einstein's conclusion in 1905 that the speed of light is a universal constant. Other colleagues included Richard C. Tolman and Paul S. Epstein, with whom Einstein could discuss various topical issues of relativity as well as his ongoing quest for a unified field theory, and William W. Campbell, who had provided one of the crucial verifications of general relativity.
The close proximity to Caltech of Mt Wilson Observatory enabled Einstein to confer with astronomers Charles E. St. John and Edwin P. Hubble who had just discovered the red shift effect and concluded that the universe was expanding, a conclusion that led to Einstein's revision of his theory of a cosmological constant.

Apart from intense scientific discussions and lectures he attended as well as delivered, Einstein also spoke at pacifist conferences and at fund-raising dinners mainly on behalf of the Jewish community.
Millikan disapproved of the political statements on pacifism, Nazism, and American domestic affairs Einstein made during his visits to the Institute. Nevertheless, Caltech's board invited Einstein to accept a permanent position at the Institute, but Einstein declined for practical reasons.

→ Einstein's expected arrival in California, as reported by the *New York Times*, December 11, 1930

CALIFORNIA SCIENTISTS AWAIT EINSTEIN'S VISIT

Expect Great Results From Meetings—Meantime Interest Centres in Big Telescope.

Special Correspondence, THE NEW YORK TIMES.

LOS ANGELES, Dec. 11—Southern California is becoming the universal peep hole for the gimlet eye of science. Strange things are going forward at the Institute of Technology where Dr. Millikan makes the atoms and the molecules lie down, roll over and say "Uncle." The visit of Professor Einstein is being anticipated by the savants at the Pasadena Research Institution with an eagerness akin to that of a small boy faced by a mysterious looking package on the day before Christmas. Something portentous may come out of the impending huddles into which the world's mightiest men of science are preparing to engage.

Just now public interest is centring in the locating of the world's greatest telescope, the 200-inch reflecting instrument, which is expected, figuratively, to bring the earth within speaking distance of the moon and some of the other planets. One of the locations is on Table Mountain 7,500 feet high, easily accessible from the university where the laboratory work will be done and 1,500 feet higher than Mount Wilson where the present 100-inch instrument, now the world's largest telescope, is located. The other site is on Palomar Mountain in San Diego County, with an altitude of 6,100 feet, comparable with Mount Wilson, seventy-five miles from the institute in an isolated section, and eight miles from the nearest village.

If the latter site is selected a large amount of road building will be required before the job of housing and transporting the delicate mechanism and priceless lens can be undertaken.

↑ With fellow physicists W.S. Adams, Albert A Michelson, Walther Mayer, M. Ferrand, and Robert A. Millikan in front of the Athenaeum at Caltech, January 7, 1931

→ From a letter to the Lebach family, January 16, 1931

« Here in Pasadena it's similar to paradise. Always sunshine and clean air, gardens with palm and pepper trees, and friendly people who smile at one and ask for autographs. Scientifically, it's very interesting and the colleagues are wonderful to me. But I'm strongly drawn back to the rough North where one can walk barefoot and one is allowed to be coarse. In contrast, here everything is formal and respectable. »

↑ Einstein writing out an equation for the density of the Milky Way on the blackboard at the Carnegie Institute, Pasadena, Jan. 14, 1931

→ On February 23, 1931, on the steps of City Hall, as thousands gathered for "the greatest civic reception and tribute ever accorded to anyone in the city" Einstein was given the key to the City of Los Angeles.

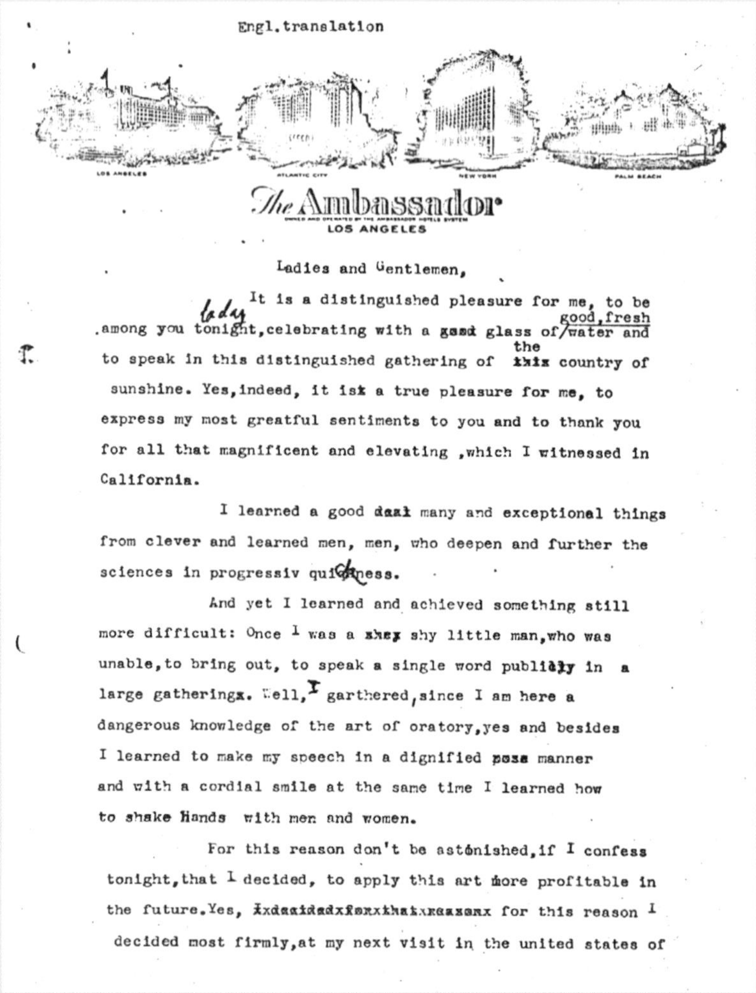

Engl.translation

LOS ANGELES ATLANTIC CITY NEW YORK PALM BEACH

The Ambassador
LOS ANGELES

Ladies and Gentlemen,

It is a distinguished pleasure for me, to be among you tonight today, celebrating with a good glass of good, fresh water and to speak in this distinguished gathering of this the country of sunshine. Yes, indeed, it isk a true pleasure for me, to express my most greatful sentiments to you and to thank you for all that magnificent and elevating, which I witnessed in California.

I learned a good deal many and exceptional things from clever and learned men, men, who deepen and further the sciences in progressiv quickness.

And yet I learned and achieved something still more difficult: Once I was a shey shy little man, who was unable, to bring out, to speak a single word publicly in a large gatheringx. Well, I garthered, since I am here a dangerous knowledge of the art of oratory, yes and besides I learned to make my speech in a dignified pose manner and with a cordial smile at the same time I learned how to shake Hands with men and women.

For this reason don't be astonished, if I confess tonight, that I decided, to apply this art more profitable in the future. Yes, Ixdecidedxforxthatxreasonx for this reason I decided most firmly, at my next visit in the united states of

→ Einstein may have hoped for a quiet period of intense research at Caltech, in association with his American colleagues. Instead, a good deal of his time in California was swallowed by social obligations. In this speech at a Los Angeles dinner in Februar 1931, he comments on his experience in a humorous way.

RESOLUTION

WHEREAS,

DOCTOR

ALBERT EINSTEIN

a citizen of the Republic of Germany, because of his personal contributions to the scientific knowledge of the world, has received international acclaim; and

WHEREAS, Doctor Einstein has accepted an invitation to visit this City of the Angels on Monday, February 23, 1931, on which day the birth of George Washington will be commemorated;

NOW, THEREFORE, BE IT RESOLVED, that Doctor Einstein be officially welcomed by the Mayor and Council of the City of Los Angeles, that the keys of the city be delivered unto him, and that he be extended cordial greetings of esteem and goodwill from our citizens.

BE IT FURTHER RESOLVED, that this Resolution be spread upon the minutes of this Council and that an engrossed copy of this Resolution be presented to Doctor Einstein by the Mayor.

John C Porter

Mayor of the City of Los Angeles.

I HEREBY CERTIFY that the Foregoing Resolution was adopted by the Council of the City of Los Angeles at its meeting held February 20, 1931.

W. J. Sanborn

President of the City Council

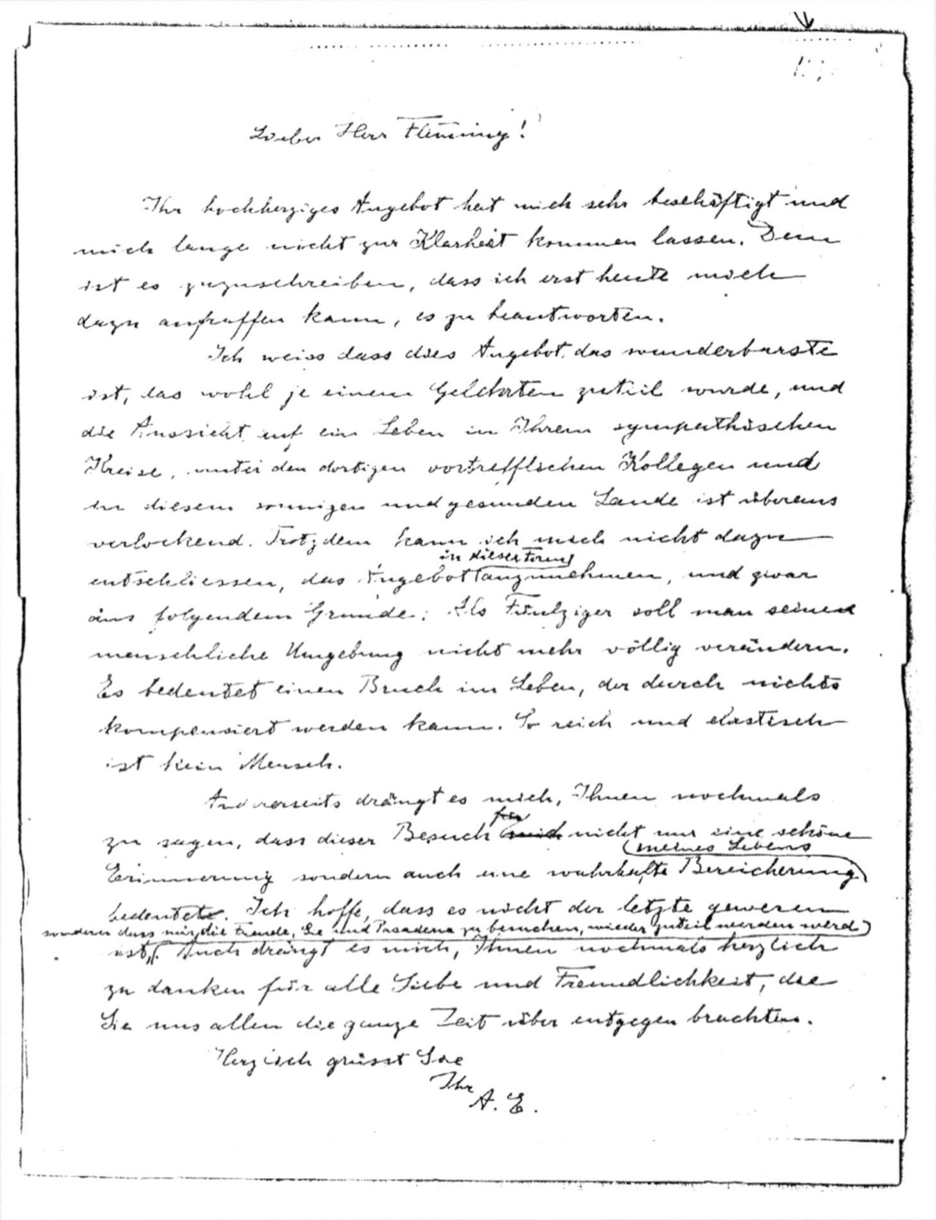

Lieber Herr Fleming!

Ihr hochherziges Angebot hat mich sehr beschäftigt und mich lange nicht zur Klarheit kommen lassen. Dem ist es zuzuschreiben, dass ich erst heute mich dazu aufraffen kann, es zu beantworten.

Ich weiss dass dies Angebot das wunderbarste ist, das wohl je einem Gelehrten zuteil wurde, und die Aussicht auf ein Leben in Ihrem sympathischen Kreise, unter den dortigen vortrefflichen Kollegen und in diesem sonnigen und gesunden Lande ist überaus verlockend. Trotzdem kann ich mich nicht dazu entschliessen, das Angebot in dieser Form anzunehmen, und zwar aus folgendem Grunde: Als Fünfziger soll man seine menschliche Umgebung nicht mehr völlig verändern. Es bedeutet einen Bruch im Leben, der durch nichts kompensiert werden kann. So reich und elastisch ist kein Mensch.

Andrerseits drängt es mich, Ihnen nochmals zu sagen, dass dieser Besuch für mich nicht nur eine schöne Erinnerung (meines Lebens) sondern auch eine wahrhafte Bereicherung bedeutete. Ich hoffe, dass es nicht der letzte gewesen ist, sondern dass mir die Freude, Sie und Pasadena zu besuchen, wieder zuteil werden werde. Auch drängt es mich, Ihnen nochmals herzlich zu danken für alle Liebe und Freundlichkeit, die Sie uns allen die ganze Zeit über entgegen brachten.

Herzlich grüsst Sie

Ihr A. E.

← Toward the end of Einstein's first sojourn in Pasadena, the chairman of the board of trustees had offered him a permanent position at the California Institute of Technology. In his answer of March 1931, Einstein emphasized the temptation that the prospect of life and work among the eminent colleagues would represent.

« Nevertheless, I cannot decide about accepting the offer in its current form for the following reason: As a fifty-year-old, one should no longer entirely change one's human surroundings. It would mean an upheaval in one's life which could not be compensated for by anything else. »

↑ Just two years later, though, nothing else but an upheaval in his life resulted in this very change.
From Einstein's letter to Arthur Fleming, March 1931

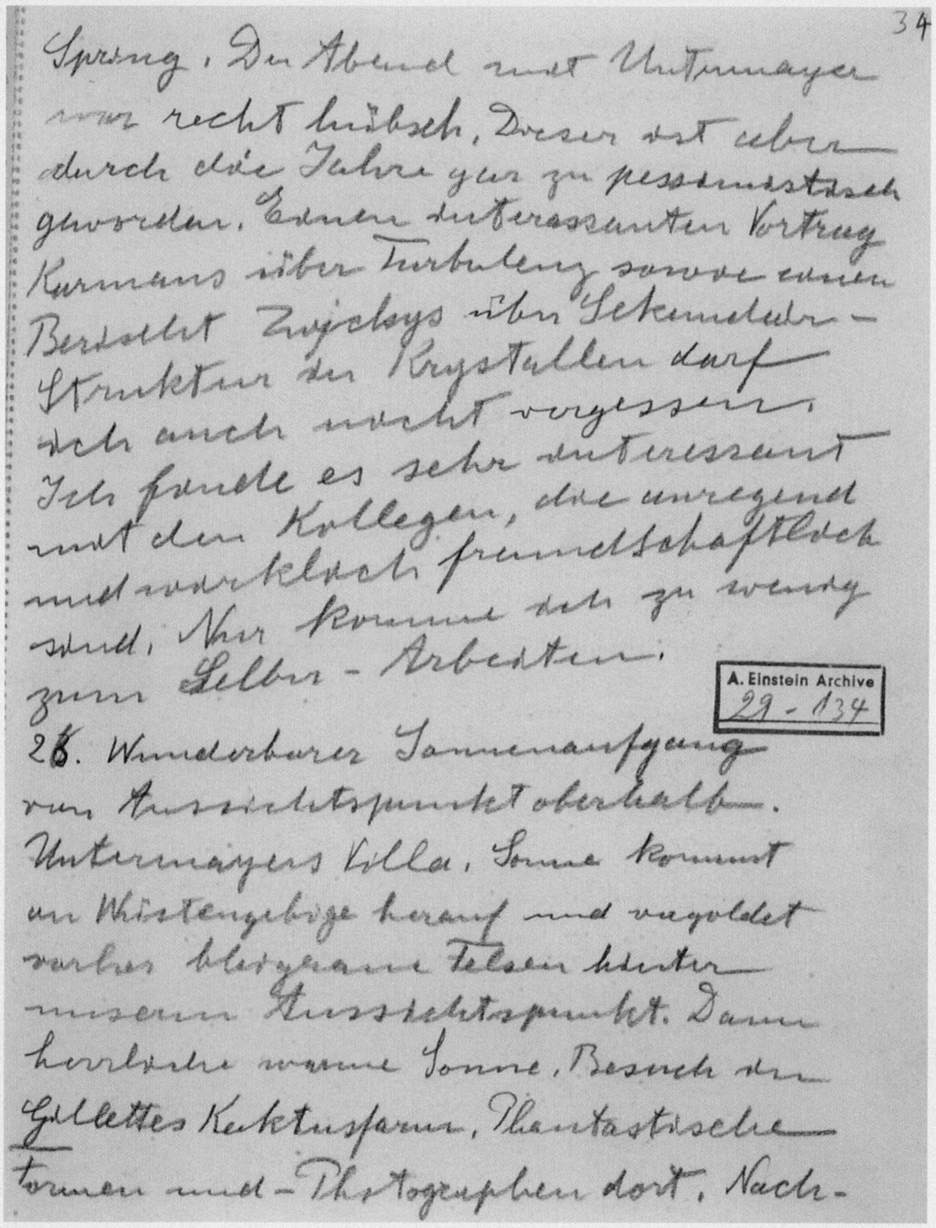
34

Spring. Der Abend mit Untermayer
war recht hübsch. Dieser ist aber
durch die Jahre gar zu pessimistisch
geworden. Einen interessanten Vortrag
Karmans über Turbulenz sowie einen
Bericht Zwickys über Sekundär-
Struktur der Krystallen darf
ich auch nicht vergessen.
Ich fand es sehr interessant
mit den Kollegen, die anregend
und wirklich freundschaftlich
sind. Nur komme ich zu wenig
zum Selber-Arbeiten.

A. Einstein Archive
29-134

26. Wunderbarer Sonnenaufgang
vom Aussichtspunkt oberhalb
Untermayers Villa. Sonne kommt
an Wüstengebirge herauf und vergoldet
vorher bleigraue Felsen hinter
unserem Aussichtspunkt. Dann
herrliche warme Sonne. Besuch der
Gillettes Kaktusfarm. Phantastische
Formen und – Photographen dort. Nach-

↓→ From his travel diary, January 26, 1931

« Amazing sunrise from the lookout point above Untermayer's villa. Sun rises past the desert mountains and bathes previously lead-gray rocks in golden sunlight behind our lookout point. Later, splendid, warm sun. Visit to Gillette's cactus farm. Fantastic shapes there and – photographers. In the afternoon drive through the desert to a ridge from where one descends to Palm Canyon, a narrow valley floor covered with palm trees which is bordered by bare rocks and scree. Many simple people were there for the trip on Sunday, approached to shake hands with me and constantly snapped shots of me. Only a mischievously looking little girl refused to pose with me for a picture. Maybe, with God's help, she will stay like that. »

→ From an unidentified newspaper, around December 1, 1932

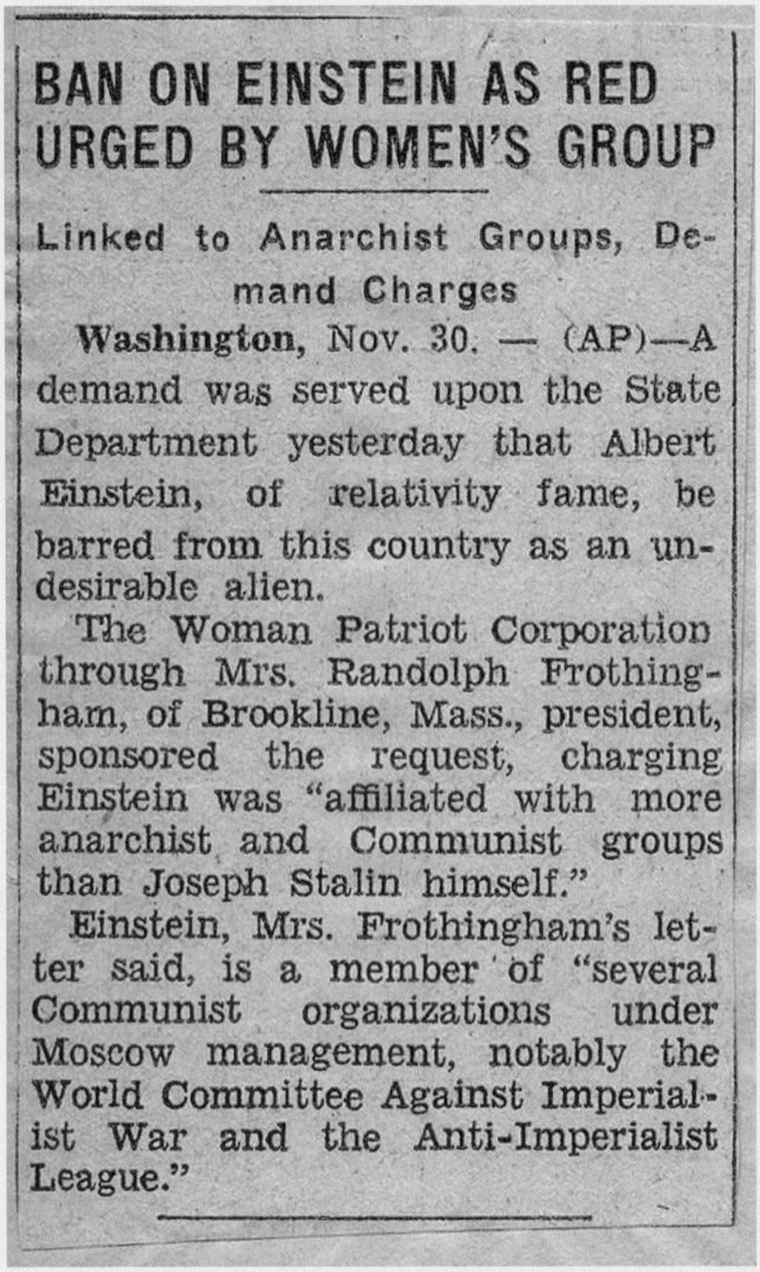

BAN ON EINSTEIN AS RED URGED BY WOMEN'S GROUP

Linked to Anarchist Groups, Demand Charges

Washington, Nov. 30. — (AP)—A demand was served upon the State Department yesterday that Albert Einstein, of relativity fame, be barred from this country as an undesirable alien.

The Woman Patriot Corporation through Mrs. Randolph Frothingham, of Brookline, Mass., president, sponsored the request, charging Einstein was "affiliated with more anarchist and Communist groups than Joseph Stalin himself."

Einstein, Mrs. Frothingham's letter said, is a member of "several Communist organizations under Moscow management, notably the World Committee Against Imperialist War and the Anti-Imperialist League."

↓→ In early autumn 1932, when it became known that Einstein would again be a part-time resident at the Institute of Advanced Study, the Woman Patriot Corporation felt the obligation to protect America from the dangerous ideas he was expected to import. They protested against his entry to the United States on the grounds of being an anarchist, the leader of the new "militant pacifism," affiliated with communist and anarcho-communist groups, and more. In October 1932 Einstein published his sardonic riposte:

« Never yet I have experienced from the fair sex such energetic rejection of all advances; or if I have, never from so many at once.

But are they not quite right, these watchful citizenesses? Why should one open one's doors to a person who devours hard-boiled capitalists with as much appetite and gusto as the Cretan Minotaur in days gone by devoured luscious Greek maidens, and on top of that is low-down to reject every sort of war, except the unavoidable war with one's own wife?

Therefore give heed to your clever and patriotic womenfolk and remember that the capitol of mighty Rome was once saved by the cackling of its faithful geese. »

AT PRINCETON

Einstein's ties with Princeton began in 1921 during his first trip to the United States, when he held a series of lectures at Princeton University.

In the early 1930s, the noted educator Abraham Flexner secured funding for the establishment of a prestigious institute for theoretical research and intellectual inquiry at Princeton. The aim of the planned Institute for Advanced Study was to enable eminent figures from the international scientific community to live and pursue work in a peaceful and productive environment, free of any lecturing responsibilities.

In the light of the threatening political situation looming over Europe, Einstein decided to accept a permanent, lifelong position at the Institute in Princeton.
In 1935 Albert and Elsa Einstein purchased the house at 112 Mercer Street, in walking distance of his office, first located at Princeton University's Fine Hall, and, from 1939 onwards, at Fuld Hall on the Institute's own campus.

Einstein's daily routine began with a leisurely stroll from his house to the office, often accompanied by his assistant, discussing work-related problems, the political situation or a book they had recently read. A decade after arriving in Princeton, Einstein acquired another walking companion, the logician Kurt Gödel. The two would talk animatedly on their way to the Institute and again, later in the day, on their way home. Hardly anything precise is known about the topics of their endless discussions, yet we may assume that they flew to great intellectual heights.

Years after Einstein's official retirement, when he still kept the routine of working daily at his office, he is reported to have said that while his interest in his own work had lessened, he now went to his office "chiefly to have the privilege of walking home with Kurt Gödel."

Einstein was obviously attracted to Princeton by its academic and intellectual life and by its quiet beauty.
Throughout his years in Princeton, a place where there was no lack of luminaries, Albert Einstein was the town's most celebrated inhabitant.

« In Princeton we have settled down really well. The place is charming, altogether different from the rest of America. [...] Here, everything is tinged with Englishness – downright Oxford Style. »

↑ From a letter by Elsa Einstein to the wife of Alfred Einstein, Hertha, February 24, 1934

→ "This house will never become a place of pilgrimage where the pilgrims come to look at the bones of the saint."
112 Mercer Street

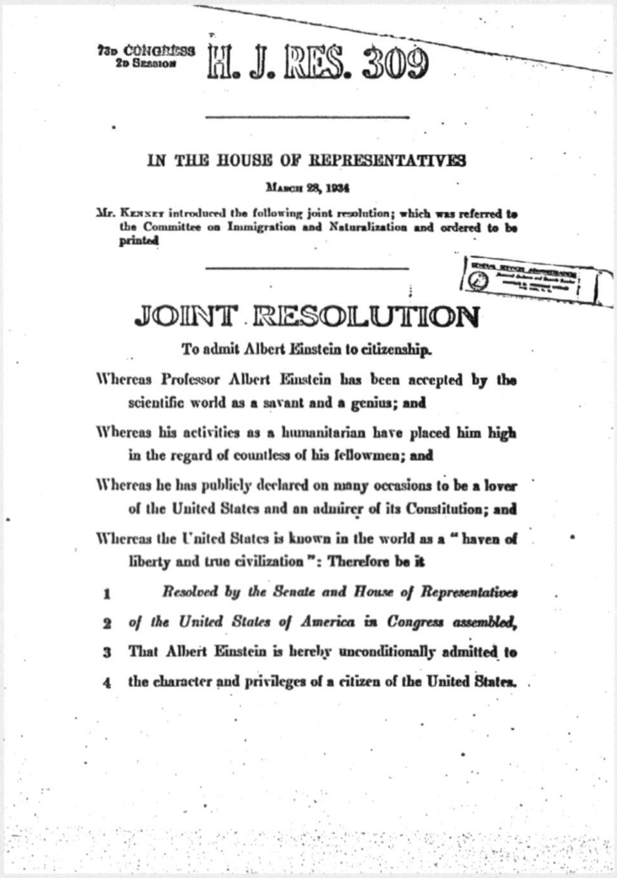

73D CONGRESS 2D SESSION **H. J. RES. 309**

IN THE HOUSE OF REPRESENTATIVES

MARCH 28, 1934

Mr. KENNEY introduced the following joint resolution; which was referred to the Committee on Immigration and Naturalization and ordered to be printed

JOINT RESOLUTION

To admit Albert Einstein to citizenship.

Whereas Professor Albert Einstein has been accepted by the scientific world as a savant and a genius; and

Whereas his activities as a humanitarian have placed him high in the regard of countless of his fellowmen; and

Whereas he has publicly declared on many occasions to be a lover of the United States and an admirer of its Constitution; and

Whereas the United States is known in the world as a "haven of liberty and true civilization": Therefore be it

Resolved by the Senate and House of Representatives of the United States of America in Congress assembled, That Albert Einstein is hereby unconditionally admitted to the character and privileges of a citizen of the United States.

← Joint Resolution of U.S. citizenship. Einstein considered the offer untimely and rejected it.

→ Albert Einstein and his step-daughter, Margot at the ceremony during which they received their U.S. citizenship, Trenton, New Jersey, October 1, 1940.
Photo by Martin D'Arcy, *Evening Times* Photographer

THE UNITED STATES OF AMERICA

ORIGINAL
TO BE GIVEN TO
THE PERSON NATURALIZED

No. 5013865

CERTIFICATE OF NATURALIZATION

Petition No. 4009

Personal description of holder as of date of naturalization: Age 61 years; sex Male ; color White ; complexion Medium ; color of eyes Brown ; color of hair Grey ; height 5 feet 7 inches; weight 175 pounds; visible distinctive marks None
Marital status Widower ; former nationality German
I certify that the description above given is true, and that the photograph affixed hereto is a likeness of me.

sign here

Albert Einstein
(Complete and true signature of holder)

United States of America
District of New Jersey } ss:

Be it known, that ALBERT EINSTEIN
then residing at 112 Mercer St., Princeton, New Jersey
having petitioned to be admitted a citizen of the United States of America, and at a term of the DISTRICT Court of THE UNITED STATES held pursuant to law at Trenton, New Jersey on October 1st 1940
the court having found that the petitioner intends to reside permanently in the United States, had in all respects complied with the Naturalization Laws of the United States in such case applicable, and was entitled to be so admitted, the court thereupon ordered that the petitioner be admitted as a citizen of the United States of America.
In testimony whereof the seal of the court is hereunto affixed this 1st day of October in the year of our Lord nineteen hundred and forty and of our Independence the one hundred and sixty-fifth.

Albert Einstein.

Seal

"This is a personal document and it is a breach of the U.S. Code (and punishable as such) to copy, print, photograph or otherwise illegally use it."
See other side

Benjamin F. Havens
Clerk of the U. S. District Court.
By Hazel K. Fries Deputy Clerk.

DEPARTMENT OF LABOR

29-121

↑ U.S. Certificate of Naturalization,
Trenton, New Jersey, October 1, 1940

« I have become a kind of enfant terrible in my new homeland because of my inability to keep silent and swallow everything that happens here. »

↑ To the Queen Mother Elisabeth of Belgium, March 28, 1954

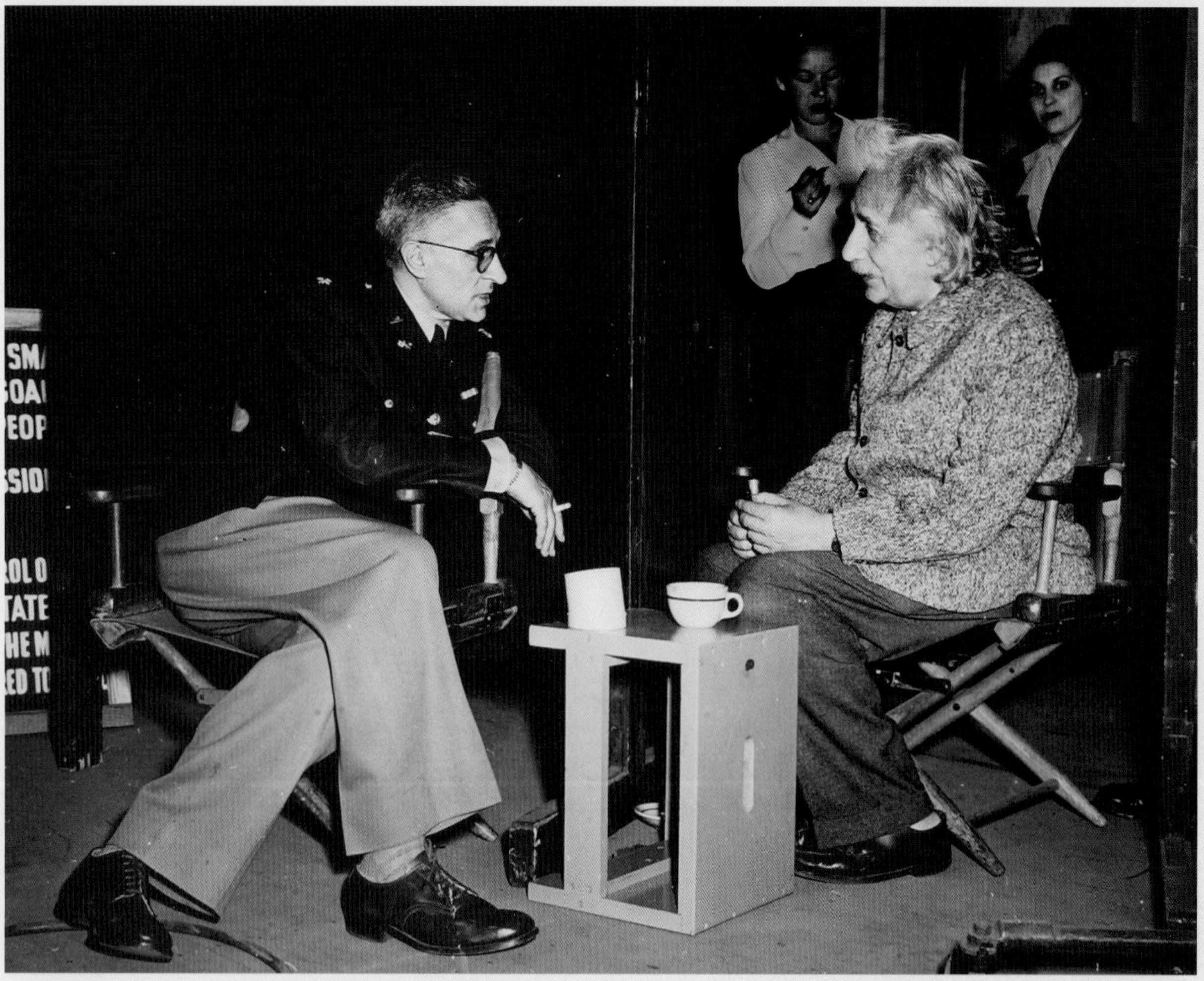

↘→ From June 1943 to October 1944, Einstein had "a sort of advisory position with the Navy." To his son he confided "It probably won't come to much because I'm very incompletely instructed about the actual duties." The Navy, however, showed more enthusiasm.

« I am in the Navy, but I was not required to get a Navy haircut. »

↓ From *On the Surface*, January 24, 1986

Einstein and the Navy:
. . . 'an unbeatable combination'

The OTS feature on ***John Bardeen*** *(18 Oct 85) mentioned Albert Einstein's work for the Navy. This work was conducted under the guidance of* ***Stephen Brunauer****, now Clarkson Professor Emeritus at Clarkson University in Potsdam, N.Y. "Several biographies of Einstein were published," says Prof.*

by Dr. Stephen Brunauer

Albert Einstein was not only the greatest scientist of our age, but also the best-loved and most admired man among all scientists. He was known not only to educated

↓ On May 24, 1943, at Carnegie Hall in New York, distinguished scholars and scientists gathered to celebrate the 400th anniversary of Copernicus. As a tribute to his memory, Copernican Citations were given to ten outstanding "modern revolutionaries."
Along with Albert Einstein, the other recipients included Orville Wright and Igor Sikorsky, two aviation pioneers, John Dewey, the most influential thinker on education in the twentieth century, Henry Ford, founder of the Ford Motor Company, Yen Yangchu, creator of a simple, easily mastered system of written Chinese, and Walt Disney, famous for his animation films.

→ Einstein and J. Robert Oppenheimer, the director of the Los Alamos National Laboratory during the development of the atomic bomb, since 1947 director of the Institute for Advanced Study, late 1940s.
Photo by Alfred Eisenstaedt

→ In December 1953, on the basis of dubious suspicions, the physicist J. Robert Oppenheimer was declared a major national security risk and excluded from the U.S. Atomic Energy Commission. His case was publicly discussed and eventually, in May 1954, commented on rather laconically by Einstein.

« The systematic and widespread attempt to destroy mutual trust and confidence constitutes the severest possible blow against society. »

→ From a letter to
Queen Elisabeth of Belgium,
November 20, 1933

« Princeton is a wonderful little spot
albeit a remarkably quaint and
ceremonious bourgeois village of tiny
stilted demigods.
Yet by breaking with social conventions,
one can gain fair privacy;
that's what I do. »

↓ Einstein and Gödel,
Princeton, 1950s

↑ Princeton, end of the 1930s

→ From a letter to the editor of the Japanese magazine *Kaizo*, September 20, 1952

« My participation in the production of the atomic bomb consisted of one single act: I signed a letter to President Roosevelt, in which I emphasized the necessity of conducting large-scale experimentation with regard to the feasibility of producing an atom bomb.
I was well aware of the dreadful danger which would threaten mankind were the experiments to prove successful. Yet I felt impelled to take the step because it seemed probable that the Germans might be working on the same problem with every prospect of success. I saw no alternative but to act as I did, although I have always been a convinced pacifist. I believe that the killing of human beings in a war is no better than common murder. »

EINSTEIN AND THE BOMB

In popular imagination, Einstein is perceived as the "father of the atomic bomb," and his famous equation $E=mc^2$ is incorrectly thought to constitute a formula for the construction of nuclear weaponry. Yet this is far from the historical truth.

Actually, only a distant connection exists between Einstein's equation and the development of the American atomic bomb with whose construction Einstein was not involved.

When Einstein devised the law of the equivalence of mass and energy in the early years of the century, he was attempting to provide a theoretical description of physical phenomena and he did not foresee any technological applications.

Three decades later, Einstein still was of the opinion that the likelihood of transforming matter into energy on an industrial scale was unrealistic in the near future. Soon afterwards, however, in a Berlin laboratory, nuclear fission was achieved and made the prospect of a Nazi bomb a looming menace.

Alarmed by the threatening news, in July 1939 Leo Szilard, himself one of the experts on nuclear fission, turned to Einstein for support, and together they drafted a letter to President Roosevelt requesting him to initiate an American nuclear research program.

There is a debate among historians, concerning the development of the atomic bomb, as to whether this letter carried the desired weight. Some argue that it was the news that British nuclear scientists had made a decisive breakthrough toward constructing the bomb that convinced the Americans to initiate a full-fledged nuclear program in 1941.

From this project to develop the atomic bomb, known as the Manhattan Project, which took place in utmost secrecy, Einstein was excluded.

As recorded by the FBI: "In view of his radical background, this office would not recommend the employment of Dr. Einstein on matters of a secret nature, without a very careful investigation, as it seems unlikely that a man of his background could, in such a short time, become a loyal American citizen." In any case, Einstein was sympathetic to issues endorsed by Communists, too, and so never received the security clearance.

He may, eventually, have drawn his own conclusions from the sudden disappearance of many of his fellow physicists, and, on the quiet, gathered some information on the progress of the project.

In spring 1945, indeed, he drafted a new letter to President Roosevelt, introducing Leo Szilard who was "greatly concerned" about the lack of communication between the scientists working on the bomb, and the politicians who eventually might make use of the bomb without being fully aware of the consequences.

Yet Roosevelt died soon afterwards and, sadly, the letter had not the intended impact on his successor, Harry Truman.

Einstein learned of the detonation of the nuclear device over Hiroshima, as did the rest of the world, by public announcement on August 6, 1945.

Albert Einstein
Old Grove Rd.
Nassau Point
Peconic, Long Island

August 2nd, 1939

F.D. Roosevelt,
President of the United States,
White House
Washington, D.C.

Sir:

Some recent work by E.Fermi and L. Szilard, which has been communicated to me in manuscript, leads me to expect that the element uranium may be turned into a new and important source of energy in the immediate future. Certain aspects of the situation which has arisen seem to call for watchfulness and, if necessary, quick action on the part of the Administration. I believe therefore that it is my duty to bring to your attention the following facts and recommendations:

In the course of the last four months it has been made probable - through the work of Joliot in France as well as Fermi and Szilard in America - that it may become possible to set up a nuclear chain reaction in a large mass of uranium,by which vast amounts of power and large quantities of new radium-like elements would be generated. Now it appears almost certain that this could be achieved in the immediate future.

This new phenomenon would also lead to the construction of bombs, and it is conceivable - though much less certain - that extremely powerful bombs of a new type may thus be constructed. A single bomb of this type, carried by boat and exploded in a port, might very well destroy the whole port together with some of the surrounding territory. However, such bombs might very well prove to be too heavy for transportation by air.

-2-

The United States has only very poor ores of uranium in moderate quantities. There is some good ore in Canada and the former Czechoslovakia, while the most important source of uranium is Belgian Congo.

In view of this situation you may think it desirable to have some permanent contact maintained between the Administration and the group of physicists working on chain reactions in America. One possible way of achieving this might be for you to entrust with this task a person who has your confidence and who could perhaps serve in an inofficial capacity. His task might comprise the following:

a) to approach Government Departments, keep them informed of the further development, and put forward recommendations for Government action, giving particular attention to the problem of securing a supply of uranium ore for the United States;

b) to speed up the experimental work,which is at present being carried on within the limits of the budgets of University laboratories, by providing funds, if such funds be required, through his contacts with private persons who are willing to make contributions for this cause, and perhaps also by obtaining the co-operation of industrial laboratories which have the necessary equipment.

I understand that Germany has actually stopped the sale of uranium from the Czechoslovakian mines which she has taken over. That she should have taken such early action might perhaps be understood on the ground that the son of the German Under-Secretary of State, von Weizsäcker, is attached to the Kaiser-Wilhelm-Institut in Berlin where some of the American work on uranium is now being repeated.

Yours very truly,
A. Einstein
(Albert Einstein)

←↙ Letter to U.S. President Franklin D. Roosevelt urging him to examine the feasibility of developing nuclear weapons, August 2, 1939

THE WHITE HOUSE
WASHINGTON

October 19, 1939

My dear Professor:

I want to thank you for your recent letter and the most interesting and important enclosure.

I found this data of such import that I have convened a Board consisting of the head of the Bureau of Standards and a chosen representative of the Army and Navy to thoroughly investigate the possibilities of your suggestion regarding the element of uranium.

I am glad to say that Dr. Sachs will cooperate and work with this Committee and I feel this is the most practical and effective method of dealing with the subject.

Please accept my sincere thanks.

Very sincerely yours,

Franklin D. Roosevelt

Dr. Albert Einstein,
Old Grove Road,
Nassau Point,
Peconic, Long Island,
New York.

↑ Franklin D. Roosevelt's reply to Einstein's letter, October 19, 1939

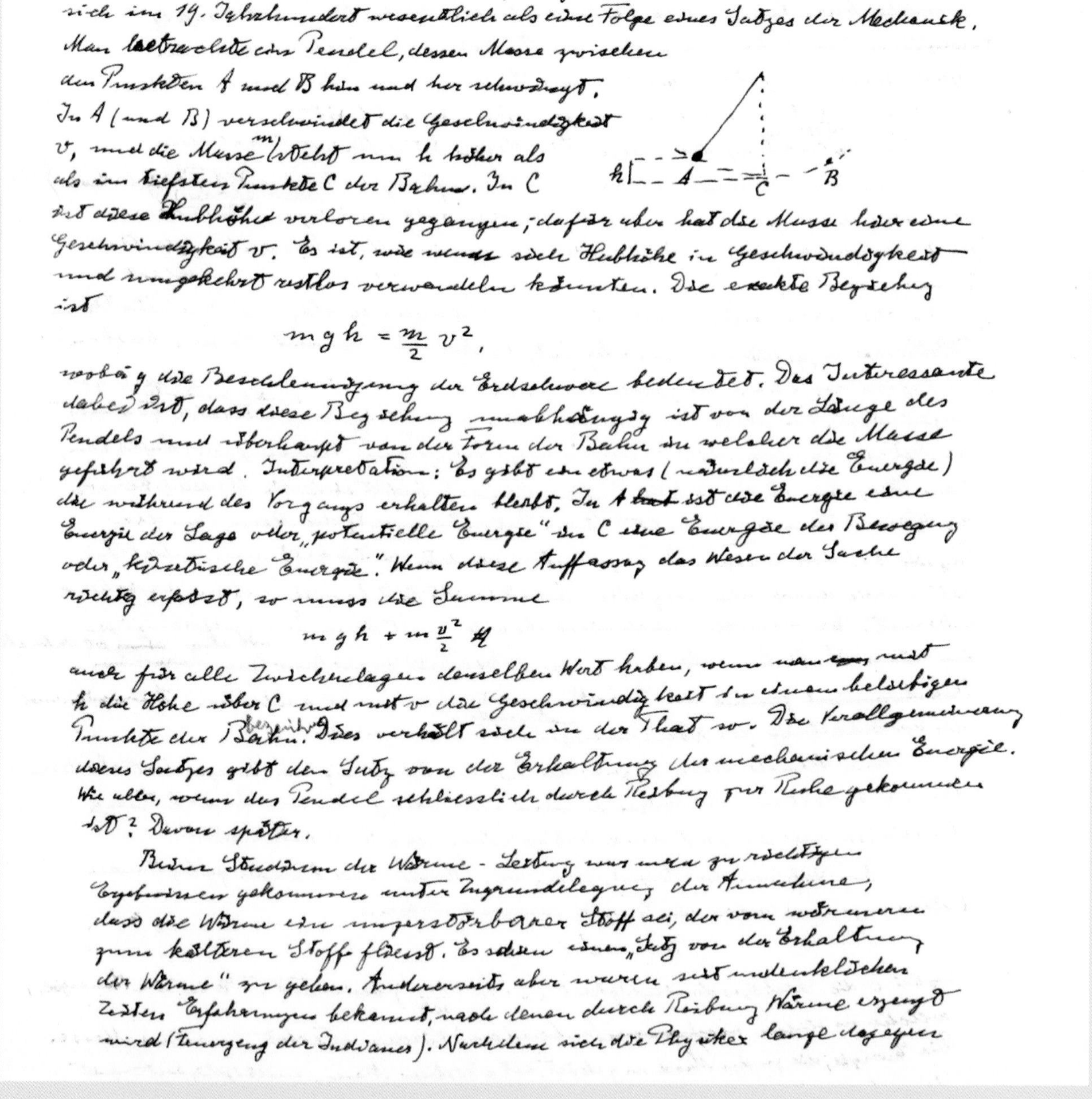

F-2 "Science Illustrated" Jan. 1946

Das Gesetz von der Aequivalenz von Masse und Energie ($E = mc^2$)

In der vor-relativistischen Physik gab es zwei voneinander unabhängige Erhaltung bezw. Bilanzgesetze, die strenge Gültigkeit beanspruchten, nämlich

1) den Satz von der Erhaltung der Energie

2) den Satz von der Erhaltung der Masse.

Der Satz von der Erhaltung der Energie, welcher schon von Leibnitz im 17. Jahrhundert in seiner vollen Allgemeinheit als gültig vermutet wurde, entwickelte sich im 19. Jahrhundert wesentlich als eine Folge eines Satzes der Mechanik. Man betrachte ein Pendel, dessen Masse zwischen den Punkten A und B hin und her schwingt. In A (und B) verschwindet die Geschwindigkeit v, und die Masse m steht um h höher als im tiefsten Punkte C der Bahn. In C ist diese Hubhöhe verloren gegangen; dafür aber hat die Masse hier eine Geschwindigkeit v. Es ist, wie wenn sich Hubhöhe in Geschwindigkeit und umgekehrt restlos verwandeln könnten. Die exakte Beziehung ist

$$mgh = \frac{m}{2}v^2,$$

wobei g die Beschleunigung der Erdschwere bedeutet. Das Interessante dabei ist, dass diese Beziehung unabhängig ist von der Länge des Pendels und überhaupt von der Form der Bahn in welcher die Masse geführt wird. Interpretation: Es gibt ein etwas (nämlich die Energie) die während des Vorgangs erhalten bleibt. In A ist die Energie eine Energie der Lage oder „potentielle Energie" in C eine Energie der Bewegung oder „kinetische Energie". Wenn diese Auffassung das Wesen der Sache richtig erfasst, so muss die Summe

$$mgh + m\frac{v^2}{2}$$

auch für alle Zwischenlagen denselben Wert haben, wenn man mit h die Höhe über C und mit v die Geschwindigkeit in einem beliebigen Punkte der Bahn bezeichnet. Dies verhält sich in der That so. Die Verallgemeinerung dieses Satzes gibt den Satz von der Erhaltung der mechanischen Energie. Wie aber, wenn das Pendel schliesslich durch Reibung zur Ruhe gekommen ist? Davon später.

Beim Studium der Wärme-Leitung war man zu richtigen Ergebnissen gekommen unter Zugrundelegung der Annahme, dass die Wärme ein unzerstörbarer Stoff sei, der vom wärmeren zum kälteren Stoff fliesst. Es schien einen „Satz von der Erhaltung der Wärme" zu geben. Andererseits aber waren seit undenklichen Zeiten Erfahrungen bekannt, nach denen durch Reibung Wärme erzeugt wird (Feuerzeug der Indianer). Nachdem sich die Physiker lange dagegen

↑ Under the title "E=mc² – The Most Urgent Problem of Our Time," the periodical *Science Illustrated* published in 1946 Einstein's article which in a more popular way seeks to explain the significance of the famous formula.

THE NUCLEAR THREAT

With the onset of the atomic era, Einstein realized that nuclear weapons were a profound risk to humanity and could bring an end to civilization. During the last decade of his life, he was tireless in his efforts to create effective international cooperation to prevent war. The "supranational organization" that he had favored already in the 1920s, he now campaigned for in the form of a world government to enforce arms control and establish an international peace-keeping force. He believed that scientists had a special responsibility to inform their fellow citizens of the perils of nuclear warfare, so far ignored by the public. In 1946, he became chairman of the Emergency Committee of Atomic Scientists whose goal was to raise funds to support a massive program of public education and policy development on atomic energy.

Einstein criticized both the U.S. and the U.S.S.R. for their cold-war policies of mutual fear and suspicion and endeavored to bring about cooperation between scientists of the two countries. Moreover, he clearly voiced his objection to the possession of the nuclear secret to be held exclusively by either power block.

One of his last political acts was his signing of a manifesto, drafted by the philosopher Bertrand Russell, which three months after Einstein's death was published under the title "Russell-Einstein Manifesto." This declaration constitutes a solemn warning concerning the horrifying consequences of a nuclear war and an appeal for nuclear disarmament. It formed the basis for the subsequent Pugwash Conferences on Science and World Affairs, which to this day bring together, from around the world, influential scholars and public figures concerned with reducing the danger of armed conflict. They seek cooperative solutions for global problems, above all for the catastrophic threat posed to humanity by nuclear and other weapons of mass destruction.

↗→ Einstein at his home in Princeton during the interview with Elliott Roosevelt, February 10, 1950. Two days later, Einstein's recorded statement on the dangers of the hydrogen bomb and his appeal for peaceful coexistence under a world government was broadcast as part of the TV show *Today with Mrs. Roosevelt.*

-2-

The ~~Thus We have come to a~~ condition of international anarchy, in which mankind lives under the constant threat of sudden annihilation. ~~It is evident that this condition cannot endure.~~

~~It~~ has led us now to a~~n~~ dangerous atomic armaments race. Therefore we of the Emergency Committee of Atomic Scientists feel it imperative to help our fellow citizens understand the new conditions.

We feel a heavy ~~sense of~~ responsibility to make clear to our fellow citizens and to the citizens of all other countries that today it is too late to think in terms of military power or technical superiority. What one group of men have discovered other intelligent and patient workers will surely learn too. There is no secret. There is no effectif ~~no~~ defense on a national basis.

The release of atomic energy has made a new world in which our old ways of thinking, our old diplomatic conventions, our old balance of power politics have simply no meaning. Mankind must give up war in the atomic era. What is at stake is the very life or death of our society.

The only armaments which could bring the world security and hope would be armaments belonging to a supra-national police force supporting world law. To that end we must work, with all our energies and also with a clear understanding for the needs of other nations ~~patience, courage, and faith in humanity.~~

###

↑ From a message to a lawyers' convention on world law, probably mid-May 1947

↑ With Elliott Roosevelt, recording Einstein's statement for the TV show *Today with Mrs. Roosevelt*, Princeton, February 10, 1950

→ From the statement of acceptance of the "One World Award," Carnegie Hall, New York, April 27, 1948

« In this time of fateful decisions, we must, above all, impress this fact upon our fellow-citizens: Whenever the belief in the omnipotence of physical force dominates the political life of a nation, this force takes on a life of its own and becomes even stronger than the very men who intended to use it as a tool. The proposed militarization of the nation not only immediately threatens us with war; it will also slowly but surely undermine the democratic spirit and the dignity of the individual in our land. The assertion that events abroad are forcing us to arm is incorrect; we must combat this false assumption with all our strength. Actually, our own rearmament, because of its effect upon other nations, will bring about the very state of affairs upon which the advocates of armaments seek to base their proposals. »

EINSTEIN'S CONCERN FOR CIVIL LIBERTIES

While America, alongside its Allies, had defeated fascism in Europe, in the United States the society was still suffering from what Einstein considered its worst disease, racism. In addition to the nuclear threat, it was the battle against racism and the spread of a cold war mentality that preoccupied Einstein in the years after the Second World War. Paradoxically, his commitment to human rights and civil liberties is best reflected in the more than 1800 pages of "evidence" the FBI accumulated on Einstein from the early 1930s until the year of his death in 1955.

Years before Senator Joseph McCarthy appeared on the national scene, and his name became synonymous with the witch-hunt of leftists and liberals, a national hysteria had created a climate in which the FBI under J. Edgar Hoover could subvert civil liberties, and red-baiting would flourish. Standing up against discrimination of minorities, and for equal treatment of white and colored people, or for freedom of speech and of independent thought, one was suspected of being communist-inspired and consequently anti-American.

↓ At Einstein's home in early October 1947 with Henry Wallace, a left-wing U.S. politician on the election trail, the only one, as Einstein wrote to a friend, who courageously, and publicly, opposed the hysterical warmongering. Einstein felt great admiration for Wallace's devotion to the fight for world peace. Also pictured are two other supporters of Wallace's election campaign: radio broadcaster Frank Kingdon and Paul Robeson, the baritone and civil rights advocate.

→↓ From Einstein's draft of a message to the National Urban League Convention, September 16, 1946

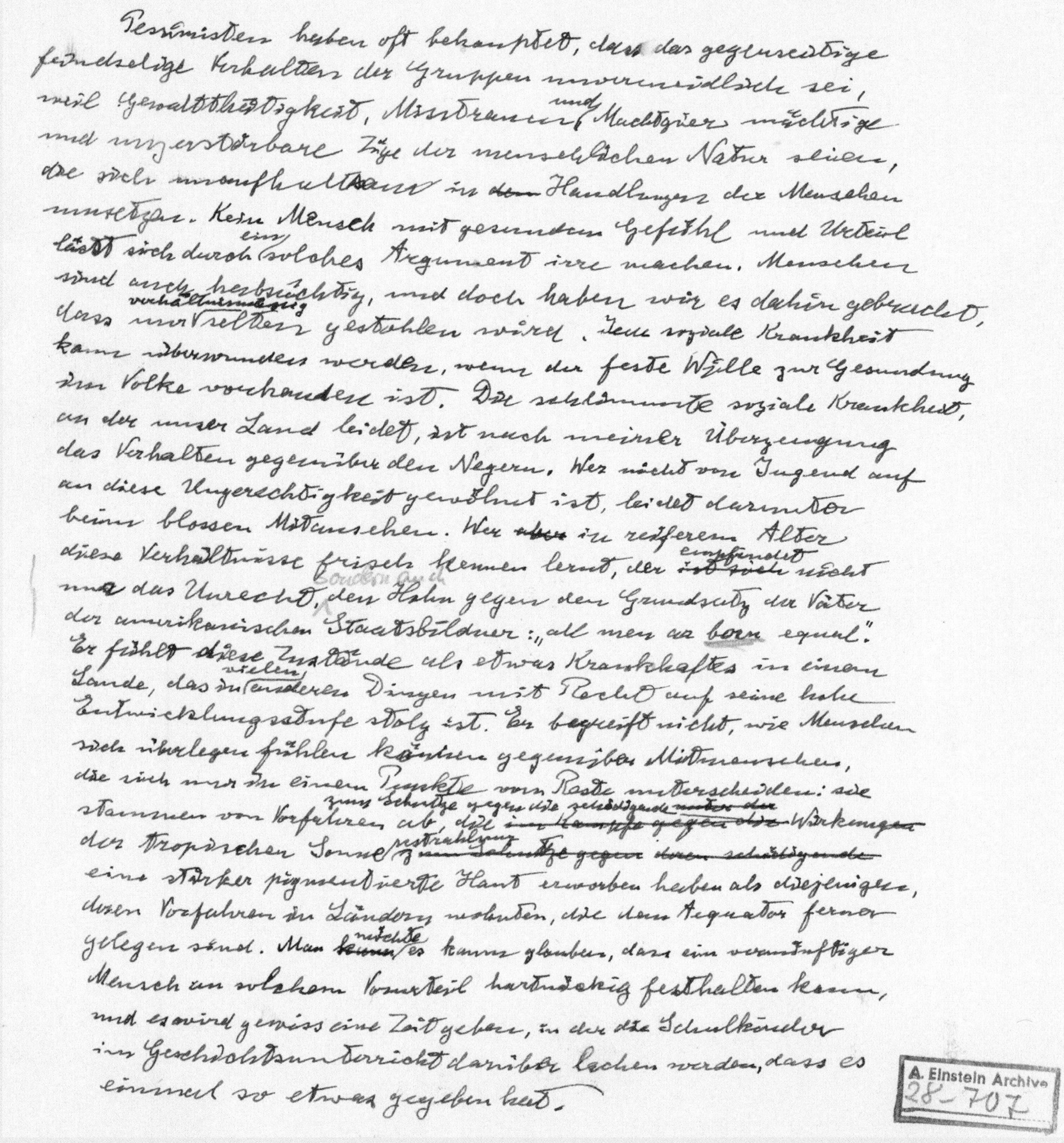
Pessimisten haben oft behauptet, dass das gegenseitige
feindselige Verhalten der Gruppen unvermeidlich sei,
weil Gewalttätigkeit, Misstrauen und Machtgier mächtige
und unzerstörbare Züge der menschlichen Natur seien,
die sich unaufhaltsam in Handlungen der Menschen
umsetzen. Kein Mensch mit gesundem Gefühl und Urteil
lässt sich durch ein solches Argument irre machen. Menschen
sind auch herrsüchtig, und doch haben wir es dahin gebracht,
dass verhältnismässig selten gestohlen wird. Jede soziale Krankheit
kann überwunden werden, wenn der feste Wille zur Gesundung
im Volke vorhanden ist. Die schlimmste soziale Krankheit,
an der unser Land leidet, ist nach meiner Überzeugung
das Verhalten gegenüber den Negern. Wer nicht von Jugend auf
an diese Ungerechtigkeit gewöhnt ist, leidet darunter
beim blossen Mitansehen. Wer in reiferem Alter
diese Verhältnisse frisch kennen lernt, der empfindet nicht
nur das Unrecht, sondern auch den Hohn gegen den Grundsatz der Väter
der amerikanischen Staatsbildner: „all men are born equal".
Er fühlt diese Zustände als etwas Krankhaftes in einem
Lande, das in vielen Dingen mit Recht auf seine hohe
Entwicklungsstufe stolz ist. Er begreift nicht, wie Menschen
sich überlegen fühlen können gegenüber Mitmenschen,
die sich nur in einem Punkte von Rasse unterscheiden: sie
stammen von Vorfahren ab, die zum Schutze gegen die schädigende Wirkungen
der tropischen Sonnenbestrahlung
eine stärker pigmentierte Haut erworben haben als diejenigen,
deren Vorfahren in Ländern wohnten, die dem Aequator ferner
gelegen sind. Man möchte es kaum glauben, dass ein vernünftiger
Mensch an solchem Vorurteil hartnäckig festhalten kann,
und es wird gewiss eine Zeit geben, in der die Schulkinder
im Geschichtsunterricht darüber lachen werden, dass es
einmal so etwas gegeben hat.

« Pessimists have often claimed that mutual hostility among groups is unavoidable, because violence, distrust and lust for power are indestructible and powerful characteristics of human nature that unceasingly influence the actions of men. No man of sound feeling and judgment is deluded by such an argument. […]
Every disease of society can be overcome if there is the firm will for a cure in the people.
The worst disease under which the society of our nation suffers, is, in my opinion, the treatment of the Negro. Everyone who is not used from childhood to this injustice suffers from the mere observation. Everyone who freshly learns of this state of affairs at a maturer age, feels not only the injustice but the scorn of the principle of the Fathers who founded the United States that 'all men are created equal.' […]
He cannot understand how men can feel superior to fellow-men who differ in only one point from the rest: They descend from ancestors who, as a protection against the destructive action of the radiation of the tropical sun, gained a more strongly pigmented skin than those whose ancestors lived in countries farther from the equator.
One can hardly believe that a reasonable man can cling so tenaciously to such prejudice, and there is sure to come a time in which school-children in their history lessons will laugh about the fact that something like this did once exist. »

↑ Einstein receiving an honorary degree from the hands of Horace Mann Bond, president of Lincoln University, Pennsylvania, a university for African Americans, May 3, 1946

→ From Einstein's address to Lincoln University students and faculty, May 3, 1947

« My trip to this institution was in behalf of a worthwhile cause. There is separation of colored people from white people in the United States. That separation is not a disease of colored people. It is a disease of white people. I do not intend to be quiet about it. »

In this period of unrelenting reaction, when hundreds were jailed, and thousands more deprived of their jobs and livelihoods because of their political beliefs, when black people fell victim to lynchings that went unpunished, Einstein did not just stand idly by, but fearlessly expressed his reprobation.

He was looked to as a sympathetic, moral figure by those summoned to appear before one of the various anti-Communist committees, panels and "loyalty review boards" and to answer questions regarding their political beliefs.
Asked for his advice on how they should defend themselves, Einstein publicly advised the accused to follow Mahatma Gandhi's principle of civil disobedience and to refuse to cooperate with the investigators.

Struck by the severe loss of intellectual freedom, in 1954 Einstein delivered his "plumber statement" which elicited great repercussions in the public sphere.

→ In 1953, William Frauenglass, an American teacher, was summoned to testify before the House Un-American Activities Committee and wrote to Einstein, asking for his advice. Einstein replied on May 16,1953. In his reply, he stressed that his advice was not to be considered "confidential," and thus, it soon found its way into the newspapers. The publication set off an avalanche of comments, pro and con, in the press as well as in letters addressed directly to Einstein.

EINSTEIN'S AXIOM

Dear Mr. Frauenglass:

Thank you for your communication. By "remote field" I referred to the theoretical foundations of physics.

The problem with which the intellectuals of this country are confronted is very serious. The reactionary politicians have managed to instill suspicion of all intellectual efforts into the public by dangling before their eyes a danger from without. Having succeeded so far they are now proceeding to suppress the freedom of teaching and to deprive of their positions all those who do not prove submissive, i. e., to starve them.

What ought the minority of intellectuals to do against this evil? Frankly, I can see only the revolutionary way of non-cooperation in the sense of Gandhi's. Every intellectual who is called before one of the committees ought to refuse to testify, i. e., he must be prepared for jail and economic ruin, in short, for the sacrifice of his personal welfare in the interest of the cultural welfare of his country.

This refusal to testify must be based on the assertion that it is shameful for a blameless citizen to submit to such an inquisition and that this kind of inquisition violates the spirit of the Constitution.

If enough people are ready to take this grave step they will be successful. If not, then the intellectuals of this country deserve nothing better than the slavery which is intended for them.

Sincerely yours,
A. Einstein.

P. S. This letter need not be considered "confidential."

→ In autumn 1954, the editor of *The Reporter* asked Einstein for a statement regarding the situation of intellectuals under McCarthy. Einstein replied with his famous "plumber statement," on October 13, 1954. Like Einstein's letter to William Frauenglass, the "plumber statement," too, was reproduced in various newspapers and provoked controversial reactions on the part of the public as well as the press.

If Einstein Were Young Again, He Says, He'd Become a Plumber

Dr. Albert Einstein has declared that, if he had his career to fashion all over again, "I would not try to become a scientist or scholar or teacher."

In a letter to the editor to be published tomorrow in The Reporter magazine, the famous physicist said he would become a plumber or a peddler to seek the independence that these vocations afford.

The letter was written in response to a request from The Reporter for Dr. Einstein's comments on a recent series in the magazine by Theodore H. White, "U. S. Science: The Troubled Quest." The series said that centers of intellectual life were troubled by recent Federal actions concerning scientists.

Dr. Einstein has been an outspoken critic of these actions. When Dr. J. Robert Oppenheimer was denied security clearance by the Atomic Energy Commission, Dr. Einstein said: "The systematic, widespread attempt to destroy mutual trust and confidence constitutees the severest possible blow against society."

Early this year he advised witnesses to refuse to testify on their activities before the legislative committee headed by Senator Joseph R. McCarthy, Republican of Wisconsin.

The text of Dr. Einstein's letter:

"To the Editor:

"You have asked me what I thought about your articles concerning the situation of the scientists in America. Instead of trying to analyze the problem, I may express my feeling in a short remark: If I would be a young man again and had to decide how to make my living, I would not try to become a scientist or scholar or teacher. I would rather choose to be a plumber or a peddler

Continued on Page 37, Column 6

EINSTEIN DECRIES SCIENCE AS CAREER

41-906

Continued From Page 1

in the hope to find that modest degree of independence still available under present circumstances."

In Princeton, Dr. Einstein's secretary declined to elaborate on this comment.

In publishing the letter, Max Ascoli, the editor of The Reporter, said that it was an honor but "hardly a pleasure to publish this letter from Albert Einstein." The comment will be freely used by enemies of the United States, he said.

But he added that the freedom to protest, which Dr. Einstein used in making his comment, can still be afforded here. Our country must maintain a good record on this score, not just a better record than do the totalitarian nations, Mr. Ascoli said in an editorial comment.

STANLEY PLUMBING & HEATING CO.
CONTRACTORS
1212 [redacted] SIXTH AVENUE
NEW YORK 19, N. Y.

JU 2-4846

November 11, 1954

Dr. Albert Einstein
Princeton University
Princeton, New Jersey

Dear Dr. Einstein:

As a plumber, I am very much interested in your comment made in the letter being published in the Reporter Magazine. Since my ambition has always been to be a scholar and yours seems to be a plumber, I suggest that as a team we would be tremendously successful. We can then be possessed of both knowledge and independence.

I am ready to change the name of my firm to read: Einstein and Stanley Plumbing Co.

Respectfully yours,

R. Stanley Murray
R. Stanley Murray

RSM:hks

← One of the many humorous reactions to Einstein's "plumber statement": Letter from the Stanley Plumbing and Heating Co., November 11, 1954

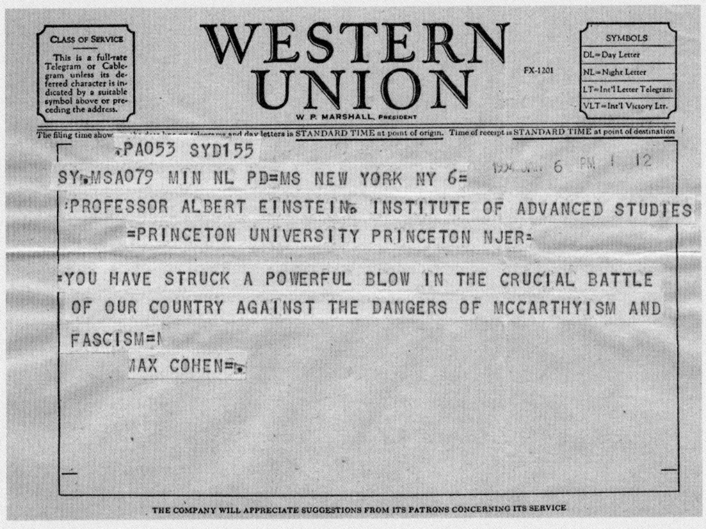
WESTERN UNION

PA053 SYD155

SY MSA079 MIN NL PD=MS NEW YORK NY 6= 1954 JAN 6 PM 1 12

PROFESSOR ALBERT EINSTEIN, INSTITUTE OF ADVANCED STUDIES =PRINCETON UNIVERSITY PRINCETON NJER=

=YOU HAVE STRUCK A POWERFUL BLOW IN THE CRUCIAL BATTLE OF OUR COUNTRY AGAINST THE DANGERS OF MCCARTHYISM AND FASCISM=

MAX COHEN=

THE COMPANY WILL APPRECIATE SUGGESTIONS FROM ITS PATRONS CONCERNING ITS SERVICE

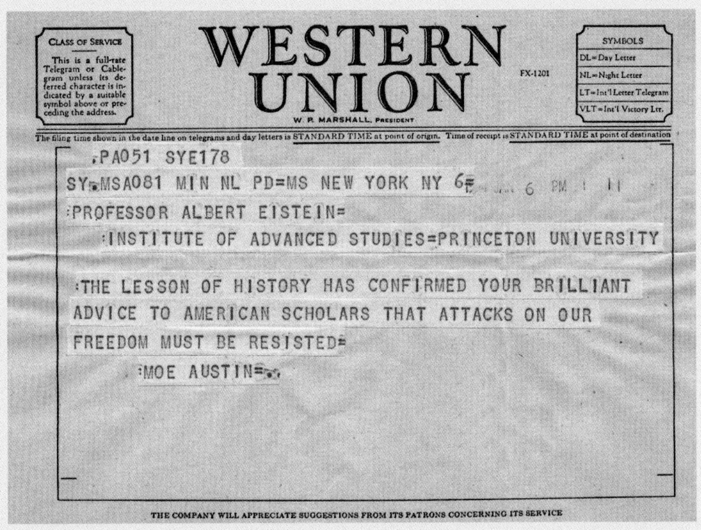
WESTERN UNION

PA051 SYE178

SY MSA081 MIN NL PD=MS NEW YORK NY 6= 6 PM 1 11

PROFESSOR ALBERT EINSTEIN= INSTITUTE OF ADVANCED STUDIES=PRINCETON UNIVERSITY

THE LESSON OF HISTORY HAS CONFIRMED YOUR BRILLIANT ADVICE TO AMERICAN SCHOLARS THAT ATTACKS ON OUR FREEDOM MUST BE RESISTED=

MOE AUSTIN=

THE COMPANY WILL APPRECIATE SUGGESTIONS FROM ITS PATRONS CONCERNING ITS SERVICE

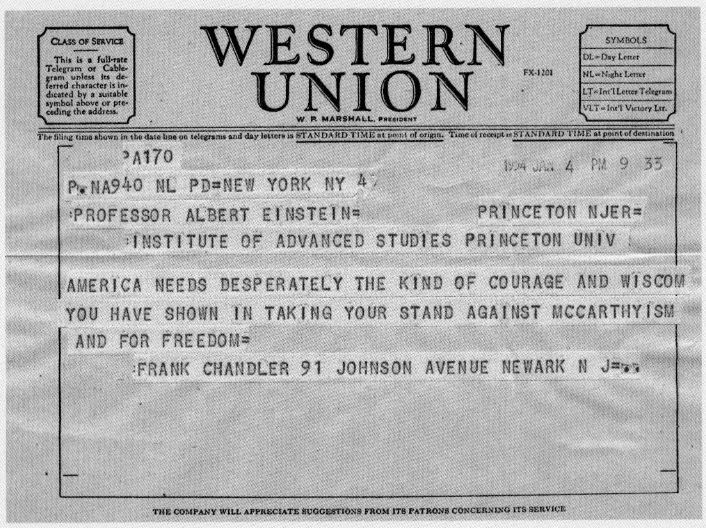
WESTERN UNION

PA170

P NA940 NL PD=NEW YORK NY 4 1954 JAN 4 PM 9 33

PROFESSOR ALBERT EINSTEIN= PRINCETON NJER= INSTITUTE OF ADVANCED STUDIES PRINCETON UNIV

AMERICA NEEDS DESPERATELY THE KIND OF COURAGE AND WISCOM YOU HAVE SHOWN IN TAKING YOUR STAND AGAINST MCCARTHYISM AND FOR FREEDOM=

FRANK CHANDLER 91 JOHNSON AVENUE NEWARK N J=

THE COMPANY WILL APPRECIATE SUGGESTIONS FROM ITS PATRONS CONCERNING ITS SERVICE

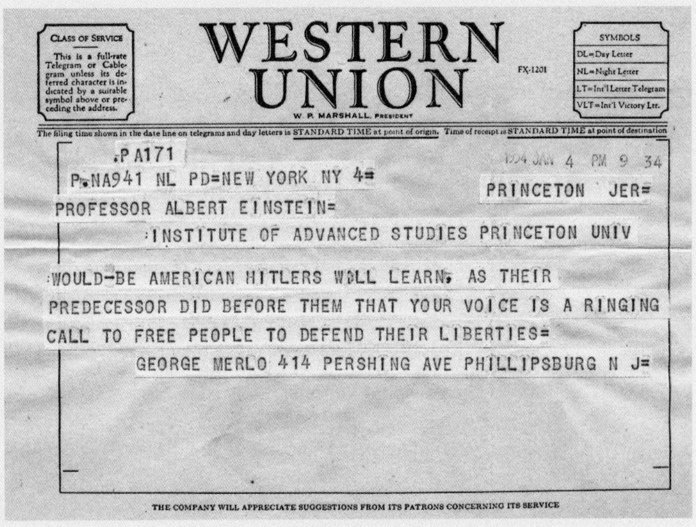
WESTERN UNION

PA171

P NA941 NL PD=NEW YORK NY 4= 1954 JAN 4 PM 9 34

PRINCETON JER=

PROFESSOR ALBERT EINSTEIN= INSTITUTE OF ADVANCED STUDIES PRINCETON UNIV

WOULD-BE AMERICAN HITLERS WILL LEARN, AS THEIR PREDECESSOR DID BEFORE THEM THAT YOUR VOICE IS A RINGING CALL TO FREE PEOPLE TO DEFEND THEIR LIBERTIES=

GEORGE MERLO 414 PERSHING AVE PHILLIPSBURG N J=

THE COMPANY WILL APPRECIATE SUGGESTIONS FROM ITS PATRONS CONCERNING ITS SERVICE

↑ Einstein received numerous telegrams and letters supporting his criticism of the reduction of civil liberties.

« Here the situation is a bit fierce at present, although ludicrous from a distance. Never a nation may have existed which had so much wealth and so much fear. It is not so innocuous a combination. One can only hope that the hangover won't bring about too much calamity. »

↑ A rather mellow description of the atmosphere in the America of the McCarthy era.
From Einstein's letter to Carl Seelig, April 14, 1954

6

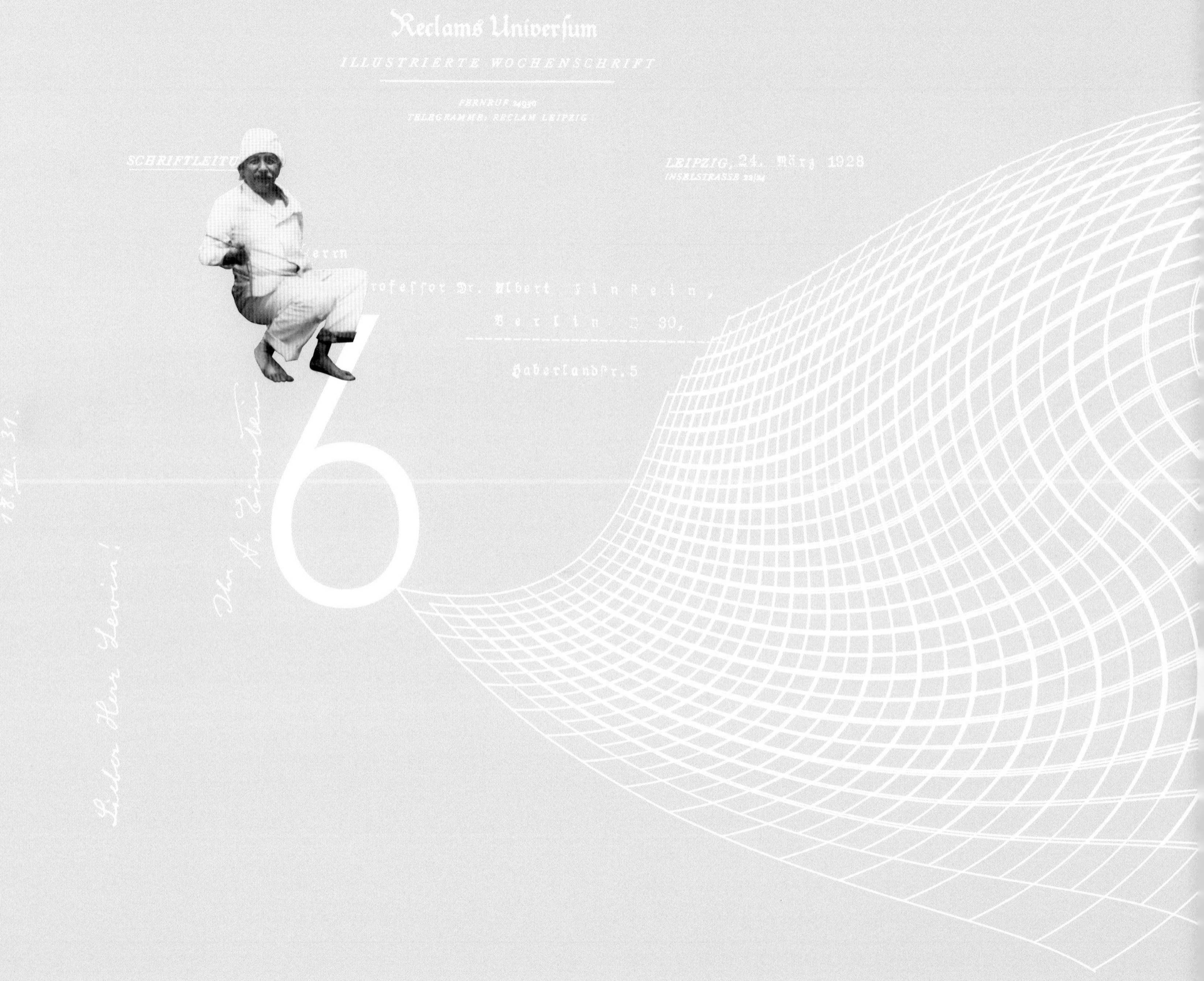
Reclams Universum
ILLUSTRIERTE WOCHENSCHRIFT
TELEGRAMME: RECLAM LEIPZIG
LEIPZIG, 24. März 1928
Professor Dr. Albert Einstein,
Berlin W 30,
Haberlandstr. 5
Lieber Herr Levin!
Ihr A. Einstein
18. VI. 31.

EINSTEIN AT LEISURE

« I even have a compass now that shines in the dark, like a fairly serious seafarer.
Yet I am not so talented in this art, and I am happy enough if I can manage to get myself off the sandbank on which I've got stuck (somewhat like in the Beethoven quartet) »

To Queen Mother Elisabeth of Belgium, February 16, 1935

↑ Playing his violin on board the *Belgenland*, December 1930

→ From a letter to his biographer Philipp Frank, spring 1940

« I took violin lessons from age 6 to 14, but had no luck with my teachers for whom music did not transcend mechanical exercise. I actually started to learn something at the age of 13 after I had fallen in love with Mozart's sonatas. Striving to reproduce their artistic essence and unique charm, I was forced to improve the technique acquired by playing these sonatas, without ever practicing systematically. Anyway, I believe that love is a better teacher than conscientiousness – certainly, at least, for me. »

MUSIC

In music, Einstein found a source of recreation and a diversion from the strains of his theoretical work and his public activities. He would resort to music when he got stuck with a problem in physics, or in moments of emotional turmoil. Sometimes, the solution to a problem would come to him while playing music.

Musical education was part of middle-class culture. Like Einstein, many of his peers and colleagues had learned to play an instrument and their gatherings afforded them an opportunity to play music together as well as to engage in intellectual exchange.

In addition to the numerous unnamed and unknown individuals with whom Einstein played music were his colleagues Max Planck and Max Born, the young violin virtuoso Boris Schwarz, and the renowned pianist Artur Schnabel. Einstein played chamber music with his friend the physicist Paul Ehrenfest in Leiden, mathematician Jacques Hadamard in Paris, a Pater Caramelli in Fiesole, or two young jazz musicians in Palm Springs. In Jerusalem Einstein "played with [an] officer in [High Commissioner Herbert] Samuel's apartment – far too long, because starved for music" and days later with the British Attorney-General, whose wife wrote: "He looked so happy while he was playing that I enjoyed watching as much as listening." And in Brussels, Queen Elisabeth waited with her violin for Einstein, sharing with him a love of Mozart's compositions.

The high value that Einstein attached to music in his own life, and his desire to instill in his sons the same joy to make music, is expressed enthusiastically in many letters to Hans Albert and Eduard.

The characteristics he appreciated in music were similar to those he favored in mathematics: purity, clarity, simplicity and balance. He revered Bach and Mozart, being his ideal composers, and enjoyed Baroque music including the works of Vivaldi, Corelli and Purcell. Yet he felt blissful with the gentle fervor of Haydn's sonatas, and with Schubert's compositions he admired their "consummate ability to express emotions." This is echoed in a remark he made in a letter to Eduard: "After all, music is for the soul and not for the intellect."
Richard Wagner's compositions, however, he abhorred, and he was unresponsive to the music of contemporary composers.

In popular mythology, Einstein as a violinist is the hero of numerous ingenious legends. This resulted in his receiving, among other letters to Einstein, the musician, a considerable number of requests relating to the physics of violin-making. At the same time gifts of musical pieces and musical instruments arrived at his door.

Opinions vary as to the quality of his playing. He himself liked to jest about his "bungling," finding it little impressive, which, however, did not at all interfere with his pleasure in fiddling.
He was probably a good amateur who had an intuitive understanding of music.

Towards the end of his life, he grew to dislike the "scratching" sounds he produced on the violin. He eventually abandoned the violin, while still improvising on the piano.

« My fiddle had to be laid aside. It may be pretty much surprised that it is never taken out of the black case; it probably thinks it has gotten a stepfather. How I miss the old friend through whom I say and sing to myself all that which I often do not at all admit to myself in arid thoughts and which, at best, makes me laugh when I see it in others… »

↑ From a letter to Julia Niggli, July 28, 1899, after Einstein had injured his right hand in an accident at the laboratory, and could not play music for several days.

← At his Berlin home, Haberlandstrasse 5, together with the cellist Francesco von Mendelssohn and the pianist Bruno Eisner, late 1920s

← At his first Princeton home, Library Place 2, with Ossip Giskin (cello), Toscha Seidel and Bernard Ocko (violin). Standing behind the musicians are Mrs. Seidel, Elsa Einstein, Emil Hilb, November 1933

Lieber Herr Levin!

Ich habe heute zwei Stunden auf Ihrer Geige phantasiert und bin völlig trunken und behext. Es ist, wie wenn ein Etwas spielte und man selbst nur den Takt dazu machte. Ich habe dasselbe Gefühl wie bei der Guarneri in Pasadena, dass ich dieses Instrumentes nicht würdig bin, dass ein wirklicher Künstler darauf spielen müsste. Ich betrachte die Geige auch wirklich nur als mir geliehen und warte, dass Sie eines Tages anders verfügen.

In aufrichtiger Bewunderung

Ihr

A. Einstein.

↑→ Letter to Julius Levin, July 18, 1931
Julius Levin – a physician, writer, musician, and amateur luthier – had "meliorated" one of Einstein's violins according to a method he himself had developed. Einstein was thrilled by the new sound, perceiving it as equal to the sound of the old Italian master instruments.
When Levin, destitute, had to leave Germany in 1933, Einstein approached various authorities hoping to collect the funds that would permit Levin to set up a luthier's school in Belgium or France. In an appraisal, however, it turned out that Levin's method of melioration caused damage to the instruments rather than improving them.– Albert and Elsa Einstein and the Queen Mother Elisabeth of Belgium, supported the poverty stricken Levin for some time out of their own pockets; yet he never got to see the unfavorable expert's report. Julius Levin died in January 1935

« I improvised for two hours today on your violin and I feel completely drunk and spellbound. It is as if a something-or-other would be playing, and oneself only adds the rhythm. I have the same feeling as with the Guarneri in Pasadena, namely that I am not worthy of that instrument, and that a genuine artist should play it. »

A. Einstein ← P. Ehren
Leiden 12 XI 21

Sonaten und Partiten

für

Violine allein

von

Joh. Seb. Bach

herausgegeben von

Joseph Joachim

und

Andreas Moser

Heft I. II. je M. 3.—

zuzüglich Teuerungszuschlag

250%

Eigentum der Verleger für alle Länder. Aufführungsrecht vorbehalten.

ED. BOTE & G. BOCK
BERLIN W. 8
Gegründet 1838

Alleinvertrieb für Italien FRATELLI CURCI, Neapel.

→ Reply to a query of the illustrated weekly *Reclams Universum* on the music of Johann Sebastian Bach, March 24, 1928

Reclams Universum

ILLUSTRIERTE WOCHENSCHRIFT

FERNRUF 24930
TELEGRAMME: RECLAM LEIPZIG

SCHRIFTLEITUNG

LEIPZIG, 24. März 1928
INSELSTRASSE 22/24

R.

Herrn

Professor Dr. Albert Einstein,

Berlin W 30,

Haberlandstr. 5

Sehr verehrter Herr Professor!

Dürfen wir Sie an unser Schreiben vom 29. v. M. erinnern, auf das wir leider noch ohne Nachricht geblieben sind? Aus redaktionellen Gründen wäre uns eine baldige Benachrichtigung sehr erwünscht, und wir hoffen gern, daß Sie den erbetenen Artikel für uns schreiben werden.

Wir verbleiben mit dem Ausdruck unserer ausgezeichneten Hochachtung

ergebenst

Schriftleitung von
Reclams Universum.

Was ich zu Bach's Lebenswerk zu sagen habe:
Hören, spielen, lieben, verehren, ~~Bewundern~~
und — das Maul halten!

« This is what I have to say about Bach's lifework: listen, play, love, revere – and keep your trap shut! »

← Einstein had inspired his friend and colleague Paul Ehrenfest with a love for Bach's music. "He opens up Bach to me," Ehrenfest noted in his diary in 1916. Einstein, who could not play piano at sight, envied his friend: "You are lucky to be able to play Bach and not have to wait until someone plays it to you." Ehrenfest presented Einstein with this collection of sonatas by Bach which Einstein – on his violin – could play at sight.

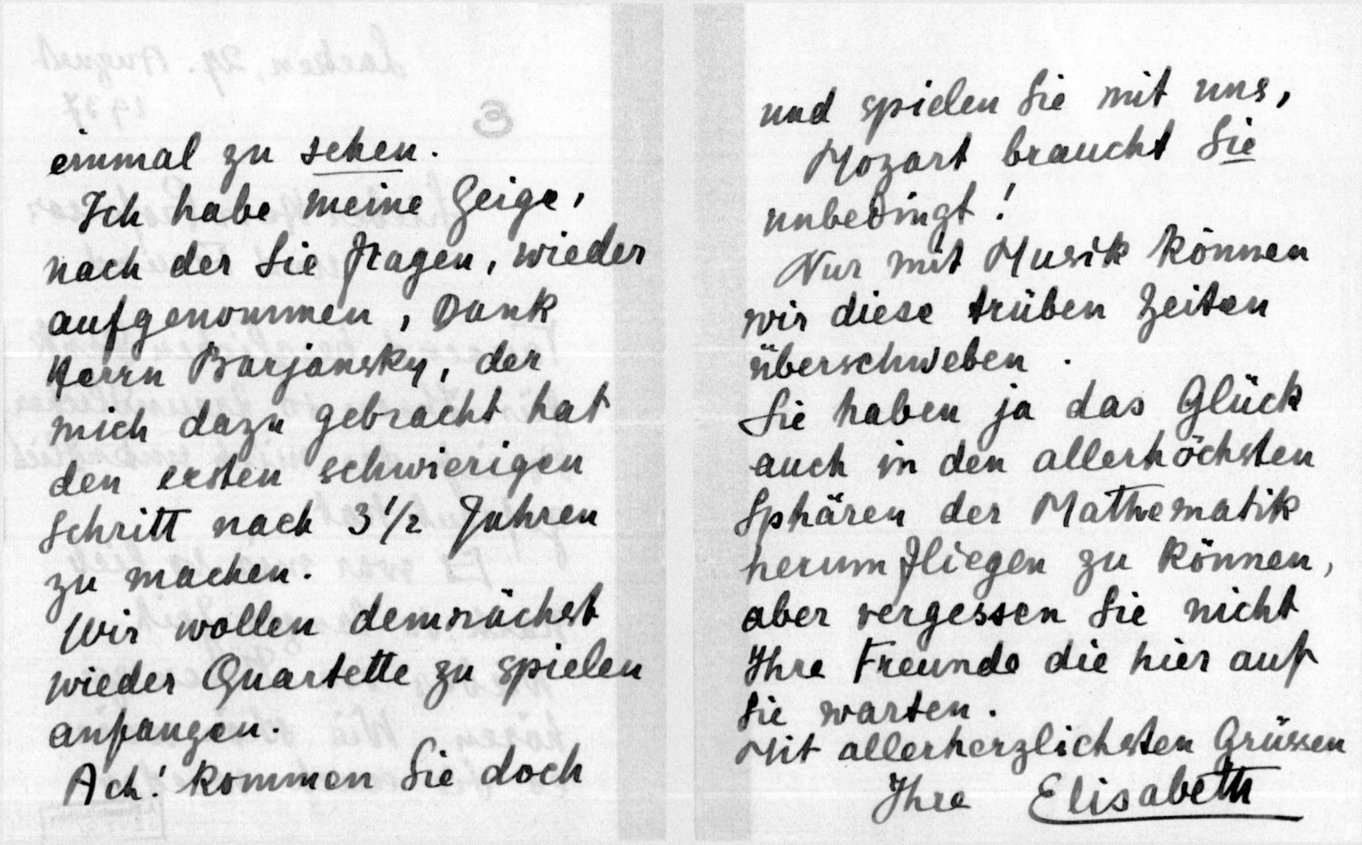
einmal zu sehen.
Ich habe meine Geige, nach der Sie fragen, wieder aufgenommen, Dank Herrn Barjansky, der mich dazu gebracht hat den ersten schwierigen Schritt nach 3 1/2 Jahren zu machen.
Wir wollen demnächst wieder Quartette zu spielen anfangen.
Ach! kommen Sie doch und spielen Sie mit uns, Mozart braucht Sie unbedingt!
Nur mit Musik können wir diese trüben Zeiten überschweben.
Sie haben ja das Glück auch in den allerhöchsten Sphären der Mathematik herumfliegen zu können, aber vergessen Sie nicht Ihre Freunde die hier auf Sie warten.
Mit allerherzlichsten Grüssen
Ihre Elisabeth

« As for my violin, that you are asking about, thanks to Mr. Barjansky I resumed playing […]
We intend soon to restart playing quartets.
Ah, do come and play with us, Mozart needs you absolutely. Only with music will we be able to glide over these gloomy times. »

↑↗ In 1929, Queen Elisabeth invited Einstein for the first time to her palace in Laeken. Similar political positions, shared also by the King, and the common love of music and philosophical questions provided the foundation for a cordial friendship between the queen and the scientist which lasted until Einstein's death.
From a letter by the Queen Mother Elisabeth of Belgium, August 27, 1937

« I would like to recommend to you a trio by Beethoven for two violins and viola (op. 82), a lively piece that I ignored completely until yesterday evening. I am delighted to learn that, with always the same ardor, you devote yourself to the arts and that you have kept loyal to the small old circle.
If I could only play a piece of Mozart with you once again. »

↑ In 1933, spending several months in Belgium before leaving for the United States for good, Einstein was a frequent guest at the queen's residence, where he used to play chamber music with her.
From a letter Einstein wrote to the Queen Mother Elisabeth of Belgium, August 12, 1939

→ Albert Einstein at the piano,
Nara, Japan,
December 17, 1922

→ From a letter to his grandson Bernhard, mid-1940s

« I am happy that you have such a lively interest in music. Cultivate it well, there is no better companion in life. I could not possibly think of my life without playing music. In tough times (and in happy moments, too) I was able to cope quite well with myself and with the world because I could always have recourse to it. It makes one free and independent. »

SAILING

As far as we know, the only sport Einstein ever had any passion for was sailing.
He became a sailing enthusiast during his student years in Zurich.
After his move to Berlin, he acquired a small boat of his own and sailed it, often with friends or his sons, on the lakes around the city.
For his 50th birthday, wealthy friends gave him a much more comfortable boat, the dinghy cruiser "Tümmler" (German for "porpoise"). During four long summers Einstein enjoyed life far from the city at his summer house at Caputh, and spent entire days on his boat.
In 1933, the Nazis confiscated the house and the boat. Sailing, though, remained Einstein's summer enjoyment also after his immigration to the United States.

His new boat was playfully named "Tinef" (Yiddish-German for "worthless thing"), a name that was completely inconsistent with what the boat actually represented for Einstein.

Sailing allowed Einstein to lose himself in thought while the wind carried him along.
His pleasure was unspoiled by cautiousness and unburdened by technical knowledge. Intriguingly, Einstein could not swim, yet he stubbornly refused to carry a life jacket.
He did not take any delight in speeding and had no desire to engage with competition. He rather enjoyed it when the breeze died down and the boat came to a standstill in a lull or ran aground. He would often keep a notebook at hand, scribbling away at scientific calculations when the sea was calm.

↑ Watch Hill, Rhode Island, 1934

↑ Still sailing along in the 1940s

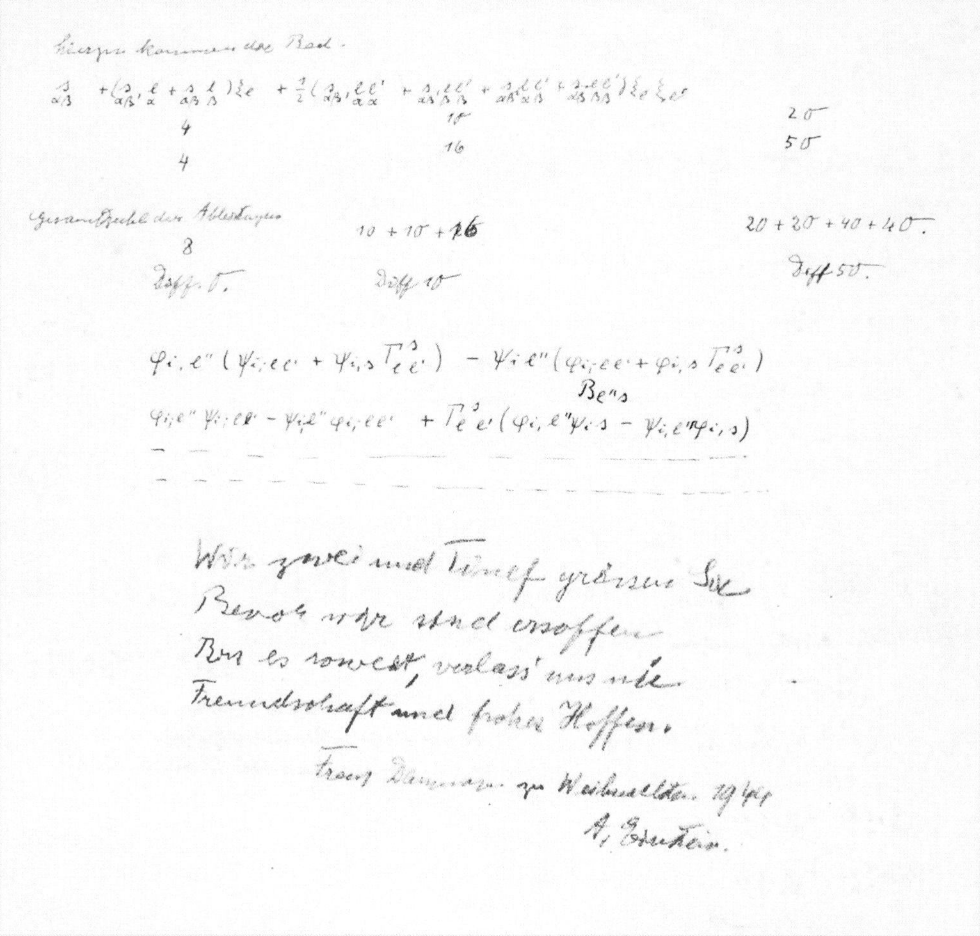

Wir zwei und Tinef grüssen Sie
Bevor wir sind ersoffen
Bis es soweit, verlass' uns nie
Freundschaft und frohes Hoffen.

Frau Damman zu Weihnachten 1944
A. Einstein.

In the summer of 1944, Einstein was sailing with three companions on Saranac Lake, in choppy conditions. When the boat hit a rock, it quickly filled with water and overturned. Einstein was trapped beneath the water under the sail, with his leg tangled in a rope. Unperturbed, he managed to free his leg and claw his way to the surface, where he was rescued by a motorboat which happened to come by. This incident, referred to in the quatrain, was not the only capsize Einstein experienced. Yet it may have been the occurrence of which it is reported that, while Einstein struggled in the water, he kept his pipe in the air so that eventually his pipe, and the pipe only, remained dry.

« Both we and Tinef send regards
As you see we have not drowned
Until such time is on the cards
May friendship and hope abound. »

←↑ Quatrain dedicated to Ruth Damman, Christmas 1944
Translation: Ze'ev Rosenkranz & Susan Worthington

« When the weather permits, we sail all afternoon, even into the open sea, and we let the waves rock us. During the morning hours and in the evening, we are working and playing music. I feel almost ashamed to pass along life so beautifully and airily, in this time of mad events. »

→ From a letter to his wife Elsa, September 7, 1923, from Kiel on the Baltic Sea where Einstein was vacationing with his sons Hans Albert and Eduard.

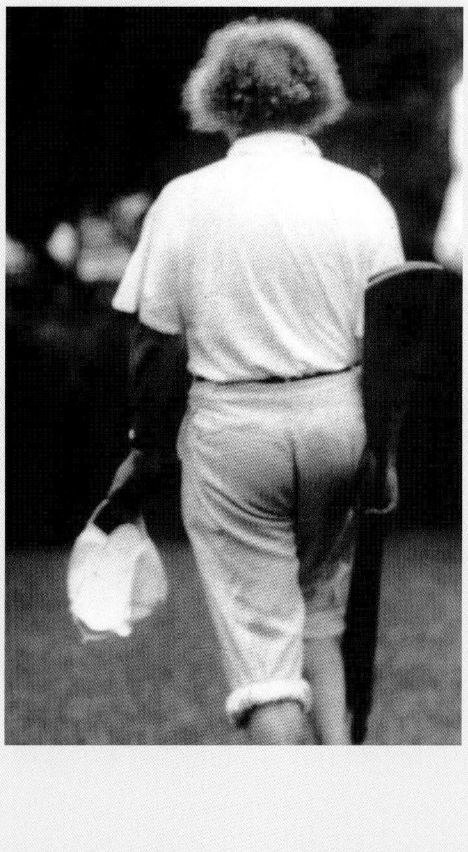

→ Huntington, Long Island, 1937

DEAR MR. EINSTEIN

7

CORRESPONDENCE WITH CHILDREN

« Dear Mr. Einstein,
I saw your picture in the paper.
I think you ought to have your
hair cut, so you can look better. »

From a letter by six-year-old Ann G. Kocin, 1951

CORRESPONDENCE WITH CHILDREN

Einstein was a subject of fascination for children all around the world. They sent him letters asking all kinds of questions and some even offered very practical advice. Many enclosed drawings, photos and small gifts. Einstein obviously enjoyed receiving these letters as he kept a large number of them. His carefully worded responses reveal his wish to foster children's natural inquisitiveness, his great affection for them and his quirky sense of humor.

In his old age, walking around Princeton, he would always greet children and babble with the babies. Children were baffled and intrigued by the eccentricity of Einstein's appearance: the unruliness of his white hair, his socklessness, his baggy coat and woolen cap.

« Dear Uncle Einstein do com at us at the school of the Jewishcommunity the boys school grade 7a. Wish yu much luck for the 50 bruday. »

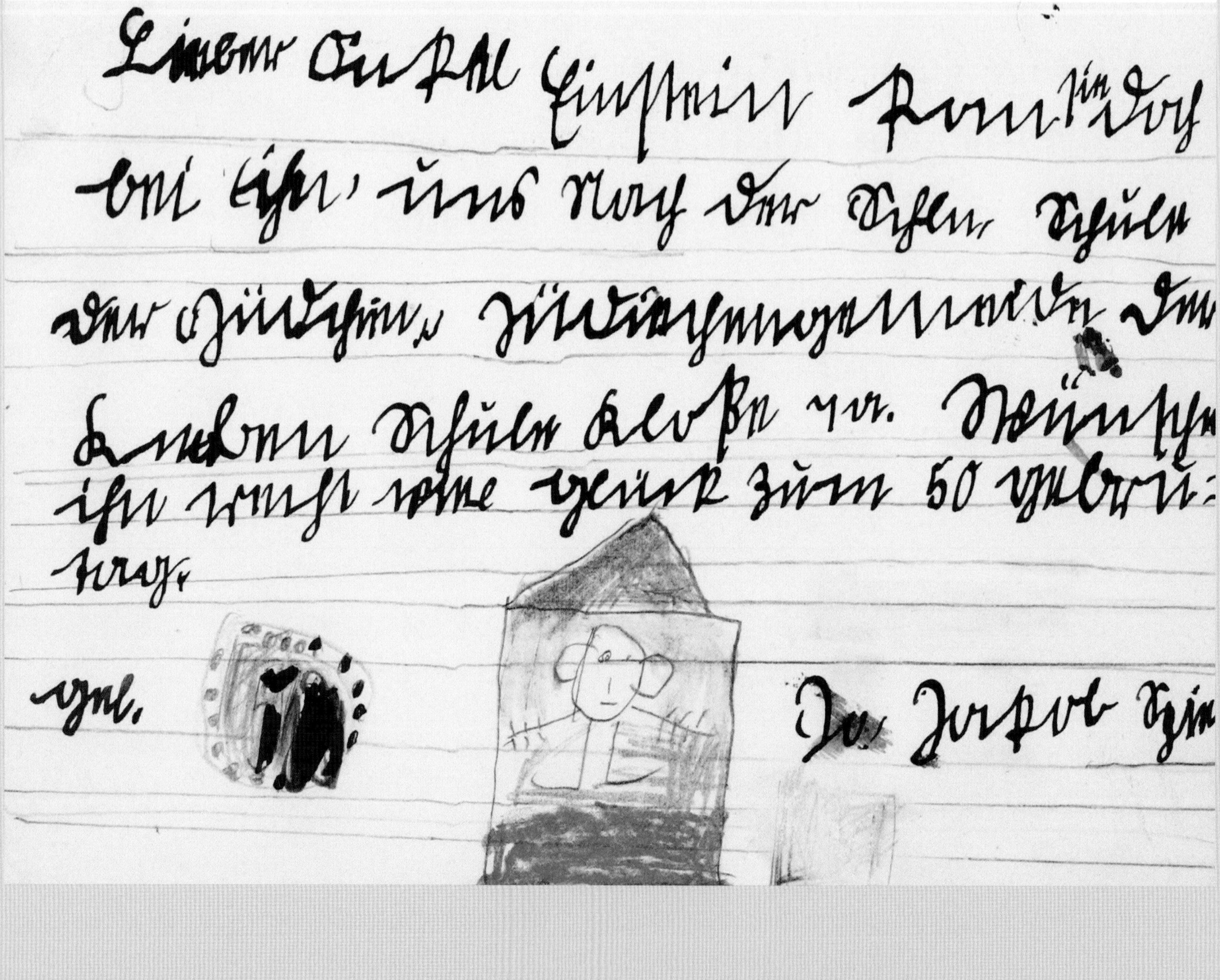

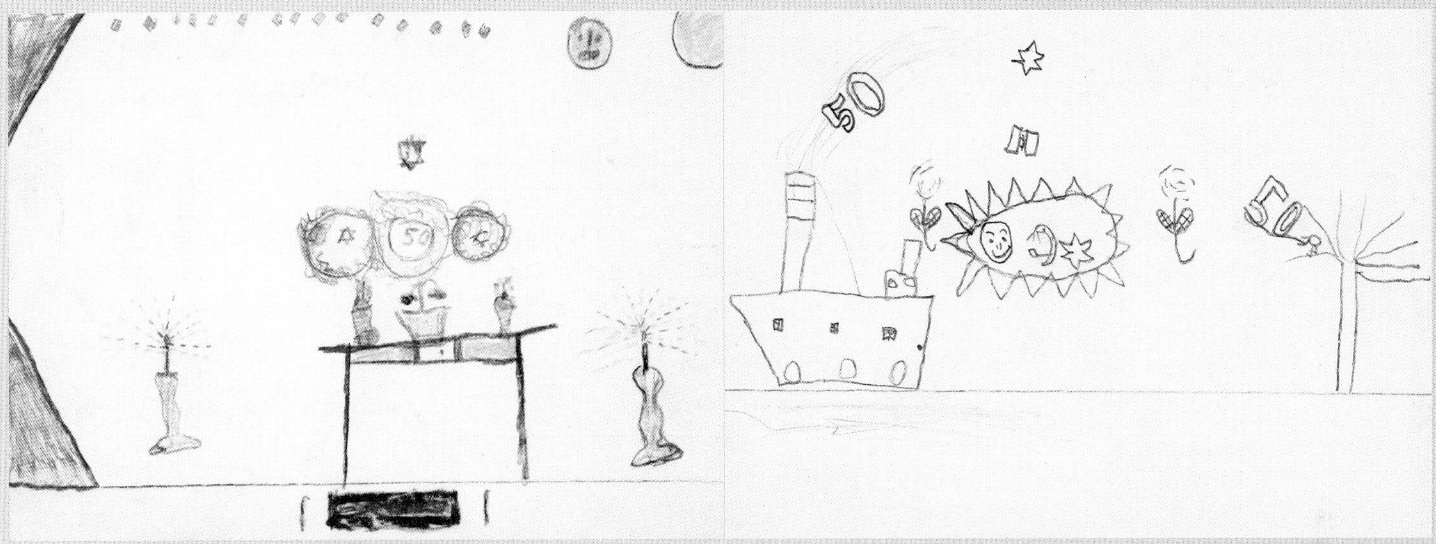

←↑ Postcards sent from Jewish
↙ schoolchildren in Berlin on the
occasion of Einstein's
50th birthday, March 14, 1929

↓ With children of the village,
Espluga de Francoli, Tarragona, Spain,
February 25, 1923
Photo by Casimiro Lana

↑ Drawings from Japanese school children for Einstein's 70th birthday, Takatsumi Primary School, Osaka Prefecture, March 1949

Monique was a refugee from France and the niece of a Princeton professor. At the age of eight, she wrote Einstein the following letter:

« Dear Professor Einstein,

When I came to this country my aunt introduced me to you. Could you tell me how old the world is and what will become of it?
P.S. You get letters from all over and I collect stamps. Could you please send me your stamps?

Monique »

June 19,1951

Miss Monique Epstein
381 Central Park West
New York City

Dear Monique:

There has been an earth since a little more than a billion years. As for the question of the end of it I advise: Wait and see!

Kind regards,

A. Einstein.

Albert Einstein

I enclose a few stamps for
your collection.

→ This was his reply:

March 26,1955

To the 5th Grade
Farmingdale Elementary School
Farmingdale N.Y.

Dear Children,

I thank you all for the birthday gift you kindly sent me and for your letter of congratulation. Your gift will be an appropriate suggestion to be a little more elegant in the future than hitherto. Because neckties and cuffs exist for me only as remote memories.

With kind wishes and regards,

yours sincerely,

A. Einstein.

Albert Einstein.

← Einstein thanks the 5th Grade of Farmingdale Elementary School, New York, for their birthday present, March 26, 1955

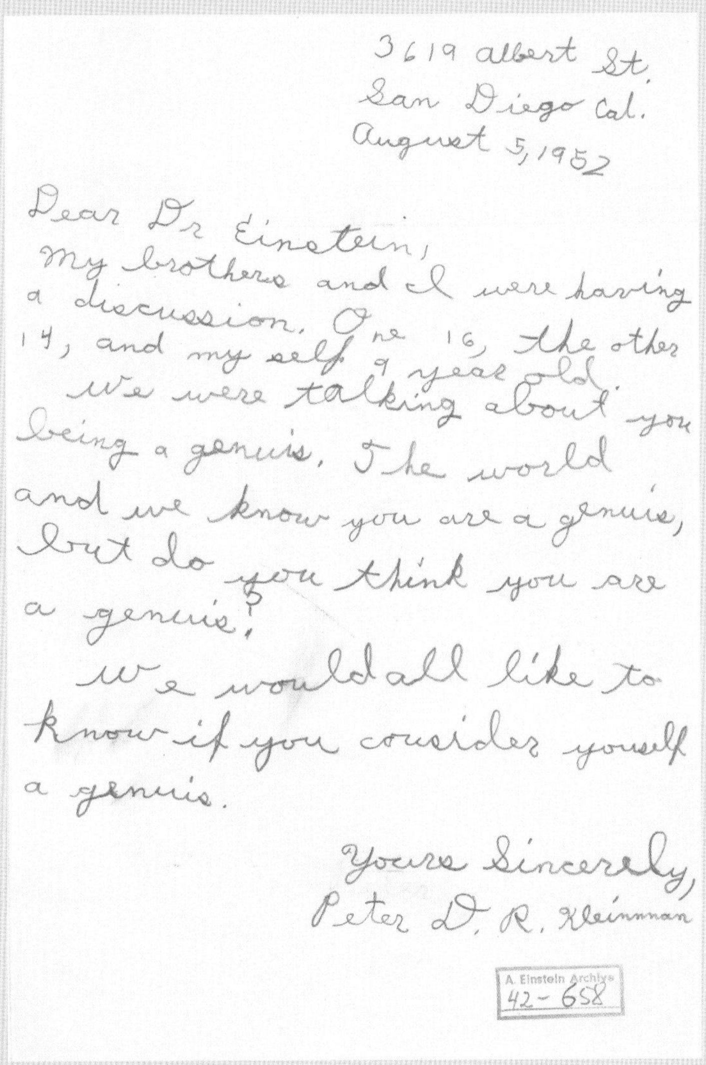

3619 albert St.
San Diego Cal.
August 5, 1952

Dear Dr Einstein,
My brothers and I were having a discussion. One 16, the other 14, and my self 9 year old.
We were talking about you being a genius. The world and we know you are a genius, but do you think you are a genius?
We would all like to know if you consider youself a genius.

Youre Sincerely,
Peter D. R. Kleinman

A. Einstein Archive
42-658

← Considered a genius by the entire world, Einstein himself might, however, have thought otherwise. Did he? That was the question, nine-year-old Peter Kleinman asked him in his letter of August 5, 1952. What may have been Einstein's reply? Did he downplay the role of ingenuity and assert that he owed his achievements mainly to a passionate curiosity, to a certain imaginativeness and to his stubbornness? Did he encourage the boys to become "geniuses" themselves by devoting their studies to subjects they truly loved?

→ Here Einstein is holding James William Pietsch, the infant son of his neighbors, July 13, 1951

← Sitting on Einstein's lap is eight-month-old John R. Steiding.
Einstein commented on the photo session: "It will certainly look like an Italian picture of the Madonna."
Deep Creek Lake, Maryland, September 1946

↑ Three little girls, unidentified so far, visiting with Einstein, around 1950

↓ A somewhat precocious entrepreneurial suggestion made by ten-year-old Louise Baker of Toronto, early 1950s

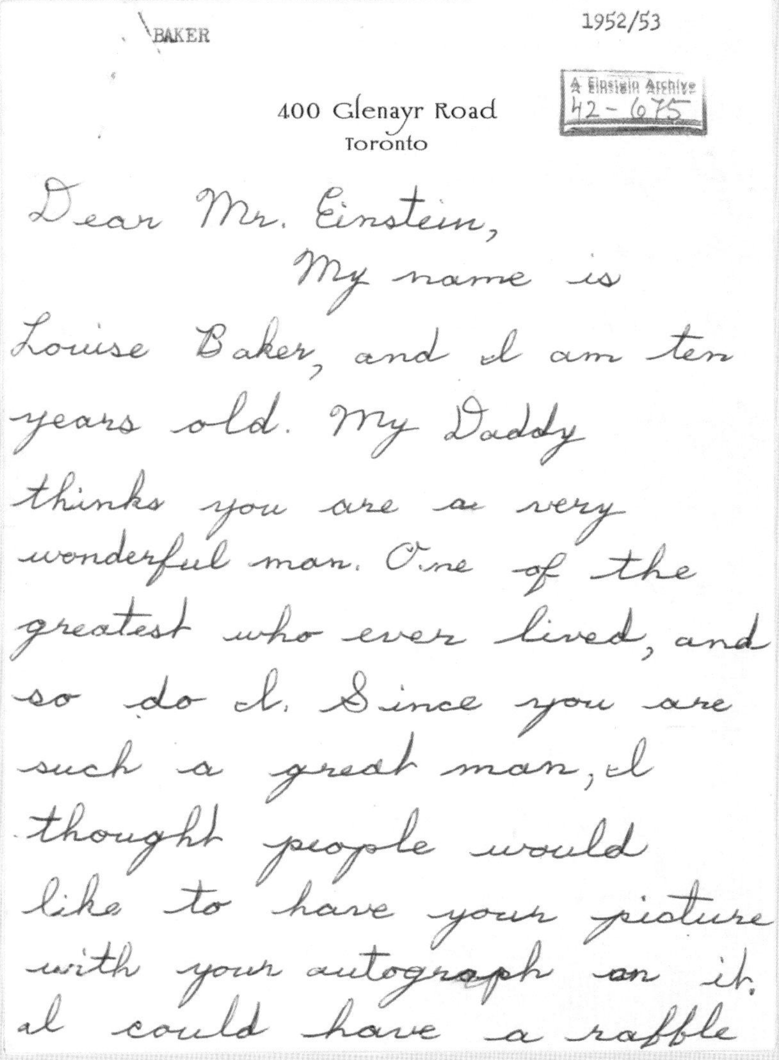

BAKER 1952/53

A Einstein Archive 42-675

400 Glenayr Road
Toronto

Dear Mr. Einstein,
My name is Louise Baker, and I am ten years old. My Daddy thinks you are a very wonderful man. One of the greatest who ever lived, and so do I. Since you are such a great man, I thought people would like to have your picture with your autograph on it. I could have a raffle

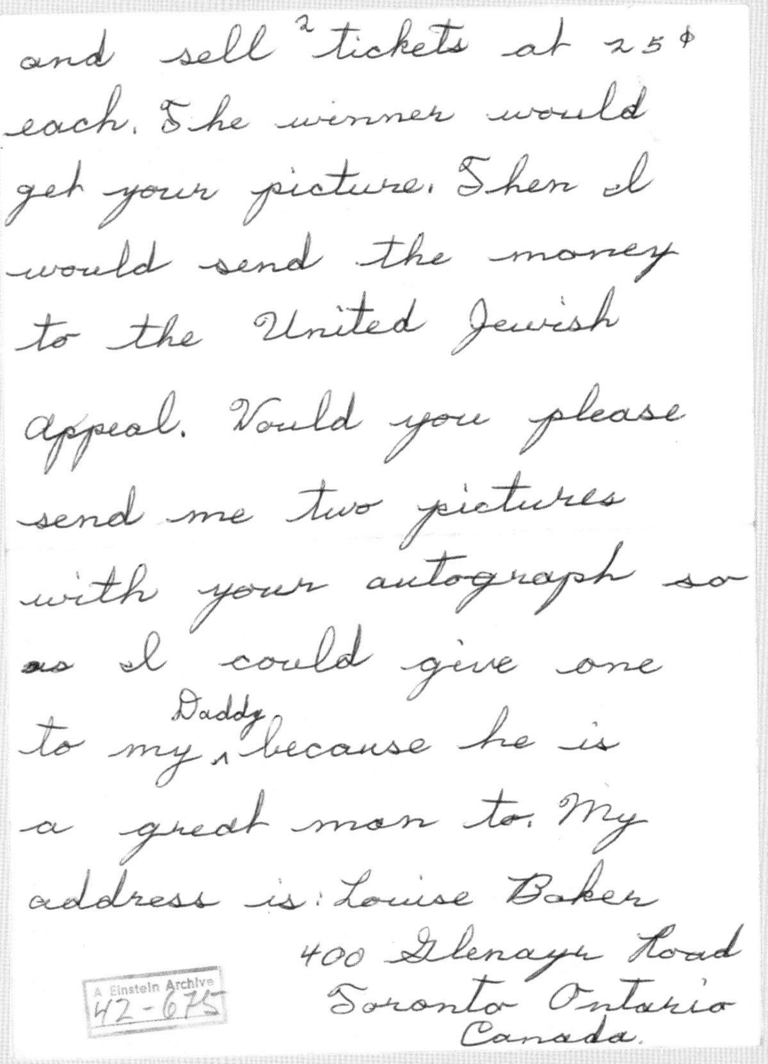

and sell [2] tickets at 25¢ each. The winner would get your picture. Then I would send the money to the United Jewish Appeal. Would you please send me two pictures with your autograph so so I could give one to my Daddy because he is a great man to. My address is: Louise Baker
400 Glenayr Road
Toronto Ontario
Canada.

A Einstein Archive 42-675

8

DEC 27
1940
Professor Relativity Einstein
Princeton
N. Jersey

THE CURIOSITY FILE

« Dear Professor,
would it be reasonable to assume that it is while a person is standing on his head – or rather upside down – he falls in love and does other foolish things? »

From a letter by Frank Wall, 1933

THE CURIOSITY FILE

Einstein's mythic stature brought with it a huge and varied correspondence.
Einstein and his secretary, Helen Dukas, relished curious and eccentric items and preserved them in the "komische Mappe" (the "curious file").

Some 700 items have been preserved, even with a special section for curious envelopes. Only very rarely does one find a reply to these unusual letters in the Albert Einstein Archives.

The files include fan mail, marriage proposals, eccentric suggestions and weird scientific theories. A less welcome side to these files is the hate mail sent to Einstein, usually anti-Semitic and anti-leftist in nature.

↓ Albert Einstein and Frank Aydelotte, President of Swarthmore College, Pennsylvania, June 6, 1938

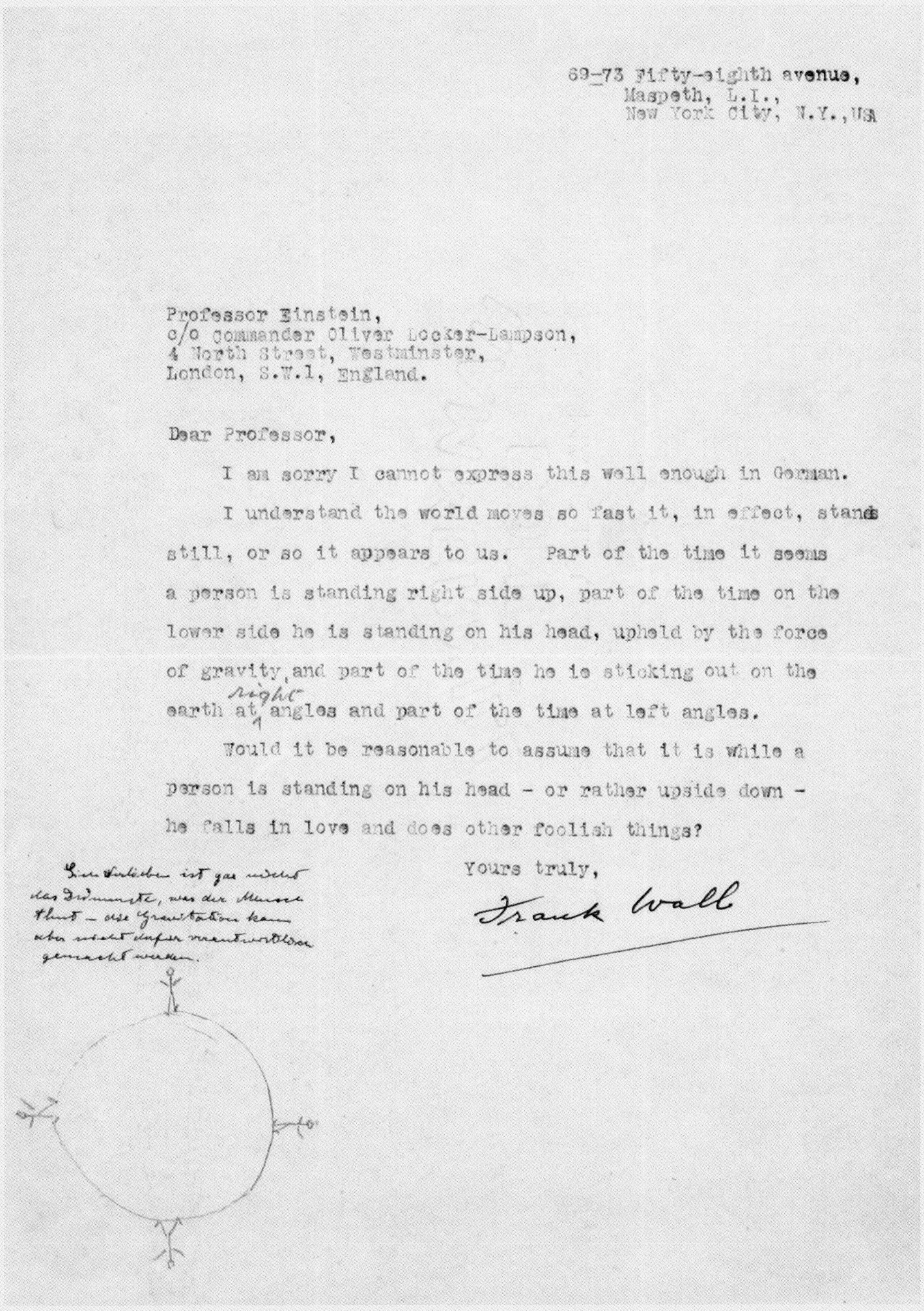

69-73 Fifty-eighth avenue,
Maspeth, L.I.,
New York City, N.Y., USA

Professor Einstein,
c/o Commander Oliver Locker-Lampson,
4 North Street, Westminster,
London, S.W.1, England.

Dear Professor,

I am sorry I cannot express this well enough in German.

I understand the world moves so fast it, in effect, stands still, or so it appears to us. Part of the time it seems a person is standing right side up, part of the time on the lower side he is standing on his head, upheld by the force of gravity, and part of the time he is sticking out on the earth at right angles and part of the time at left angles.

Would it be reasonable to assume that it is while a person is standing on his head – or rather upside down – he falls in love and does other foolish things?

Yours truly,

Frank Wall

Sich Verlieben ist gar nicht das Dümmste, was der Mensch thut – die Gravitation kann aber nicht dafür verantwortlich gemacht werden.

←↙ A rather idiosyncratic view of Einstein's theory of gravitation. Letter from Frank Wall, New York, 1933 and Einstein's drafted response

« Falling in love is not at all the most stupid thing that people do – but gravitation cannot be held responsible for it. »

→ On behalf of The Shoe Club, Inc., New York, J.J.Murray requests Einstein's right shoe. February 7, 1936

K. W.

The **SHOE CLUB**, *Inc.*

HOTEL McALPIN
NEW YORK

TELEPHONE:
PENN 6-5700

February 7th
1 9 3 6

Professor Albert Einstien
Institue for Advanced Studies
Princeton, N. J.

Dear Professor Einstien:

In behalf of the Shoe Club, the outstanding organization in the shoe industry comprising a membership of 400 leather tanners, manufacturers of mens and womens shoes and retail merchants and buyers, we are asking an unusual favor, to start a collection of shoes worn by outstanding persons.

The Shoe Club feels that a collection of shoes that have been worn by men of renown will be an inspiration to the younger members of the shoe industry not only in craftsmanship, but to show them that their livelihood is of a service to mankind that they can be proud of.

Would you be kind enough therefore, to send us one of your old shoes, preferably the right shoe, and also fill out the enclosed autograph? This shoe will be permanently preserved and on display in our headquarters at the Hotel McAlpin, New York City.

Thanking you in advance for complying with this request, I am,

Very truly yours,
THE SHOE CLUB INC.

F. J. Murray
F. J. Murray
Executive Secretary

FJM:SH

→ In 1931, Albert and Elsa Einstein visited Warner Bros. film studios, Hollywood, where they were introduced to the magic of movies first hand.

DURBAN
SUID-AFRIKA
SOUTH AFRICA
Prof. Albert Einstein
Master Tailor of clothes for vacumm Space
Princetom University
Pricetom
New Jersey
United States of America

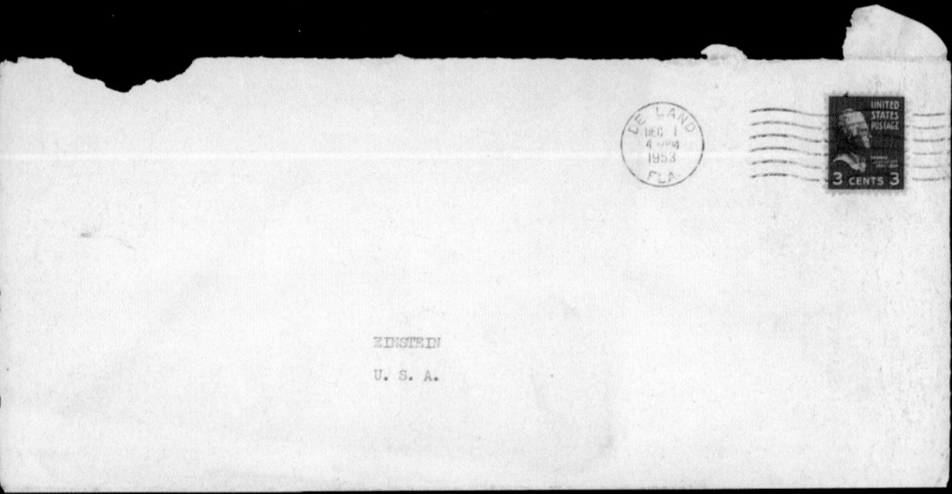
DE LAND
DEC 1
4 PM
1953
FLA.
UNITED STATES POSTAGE
3 CENTS 3
EINSTEIN
U. S. A.

R 435
GRAM
Mr. Einstein
The atomic scientist
U. S. A
DEV.
No. 1/BT.
1 rupiah
INDONESIA
AIR
INDONESIA
7 1/2
SEN

RIDGEWOOD
DEC 27
1940
Professor Relativity Einstein
Princeton
N. Jersey

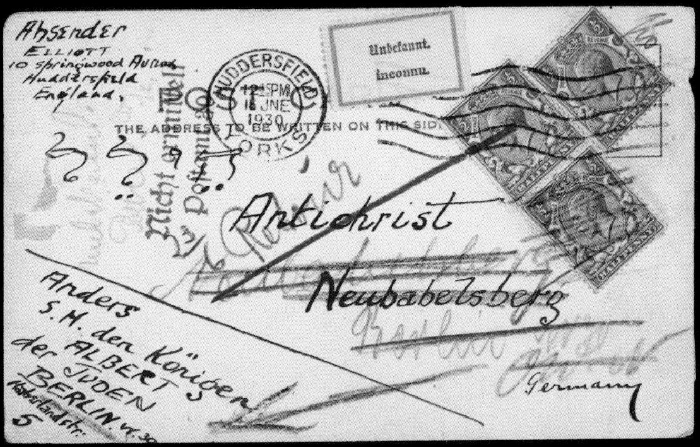
Absender
ELLIOTT
Huddersfield
England
Unbekannt.
inconnu.
HUDDERSFIELD
1930
YORKS
THE ADDRESS TO BE WRITTEN ON THIS SIDE
Antichrist
Neubabelsberg
Germany
Anders
S.M. den Königen
der JUDEN
ALBERT
BERLIN

UNITED STATES POSTAGE
SPECIAL DELIVERY
Dr. Albert Einstein,
Chief Engineer of the Universe,
School of Advanced Study,
Princeton, New Jersey,
C.C.C.P.
Special —
— Delivery

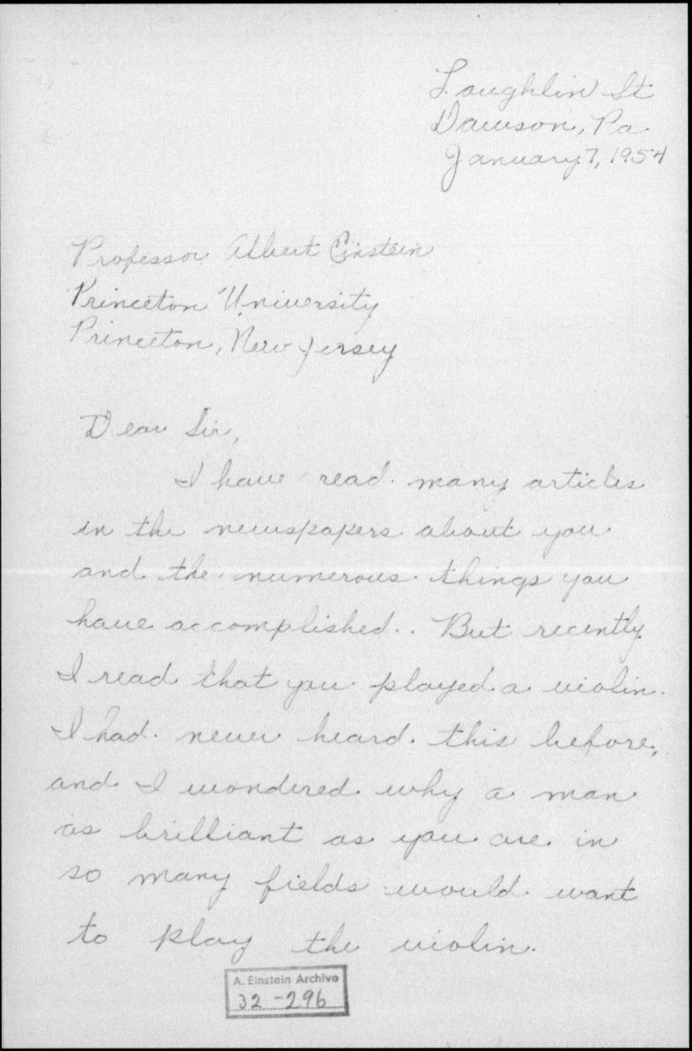

Laughlin St
Dawson, Pa.
January 7, 1954

Professor Albert Einstein
Princeton University
Princeton, New Jersey

Dear Sir,

I have read many articles in the newspapers about you and the numerous things you have accomplished. But recently I read that you played a violin. I had never heard this before, and I wondered why a man as brilliant as you are in so many fields would want to play the violin.

A. Einstein Archive
32-296

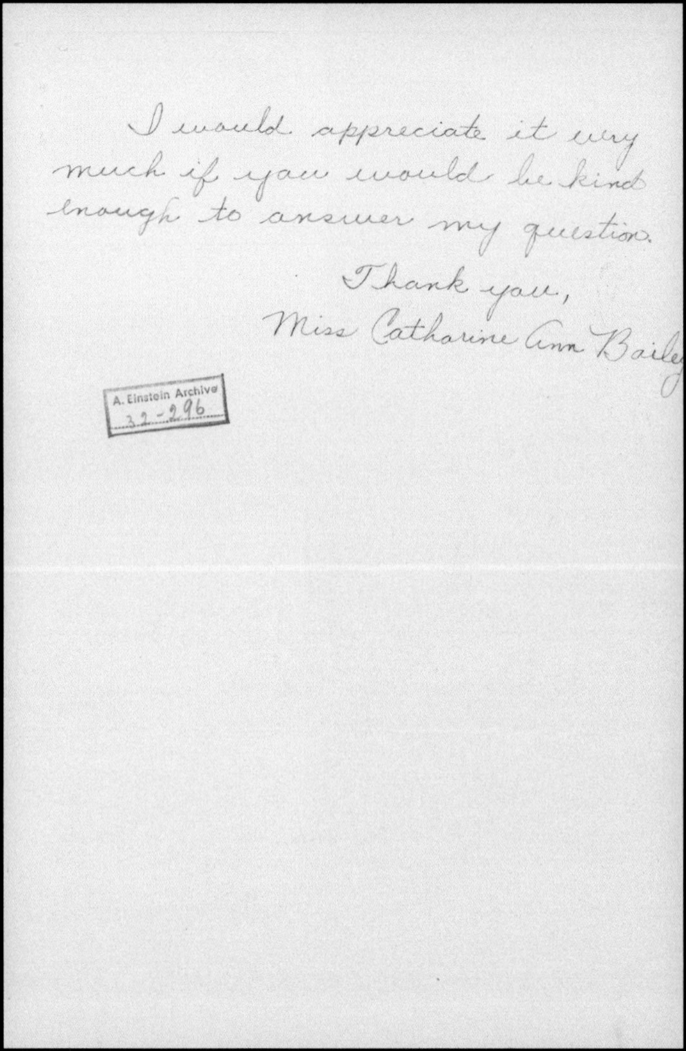

I would appreciate it very much if you would be kind enough to answer my question.

Thank you,
Miss Catharine Ann Bailey

A. Einstein Archive
32-296

↑ Are brilliance and playing the violin really inconsistent with one another?
Letter from Catherine Ann Bailey, January 7, 1954

↑ Einstein, mathematician Adolf Hurwitz and his daughter Lisbeth, Zurich, around 1912

← In a most flowery letter Reverend Mark Weiss from New York confides that he has composed a march based on old Jewish themes, and dedicates it to Einstein. His happiest moment, the reverent Reverend writes in a fumbling yet awestruck German, will be the day Einstein accepts this present as evidence of the loyal donor's admiration.
It is obvious that the Reverend was not aware of Einstein's distaste for marches:
"That a man can take pleasure in marching in fours to the strains of a band is enough to make me despise him."
Musical score sent by Mark Weiss, April 15, 1931

E. S. Moses

S.S. John M.Schofield, at sea,
Proceeding from Brake,Aldenberg,Germany,
to New York City, August 3, 1946.

Professor Albert Einstein,
Princeton University,
Princeton, New Jersey.

My dear Professor Einstein:

Forgive me if I seem presumptuous in addressing you, but I have heard of your keen sense of humor and believe that the following true anecdote may give you a friendly smile.

Our ship has just delivered a cargo of some 309,000 bushels of relief wheat to the grain elevators at the village of Brake, Port of Bremen. Our last night the Boatswain and the Carpenter, two old time sailors came back from shore a little the worse for wear, with a little kitten about six weeks old. When they sobered up the next morning they decided to become joint foster parents of the kitten. The poor kitten must have been getting a meagre diet and seemed weak and starving so they fed him one can of evaporated cream for breakfast, a can of sardines for dinner and several slices of liver sausage for supper. Naturally the cat grew strong and playful and much attached to its foster parents. One day a young seaman tried to play with the kitten who promtly scratched him. Very much surprised the seaman called out "That cat is crazy" The Carpenter indignantly cried "Sure, that cat is crazy like Einstein. Wasn't he smart enough to leave Germany and come to the United States?" So you have an eight weeks old kitten as a namesake. He has been formally, respectfully and affectionately christened "Professor Albert Einstein " by a bunch of hard boiled sailors whose conception of"relativity"is a euphemistic synonym for "kinship"

Very respectfully,
Edward S. Moses

Edward S.Moses,
ChiefEngineer,
S.S.John M.Schofield,
Waterman S.S.Company,
19 Rector Street,
New York City.

↑ The Chief Engineer on the *S.S.John M.Schofield* informs Einstein of a namesake of his who happens to be a cat. Letter from Edward S.Moses, at sea, August 3, 1946

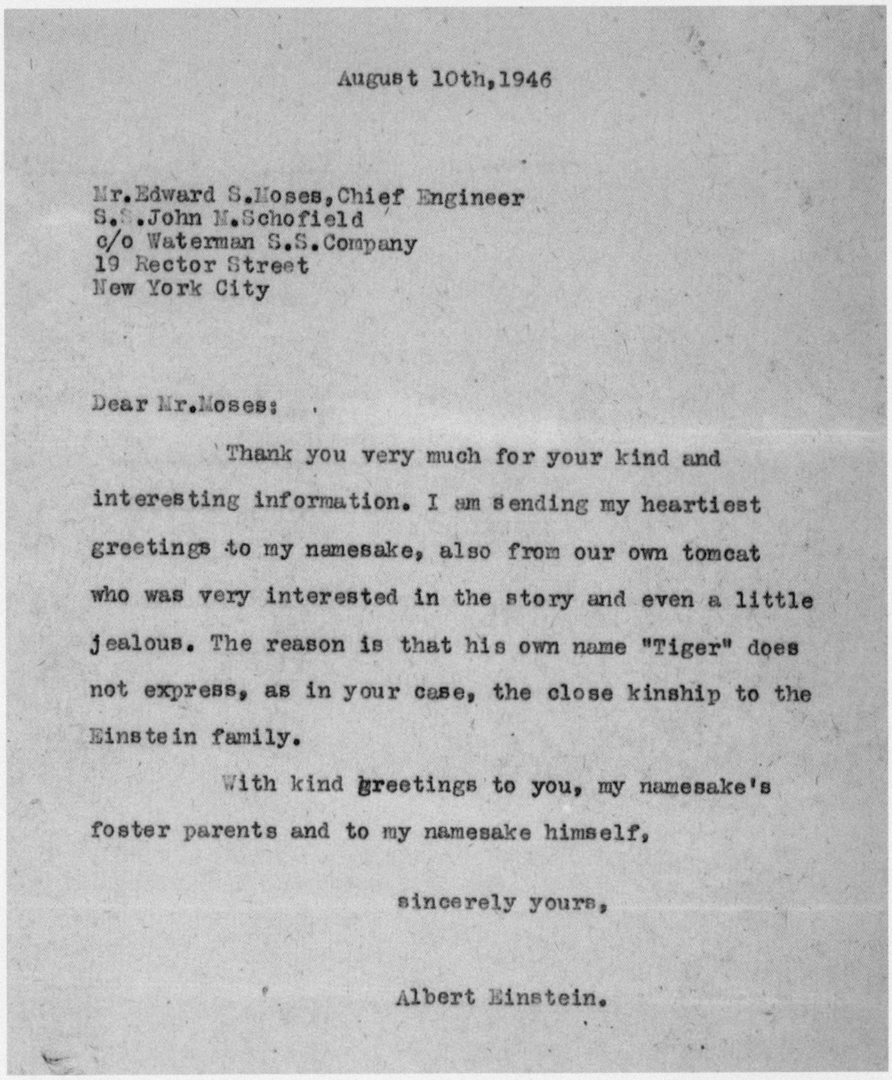

August 10th,1946

Mr.Edward S.Moses,Chief Engineer
S.S.John M.Schofield
c/o Waterman S.S.Company
19 Rector Street
New York City

Dear Mr.Moses:

Thank you very much for your kind and interesting information. I am sending my heartiest greetings to my namesake, also from our own tomcat who was very interested in the story and even a little jealous. The reason is that his own name "Tiger" does not express, as in your case, the close kinship to the Einstein family.

With kind greetings to you, my namesake's foster parents and to my namesake himself,

sincerely yours,

Albert Einstein.

← Einstein's reply to the Chief Engineer, August 10, 1946

→ Riding a bicycle in Santa Barbara, California, February 1933

↑ Albert and Elsa Einstein visiting Hopi House at the Grand Canyon where Indians demonstrated their arts and posed for pictures with tourists. An apocryphal story claims that the Hopis addressed Einstein as "The Great Relative," yet it is more likely that this pun was invented by a creative journalist. February 28, 1931

Hetzer Einstein nun in Europa auf dem Kriegspfad.
Professor Albert Einstein, der in Amerika ehrenhalber zum Indianerhäuptling ernannt wurde, befindet sich nun „in Europa auf dem Kriegspfade". Bei seiner Landung in Le Havre erklärte er, daß er nicht mehr nach Deutschland zurückkehre, solange die „faschistische Regierung" an der Macht sei.

→ In 1933, a German cartoonist alludes to the above photograph and presents Einstein "on the warpath" against the fascist German government.

↑ In his Princeton garden with a delegation from the American Continental Club, 1941
Photos by Trudi Dallos

The very month he assumed office in 1933, the Nazi mayor of Einstein's native city, Ulm, renamed the street from Einsteinstrasse to Fichtestrasse, thus replacing the unwanted Jew by a more convenient "Aryan" philosopher.
After the war and the defeat of the Nazis the new mayor of Ulm did not hesitate to restore the street's previous name.
Einstein's comment on this incident reads:

« I had heard the droll story of the street names at the time and it caused me no little amusement. – I think that a neutral name such as "Windfahnenstrasse" (Weather Vane Street) would be better suited to the political mentality of the Germans and would make further relabelling in the course of time unnecessary. »

→ From two letters to Einstein of March 20 and August 25, 1946, respectively, quoted in a letter from Leopold R Hirsch to Einstein's trustee Otto Nathan, August 20, 1960

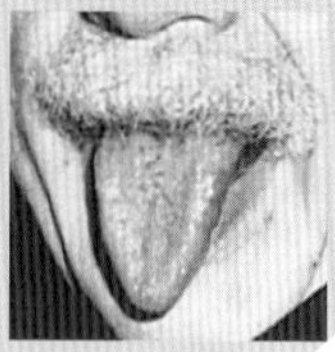

A. Einstein

9

EINSTEIN THE MYTH

« All sorts of fables are attributed to my person, and there is no end to the number of ingeniously devised tales. »

From a letter to the Queen Mother Elisabeth of Belgium, March 28, 1954

THE CREATION OF THE MYTH

Albert Einstein is a powerful mythical figure, a universal cultural icon and his name passes as a synonym for "genius." In popular mythology, Einstein plays contrasting roles: saint and demon, wise old man and free-spirited child, sorcerer and philosopher. There is a basic duality to the Einstein myth: Einstein is perceived as having unleashed the best and the worst in science and human nature.

Albert Einstein became famous overnight. When sensationalist reports of the verification of his general theory of relativity appeared in the international press shortly after November 6, 1919, readers may have received the impression that all the mysteries of the cosmos were finally unraveled. From then on, the press reported his every move and the general public became fascinated by this man who had overturned the traditional concepts of time and space. They were intrigued by his quirky appearance and quaint utterances.

Einstein's scientific lectures turned into social events and attracted audiences whose understanding of Einstein's physics may hardly have been different from the popular idea that "everything is relative." Others, as was the case in Japan, may have expected Einstein to lecture on the relations between the sexes.

Whoever was in possession of a camera hunted for an occasion to take a snapshot of the celebrity, preferably together with the camera owner.

On his trips abroad, the masses flocked to see him: cheering young girls with arms full of flowers in the United States, awestruck and silent crowds in Japan.

Einstein enjoyed enormous popularity among Jews: he was celebrated as the embodiment of the Jewish intellect and the greatest Jew of his time. In reaction to this adulation, Einstein self-mockingly termed himself a "Jewish saint."

Yet he was also vilified: anti-Semitic circles in Germany launched vitriolic attacks against him and his allegedly misguided and untenable "Jewish Physics" and Henry Ford's Dearborn Independent hid its slander behind the seemingly unbiased head-line: "Is Einstein A Plagiarist?" Already in 1921, the incitement culminated in a German newspaper's call for Einstein's murder.

Various factors contributed to the creation of the Einstein phenomenon: Apparently universal and absolute truths which had been valid for about three hundred years were dramatically overturned by Einstein. A special mystique came to surround his reputedly incomprehensible theories. He was ascribed sorcerer-like qualities: having discovered a magic formula, a key that opened the single secret of the universe.

The contemporaneous expansion of the mass-media eventually allowed these factors to take such a broad effect. After the First World War, a war-weary public was searching for a new kind of hero. Einstein proved to be tailor-made for this role, with his anti-militarist views, bohemian appearance, gentle manner and playful sense of humor.

In a wider cultural context, and not unrelated to each other, the arts, architecture, philosophy and psychology were simultaneously creating their own revolutions in the approach to time and space. Picasso and Braque invented cubism, Schönberg replaced tonality by dodecaphony, Bergson developed a new concept of duration and Freud formed his theory of psychoanalysis.

« There was a young lady named Bright,
Who traveled much faster than light.
She started one day
In the relative way,
And returned on the previous night. »

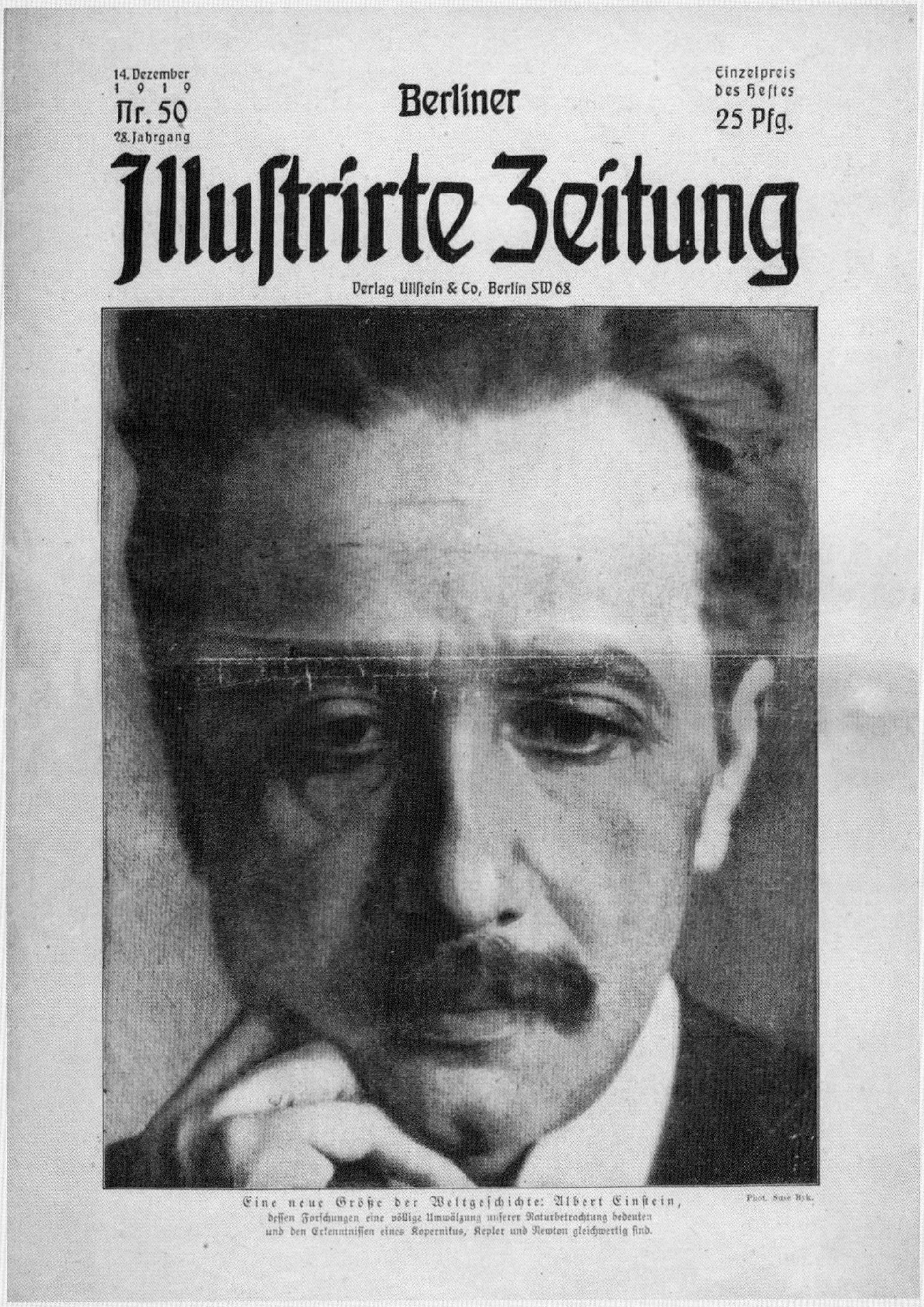
14. Dezember 1919
Nr. 50
28. Jahrgang

Berliner

Einzelpreis des Heftes 25 Pfg.

Illustrirte Zeitung

Verlag Ullstein & Co, Berlin SW 68

Eine neue Größe der Weltgeschichte: Albert Einstein, dessen Forschungen eine völlige Umwälzung unserer Naturbetrachtung bedeuten und den Erkenntnissen eines Kopernikus, Kepler und Newton gleichwertig sind.

Phot. Suse Byk.

← A new celebrity in world history: Albert Einstein. On December 14, 1919, Einstein's portrait appears for the first time on the cover of a German periodical.
The caption reads:
His research signifies a complete revolution in our concepts of nature and is on a par with the insights of Copernicus, Kepler, and Newton.

→ From a letter to Marcel Grossmann, September 12, 1920

« The world is a strange madhouse. Currently, every driver and every drover is debating whether relativity theory is correct. »

Shortly after the newspapers had discovered that any report about Einstein paid off, the journalist and socialite Alexander Moszkowski, known mainly as the editor of a popular humor magazine, announced his book *Conversations with Einstein*. Having learned about the forthcoming book from friends, Einstein tried to stop its publication.

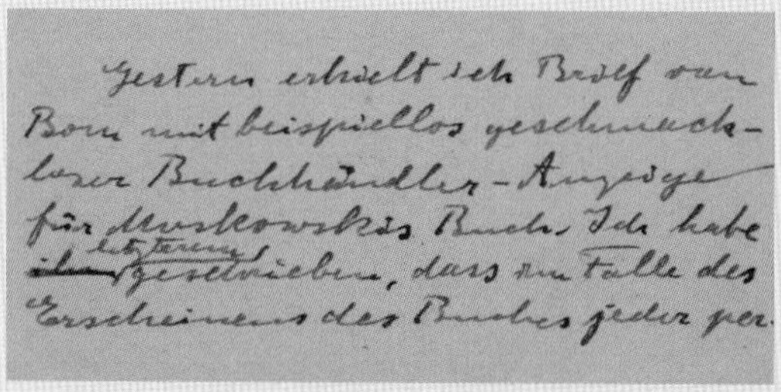

Gestern erhielt ich Brief von Born mit beispiellos geschmacklosen Buchhändler-Anzeige für Moszkowskis Buch. Ich habe letzterem geschrieben, dass im Falle des Erscheinens des Buches jeder per-

« I wish I had the eloquence of an angel so as I could make the consequences clear to you. [...]
This book will constitute your moral death sentence for all but four or five of your friends. It could subsequently be the best *confirmation of the accusation of self-advertisement*. We, your friends, are deeply shocked at this prospect. »

↑ From a letter by Hedi Born, October 7, 1920

« Yesterday, I received a letter from Born with a singularly tasteless bookseller's advertisement for Moszkowski's book. I wrote [him] that in the event of the appearance of the book all personal contact with him would be cut off. I refrain from legal prosecution [...] because this would only increase the scandal. »

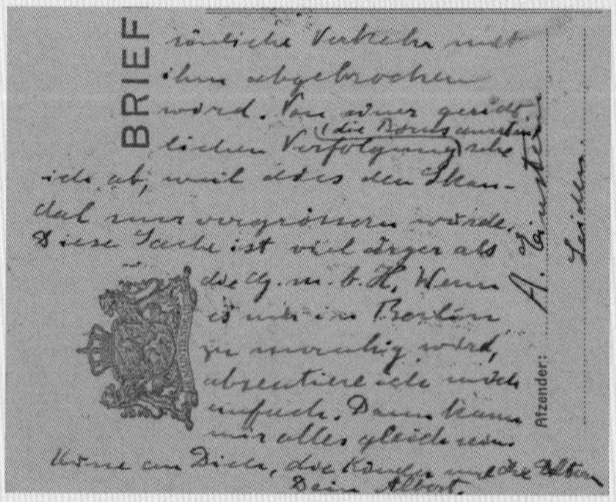

BRIEF

sönliche Verkehr mit ihm abgebrochen wird. Von einer gerichtlichen Verfolgung (die Borns anraten) sehe ich ab, weil dies den Skandal nur vergrössern würde. Diese Sache ist viel ärger als d. Weyl.-u. B.-H. Wenn es mir in Berlin zu mauelig wird, absentiere ich mich einfach. Dann kann mir alles gleich sein. Küsse an Dich, die Kinder und die Eltern Dein Albert.

Absender: A. Einstein Leiden

↑ Postcard to his wife Elsa, October 26, 1920

Einstein

Einblicke in seine Gedankenwelt

Gemeinverständliche Betrachtungen über die Relativitätstheorie und ein neues Weltsystem

Entwickelt aus Gesprächen mit Einstein

Von

Alexander Moszkowski

1921

Hoffmann und Campe / F. Fontane & Co.
Hamburg Berlin

88-50/15

← The book nevertheless was published and Einstein stated that it had done him more harm than the attacks of the anti-Semites the previous year.

« Imagine you have a casual chat with someone about various things, and then this someone sets about pinning your words down black on white just like he recalls them, and what is more, he adds a significant odor of adulation. – Offhand, I may have replied to some of Moszkowski's propositions just as the whim and a spirit of contradiction inspired me at the very moment. »

↑ From a letter to F. Siemens, February 1921

↑ Einstein and two unidentified people who may, like so many others, have jumped at the chance to appear in a picture together with the famous scientist.

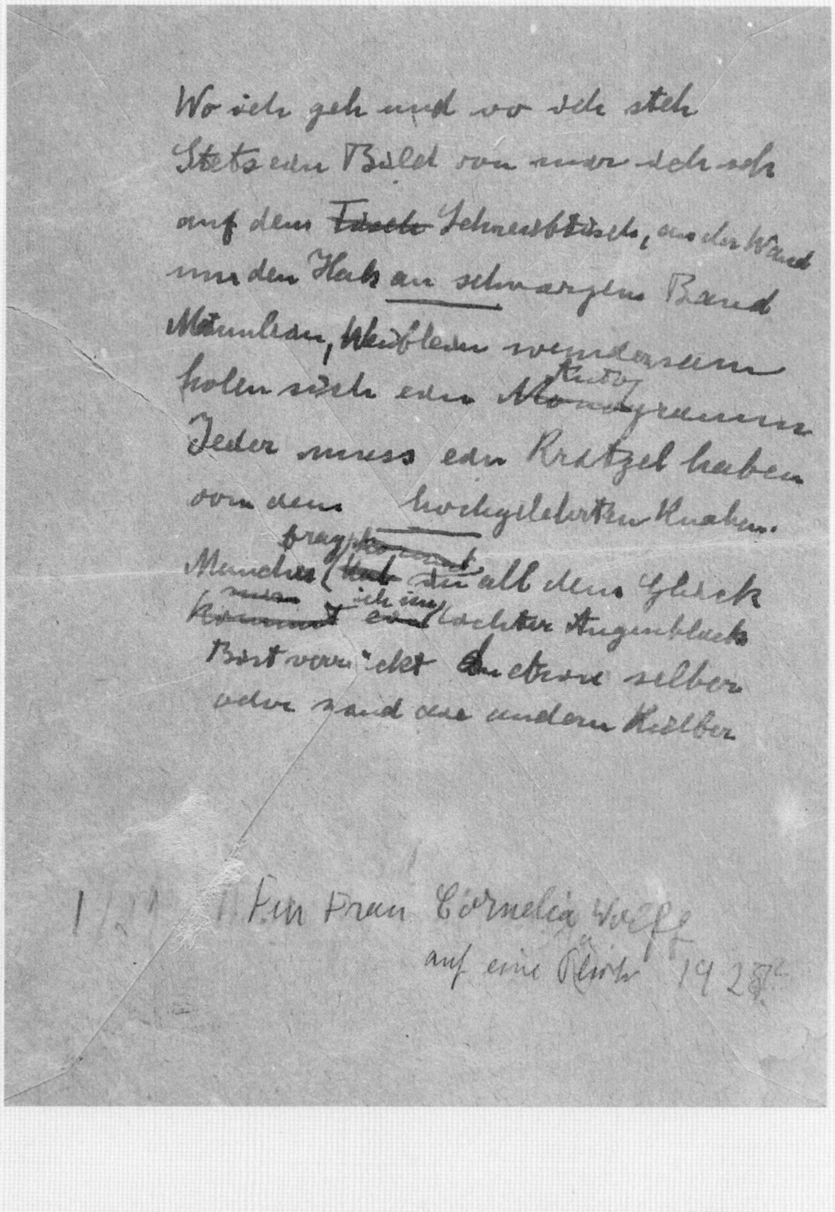

Wo ich geh und wo ich steh
Stets ein Bild von mir ich seh
auf dem Schreibtisch, an der Wand
um den Hals am schwarzen Band
Männlein, Weiblein wundersam
holen sich ein Autogramm
Jeder muss ein Kritzel haben
von dem hochgelehrten Knaben.
Manchmal frag ich in all dem Glück
ich im lichten Augenblick
Bist verrückt du etwa selber
oder sind die andern Kälber

1/21 Für Frau Cornelia Wolff
auf eine Reise 1920

« Wherever I go and wherever I stay,
There's always a picture of me on display.
On top of the desk, or out in the hall,
Tied round a neck, or hung on the wall.

Women and men, they play a strange game,
Asking, beseeching: "Please sign your name."
From the erudite fellow they brook not a quibble
But firmly insist on a piece of his scribble.

Sometimes, surrounded by all this good cheer,
I'm puzzled by some of the things that I hear,
And wonder, my mind for a moment not hazy,
If I and not they could really be crazy. »

Translation: Helen Dukas & Banesh Hoffmann

↑↗ On the ubiquity of his image. Verse dedicated to Cornelia Wolff, January 1920

↑ Surrounded by journalists, Pittsburgh, December 28, 1934

→ From "Some Impressions of America," 1931

« The cult of individuals is always, in my view, unjustified. To be sure, nature distributes her gifts unevenly among her children. But there are plenty of the well-endowed, thank God, and I am firmly convinced that most of them live quiet, unobtrusive lives. It strikes me as unfair, and even in bad taste, to select a few of them for boundless admiration, attributing super-human powers of mind and character to them. This has been my fate, and the contrast between the popular estimate of my powers and achievements and the reality is simply grotesque. The awareness of this strange state of affairs would be unbearable but for one pleasing consolation: it is a welcome symptom in an age which is commonly denounced as materialistic, that it makes heroes of men whose goals lie wholly in the intellectual and moral sphere. This proves that knowledge and justice are ranked above wealth and power by a large section of the human race. »

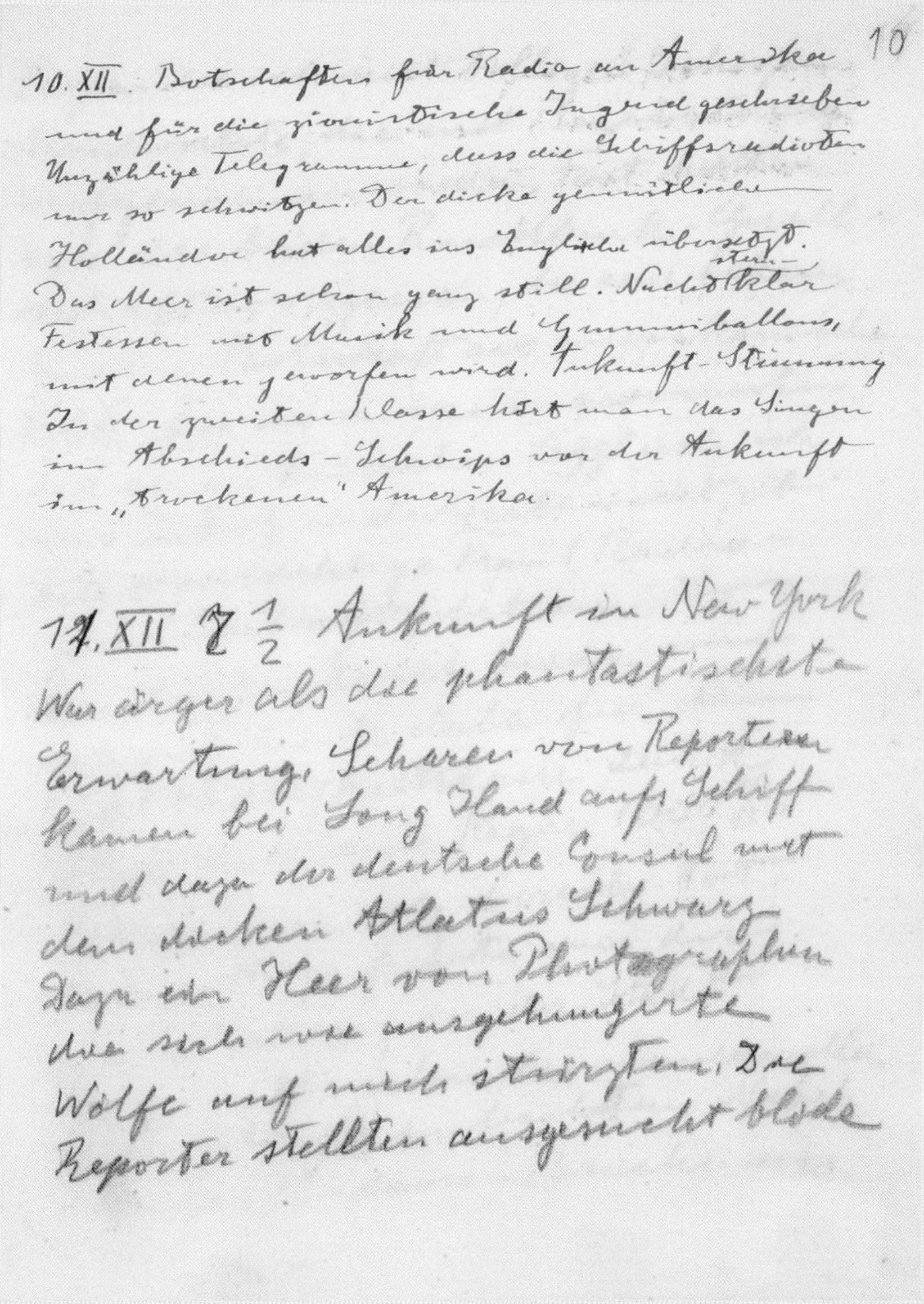

10. XII. Botschaften für Radio an Amerika
und für die zionistische Jugend geschrieben
Unzählige Telegramme, dass die Schiffsradioten
nur so schwitzen. Der dicke gemütliche
Holländer hat alles ins Englische übersetzt.
Das Meer ist schon ganz still. Nachts stern-klar
Festessen mit Musik und Gummiballons,
mit denen geworfen wird. Ankunft-Stimmung
In der zweiten Klasse hört man das Singen
im Abschieds-Schnaps vor der Ankunft
im „trockenen" Amerika.

11. XII 7 1/2 Ankunft in New York
War ärger als die phantastischste
Erwartung. Scharen von Reportern
kamen bei Long Island aufs Schiff
und dazu der deutsche Consul mit
dem dicken Adlatus Schwarz
Dazu ein Heer von Photographen
die sich wie ausgehungerte
Wölfe auf mich stürzten. Die
Reporter stellten ausgesucht blöde

« 11.XII 7.30 a.m. Arrival in New York. Was worse than my most fantastic expectations. Swarms of reporters boarded the ship at Long Island as well as the German Consul with his fat adjunct Schwarz. In addition, an army of photographers who pounced on me like starved wolves. The reporters asked outright stupid questions to which I responded with cheap jokes which were greeted enthusiastically. »

↑ On being "mobbed" by the press upon his arrival in New York. From his travel diary to the U.S., December 10/11, 1930

↑ Albert and Elsa Einstein with Charlie Chaplin at the premiere of *City Lights*, Los Angeles, January 30, 1931
Photo by Emil Hilb

In reaction to the crowds gaping at both men in front of the theater, Chaplin remarked to Einstein:

« These people applaud me because everyone understands me, and they applaud you because no-one understands you. »

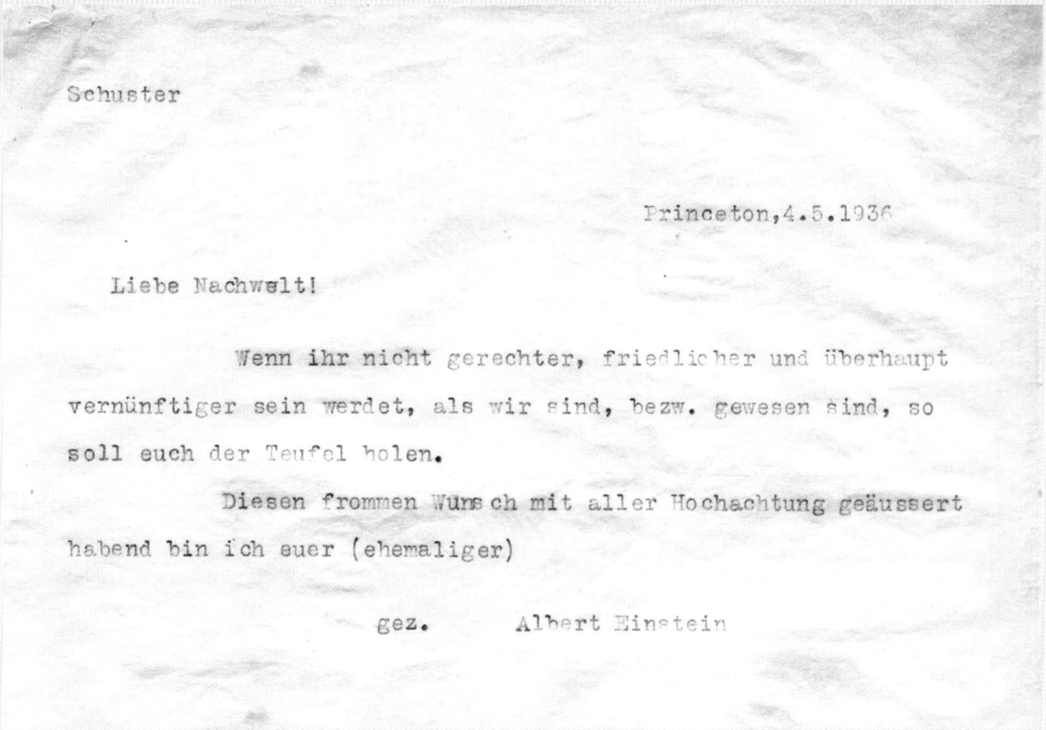

Schuster

Princeton,4.5.1936

Liebe Nachwelt!

Wenn ihr nicht gerechter, friedlicher und überhaupt vernünftiger sein werdet, als wir sind, bezw. gewesen sind, so soll euch der Teufel holen.

Diesen frommen Wunsch mit aller Hochachtung geäussert habend bin ich euer (ehemaliger)

gez. Albert Einstein

↑↗ Message to posterity written on parchment and placed in an air-tight metal box in the cornerstone of the house of the American publisher, M.L. Schuster, May 4, 1936

« Dear Posterity,

If you have not become more just, more peaceful, and generally more rational than we are (or were) - why then, the Devil take you.
Having, with all respect, given utterance to this pious wish,
I am (or was)
Yours,

Albert Einstein »

↓→ Sculptor Sir Jacob Epstein with his bust of Einstein. Einstein posed for the artist in September 1933 when hiding in a hunting lodge in Norfolk on the British coast. In a letter to his wife Elsa of September 27, 1933, he expresses a rather limited enthusiasm for this tribute he had to pay for his stardom:

« I still enjoy the time to the fullest although, much to my regret, I am going to be sculpted by a reputedly very important crocker. So far it looks Mexican. »

THE MYTH IN THE NUCLEAR AGE

With the onset of the atomic era after 1945, the Einstein myth gained a new dimension. When the "Cosmoclast Einstein" looked from the cover of *Time Magazine* of July 1, 1946, with a menacing mushroom cloud looming over his head, every reader realized that this man was to be believed to have created the threat of a nuclear holocaust.

Although this is a gross distortion of Einstein's role, it fulfilled the public's need to express its disillusionment with scientific and technological "progress." Einstein embodies the dilemma of scientists in modern times: those who generate pure knowledge can no longer operate in a moral vacuum disconnected from society, a society that may usurp knowledge that it is inadequately equipped to handle.

While initially many held Einstein responsible for the atomic disaster, increasingly, though, he was perceived as a saint suffering on behalf of humanity. His soul-searching eyes, his crown of white hair and even his habit of not wearing socks further contributed to the image of a benevolent sage.

Einstein's political campaigns on behalf of nuclear disarmament and civil liberties rendered him a moral authority for the post-war generation. Einstein's active commitment to societal change also had particular resonance among Jews: he became a symbol of Jewish morality and social conscience.

In the post modern period, Einstein features prominently in newspaper articles, films, plays and operas, and stares from stamps, coins, T-shirts and advertisements. His appeal is so strong that impostors who pose as his son or grandson elicit a cult-like interest in Istanbul, St. Petersburg and elsewhere, while American newspapers wisecrack: "Einstein's Son? It's a Question of Relativity."

His pop culture image is a depoliticized and trivialized one: alongside Mickey Mouse and Marilyn Monroe, the bumbling professor with the tousled hair has become one of the major cultural icons of our era.

An example of his enduring mythic status was *Time Magazine's* choice of Einstein as "Person of the Century" in 1999.

As hardly any other, Einstein's persona epitomizes the combination of the 20th century's major challenges: the scientific revolutions and the atomic peril, the Nazi frenzy and the persecution of the Jews, and the ambivalent power of science.

In the World Year of Physics 2005, dedicated to Albert Einstein, many exhibitions and new publications shifted from the mythical figure, from the "brazen lies and utter fictions" that had been spread already during Einstein's lifetime, to a more realistic and comprehensive image of his multi-faceted personality which eventually may supersede the image of the genius who showed his tongue to the world.

« I am generally regarded as a sort of petrified object, rendered blind and deaf by the years. I find this role not half bad, as it corresponds fairly well with my temperament.

One feels as if one were an Ichthyosaurus, left behind by accident. »

→ From letters to Max Born, April 12, 1949, and May 12, 1952

↑ "Einstein meets Monroe"
© Quint Buchholz 1985

Marilyn Monroe suggests to Einstein: What do you say, professor, shouldn't we have a little baby together: what a baby it would be – my looks and your intelligence!
Einstein: I'm afraid, dear lady, it might be the other way around...

Insignificant encounter of an aged fiddler with a moonstruck college student or romantic tête-à-tête of The Beauty and The Genius?
There are no indications that such an encounter occurred in the real world, yet the fantasy of their conjunction has become an urban legend.
For over half a century speculation has not died down as to whether the union of these two pop idols may even have resulted in the birth of a child.

→ From a letter to Mervin Ruebush, who asked Einstein for his permission to use Einstein's name to advertise his cure for stomach aches, May 22, 1942

« I have never given my name for commercial use even in cases when no misleading of the public was involved, as it would be in your case. I, therefore, forbid you strictly to use my name in any way. »

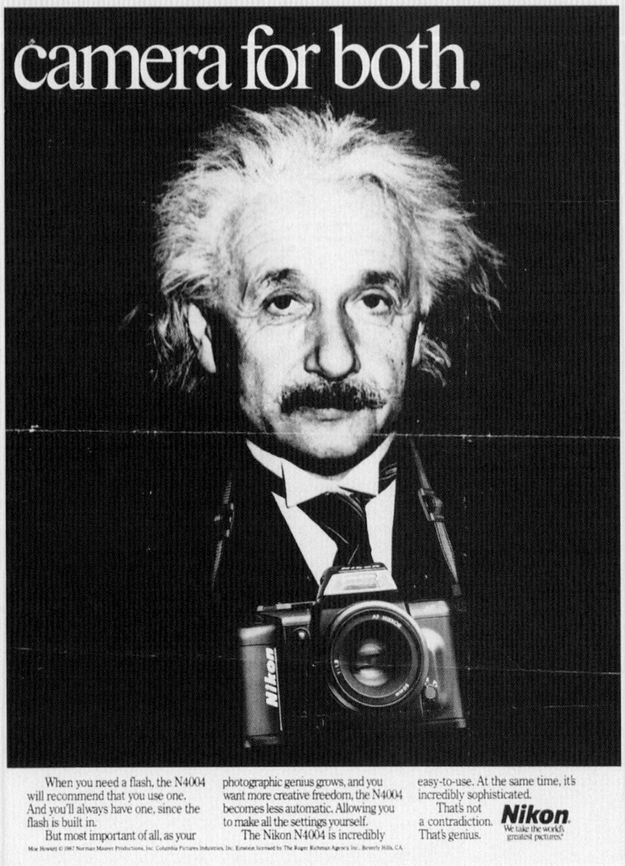

IT'S LIKE G.Q.
WITH A HIGHER I.Q.
Esquire
THE ONLY INTELLIGENT
MEN'S MAGAZINE.

School.
Supplies.
OfficeMax.
what's your thing?

SPIEGEL
Nr. 50/13.12.99 · 5,00 DM
CHLEUSSER-AFFÄRE:
Die fliegenden
Genossen von NRW
DAS GEHIRN
DES JAHRHUNDERTS
Wie Albert Einstein
aus Gedanken ein Universum schuf

The Brain of the Century

After Einstein's death, an autopsy was performed during which the pathologist Thomas S. Harvey removed Einstein's brain. This was done without either Einstein's permission or the prior permission of his close relatives or trustee. Subsequently, permission was given on condition that the brain be used only for scientific research and that the results be published in scientific journals of high standing.

Over the years, Thomas S. Harvey, who was keeping Einstein's brain as somewhat of a personal trophy, distributed slices of it to dedicated scientists, but also to Einstein enthusiasts. Yet only a few neuroscientists were willing to examine the parts of the brain that Harvey provided. Three scientific studies were eventually published, each of them offering a different explanation of Einstein's brain's pecularity. However, none of the researchers would confirm unequivocally and beyond controversy Harvey's hope that Einstein's genius could be deciphered from his brain's anatomy.

The odyssey of Einstein's brain, cut into more than 200 chunks and stored in jam jars of formaldehyde, provided the material for a novel and a movie.

→ In 1996, Harvey delivered the remaining pieces of Einstein's brain to Princeton Hospital, from where their journey had set out four decades earlier.

« From the outset I tell you that I would not grant you permission to [make] either of the two movies you suggested. My personal life is astonishingly meager with regard to events that could be exploited for such a purpose. […] Not even Shakespeare dared to engage with a play in which the hero would be a simple unassuming professor of philosophy. Such a life is like an ocean without a surf. »

↑ From a letter to P. Gordon, March 25, 1944

« To my regret I cannot give any cooperation or consent for the making of a motion picture concerning my personal life. The reason is that I am trying hard to avoid any publicity concerning my person. »

↑ From a letter to H. Bellit, December 15, 1943

« I am very sorry to say that I cannot give my consent to any film which tries to represent my personal life. There has been already too much publicity about my person and I have to try to stop it. »

↑ From a letter to D.M. Noyes, April 29, 1947

↑ On Einstein's 72nd birthday, March 14, 1951, UPI photographer Arthur Sasse was trying to persuade the celebrant to smile for the camera. Having smiled for the photographers many times that day, Einstein stuck out his tongue instead.
This image, showing the serious scientist in a moment of levity, has become an icon in pop culture. The original photograph was taken with Einstein sitting in a car between Marie Osgood Aydelotte and Frank Aydelotte, the former president of Swarthmore College and director of the Institute for Advanced Study.

↑ Princeton, early 1950s

« One lives under persistent tension until one eventually sails off. Yet I can take comfort in the conviction that the essence of what I made has become a fundamental asset of our science. »

↑ From a letter to his sister, Maja, August 31, 1935

APPENDICES

THE ALBERT EINSTEIN ARCHIVES

THE HISTORY OF THE ARCHIVES

Albert Einstein was not the sort of person to retain every piece of paper that passed through his hands. He made no systematic attempt to preserve his papers prior to 1919. As a result of his dramatic rise to fame in November 1919, his correspondence increased vastly and he employed his stepdaughter, Ilse, as his secretarial assistant. She achieved the first semblance of well-ordered files. In April 1928, Helen Dukas came to work for Einstein and began to preserve his papers more systematically. However, not even then were copies of all outgoing correspondence kept.

Shortly after the Nazis' rise to power in 1933, Einstein's papers were rescued from Berlin by Einstein's son-in-law, Rudolf Kayser, with the help of the French Embassy. The material was brought to Einstein's new home in Princeton and kept there until well after his death. With a few exceptions, the material left at Einstein's summer house in Caputh outside Berlin was destroyed in order to prevent it falling into the hands of the Nazi authorities.

Einstein's Will of 1950 appointed his secretary, Helen Dukas, and his close associate, Otto Nathan, as trustees of his estate. Nathan was also appointed as sole executor. Following Einstein's death in 1955, Dukas and Nathan devoted themselves tirelessly for more than a quarter of a century to organizing the papers and acquiring additional material. As a result of their efforts, the Archives grew threefold. In the 1960s, Helen Dukas and Gerald Holton of Harvard University started to systematize the material, thereby rendering it accessible to scholars and preparing it for eventual publication in *The Collected Papers of Albert Einstein*, a joint project of The Hebrew University and Princeton University Press.

In 1982, the Einstein Estate vested all literary rights in The Hebrew University and Einstein's personal papers were forwarded to the Jewish National & University Library in Jerusalem. In subsequent years, additional material was dispatched from Einstein's Princeton residence, namely his personal collections of reprints, photographs, medals, and diplomas as well as his private library, including sheet music and records.

In 1988, the Bern Dibner Curatorship for the running of the Albert Einstein Archives was established by the Dibner Fund of Connecticut, U.S.A.

In July 2006, more than 1000 letters to and from family members, presumably the last large lot of original archival material, which had been sealed for twenty years after the death of Margot Einstein, was made accessible at the Albert Einstein Archives.

THE IMPORTANCE OF THE ALBERT EINSTEIN ARCHIVES

The Albert Einstein Archives is an extraordinary cultural asset of universal importance for humanity and of national importance for Israel and the Jewish people. Representing the intellectual and personal record of a creative genius whose thinking profoundly changed our perception of the universe, it is of inestimable value.

The Albert Einstein Archives contains the largest collection of original manuscripts by Einstein in the world and includes his vast correspondence with the most influential physicists and intellectuals of the 20th century. The Archives continues its exhaustive compilation of material about Albert Einstein.

The Albert Einstein Archives constitutes an extremely valuable historical resource. It is considered one of the most significant sources for the history of modern physics. In addition, the Archives is an especially important source for the history of such movements as pacifism, socialism and Zionism as well as for German, Jewish, European and American intellectual, political, and social history of the 20th century.

Einstein did not wish that any physical monument or memorial be erected in his name. The preservation of his papers, which most authentically reflect his ideas and person, affords a far more fitting means of maintaining his legacy.

↑ Einstein's desk at Fine Hall, as he left it a few days before his death, 1955
Photo by Alan Windsor Richards

BIBLIOGRAPHY

Given the fact that there are thousands of publications related to Einstein, we have attempted to make a judicious selection of reliable sources for further reading.

PRIMARY LITERATURE

The Collected Papers of Albert Einstein

Every document in *The Collected Papers* appears in the language in which it was written, while the introduction, headnotes, footnotes, and other scholarly apparatus is in English. Upon release of each volume, Princeton University Press also publishes an English translation of previously untranslated non-English documents.

Vol. 1: *The Early Years (1879–1902),*
ed. by John Stachel et al., Princeton 1987.

Vol. 2: *The Swiss Years: Writings (1900–1909),*
ed. by John Stachel et al., Princeton 1989.

Vol. 3: *The Swiss Years: Writings (1909–1911),*
ed. by Martin J. Klein et al., Princeton 1993.

Vol. 4: *The Swiss Years: Writings (1912–1914),*
ed. by Martin J. Klein et al., Princeton 1995.

Vol. 5: *The Swiss Years: Correspondence (1902–1914),*
ed. by Martin J. Klein et al., Princeton 1993.

Vol. 6: *The Berlin Years: Writings (1914–1917),*
ed. by A. J. Kox et al., Princeton 1996.

Vol. 7: *The Berlin Years: Writings (1918–1921),*
ed. by Michel Janssen et al., Princeton 2001.

Vol. 8: *The Berlin Years: Correspondence (1914–1918),*
ed. by Robert Schulmann et al., Princeton 1998.

Vol. 9: *The Berlin Years: Correspondence (1919–1920),*
ed. by D. Buchwald et al., Princeton 2004.

Vol. 10: *The Berlin Years: Correspondence (May-December 1920),*
ed. by D.Buchwald et al., Princeton 2006.

Einstein's miraculous year: five papers that changed the face of physics. Ed. by John Stachel. Princeton, N.J. 2005.

Einstein's 1912 Manuscript on the Special Theory of Relativity. Facsimile edition. New York 2004, c1996.

Einstein's Annalen Papers: The Complete Collection 1901–1922. Ed. by Jürgen Renn. Berlin 2005.

Einstein, Albert: *Akademie-Vorträge*. Sitzungsberichte der Preußischen Akademie der Wissenschaften 1914–1932. Ed. by Dieter Simon. Berlin 2005.

Einstein, Albert: *Relativity – The Special and the General Theory*. New York 2005.

Einstein, Albert: *The Meaning of Relativity*. Fifth Edition, including *The Relativistic Theory of the Non-Symmetric Field*. Princeton, N.J. 2004.

Einstein, Albert / Infeld, Leopold: *The Evolution of Physics: From Early Concepts to Relativity and Quanta*. New York 1967, c1938.

Einstein, Albert: *About Zionism*: speeches and letters. Ed. by Leon Simon. London 1930.

Einstein, Albert: *Ideas and opinions.* New York 1994, c1954.

Einstein, Albert: *Autobiographical Notes*. Ed. by Paul Arthur Schilpp. LaSalle, Ill.1979, c1949.

Einstein, Albert: *Einstein on Peace*. Ed. by Otto Nathan and Heinz Norden, New York 1981, c1960.

Einstein, Albert: *Albert Einstein, the human side*: new glimpses from his archives. Ed. by Helen Dukas and Banesh Hoffmann. Princeton, N.J. 1981, c1979.

Einstein, Albert / Freud, Sigmund. *Why War?* Chicago 1978, c1933

Albert Einstein / Mileva Marić – The Love Letters. Ed. by Jürgen Renn and Robert Schulmann. Princeton, N.J. 1992.

Einstein, Albert: *Letters to Solovine*. Ed. by Maurice Solovine. New York 1993, c1987.

Einstein, Albert / Born, Max: *The Born-Einstein letters; from 1916 to 1955*. Ed. by Max Born. Basingstoke, 2005, c1969.

Einstein, Anschütz and the Kiel Gyro Compass. [Einstein's correspondence with Hermann Anschütz-Kämpfe]. Ed by Dieter Lohmeier and Bernhardt Schell. Kiel 2005, c1992.

Elie Cartan / Albert Einstein: *Letters on absolute parallelism, 1929–1932*. Ed. by Robert Debever. Princeton, N.J. 1979.

Letters on wave mechanics: *Schrödinger, Planck, Einstein, Lorenz*. Ed. by Karl Przibram. New York 1967.

Einstein, Albert / Sommerfeld, Arnold: *Briefwechsel*, ed. by Armin Hermann, Munich 1968.

Einstein, Albert: *Verehrte An- und Abwesende*, Audio-CD, Cologne 2003.

SECONDARY LITERATURE

Abraham, Carolyn: *Possessing Genius: The Bizarre Odyssey of Einstein's Brain*. Toronto 2001.

Aichelburg, Peter C. et al. (eds.): *Albert Einstein: His Influence on Physics, Philosophy and Politics*. Braunschweig 1979.

Bernstein, Jeremy: *Albert Einstein And The Frontiers Of Physics*. New York 1996.

Bodanis, David: *$E=mc^2$: A Biography of the World's Most Famous Equation*. New York 2000.

Clark, Ronald William: *Einstein; The Life and Times*. An Illustrated Biography. New York 1984.

Fölsing, Albrecht: *Albert Einstein, a Biography*. New York 1997.

French, Anthony Philip (ed.): *Einstein: a Centenary Volume*. Cambridge, Mass. 1979.

Grundmann, Siegfried: *The Einstein Dossiers*. Science and Politics – Einstein's Berlin Period. Berlin et al. 2005.

Hentschel, Ann M. / Graßhoff, Gerd: *"Those Happy Bernese Years."* Bern 2005.

Highfield, Roger / Carter, Paul: *The Private Lives of Albert Einstein*. New York 1994, c1993.

Hoffmann, Banesh: *Albert Einstein, Creator and Rebel*. With the collaboration of Helen Dukas. New York 1974, c1972.

Holton, Gerald / Elkana, Yehuda (eds.): *Albert Einstein: Historical and Cultural Perspectives*. The Centennial Symposium in Jerusalem. Princeton, N.J. 1982.

Holton, Gerald: *Einstein, History, and Other Passions*. The Rebellion Against Science at the End of the Twentieth Century. Reading, Mass. 1996.

Howard, Don / Stachel, John (eds.): *Einstein: The Formative Years, 1879-1909*. Boston 2000.

Infeld, Leopold: *Albert Einstein. His Work and Its Influence on Our World*. New York 1983.

Isaacson, Walter: *Einstein – His Life and Universe*. New York 2007.

Jammer, Max: *Einstein and Religion*. Physics and Theology. Princeton, N.J. 1999.

Jerome, Fred: *The Einstein File*. J. Edgar Hoover's Secret War Against the World's Most Famous Scientist. New York 2002.

Jerome, Fred / Taylor, Roger: *Einstein on Race and Racism*. New Brunswick, N.J. 2005.

Kramer, William M.: *A Lone Traveler: Einstein in California*. Los Angeles, Ca. 2004.

Levenson, Thomas: *Einstein in Berlin*. New York 2003.

Pais, Abraham: *"Subtle is the Lord-- "*: The Science and the Life of Albert Einstein. Oxford 1982.

Pais, Abraham: *Einstein lived here*. Oxford 1994.

Popovic, Milan (ed.): *In Albert's Shadow*. The Life and Letters of Mileva Mariç. Baltimore 2003.

Renn, Jürgen (ed.): *Albert Einstein, Chief Engineer of the Universe: One Hundred Authors for Einstein*. Weinheim 2005.

Renn, Jürgen (ed.): *Albert Einstein – Chief Engineer of the Universe: Einstein's Life and Work in Context and Documents of a Life's Pathway*. 2 Volumes. Weinheim 2005.

Rentsch, Ivana / Gerhard, Anselm (eds.): *Musizieren, Lieben – und Maulhalten:* Albert Einsteins Beziehungen zur Musik. Basel 2006.

Robinson, Andrew: *Einstein, A Hundred Years of Relativity*. Bath 2005.

Rowe, David E./ Schulmann, Robert (eds.): *Einstein on Politics*. His Private Thoughts and Public Stands on Nationalism, Zionism, War, Peace, and the Bomb. Princeton, N.J. 2007.

Sayen, Jamie: *Einstein in America*. The Scientist's Conscience in the Age of Hitler and Hiroshima. New York 1985.

Schilpp, Paul Arthur: *Albert Einstein, Philosopher-Scientist*. La Salle, Ill.1988, c1970.

Seelig, Carl: *Albert Einstein: A Documentary Biography*. London 1956.

Stachel, John: *Einstein from "B" to "Z"*. Boston 2002.

Stern, Fritz Richard: *Einstein's German World*. Princeton, N.J. 1999.

Yourgrau, Palle: *A World Without Time: The forgotten Legacy of Gödel and Einstein*. New York 2005.

CREDITS

The documents and photographs reproduced in this book come primarily from the Albert Einstein Archives. We gratefully acknowledge the following individuals and institutions who provided us with permission to use their materials for this volume.

In some cases we have been unable to identify the source of a document. Any information leading to proper identification of those items is most welcome and will be duly noted.

Archives du Palais Royal, Bruxelles: 206

Archivo General de la Administración, Alcalá de Henares, Madrid: 213

Associated Press, New York: 243

Berlin-Brandenburgische Akademie der Wissenschaften, Berlin: 107

Central Zionist Archives, Jerusalem: 144, 161

City of Los Angeles: 173

Corbis-Bettmann, Seattle: 104

Douglas Heggie, Edinburgh: 102

École biblique et archéologique française de Jérusalem: 142

Eidgenössische Technische Hochschule, Zurich: 64-65

El Tovar Studios (Fred Harvey Company): 40, 232

Emilio Segrè Visual Archives, American Institute of Physics, College Park, MD: 92, 93, 97, 183

Erbengemeinschaft Prof. Dr. Max Planck, Germany: 91

Franklin Toker, Pittsburgh: 13

Historisches Museum, Bern: 42, 44, 46-47

Kenji Sugimoto, Japan: 19 (1922)

Leo Baeck Institute, New York: 34, 38, 116, 222, 229, 231, 239

Lotte Jacobi Collection, University of New Hampshire: 101, 207

Lucien Aigner Estate, Washington: 50, 98, 148

Museum of Modern Japanese Literature, Tokyo: 205

Neil Kleinman, Philadelphia: 217

New York Times. New York Times Pictures, New York: 170, 240

Niels Bohr Archive, Copenhagen: 95

Paterson Marsh Ltd., London: 123

Paul Haupt Verlag, Bern: 39

Quint Buchholz, Munich: 245

Schweizerische Landesbibliothek, Bern: 17 (1903), 32 (left), 60, 66

Sidney Harris, New Haven: 69

Spiegel Verlag, Hamburg: 248

Staatsarchiv, Aarau: 58-59

Stadtarchiv Ulm: 22, 28

Ullstein Bild, Berlin: 81, 237

United Press International, Washington: 192, 251

Werner-Heisenberg-Archiv, Munich: 95

Zentralbibliothek für Physik, Vienna: 94

$E = \frac{mc^2}{\sqrt{1-\frac{v^2}{c^2}}}$